Gordon Burn is the author of two novels, *Alma Cogan* (which won the Whitbread Best First Novel Award in 1991) and *Fullalove*. He is also the author of two works of non-fiction, *Somebody's Husband, Somebody's Son* and *Pocket Money*. He was named columnist of the year in the 1991 Magazine Publishing Awards for his sports column in *Esquire*. He was born in Newcastle in 1948 and lives in London.

Praise for *Happy Like Murderers*:

'Burn's writing is conversational, warm, alive to the contours of narrow lives . . . The violence, when it comes, is exactly drawn and terrifying . . . Burn's sentences are short, neutral to the point of blankness, and they circle the themes here, steadily closing, like Fred West searching the Gloucester one-way system for hitch-hikers . . . The result is a kind of history, a black shaft sunk through Britain during the last half-century . . . Burn's main justification for studying them like this is, it seems, simply to write his best book.' *Guardian*

'This terrifying book . . . Burn has researched with great care every detail (my God, the detail) of what went on in the Wests' house for decades . . . It is horrible, and there is always unease about why any writer should take such a long journey into uncleanness. But Burn does not embroider the facts: he uses his imagination only to try and understand the Wests, especially Fred.' *The Times*

'Burn sets their story in the wider context of rapid and drastic postwar migration, social disintegration and dislocation. His strange and powerful book explores the urban flipside of a world that promotes individual choice to a moral imperative but which simultaneously dismantles rural systems of surveillance, coercion and restraint . . . *Happy Like Murderers* generates its own unnerving poetry.' *Daily Telegraph*

'Gordon Burn's *Happy Like Murderers* . . . is a highly sophisticated literary construct . . . He has now told the story of the Wests as if it were his own fiction . . . It will be seen at once that this is powerful writing. Burn's approach has given him some real intuition into the world the Wests inhabited, physically, socially and psychologically.' *Evening Standard*

'After the race to be the first in print with the worst on the Fred and Rose West case comes Gordon Burn's volume, the result of vast research and deep, dread reflection, and it's the best by far . . . As well as being a powerful piece of prose about how human beings are placed, brutalized and finally defined, it is also a book of fierce humanity which is as much about the victims who lived and died as the supposedly human beings who tormented and killed them.' *Time Out*

'We are not so far removed from the Wests as we might like to believe . . . they were part of our society, products of our culture, people formed and warped and influenced, and more importantly, sheltered by the structures and values we have built and continue to rely on . . . There is much here that will make your blood run cold.' *Glasgow Herald*

'*Happy Like Murderers* is . . . startlingly (worryingly) original and fearless and distressing . . . This could be fiction. Open a page at random and it could still be fiction, almost: we hear the voices of the characters, slide unnervingly under their skin, into their minds. There are angry, verbless sentences; one-word sentences hammering things home: snatches of dialect, mimicked and repeated, the burry Gloucestershire dialect. We are very close-up in this book . . . He makes us look at the facts and won't let us look away . . . He has a novelist's flair for making us understand, the way no one else has managed to do, what the relationship was like between the couple.' *Observer*

'Unsettlingly, Burn shows that theirs was a world where dozens of men were eager to make use of the sex on offer in the West household . . . And as for the content. I mean it as a tribute to Gordon Burn when I say that it is numbingly, hauntingly horrible.' *Mail on Sunday*

Happy Like Murderers

GORDON BURN

faber and faber

First published in 1998
by Faber and Faber Limited
3 Queen Square WC1N 3AU
Open market paperback edition first published in 1999
This paperback edition first published in 1999

Typeset by Agnesi Text, Hadleigh
Printed in England by Mackays of Chatham plc, Chatham, Kent

A CIP record for this book
is available from the British Library

ISBN 0-571-19720-5

2 4 6 8 10 9 7 5 3 1

Happy Like Murderers

Chapter One

Quedgeley is a suburb on the southern edge – the Bristol side – of Gloucester. And Carol lived in Quedgeley until the age of four, in a big house surrounded by several acres. Just before she was born, though, the big house had been broken up into bedsits, and the fields closest to the house had become a caravan park.

In those days – it was the years following the war; the mid-fifties – box-shaped prefabs had been put down on the bombsites and patches of wasteland to provide accommodation for all the demobilized servicemen and their instant young families; and caravan sites had sprung up in fields adjoining many towns and villages for the same reason.

The site at Quedgeley Court was one of these. The 'vans, as the occupants called them, weren't holiday 'vans, but were occupied all the year round by large, unruly, poorer-off families. Although they had no real reason to, the families living in the house, whose interior walls were no thicker than the caravan shells, considered themselves a slight cut above the 'van people, who slept in beds that by day became cabinets and tables, and who had to share facilities for bathing and so on.

They were circumstances that intrigued Carol, who would go through her whole childhood and teenage years without knowing what it was like to have anywhere to think of as purely her own. Growing, often warring, families, strangers to each other, were squeezed into living spaces in which every intimate sound was overheard, while green fields stretched away on all sides, apparently doing nothing, towards the horizon.

Carol's mother's name was Elizabeth. She would have liked her neighbours at Quedgeley Court and others to call her 'Liz', but at this point in her life she always got 'Betty', a name apparently better suited to a pub cleaner, which is what she occasionally was, and a single mother.

Betty Mills had had two children before Carol. The first, Christopher, was what was then known as a 'blue baby'; he had a hole in the heart and lived for only about a year. He also had six fingers on each hand and six toes on each foot, and for his short life was fostered out to a woman called 'Nanny' Munroe who lived on Barnwood Road in Gloucester, close to the Black Dog pub where Betty Mills worked, which made it easy for her to see him. She still got to spend time with Christopher but he couldn't live with her.

Her second son, Phillip, was born in 1953, a year and a half before Carol. Because he was overdue, Phil arrived bright red and covered in fine white hair from head to foot, compared to Carol, who was a big bonny baby with beautiful black curly hair. Their mother was always telling them and other people this as a way of showing how they had been different from the word go, and Phil used to hate it. Used to hate *her*, Carol was sure, for being their mother's favourite. When she was two, Phil fed her bacon rind and she nearly choked to death. She often wonders now if that was his first show of dislike towards her. In years to come, if it ever happened that they were out at the same place together and his friends were showing an interest, he got that he would pretend to throw up when she walked past him and call her names under his breath. He showed a frightening contempt for her which escalated during her teens. So no closeness there.

The blue baby's, Christopher's, father was not the same as Phillip's and Carol's. Phillip and Carol were conceived from the same man, but he was not the man to whom Betty Mills was married at the time.

Her domestic situation was complicated, but complicated in the straightforward way the system would gear itself to handling in the upheavals of the next twenty or thirty years, in a time of more and more multi-parent and serial-parent, accidental, mongrel families.

Betty Mills was married to a man called Raine, and this was the name her children had been given. Albert Raine was a merchant seaman. He was also homosexual. She hadn't known this of course when she married him, but Betty soon deduced it from the friends he brought home. Phillip's and Carol's natural father, who Betty had been seeing without Bert Raine knowing, was an Irish roadman called Michael Mahoney.

Until the opening of the Severn bridge, Gloucester was the lowest crossing point on the river Severn and all traffic from southern England travelling into South Wales passed through the centre of the city. Likewise traffic travelling the north–south route prior to the opening of the M5 motorway. The main shopping streets were permanently choked with tarpaulined, long-haul trucks and lorries, belching fumes, shedding dirt. Michael Mahoney was part of the post-war programme of resurfacing and reconstruction. He was the foreman of a gang of labourers who were laying new roads in Gloucester.

He had made it clear to Betty Mills when Phillip was on the way in 1953 that he couldn't marry her because, leaving aside the fact that she was married herself, there was a girl at home in Cork to whom he had given his promise. But Carol came along eighteen months later, and Betty Mills and Michael Mahoney were still on some kind of terms during the years she was living at Quedgeley Court in the late fifties.

Most of the 'van dwellers were eventually rehoused on the sprawling satellite estates that had been going up at Coney Hill and White City in Gloucester. But, after a brief period doing menial work on a farm in Painswick and living there with the children, in 1959 Betty Mills found herself having to move in for a time with Michael Mahoney in his council flat in Matson.

It was the kind of rootless and insecure existence that would have bred anxiety in most people. And it is probable that Betty Mills wasn't as unalive to the sense of perilousness and drift in her life as she liked to appear. But stop-gapping and tiding-over, a total absence of stability or direction – this was the only way of living she had known. It was the kind of scraping by she had grown up to expect. It was what life had handed her. Hanging on to her children was her only object and aim. When times were bad she would swear to them that she would never put them away or leave them. Really swear it. And this puzzled them, because at that time they were ignorant of the details – what they call 'the roots and shoots' – of Betty's background.

Her own mother had had a string of children by different men. They were born in special homes for unmarried mothers usually adjoined to a workhouse, then passed over to the authorities for rearing. Betty was born in 1928 and she was the youngest. Two brothers, Syd and Ben, were already in an orphanage, and she soon joined them. Hampton Home, 1 Peewitt Lane, Evesham. Eight boys in one house; eight girls in the other. They lived in separate cottages next door to each other and, although the boys knew that Betty was their sister, they never really had anything to do with her, and vice versa.

As soon as she was old enough, Betty was put to work fetching and carrying, scrubbing floors, skivvying. Every day the same as any other in the flattened landscape of her life. And then, when she was four, an older sister who had gone into service on the Isle of Wight came on a visit. She said she had come to take Betty and her brothers to see their grand-parents in Salford Priors in the Vale of Evesham.

They set out on foot and were still walking in open country when dusk started to come down. Even as an old man Syd Mills would remember walking for ever until they came to a wood where the two brothers and the two sisters slept outside the fence. When they woke, they crossed a newly ploughed field towards the lighted windows of a house in the distance. Syd, only six then, could remember looking through the window and seeing a small old man, a big old woman and a man with his feet up on the iron range.

But they were not made welcome. They had walked all the previous night and slept under a hedge before continuing their walk to Gramma's just to be made to feel unwanted. They were greeted at the door with a 'What do you want?' Syd and Betty spent the night on the sofa sleeping spoon fashion and he would always remember waking up in the morning and hearing his mother singing 'The Old Rustic Bridge by the Mill' as she cleaned the grate in the hearth.

More than twenty years later, Betty Mills would repeat the trek, only this time by bus and with Phillip and Carol in tow. She had lost contact with all her brothers and sisters as they left the home and went off to the army or wherever was their destination, but she had found her mother and wanted to show her children off to her. Her mother, though, had got married by this time and didn't want her in-laws to know about her previous life as it could only make trouble for her. They were turned away and the door shut in their faces.

It would take Carol many years to realize the hardships her mother had endured as a child, never being shown affection, being rejected. She would realize then how lucky she herself had been, having a mother who always told her that she was a beautiful baby and always would be beautiful. Her favourite line, used so often when Carol complained that she had no nice clothes to put on, was 'Carol, it doesn't matter what you wear. If you wore a sack you'd still look beautiful.'

Carol was four in 1959 when she, her mother and her brother moved in with her natural father, Michael Mahoney, in his flat in Matson. Carol knew that this man, and not the man whose name she carried, was her 'real' father, and because of that she loved him. He was big, tall and strong with her own thick dark hair, and she thought of Michael as looking like Clint Walker in *Cheyenne* on the television. He drove a motorbike with a side-car and raced her around the countryside in it. Sometimes she even got to sit up behind him on the pillion. She has always been drawn to motorbikes and the men who ride them, probably because of that connection.

Among her lasting memories of what she would continue to think of as her dad's flat were the big picture of Mary and Jesus with the follow-you eyes hanging in the living room, and the accordion in Michael's room which she was told would be hers one day, but which she was forbidden to touch without him being present.

And then, through no fault of her own, although she believed it was – there had been a blow-up over some shillings kept in the kitchen for the gas meter which she had taken and which had resulted in Michael being angry enough to raise his voice to her – it was again time to move on. Her dad had said she was a bad girl and that he didn't want a bad girl living with him. But that wasn't why they were going. Betty and Michael had had an understanding from the beginning that this living together as a family could only ever, for their own undisclosed reasons, be a temporary arrangement.

Betty was thirty-one or thirty-two by now. Carol was four; Phillip, six. From Michael Mahoney's they went to stay with Joan and Jimmy, the Bradys, an Irish Catholic couple they had known back at Quedgeley Court and who, despite the move, were living in what were fast becoming overcrowded conditions. It was while lodging with the Bradys that Betty met the man who was going to be her next husband and the father of her second family. He would also of course be the stepfather of her existing children.

Alf Harris had fair hair that was turning grey. He was twelve years older than Betty Mills and he wore a trilby hat and a suit, as Carol noticed. She also noticed that her mother spent most of the time in the outside toilet on the afternoon of that first meeting. Carol knew that was where she was because she was out in the garden herself waiting for the trains going past the end of it, into and out of Gloucester station. She enjoyed scaring herself standing so close to the noise. Betty came indoors when the men went along the street to the pub, but she went quiet and shy again when they came back. It was only a couple of weeks, perhaps three, before she told Phillip and Carol that Mr Harris was going to be their new dad, and only six weeks until she married him.

'Imagine you come from the city, and you're suddenly down here with all these strange people you have to call brothers and sisters and dads an' that.'

Having, at the age of five, discovered her 'real' father, Carol wasn't ready to surrender him. The other thing she wasn't ready for was the fight to get noticed against the competition of a ready-made brood of brothers and sisters. The third was the move from Gloucester out into what, even at her age, she was townie enough to regard as hillbilly country.

Thanks to the work of Dennis Potter – his television plays and interviews and essays – we have a fuller picture of what it has been like to live in the Forest of Dean in the last half a century than in possibly any other geographically discrete part of England.

The Forest is about twelve miles by road from Gloucester ('a city one would always want to get out of as quickly as possible', Potter wrote), on the other side of the river Severn.

The river Wye makes the western boundary of 'this little country on its own', and Wales is just across Offa's Dyke. Throughout his life, Potter circled endlessly around the theme of the Forest's seclusion and physical isolation and the inwardness it has bred in the people who live there. The muttonheadedness of Foresters resulting from inbreeding and incest ('couldn't find his arse with both hands') was until quite recent times a standing joke in towns in the surrounding area. The closeness to the Welsh borders accounts for a dialect that is more or less unintelligible to non-Foresters.

The insularity was something that Potter, typically, both celebrated and deplored. (At the age of ten, 'between VE day and VJ day', he had been molested – 'abused out of innocence' – by an older male relative, an event he didn't mention to anybody for more than thirty years.)

The first film Potter made for the BBC was a documentary about the encroachment of the modern world into a way of life that had turned for generations around the same old Forest immutables: chapel, rugby football, the brass band, the pub and the choir. A Woolworths, 'a new candy-coloured shop called simply "Do It Yourself"' and a Co-op supermarket had opened in Cinderford; and there was a coffee bar called the 'Telebar' at the bottom of the town, down the hill past the war memorial, Potter noted regretfully. Its main draw, a black-and-white television, had recently been superseded by a Sputnik-design juke-box aglow with cheap cascading colours. 'The young people in the room jigged their feet and snapped their fingers, with something of the saving grace of self-parody, talking spasmodically in broad Forest accents: "If thou's ask me, thik box could do wi a good butt ash round the back on in."'

This was 1961, a year after Betty Mills had married Alf Harris and moved to Cinderford.

Harris was a miner at the Northern United, one of the deep

shaft pits that before the war had provided jobs for almost all able-bodied men in the Forest; pick-and-shovel pits kept going by grinding shiftwork. He would have a wash or shower at work before cycling home along the paths in the thick clumps of forest between pit and village. But there would still be coal dust around his eyes and in his ears, as Carol noticed with her eye for noticing. He never got really clean. His skin was always a kind of yellow. Black circles around his eyes and bright blue eyes shining through.

Harris had a Forest job and, away from work, followed pastimes that rooted him firmly in the community of the Forest. He had built a shed and made it his workshop. ('Come in, o' but, cast thee eyes over my abode.') He used to build things. Shelves, doors, tables . . . He'd get a couple of old chairs, take the legs off, put a new top on and make a table. Toboggans. Breakfast bars when they came in. Hen coops. Dog kennels. Even Carol had to admit. He was quite handy, actually.

Harris used to breed white Canadian rabbits. He had chickens; bred chicks. When they moved, from the third-floor flat in Grenville House where he was first living with Betty Mills to a house with a bit of garden, he borrowed two wild ponies from a neighbour to get the grass down. Tied them to poles in the garden so they went round in circles cropping. One of the bastards nearly choked itself on its straps during the night and he had to go out in the dark and unwind it. Bloody kids all hanging out the windows watching.

Brass. That was another of his interests. He collected brass in all shapes and sizes and worked out a way of getting the kids to keep it polished for him by turning it into a competition. Newspapers out on the table, and ready, steady, rub, who's got the shiniest?

Autumn came, he would be out collecting wood from the nearby forest. He had knocked up a little kind of box-buggy thing that ran on pram wheels, and sometimes he would allow Carol to ride in it on the way there if she wasn't jibing him with not being her real father and he wasn't lashing out at her and they were enjoying one of their truces. On the way home she'd help drag it if it wasn't too heavy.

The marriage between Betty Mills and Alf Harris was a transaction of sorts, and obliquely acknowledged as such by both parties: she had no home; he had children to look after.

Harris was a widower. His wife had died of cancer in her thirties. The children of that first marriage had been put with relatives after the death of their mother. But now that their father had another woman, they gradually started drifting back home. Chrissy, nine; Keith, eleven; Josephine, fifteen; Raymond, sixteen. Phil and Carol had met Mr Harris only twice and suddenly he was their dad and they had gained three older brothers and a sister. Now they were no longer three, but part of a large family, shut off in the Dean Forest.

Almost straightaway there were problems. It would have been more surprising had there not been.

It was Carol, Phil, Chris and Keith at first, all rubbing up against each other, jockeying for position. When they first went to live in Cinderford ('Zinnerfud'), their mother would put Phil and Carol on the double-decker Red and White bus to Gloucester about once a month. Michael Mahoney would meet them and take them shopping for toys and clothes and generally spoil them. Naturally they couldn't see why this didn't go down very well with the have-nots back in 'the sticks', as Carol still calls the Forest, although she has lived there now for forty years.

Then something happened and Michael Mahoney stopped seeing them. All they knew was their stepfather told them that their dad didn't want to see them any more; didn't want nothing to do with them. Later they would discover that their father had tried to keep in touch with them but all his cards and letters and small presents of money had been intercepted. At the time, though, Carol couldn't think what bad thing she had done to make him not want to see her. She started to feel life going downhill for her from then on.

Then, only months after getting married, her mother announced that she was expecting a baby. That would turn out to be Suzanne, Carol's first Harris sister.

Carol was still five when Suzanne was born. She was six when she started spending time with a neighbour, an elderly friend of Alf Harris's.

She would sometimes be left in his care while her mother and Alf went shopping. He gave her cuddles. She'd sit on his lap and watch TV. Then one day Alf got really angry and he was shouting at the old man and the old man was crying and Carol was dragged out of his house. She would remember feeling very upset about seeing him cry. Later her mum and dad told her she was not to go round there again as they had been doing something very bad, but that the old man couldn't help it as he was not right in the head. If they'd done something bad and he wasn't to blame, then she must be. That's how she figured it. The first time she had been made to feel bad about herself. She takes consoling from an elderly family friend she likes and trusts. He interferes with her. Life going downhill.

About three years later, which would make her ten, there was to be another incident with another man, this time a friend of her mother's. That is, the *father* of a friend of her mother's. Another elderly man. This one's trick was to keep a bag of sweets in his pocket and invite her to put her hand in his pocket and get one out. As she did, he pushed her hand down on to his penis which was hard, and held it there. This time she didn't tell anyone about it until years later.

Sometime in 1962, when Suzanne was only a few months old and Betty was already pregnant or about to get pregnant

13

with the twins, Angela and Adrian, she walked out on Alf Harris. Put Suzanne in the pram, sat Carol on the pram, grabbed Phillip by the hand and started walking. They got as far as Westbury-on-Severn, which is six miles, seven miles from Cinderford. Reached the police station there and got sent back. She had nowhere to go, so they brought them back. Some childhood memory of walking.

Quite soon after this – Carol assumed he must have hit her or something – Betty left again and they actually did stay in a caravan on some site in Gloucester somewhere. Carol can remember being there. She can remember being scared of the caravan, being wary of it and having the curtains drawn. She thinks it was because they were waiting for her stepfather to find them.

With Angela and Adrian, it made eight children in the Harris home, three of them under the age of three. Carol noticed a change of smell on her mother. She started to smell of babies. Betty suffered an ectopic pregnancy in 1963, and in 1964 gave birth to another set of twins, Richard and Robert. Five children in four years and a daughter who had started cheeking up the man she refused to think of as her 'dad'. Carol was very pretty and very bright and always looking for an excuse to tell Alf Harris that she didn't have to do what he told her to because he wasn't her real father. Which would earn her a smack. She could be fiery.

Betty was starting to slap Alf's son, Keith, around and being hard on Christopher, who was in trouble with the police. She was getting quite nasty with Keith and Chrissy. Then Alf would be picking on Carol, and she'd be rebelling against him. He smashed her head into the wall and ruptured her eardrum.

Into this turmoil in the flats – Hill Dene council estate in Cinderford had a bad name for being a rough area – stepped Alf Harris's oldest boy, Raymond. Raymond was about eighteen and Carol was about eight, and they were at each other's throats straightaway.

He'd sit in front of the fire when he got home from work and take his socks off and pick the skin off his feet and his pimples and either flick them into the fire or over Carol. Carol's mother would tell him off but he just did it all the more. So that was gross, even without the smell and the fact that he was monopolizing the heating. In those days the fire was all the heating they had, so they'd all try and huddle round it, but he'd be there with his smelly feet and that would put you off. He'd come in and take his boots off and put his feet up on the range and then the smell would come up from them. 'Tell Raymond to move his feet, mum.' The start of another cosy evening in front of the fire.

Raymond and Betty got that they would argue on sight and because Carol was a 'mummy's girl' he'd do what he could to antagonize her so she'd complain to her mother and that would start a fight. He'd push her or whatever, and then Alf Harris would come in on it.

The worst thing Raymond used to do, though, was tell Carol that he'd put bogeys in her porridge. Alf Harris used to make them up porridge, and Carol couldn't stand it but she had to eat it. It was slimy. And Raymond if he was around would come in and say, 'I've just blown my nose into that.' And that used to make her feel sick, and sometimes she was sick. Then her stepdad would slap her one for playing up and not eating her food. Then her mum would start on him. This is how it happens in big families.

It got that Carol hardly ate anything. Then she started suffering with heavy nosebleeds nearly every day. It was nothing for her to soak two towelling nappies with the blood she lost. Sometimes it was so profuse that she'd choke. She'd get clots in her nose blocking the air off and her mouth would fill up with blood and she'd panic. If she blew her nose it just got worse. So – and she was aware that it was a filthy habit – she'd remove the clots by hooking them out with a hairgrip.

One day her brother Raymond came in as she was doing this and he gave her a smack around the head and told her off for being a dirty bitch; nothing but a filthy little bitch. He had a fit on her in front of her friend. Slapped her face and made her sit on a chair with a nappy under her nose and if she moved he'd hit her around the head, disgusted by this polluting substance which perhaps in his adolescent's mind he was associating with menstrual blood. 'Sit there and don't move. Move and I'll hit you again.' Then she choked coughing and the blood splattered over the carpet and he punched her in the stomach.

That was the last straw for Betty when she found out about it. She said she'd take Carol and Phillip and leave, but she didn't. She'd just discovered she was pregnant again.

The only one of Alf Harris's children who hadn't come home to live was Josephine. She had gone on living with her aunt Marje and her husband uncle Ralph Trigge. In 1963, when Betty's first set of twins were a year old, Josephine got pregnant and married her long-term boyfriend John Thomas. They took Raymond and his girlfriend on honeymoon on a boat with them. A few days later there was a lot of visitors and the police came to the flat. The honeymoon was cut short. Raymond had gone missing at sea. One night Ray went out on the deck alone to do something, and the sail pole hit him, knocking him out and overboard. He'd had a few drinks. His body was washed up nearly a week later. Carol was about ten years old then and she found her mother crying at a neighbour's, and she was told Ray was dead. She was so happy she laughed and said 'good' and got another good hiding for that too. She couldn't disguise her happiness that he wasn't coming back. Did a few 'yeh!'s and a little dance. She was generally obnoxious. Mrs Mathews, the neighbour, smacked her face and threw her out of the door saying she was a wicked girl. Later that day she got another good hiding off Alf. She was just so relieved that at least one of her bullies was gone. She'd often wished that Alf would just die and that they could all be happy again. The hidings got worse and more frequent.

One thing she hated Alf for was he made her wear a pair of hobnail shoes to school. They were great clumpy things with laces and there were studs under the soles and heels and they made loud clip-clop noises when she walked. It was a sound that had been a familiar one for generations around the villages in the Forest but, with the gradual closure of the pits, it was fast dying out. The clamp, clamp of steel-toed pit boots could be heard minutes before the men came by, and children would rush to the windows in Coleford, Coalpit Hill, Cinderford, Coalway, eager to see the coal-black faces. The miners would walk home from the evening shift with carbide lamps or candles encased in jamjars, often singing hymns or band tunes, their boots ringing out.

But that was history. Carol was eight in 1963; nine in 1964. The Twist had been and gone. The Beatles were making the Liverpool sound international. *A Hard Day's Night* had already played at Cinderford's flea-pit cinema. She wanted something a bit less pre-historic in the shoe department; something more up to date and modern. But every time she raised the subject, Alf said she would have to wear the hobnails until they wore out. That would be when she was an old lady of twenty as far as she was concerned at the time.

Behind where they lived used to be all meadows. There was a field with a pond in it where in the spring they'd go to collect tadpoles. There was a conker tree and a derelict wall, which they'd climb on to watch the big black horse that grazed there. The horse was called Chris. He was quite wild and most people avoided him, but Carol didn't. She'd sit on the wall for hours trying to entice him over with grass. They got used to each other. Carol felt they had something in common, her with her bullying at home and him with the spiteful boys that threw stones at him. Those boys had made him nervous and then he turned nasty. She started to treat some younger girls nasty, she didn't know why. Probably because she was too small to hit Alf and so she picked on others even weaker and smaller, needing to take her unhappiness out on somebody.

But she wasn't miserable all the time. It wasn't all fighting and abuse at their flat at 95 Hill Dene, later named Grenville House. Whenever anybody brought home a new baby, say, or got married, the whole flats came out to welcome them home or see them off, whichever the case might be. They had decent neighbours, all struggling to keep their heads above water, and there were many laughs and good times.

When Carol was eleven, the family moved to a three-bedroom council house on the same estate. Alf Harris had lost his job the previous year, due to an accident at work down the pit which meant he couldn't use his hand to grip any more. He had a bedroom to himself in the new house. Carol shared a double bed with one of her sisters and her mother slept in another double bed in the same room with a second sister. Betty had stopped sleeping with Alf by then. There were two doubles and a single bed in the third bedroom for the boys.

In addition, Alf also had his big shed in the garden to retreat to. His workshop. The shed became very popular with the boys in the neighbourhood, who would want to sneak in for a look when he wasn't there. Alf was a regular reader of *Parade* magazine, and he had plastered the walls with its pages of pin-ups. They weren't *bad*, in the pornographic sense. There was no hair. Just topless. *Parade* was a kind of working man's *Playboy*. But they were in full colour, and at the time that kind of thing was still considered quite racy. Carol would certainly notice her brothers' mates trying to get in to have a look around there. Cop a look when they thought nobody was watching.

Whenever Carol had to go in the shed herself, to take Alf a cup of tea or something, it would always bring a touch of heat into her face and she would shyly look away from the pictures of oiled and bare-breasted women. In the years to come she would get persistent requests to do glamour modelling herself. She would be crowned Cinderford Carnival Queen in 1977 and ride through the streets on a camel. And that would bring in a steady stream of offers of catalogue and lingerie work, eventually leading to topless modelling and a try-out for Page Three in the *Sun*.

Up to the age of fourteen, though, she had no body-confidence. She started to worry that her body wasn't developing at the same speed as everybody else's. Even Jenny Powell had boobs and she was the tiniest girl in their class. Carol had no boobs and no pubic hair and no periods. She hated the fact that she didn't even need a 32AA bra yet. She was mates with all the boys in her class. One of the boys. That was her.

Then when she was thirteen she was involved in an incident that further undermined her confidence. It gave her a knock. She had taken the bus from Cinderford into Gloucester to go swimming at Barton Baths. She had gone as part of a group that included one of her brothers and some of his friends and a friend of her own called Dawn from the flats. Instead of going straight back home when they finished swimming, they decided to go to Gloucester Park. While she was with Dawn in the women's toilet in the park, Carol was assaulted by an older man.

Dawn was inside the cubicle and Carol was waiting and the man suddenly rushed at her, making strange throaty noises and grabbing. They struggled to the floor, his hands grabbing inside her pants, her hands grabbing his, trying to bend his fingers backwards to get him off. She was sliding down the wall and trying to scream but no noise was coming out. Dawn, who was tiny for her age, jumped on his back but she couldn't pull him off. All the time he was making strange groaning noises, so Dawn ran out and grabbed two passers-by and they dragged him away. By the time the police arrived a crowd had gathered, among them a gang of young men. The man who had attacked her was sobbing and crying, and the men in the gang were jeering and going 'Gwan, let the poor bugger go.' The man was charged with indecent assault and found guilty. He was fifty-four years old and a mental patient from Coney Hill hospital and had done this kind of thing before. But once again Carol had been made to feel that it was her fault. She kept reliving the sensation of travelling backwards through the air before hitting the wall and of then being under the man with Dawn on top of the man and the man clawing sharply at her under her skirt. And then the fact that it wasn't her but the man who was crying and the voices calling out to let him go.

In the immediate aftermath of this attack, two strange but possibly connected things occurred: Carol started to have morbid thoughts about ending up in the papers as a murder victim; obsessively thinking that her picture would be on the front page of some paper because she'd been found dead. 'I *know* I'm going to be famous,' she started telling friends after the incident in the park. 'But it's going to be for being a body.' At the same time, she realized that for the first time ever the older boys at school were taking a bit of notice of her. But when she found herself alone with a boy, in the woods or just innocently walking at the edge of the forest, she'd inevitably end up looking, scrutinizing the shadows and the undergrowth, terrified she was going to find a body.

When she was fourteen, she started going out with a

sixteen-year-old, Clive Kibble, and, after a few months, lost her virginity to him. Clive taught her how to ride a motorbike and a scooter and at the beginning they'd spend hours tearing around the tracks in the wood and the green outside his home. After the sex came into it, though, it just seemed to spoil things for her. She was always making him cry by being nasty to him and being jealous. She changed so much she didn't even like herself.

Puberty, when it happened, came very quickly. She went from nothing straight into a 34A bra. She started getting a great deal of male attention, and by the time she was fifteen was known as 'Jailbait of the Year' in Cinderford and the surrounding area. This led to her getting picked on a lot by other girls whose boyfriends found her attractive. One girl had a car pull up, Carol was dragged into it and had the doors slammed on her legs. She was beaten up while in the car and then thrown out of it. She was carried home by some of her brothers' friends and Betty went hysterical.

She was a well-fancied woman – 'a well-flirted filly', as she herself puts it. Maybe it was her body language or whatever it was. But from the age of fourteen she started to get an abundance of male attention, and with the male attention you got the girlfriends following behind, like threatening. She couldn't help it. If Carol went to a disco, nine out of ten times some girl would hit her when she went in the toilets on account of her boyfriend's wandering eye. If their men *looked* at her, she'd be the one to blame; the one who'd get the smacked face or the head cracked against the mirror or the lavatory.

At the age of fifteen, she started seeing a local biker. She used to go to work with his mum apple-picking. His name was Graham and he was eighteen and she was the only girl in their crowd when they went to the pictures or to Mallory Park motorbike races. Carol went out with Graham for a year but as soon as they had a sexual relationship going she started getting jealous again and insecure, and that was what finally ruined that relationship, her bad jealousy tantrums.

After it ended, she was in danger of going quite seriously off the rails for a while. A woman called Kate with a house in the woods and a bad name said she wanted Carol to babysit for her. Carol said OK with no thought about what she might be getting herself into. The woman's husband had left her and she would go out with several different men and they'd come back to her place after the pubs had closed and more often than not it would turn into a party. Of course some of these men or their friends would get after Carol but she was still only fifteen and they were all too old for her. They all tried it on and on one or two occasions she gave in to get rid of their attentions. If she got tired of fighting off a man she would give in just to get rid of him, or she'd have had too much to drink and it just happened.

She wasn't capable of dealing with their sexual advances and she earned herself a bad reputation. Which led to more and more unwanted admirers. She didn't like to say no because she thought they would think she was childish. 'Then I turned into a wild child,' she says. 'I slept around a lot.' Her brother Phillip, who had never been close to her, her one full blood relative after her mother, started referring to her as a slut. Still life was going in one direction only, and it wasn't up.

A solution seemed to be to get right away from Cinderford and the Forest for a while. Southsea, near Portsmouth, may not have been the perfect destination, and Doreen Bradley certainly wasn't the ideal companion. But those were the only options available, so Carol left school and went. It was the furthest from home she had ever been before. It was the first time she had ever been away from home by herself.

The Bradleys lived at the end of Northwood Close, the

cul-de-sac into which Alf Harris had moved his family in the mid-sixties. But they were anyway unavoidable on the Hill Dene estate. The Bradley family were better known as the 'Cinderford mafia', or, sometimes, 'the most hated family in the Forest of Dean'. So many people in town were said to be on antidepressants because of them. What made them unusual was that they were a female- rather than a male-dominated clan. Sisters, mothers, aunts, nieces: they were all as likely to be weapon-carrying, and as capable of knocking heads together, as men. You wouldn't want to cross them. One example: a couple of them went into the Miners' Institute one night, tore this woman's jewellery from round her neck and stuffed it down her throat. Her crime: letting it be known that she was thinking of sending her son to a fee-paying school out of the district. The Bradleys would fight each other all the time as well as picking on everybody else, even women with pushchairs. Anybody. This was Doreen's family.

Doreen Bradley had been at school with Carol. She was still fifteen, nearly sixteen, and had yet to start coming up through the family business. She needed a friend of her own age to make the move with her to Southsea, where an older sister, Edith, known as 'Deedee', already lived.

Deedee was running a good line in ripping off the Co-op, where she worked. Something to do with milk tokens. She had found Doreen a job working there with her. Carol started working in a textiles shop, and at night she and Doreen ran around and had fun.

Southsea of course was full of sailors. Clubs and cafés and rowdy bars and rowdy, rough-housing sailors. Carol went out with a few and then some, but only fell in love and into bed with one. His name was Steve Riddall, known to his mates as 'Jimmy Riddle'. They met in a club on the sea front where Carol shouldn't have been, being still under-age. They were both often in 'Joanna's'. He always danced and sang along to the song 'Little Girl, Please Don't Wait for Me', a Diana Ross number. He was short, dark and handsome, and nobody loved him more than he did himself. Carol was never under any illusions: she was always just going to be another notch on the hammock for Steve.

When he was away on patrol with his boat she wrote to him. And then one night the opportunity arose and they slept together in a narrow single bed at Deedee's. Doreen had got the double. But Deedee found out about them having men back to the house while she was away and there was a flare-up. She tried to stop Carol seeing Steve one last time to say goodbye before he left for sea, and so Carol left Deedee's place and got a bedsit.

Before long Doreen also got kicked out of Deedee's for continuing to meet up with Carol against her sister's orders. By that time, though, Carol had lost her job because of persistent oversleeping, and that led to her losing the bedsit, which left both Carol and Doreen homeless.

A family Doreen knew in Southsea put them up for a while, and then another acquaintance let them stay in his place while he was away for a week. When they were there they steamed open an envelope containing a cheque belonging to another tenant, and used that as the down payment on somewhere to live.

It was the attic floor of a three-storey house. The kitchen was on the landing, with two doors leading from it into a living room and a bedroom. The kitchen consisted of a sink with a gasket heater for hot water which didn't work. There was a two-door unit under the sink to keep food in which was filthy, a fridge, and two meters for gas and electricity. These needed feeding all the time and there was no money to feed them. The inside of the fridge was covered in fur.

The furniture in the living room consisted of an oil slick of a settee and a broken armchair. In the bedroom were two beds positioned in an L-shape and a listing chest of drawers. When Carol fell into her bed on that first night it collapsed underneath her. She had to stack it back up on its pile of bricks and they ended up laughing themselves to sleep. Laughing until their throats were sore and they were gagging and felt they couldn't breathe.

The next day they set about cleaning the place up. The water took up all the money they had put into the meter the night before and it still wasn't that hot. They opened the roof window and it fell in on them and they had to put cardboard up. Carol cut her arm. A cupboard door fell off.

Doreen had got a job in a Kentucky shop. They relied on the chicken Doreen brought home after work as their main meal. Carol still couldn't find a job, and then Doreen was laid off. They had no income and were running out of food and spent most of their time wrapped up in bed looking at magazines the previous tenants had left behind.

They were down to eating Weetabix spread with margarine and just about at the end of their sense of humour when they were woken one morning by the kind of loud banging at the bedroom door that is made only by the police. They didn't know what they'd done. A voice ordered them to open up.

But it was all right. It turned out that Carol's mother was worried about her. She had contacted the Southsea police to ask them to find her and tell her to get in touch. Before she could, though – Betty and Alf weren't on the telephone, and Carol hadn't made her mind up what to write – they received a second visit from the police. This time they told them that Doreen's father had had a stroke and Alf Harris had had a heart attack, both within hours of each other, which Doreen and Carol thought was weird and unbelievable. They were neighbours, living just a few yards from each other, and they were both critical at the same time. They could die.

They got the news at eight at night, and by nine o'clock they were standing with their thumbs out, penniless, and relieved to have an excuse to be hitching home to Cinderford.

In the event, both fathers survived, although Doreen's would be confined to a wheelchair for the rest of his life. Carol surprised herself at how badly she wanted Alf to pull through. After all they had spent the whole of the previous twelve years locked in a bitter battle with each other. 'Hating each other' wouldn't be putting it too strongly. And now she found herself praying that he would survive. Literally that: closing her eyes and sending up a prayer. That was June 1972. Carol continued writing to the disco dreamboat, Steve 'Jimmy Riddle' Riddall, on his coastal-patrol vessel, and she'd get the occasional letter from him dropping through her door in Cinderford. A letter from Steve would always bring a lift to her day.

Just before her sixteenth birthday in October 1971, Carol had cut all her hair off. She had always been known for her hair, which was dark and lustrous and which she had always worn long. People identified her with it, and even years later as a middle-aged woman she'd meet men in Cinderford who would tell her, without the benefit of a few drinks in them, how they had dreamed of touching her pretty black hair. Men will come up to her now, look at her long dark hair, and say, 'Oh Carol, you're looking good.'

For a long time between the ages of fifteen and sixteen she had hovered between pretty and brutal. She was aware that the conventional sexiness of tousled-looking, flowing hair got her the attention. At the same time she knew that it didn't go with the clothes she had started wearing. More to the point, she wasn't sure she wanted that sort of attention any more, and the problems it inevitably brought. For a while she had tried combining being a skinhead with having long hair and of course it didn't work. So she had it all cut off. Really short. Brutal, with a spiky hogsback crown and a razor parting. So short her mother didn't recognize her. Crombie topcoat, pink gingham Ben Sherman shirt, eight-hole Dr Martens, scary hair. That was the new-look Carol.

Emboldened by their Southsea adventure, Carol and Doreen started travelling by thumb to discos in Gloucester and all around the area. Carol loved dancing. Discos were her thing, and she was prepared to travel miles to go to one.

Quite soon after they came home, Doreen's older sister, Kathy, asked them if they wanted to go with her to meet her new boyfriend Taffy. He worked on a fairground that was then on the Ham at Tewkesbury. It wasn't a straight run from Cinderford to Tewkesbury. It usually meant going via Gloucester. But it was a route that Doreen and Carol had travelled a number of times before and they had found that it could be done quite easily.

While they were at the fair on that first occasion, saying their hellos to Taffy, Carol and Doreen fell in with two local lads, Tony and Rob. Carol really liked Tony. He was a skinhead. He wore bleached-out cropped-leg trousers, a bomber-style jacket and big cherry-reds. An all-out skin. In addition he had the biggest blue-grey eyes she'd ever seen on a man and full, Mick Jagger lips. Tony had this cool, no-nonsense way about him, and even though he was only sixteen years old he got a lot of respect from the town hardcases both older and younger than himself. He had a rep in town. You don't mess with Tony. A fair bloke, but you don't mess with him.

Carol and Doreen started to go out there two, maybe three times a week, just to walk around, go to the café, maybe sometimes the occasional pub disco. It was always them hitching to Tony and Rob in Tewkesbury rather than the other way around because it was a fact that girls could get lifts more easily than boys. How many drivers were going to stop to offer lifts to what looked like two yobs with big boots, bullet heads and braces? Whereas with girls it just wasn't a problem. Carol even started to get her regulars; people who would recognize her, give her the flashing lights sign and stop to pick her up.

If Doreen couldn't make it, she had a couple of other friends who would usually go with her. But when they all got themselves local boyfriends, or they didn't fancy coming, or it was getting colder, Carol used to set off on her own. Whatever it took.

She didn't like going alone, but she wasn't worried about it. She always took basic precautions. She always wore trousers, for instance. Rule one: always wear trousers hitch-hiking. When she didn't, because she was planning on going dancing, she would have a long coat on that covered up her legs; they had what she and her friends called the 'Nazi coats' – maxi-coats – as well then. If anything, the return leg to Cinderford late at night was easier than the outward journey to Tewkesbury. There were two men who would be going to work on a nightshift and they usually dropped her off in Gloucester, then she would get a lift home from there easily.

Tony Coates was an apprentice at a place in Tewkesbury where they repaired JCBs, heavy plant, and tractors. He lived with a couple who had children. Their house was a council house and therefore small, so Tony and Carol didn't go back to his lodgings very often. They didn't really do anything. Often she just sat in his workshop and watched him do work, and was happy doing that. They were happy enough just to be able to spend time with each other without being held to account.

There was a little park going into the council estate where Tony used to lodge. Directly opposite was a pub called the Gupshill Manor. And it was at this same spot by the park that Tony used to leave Carol between ten thirty and eleven to begin hitching home. He used to leave her there so that if she didn't get a lift she could easily walk to where he was living. But she was always lucky and was usually on her way within quarter of an hour.

In September 1972, when she got into Fred West's grey Ford Popular, Carol was still a boyish-looking girl. She had allowed her hair to grow out over the summer that was bringing her to her seventeenth birthday, but not in a uniform way. It was still very short on the top but now long and feathered down the sides and back, copying a hairstyle made popular by Dave Hill of Slade. She had plucked her eyebrows really thin, and her clothes too were influenced by glam rock and Slade. Long hair, short fringe, platform shoes, big flared trousers; garish stripes, Rupert Bear checks, fluffy jackets with jumbo zips. Boyish girls, girlish boys. Carol had always had a small waist and slim hips. Gender-bending. Bolan and Bowie. That was then the thing.

The couple who stopped to pick her up that night, though, looked pretty straight. The woman, Carol would discover in the course of the brief time she was with them, was only two years older than herself, but if anything she looked younger. Too young, it would occur to her, to be partnered with the man who was driving, who looked old enough to be her father. And when the car came to a stop opposite the Gupshill Manor, it was the woman who wound the window down and spoke. She turned and said something to the driver and then she said OK then, they would give her a lift. The woman got out and tipped up her seat for her, tipped it so that the back dropped forward in a skewed way towards the driver, and Carol hopped in the back.

'Why ain't your boyfriend took you home?' the man said, talking to her through the mirror. He was smoking a roll-up and clocking her. 'Don't your boyfriend take you home?' On the journey the woman asked Carol all about herself, what she was doing in Tewkesbury, whether she lived at home and did she have a job. The answers were: Tony, yes, and no because she had just come back to the area after being away in Portsmouth.

'Ooh – we could do with somebody to help out looking after our children.' She could see the man had a kind of gypsyish look – tight dark hair and a wide turned-up nose. A bit of a dark gap in the middle of his smiley teeth. 'Just a bit of housework and helping Rose really round the 'ouse.'

And Carol goes, 'Ooh, that would be nice', kind of casual. Her ambition was to be a nanny or a model.

There was a bit of smell coming up off the man, not offensive; tobacco and something else.

The woman told Carol they were married and had three children, all girls. Carol told the woman that they had ten in her family, including two sets of twins. That was always the thing at the time – two sets of twins was quite unusual. So that kind of conversation.

Having babies had already started to thicken the woman's figure. That explained the slightly pear shape Carol had noticed when this Rose got out of the car; the broadening, the hint of droop. She was quite pretty but she wore her hair in a short, plain, single-parted cut, about down to her collar. A middle-aged style, in other words, for what was still really a pretty young girl.

The couple didn't drop her when they got to Gloucester, although they lived there. They took the bridge over the river, followed the road up into the high, sloping villages of Dean Forest, and brought her all the way home to Cinderford. By the time they arrived there it had been agreed between them: Carol would move in with them to help look after Anna-Marie, Heather and baby May.

The Wests themselves had only recently moved into their house in Cromwell Street, close to Eastgate market and the main shopping streets in Gloucester. When she turned up there a few days later, Carol was impressed first of all to find herself standing in front of a house in a street full of houses.

Nanny Munroe, the woman who had looked after her mother's first baby, Christopher, until he died, was the only person she had ever known at that point who lived in a *house* house. That is, a house that wasn't owned by the council. Mrs Munroe's had a great big cellar where she used to keep her labradors. You'd come out of there and go upstairs and upstairs and upstairs, and it was huge. Now this house where she was going to be living gave her the same good feelings. These were of solidness and space. It wasn't prefabricated or fast built. It was old. You sensed the depth of its foundations and the weight of its thick walls.

It was only eventually that she realized how close it was to the park; that from the pavement in front of 25 Cromwell Street it was possible to look beyond the spiked railings of Gloucester Park to the lavatories where she had been assaulted by the man from Coney Hill mental hospital, thrown backwards through the air by him, four years earlier; that winded sensation when she struck the wall when she was thirteen. The damp floor.

The toilet building was black and white with black beams running up and across it. It was recently built but had been made to look lumpy like a traditional timber-framed building you would expect to find in a postcard village out in the country somewhere. There was a tree-lined path leading to it.

Although it was the obvious place to take them, Carol would avoid the park, walking past it or around it, when she was out with the pram on her own, treating the West children to some air.

Chapter Two

Gloucester Park runs from Cromwell Street to the round-about on the main road going south out of Gloucester, a distance of about two hundred yards. It is a Victorian park with a white-stone memorial to the dead of the two wars set in a crescent shape into the north-east corner. Away from the road, looking straight along Wellington Street, the street next to Cromwell Street, is a statue of the founder of the Sunday School movement, Robert Raikes; an unremarkable, weathered public monument standing on a high plinth, and noticed by more or less nobody at all.

The park is bare land. The word 'field' probably describes it best. Although it is Victorian, there is none of the dark-green Victorian gloom; no special architectural or landscaping features; no secret places or notorious areas. It is a flat field crossed with paths without very much to break up the flatness. There was a popular café once that stood near the centre but it was closed down some years ago because of the amount of drug-taking and drug-selling going on there.

Every summer since the war, a fair has opened in the park on the last Saturday of July and played for a fortnight. It sets up in the centre and, after dark, becomes an island of light and noise surrounded on all sides by intense blackness. From inside the fair, the house lights in Cromwell Street are only blurrily visible. The brighter lights thrown off by some of the newer rides, laser-like flashes and colours, fail to penetrate the darkness as far as the statue on its plinth or the perimeter railings.

The open flatness of the park is at one end of Cromwell Street and, until fairly recent years, 'Tommy Rich's' was at the other.

The Sir Thomas Rich school opened towards the end of the last century and for seventy-five years occupied a large site between Cromwell Street and Eastgate Street, one of Gloucester's busiest shopping streets. Unlike many of the muscular municipal buildings that were being erected nearby in the same decade – the library, the art gallery, the Guildhall, the City Museum – Tommy Rich's was built in rich red brick rather than blank grey stone. Its Victorian bulk seemed connected to Gloucester Park, a hundred yards away, in much the same way that the great houses of the previous century were connected to their formal gardens. Except, interposed between the school's grandness and the park's greenness, were three narrow streets of terraced and semi-detached houses.

Sir Thomas Rich's School was opened in 1889, and Cromwell, Wellington and Arthur Streets were all also built around that time. The villas of Brunswick Square would remain the most desirable places to live in the Gloucester Park area. There had been an attempt at the beginning of the century to set Gloucester up in competition with Cheltenham as a spa town and tourist centre, and Brunswick Square, apparently perfectly situated to benefit from 'a perpetual current of fresh and wholesome air' from the Severn, had been built as a speculative development next to the spa. The houses' iron palisades and Grecian pilasters were seen as a mark of their owners', and the area's, conspicuous prosperity and respectability.

The houses in Cromwell Street and its close neighbours had little of any architectural merit to recommend them. Modest on any reckoning, they seemed further diminished by the municipal magnificence by which they were surrounded.

The vast warehouse buildings in the docks were also close by and, again, in terms of scale, the houses in Cromwell Street and its near neighbours were dwarfed and made to seem insignificant. And not just dwarfed; also darkened. A darkness that contrasted with the strong light and big horizon of the park, which was always visible. This narrow aspect opening on to so much space. It felt like living in a canyon. But, for fifty years, the area between the school and the park was a well-to-do part of the city inhabited by business people and professionals.

Tommy Rich's gave what the residents considered 'tone' to the area; Sir Thomas Rich's School at one end of Cromwell Street; Fords' garage, with its ramped approach and red, white and blue pumps, owned by the two Ford brothers, at the other.

Even after Cromwell Street had ceased to be neat, quiet and respectable, even after the very name had become synonymous with corruption and human cruelty almost beyond imagining; even then pockets of quiet respectability would persist at the school end of the street.

Years after Tommy Rich's had been demolished and the playground turned into a pay-and-display car park for town-centre shoppers, you could still find fresh paintwork, scrubbed steps, laundered curtains, polished handles, shrubs protected against the weather by plastic bottles and supermarket carrier bags fitted over them at this end of Cromwell Street. Signs of self-respect and ingrained tradition; symbols of standards upheld against the scrappy lives and crude interferences and boom-boxes disturbing the peace; a defence against the loud obscenities rattling the windows in the middle of the night.

Mr and Mrs Miles have lived at 43 Cromwell Street for fifty years. Theirs is the house that abuts the perimeter wall of what used to be Tommy Rich's (although the school is gone, the wall is still there). The windows at number 43 are filled with trailing plants hanging in baskets. Other plants, some swathed in cellophane, others standing in tin biscuit boxes, line the window ledges. Mr Miles, a retired civil servant, grows flowers in beds that run around two sides of his house. He is often to be found on his knees on the pavement, pruning and trimming, forking and sifting, tending his little bit of suburbia.

Mr Miles's special talent is for growing roses – roses of vivid colours: bright crimsons and yellows set against the singing green he has painted the timber frame of his house and almost hallucinatory in this dingy backwater. Big-headed roses trained around thick cane poles.

The flowerbeds are a few inches high and two feet deep and sit right on the pavement. Invariably Mr Miles's first task of the day is picking out the litter; taking away the cigarette packets and hamburger cartons, the lager cans and sweet wrappers that have been discarded there over the previous twelve hours. He does this not angrily, but routinely, before he moves on to anything to do with the care of the plants.

Many years ago, when the Mileses first came to Cromwell Street, there had been allotments all along the backs of the houses, on the spit of land separating Cromwell Street from the then very desirable St Michael's Square. The strip of paved road running down the side of the Mileses' house is an access road for Gloucester Art College. But they remember it when it used to be 'Muddy Alley', the rough track leading into the allotments. And it is possible that Mr Miles's show of roses is an attempt by him to preserve a piece of that old landscape, a last trace of what used to be there before it was levelled and paved over.

Mr and Mrs Miles have a friend who used to take in washing seventy years ago for the people who then lived in their house at 43 Cromwell Street. There are two attic bedrooms where the maids used to sleep. Their friend has told them you used to hear the maids running along the corridor, their feet clattering on the brown-and-yellow-pattern mosaic tiles. They think their employer could have been a doctor. Anyway it was the professional classes.

Sir Thomas Rich was the founder of the Blue Coat School in Gloucester. The boys wore blue hats and blue jackets and the tradition passed down through the generations. Three hundred years later, boys in blue coats were still dragging their feet past Mrs Miles's front-room window on their way to school. The ten-to-nine morning bell rang punctually in the lives of everybody in the area. In 1964, Tommy Rich's moved to a northern suburb of Gloucester, although it would be a further ten years before the school buildings were finally taken down.

Throughout the sixties and seventies, Mr and Mrs Miles watched their friends and neighbours – the McCalls, the Jameses, the Taylors – gradually move out. When they went, they tended not to take very much with them. The better pieces went for sale in Mott's Salerooms in Wellington Street around the corner. The rest – old sofas and tables, curtains and clothes, pictures and ornaments, china and cutlery – was left behind for the new people to use or not use, to keep or to throw away. The old belongings were shabby and shameful, unworthy of the new life that was to begin. People left behind in the old houses a prodigious amount of what they considered junk.

Friends and family and workmates and colleagues and sisters and brothers moved out. Friends and monsters and beasts and thugs and vandals and child-molesters and weirdos and alkies and addicts and scroungers and thieves and liars and cheats and hooligans and drop-outs and no-hopers filled the empty spaces. It started to feel that way anyway to the marooned older residents. 'Ne'er-do-wells' as Mr and Mrs Miles cautiously refer to the new neighbours. People with sitting-up or lying-down mattresses in the small cement front gardens. People who are in the courts every week.

A hitman hired to murder two Gloucester lovers at Barrow Wake beauty spot in November 1991 lived at 1 Cromwell Street, formerly the Commercial School. The pair were trussed up, and pushed over a cliff in a burning car.

One night a drunk put his fist through the window panel of Mr and Mrs Miles's front door, a first in more than forty years of living there. This would be around the time of what they regarded as the riot. School House – the headmaster's house at Tommy Rich's – in recent years has become Winnie Mandela House, a hostel for homeless young people with bright Rastafarian colours painted on the front of it. And Winnie Mandela House acquired as overspill accommodation the small house next door to Mr and Mrs Miles. On the night of the riot they used the stakes from Mr Miles's roses to batter down the hostel door.

There was a time when most of their neighbours from aroundabout would join the Mileses standing on Park Road for the march past and the solemn ceremonial at the war memorial on Remembrance Sunday. No more. Such an archaic act of public remembering can have no appeal for the shifting population of a place whose main reason for being has become its capacity for overlooking; for wiping out and forgetting.

For five years from 1927, Eddie Fry, destined to be known as 'The Pocket Hercules' and 'Gloucester's Midget Strongman', walked along Cromwell Street on his way to the back playground entrance of Sir Thomas Rich's. He was aged eleven to sixteen then and would return to Cromwell Street to live a few years later when he married Doris Green, the girl at number 25.

Eddie's father was the Son of 'Fry and Son', bakers, of 41 Southgate Street. The shop was just a short stroll away from Tommy Rich's and the family lived over the premises. Eddie had attended the British School in Wellington Street until he was eleven, and then his father paid for him to become a Richian – it was like a calling card in the city; there was an association, the 'Old Richians' – in an attempt to knock some of the rough edges off him.

When the plan wasn't succeeding, at the age of fourteen Eddie was made to work in the bakehouse from six in the morning until eight and then have his breakfast and change into the blue cap and blazer to go to school. After school he had to do his homework and then go back in the bakehouse and clean and grease bread tins before the nightshift came in.

He left school at the end of the term following his sixteenth birthday in 1932 and worked full time in the bakery until a persistent skin complaint of the dermatitis type saved him. He was advised to give up the bakery trade, but his father, as it happens, was just about to tell him to get out of the house and the shop; out of his life. Eddie bought a small tent and a motorbike and went and lived in Cranham Woods. Later he moved to a wooden shack on the banks of the Gloucester and Sharpness canal at Hardwick near Gloucester, a little way from the Pilot Inn.

It was around this time that he became very friendly with a young lady called Doris Green. The year was 1938. Her parents had retired three years earlier from the sweet shop they used to run in Lydney, in the Forest of Dean, to live in Cromwell Street in the centre of Gloucester. Number 25 was one half of a house, which, because of the way the pitch of the roof was recessed, looked like a box from the front. The box effect was emphasized by the fact that the doors to numbers 23 and 25 didn't open from the street, as the front doors to all the other houses did, but were around the side.

In the case of number 25, this meant going down the alley-like path separating the house from the next-door mission hall. The boundary of the church land was marked by a high wooden fence, although the hall itself was little more than a shanty building, roughly constructed of wood and corrugated sheeting. As a result, you could hear the singing inside number 25 on those days when there were services. The sound used to come through quite well and it always made for a restful atmosphere which made Mrs Green and the members of her family feel blessed. There was very little other noise to compete with it in those days. The street was quiet and calm. Mr Green, Doris's father, looked after the key to the mission hall and acted as a kind of warden.

25 Cromwell Street was rented from the King agency for seven shillings and sixpence a week. Freddie King – Alderman King – owned a number of properties in the area, and had his rents collected for him by a Mr Cyril every Friday. Every Friday at ten or ten thirty at the latest. He was punctual. Mrs Green would be on the King books for thirty-six years, from 1935 all the way through to 1971. And for many, many years the rent on 25 Cromwell Street never went up from the original seven and six.

Doris's father was a church man, and Eddie knew without him ever having to say anything that he disapproved of the way he lived. He may have been an Old Richian, but the fact was he was living in a wooden shack on the canal bank and driving their daughter around in an Austin 7 Fabric Saloon for which he had given five pounds. But the aspect of Eddie that almost certainly set the loudest alarm bells ringing was the fact that, two or three years earlier, at the age of eighteen, he had joined the boxing club at the India House public house in upper Barton Street.

Eddie was eight stone and five foot nothing, but he trained with most of the old boys: Harry Hewlet, Tosh Wells, Billy

Wagner, Harry Smith, Doug Watkins. He also had a round or two with Hal Bagwell and several other well-known boxers, not forgetting Johnny Thornton. But he couldn't seem to put his heart into boxing as he didn't like punishing people, but he enjoyed the keeping fit. So he concentrated on developing his body. He took up body-building.

He did at least one hour's training in his bedroom every night and still went to India House boxing club two nights a week. After about a year he had developed a very strong and fit, well-musculated body. He was still short, but he had developed his upper body to impressive proportions. In 1937, the year before he started seeing Doris Green, Eddie gave his first public show as a strongman in the skittle alley running alongside the bar in India House. A report with pictures was published in the *Citizen* newspaper and it wasn't long before he was in demand to give shows at clubs, pubs, mission halls and the city hospitals. He gave his first theatre show at the Theatre Deluxe in Northgate Street in Gloucester. A man called Wyndam Lewis played him on stage with 'The Entry of the Gladiators' on the great Wurlitzer organ and continued with a waltz while Eddie held the springs, ten strands of spring whose combined tension weight was more than six hundred pounds, expanded at arm's length. This brought a big round of applause. His other feats included having somebody strike a sledge-hammer on to the three-hundredweight anvil he was supporting on his chest and inviting six heavy men to jump on his stomach. It was a talent show and he took second place.

If, as he suspected, he had always been 'too rough and ready' for his father, a future High Sheriff and Deputy Mayor of Gloucester, Eddie was definitely stronger meat than Mr and Mrs Green had been hoping for as a son-in-law. Sensing that their daughter was showing signs of wanting to spend the rest of her life with a boy who was going to grow old with a bed of nails stored away in his wardrobe, who would be photographed lying on it on his eightieth birthday, bare chested and with a woman in sharp heels standing on his stomach, they made it clear that he was no longer welcome at 25 Cromwell Street.

But Doris Green married Eddie Fry anyway. The wedding took place in February 1939, and their son Brian was born five months later. By then Doris and Eddie had found a flat in Cromwell Street numerically right next door to her parents. Numbers 25 and 27, though, had the mission hall standing in between them.

When Doris came out of hospital, she took the baby and went to stay with her parents. Mr and Mrs Green wouldn't let Eddie see his son and, whenever he tried, told him the same thing: that he wasn't wanted there.

Things continued in this fashion for more than a year, with Doris living on one side of the mission hall with her baby and her mother and father, and Eddie living on the other side on his own.

Eddie was working at the Gloucester Aircraft Company as a fitter in the wing shop when he was enlisted in October 1940. He was sent to Blackpool to do his basic training with the RAF and billeted in a house opposite the Central Pier. His wife was allowed to join him there and it was at Mrs Adshead's in Blackpool that they enjoyed their last period of intimacy together. Doris went back to living with her mother and father in Cromwell Street when they returned to Gloucester. Eddie sold up everything at number 27 and two weeks later was posted to Exeter. The letters he wrote to Doris from there all went unanswered.

By the time the war was over, Doris Fry had had another son with another man and it became clear to Eddie that her parents had won. They had achieved what they wanted and the relationship was over. Eddie left Gloucester then for several years with the idea of following wherever his body-building talents led him.

It is worth following Eddie Fry for a while on his travels, because they reveal some striking coincidences of interest between him and the next long-term resident of 25 Cromwell Street, Fred West, despite an age difference of twenty-five years.

For example, their life-long attachment to caravans and mobile accommodation and what Eddie Fry calls 'living vans': vans and other commercial vehicles converted to domestic use. Also of course for use as 'love wagons'.

In the forties, Eddie took a high-sided Luton Motor Van, previously used for moving furniture, and converted it into a mobile living room. He put in a window high up so nobody could look in. He had a bed in there and a little table and it was all done out for electronics. He put board on the walls and covered it in wallpaper. Thirty years later, Fred West would carry out the same kind of conversion on a former Group 4 Ford transit van, welding the security chutes up, cutting in windows, boarding up the inside with chipboard, and adding a chipboard table for the children to play on. He customized all the vans he owned in this way.

Both Eddie Fry and Fred West were keen motorbike riders as young men, and they would both link the key events of their lives to the bikes or cars they were driving at the time. For more than twenty years Eddie drove a Bentley around town. He thought it was the appropriate transport for 'the most well-known man in Gloucester', which is what he considered himself to be at that time. The Bentley had once been the property of the children's writer, Enid Blyton, and it was put through many resprays during the years that Eddie had it: black, Rolls-Royce 'regal red', glittering gold, back to black for the last couple of years in Eddie's possession. He saw the golden floor in the reception area of a shop and walked out of there and had the car sprayed 'colonial gold'. With the light on it, it would appear to have specks all through it. 'Look at all the people I got mixed up with,' he would say. 'All the big high people. Two out of three people I meet know me.'

At one point in the early sixties, Fred West had got away from Gloucester and had gone to live in Scotland. He drove a Mr Whippy ice-cream van around Glasgow. Twenty years earlier, Eddie Fry had escaped to run a cockles and whelks stall at weekends outside a pub in Wandsworth, in south London. Rented a lock-up garage, managed to find two ice-boxes to keep the shellfish fresh, drove the living van to Billingsgate market in the middle of the night on Thursday mornings for stock. During the week, he did his strongman act in the pubs, sending the hat around afterwards for tokens of appreciation. There was a period selling yo-yos and monkeys on a stick for a couple of men he met in Shepherd's Bush. That was it. Nothing too steady. Ducking in, ducking out.

In those days Eddie considered himself a showman. And he lived on caravan sites with showmen. Gypsies and showmen. Travelling people. Pat Kane, seventy-three, a retired Punch and Judy man, and Minnie Mills, widow of Harry Mills, tinker and grinder, were among his neighbours in the 'caravan colony' in Manley's Yard by the railway line in Battersea. He shared his caravan for more than a year with a homeless girl called Renie Richardson who he had met one night when he was busking in a pub in Clapham. He married his second wife while he was living on a tinkers' site in the East End and eventually moved with her to a site in Barnwood, just outside Gloucester. There were other caravans in Longford, behind Longford Garage, and on a site by Hawkes the Bakers on the Bristol Road.

These were not caravan 'parks' or 'mobile-home communities'. Just derelict parcels of land with few amenities, hidden away out of sight, sometimes in the countryside, but just as often in the heavy industrial suburbs. Hole-in-the-ground toilets and puddles of sump oil and tools left to rust. For most of the sixties, and virtually up to the time he moved into Cromwell Street in 1972, Fred West lived in trailers and small 'snailback' caravans on sites of this type.

He was itinerant and, although of fixed abode, remained, like Eddie Fry, itinerant throughout his life. After his permanent return to Gloucester in the fifties, Eddie made his living for forty years in the waste trade: collecting, baling and selling cardboard, waste paper, rags, hessian sacks and, eventually, scrap metal.

He got his start in the business as a young man going around Barton Street collecting cardboard and paper. He stored it in a disused bakehouse close to where he lived. Even in retirement, now a man in his seventies, he couldn't resist the lure of making money out of junk. He bought a small Mazda pick-up truck and would ride around Gloucester and Stroud and Cheltenham and the villages of the Forest of Dean looking for bits of scrap iron to throw in the back.

Fred West had this same scavenging eye. He was always stopping to pick up bits of rope and electrical cable from the roadside. Clothes line and rope and bits and pieces of rubbish. He'd pick up stuff and have a lot of rubbish in the house. Like Eddie, he enjoyed cruising, looking to make something out of nothing. He had an eye for spotting use in something that had been discarded by everybody else as useless.

Eddie Fry never completely lost touch with Brian, the son he had with Doris Green. Brian would occasionally be allowed to visit his father in whatever circumstances he then happened to be living. As head choirboy at St Mary de Crypt in Gloucester, Brian found such things as jaunts to Billingsgate market in the middle of the night and taking the hat round in pubs for his father and Eddie's alternative way of life very eye-opening.

But mostly Brian Fry went on living with his grandparents and his mother at their home at 25 Cromwell Street, knowing only that something had gone 'radically wrong' between his father and his mother after he came along. When his grandfather died and his mother remarried and moved with her new husband to another house in a different part of Gloucester, Brian would continue living at Cromwell Street with his grandmother, Mrs Green. His mother always worked at RAF Records in Cheltenham Road and his grandmother had brought him up because his mother worked so much. He always thought of his grandmother as his mother. She was the mother figure to him.

Mrs Green – her first name was Amelia – was the heart of the family. A tough matriarchal presence. Pictures from the time show a substantial woman in a felt hat and flower-patterned pinafore down at the bottom of the garden feeding her chickens. And, for the Greens as a family, number 25 was the main meeting point. Whether it was a birthday, Christmas or whatever, everybody came together at Cromwell Street. There were a lot of sons and daughters, cousins, aunts and uncles, and that's where they all met.

Brian had an uncle who was the projectionist at the picture house in Lydney in the Forest of Dean. And it was from this uncle, his uncle Raymond, that he picked up an interest in photography and cameras at an early age. He was bought his first camera when he was about nine, and it got into his system. He moved from still photography to 9.5-millimetre home movie-making, an unusual gauge, now extinct, and soon started to combine this with other interests of his. He was a railway enthusiast. He followed the steam. And he started taking his camera to steam fairs and rallies.

He captured all the changes that were happening in Gloucester in the fifties and sixties. When the coach station was moved out of King's Square in the centre of town and replaced with benches and fountains, Brian was there with his camera for the official reopening. Whatever it was – royal visits, falconry displays or dry-stone-walling demonstrations in the park during Carnival Week – the chances are Brian would be somewhere in the crowd, filming.

The downstairs front room at Cromwell Street was his grandmother's 'special room'. She called it this: her 'special room', furnished quite formally and kept for special occasions. Even so on the floor there was only oilcloth which it was Brian's job to keep clean with lavender polish. There were mats in there – rag rugs – but no carpets. Pride of place was reserved for a gypsy caravan that had been made for Mrs Green when she was a young girl; one of the boys she was courting had made it for her to try and woo her into marriage. It was made of fretwork and it was the centrepiece of the stout, bow-fronted little china cabinet.

The front room, on a level with Cromwell Street and facing out on to it, was on the left as you came in the front door (which of course was actually around the side of the house). On the right as you came in was another room of a similar size. And the Greens lived mostly in there, facing the garden. There was a couch and a door leading down three steps into the kitchen, which was housed in a single-storey brick building jutting out into the garden.

It was in the back room that Brian started giving his film shows on Sunday evenings. The audience consisted of his family, and for a screen he used a bit of cardboard painted up with a professional-looking black border. In the early days it was all amateur footage, but the equipment he shot it with and showed it on was professional standard: he had a Pathé H camera and a Pathé Son sound projector.

In 1955, when he was sixteen, Brian was taken on as rewind boy at the Hippodrome cinema, only a short walk from Cromwell Street in the city centre. But he had been there only five months when the Hippodrome burned down. He moved to the Ritz in Barton Street and made steady progress from rewind boy to chief operator. But the Ritz used to share the news with another cinema, the Regal in King's Square. And at the beginning it was Brian's job to run between the cinemas carrying reels of Pathé newsreel in a can. The audience at the Ritz would see it, and then Brian would make the dash across town to make second house at the Regal.

The perk in those mainly televisionless days was that he sometimes got to keep the news over the weekend and so was able to regale his family with footage of the latest world happenings – Derek Ibbotson recapturing the mile record in 1957, the swearing in of President Kennedy in 1961 – instead of the latest of his own hand-shot sequences commemorating the Great Age of Steam.

Brian slept at the top of the house. The simple layout of two rooms, back and front, a single window in each, was repeated on the two upstairs floors, and Brian slept in the top-floor bedroom overlooking the street. But as a boy, and even later, he spent a lot of time at the bottom of the house, in the cellar.

Immediately under the back-living-room window, in the garden, was a heavy trapdoor made of wood. This opened into a coal hole, and the coalman used to come about once a fortnight, on a Friday, and drop four hundredweight of coal in there. He'd park in the street and carry the bags on his back down the alley, between the mission hall and the front door. Mr Cook, the coalman, came all through the summer so that stocks built up. It was all coal fires in those days, and in the winter months that was the amount that was needed. The coalman would stack the bags as he emptied them so that they could be counted and in that way hope to avoid any misunderstandings.

There was a flight of stone steps under the trapdoor going down into the cellar and afterwards somebody, usually Brian, used to go in there and shovel the coal off the steps and heap it against the wall. The coal was brought to the upstairs living room as it was needed in a narrow-necked zinc scuttle. There was a door to the right of the stairs in the hall, facing the front door, and Brian would go down into the cellar and carry coal up for his grandmother.

The coal was in the part of the house immediately under the back living room, which was half of the cellar. Brian's model railway took up most of the other half, the part under his grandmother's best room, at the front. He had a model railway permanently set up down there. Hornby Double-o. He had two trains: a small 060 truck, and *The Duchess of Atholl*. Still has them. The track was set up on a big tabletop measuring eight feet by four that Brian's uncle had made him. A big chipboard trestle with the legs packed to counter any wobble. This was necessary because the floor in the cellar wasn't even. The floor was red brick. But it was as if the bricks had been laid and then something had happened – some settling, a small shifting – to cause the bricks to lift a little and the ground to go uneven.

There was no window, only a narrow vent, but Brian's uncle Ray had rigged him up a light. And that is where he would spend much of his time, and not only as a boy, but also later.

He remembers when he was down there being able to hear the piano and the singing from next door at the church. The lusty singing from *The Seventh-day Adventists' Hymnal* by the choir of elderly West Indian men and women; the women in dark skirts and white blouses and wide-brimmed black or white hats; the men, even in hot weather, in formal suits, mostly of metallic fabrics, and collars and ties, singing counterpoint. 'Amazing love!' Hymn number 198. Being a choirboy himself for eight years, Brian recognized some of the songs. Their Sabbath was actually the Saturday. And sometimes Brian would see them congregating on the pavement outside the church late in the morning, in lively, chattering, nicely dressed family groups.

Brian wouldn't get married until he was thirty, in 1969. There were stays at various properties Eddie Fry had acquired in and around Gloucester. But they never amounted to anything. Brian always went back to living with his grandmother at Cromwell Street. There was no real wanderlust there.

Towards the end of her life, when the stairs became a problem, Mrs Green moved her bedroom into the ground-floor room at the front of the house. Brian moved down a floor to be near by if she needed him in the night. The house was nowhere near as big as it looked from the street. The rooms were very small and his grandmother only had to make a noise turning in bed for him to hear it. When he was little, she would come out into the hallway to get him up for school. She'd call up the stairs to the top room where he was sleeping, and always one call would do it.

Mrs Green died in what had formerly been her 'special room', in February 1971, and was buried from Cromwell Street. She was eighty-four. It ended a connection with the house that had lasted for thirty-six years.

Many years later, when all its openings have been blocked, the doors and windows walled up as a result of the terrible discoveries that have been made there, petty criminals will give tours of Mrs Green's old home by torchlight to paying visitors, entering under cover of darkness. More than a few of the visitors, battle-hardened media people, will be afraid to descend the stairs into what was once the place where a boy came to watch his trains go round. The shadows leaping and the floorboards groaning like some cheap, churned-out horror movie.

Even after he had married and moved away from the area, Brian Fry found himself parking his car in Cromwell Street whenever he went into town to go shopping. He used to park in Cromwell Street or Wellington Street and then walk across what used to be the playground at Tommy Rich's to the shops around the Cross. And of course he was curious. Many times when he was passing he felt like knocking and asking the people who were living there then if they would mind letting him have a look at the place. His old home. On more than one occasion he took some steps towards the front door. But always something stopped him. The quiet possibly. It was just that quiet. Call it an intuition.

For some years there was no sign of any structural alteration to 25 Cromwell Street, or none anyway that was visible from the street. Quite quickly a cladding skin did appear, biscuit in colour with a gravelly texture, the cheapest form of cladding. It evened out the old weathered brickwork and pointing, giving the outside of the house an overall blankness and flatness, a featureless uniformity it had never had. Only the stepped sandstone lintels above the windows were left as the slightest decorative interruption.

After a while an iron gate appeared, silver-painted and worked in scrolls, with only its height perhaps – it was head height – alluding to a bleaker purpose. It was fixed at one side to the wall of the house and at the other to the wall of the church. A double gate with two opening parts to it.

But Brian Fry can honestly say that he had those feelings even not knowing what he now knows. It was the quiet that disturbed him. And the presence of the gates. In fact two sets of gates. Low black metal ones at the pavement, with spear-tips painted gold; high, arched silver ones with a heavy lock on, some feet behind them, between the house and the church. The door to his grandmother's house – to virtually all the houses in Cromwell Street – had always been open. In his day the door was open and you'd walk up the alleyway and straight in.

So there were no major changes. And yet the feeling persisted. And it was stronger than the normal resistance to having the place of your childhood and your first memories meddled with. It was stronger than that. It was the sensation of the homely turned unhomely; the familiar turned strange. A web of strangeness seeming to enclose what had long been unconsciously a part of him.

By the eighties, Brian had stopped going by his old home altogether. He didn't want to give himself that feeling. He started using a way into town that took him away from Cromwell Street rather than past it, which had always been his habit.

You never saw anybody, that was what got him. He believed there were several children living in the house, but you never heard a sound.

Chapter Three

Anna-Marie was eight, Heather was two, and the baby, May June, was four months. Anna-Marie was the daughter of Fred West's first marriage, and Carol found her clinging. If they sat next to each other on the sofa Anna would play with Carol's hair and when she was standing talking to her she would touch her hair or her arm. Very touchy. Always touching and wanting to cuddle up.

And Carol had to share a bedroom with Anna-Marie. She really thought she was going to get her own room when she saw the size of the house. Some personal space for the first time in her life at the age of nearly seventeen. And she ended up sharing with Anna-Marie. So that was a let-down for a start.

Between Mrs Green dying in the winter of 1971 and the Wests moving in in September 1972, 25 Cromwell Street had been let out as bedsits. The King agency had sold the house to an elderly Pole called Frank Zygmunt who had been steadily amassing properties all over Gloucester. The Wests had been living in another of Mr Zygmunt's houses in Midland Road, on the other side of Gloucester Park, when the offer of Cromwell Street came up. They had had the ground floor of the house. Two rooms and a kitchen.

Fred West was working in a factory and earning extra money by being on call to Frank Zygmunt as a jobbing builder. There was a bond between the Wests and Mr Zygmunt, and he was trying to do what he could to help them. With Frank Zygmunt's help (a loan of £500, plus pushing forward the mortgaging process and the paperwork that Fred West was incapable of taking care of himself), West completed the purchase of 25 Cromwell Street in July 1972, and moved in with his family a few weeks later. A few weeks after that Carol Raine joined them as a mother's help or – the word they preferred, and she wasn't going to argue – 'nanny'.

After Mrs Green's death, Zygmunt had rented the house to students. He quite quickly evicted them for mess and nuisance and non-payment of rent. He had done the minimum needed to make the house suitable for quick multi-occupation. The walls, the floors, some of the furniture, even the curtains were as Mrs Green had left them. Not able to afford major (or even minor) redecoration, the Wests in turn fitted their few possessions in around the dated wallpapers and faded linos and skimpy floor coverings.

Fred West had decided that letting out rooms would see them through their short-term but pressing financial difficulties. They were still sometimes living on chips and bread and butter. It seemed like Rose and the children were always hungry.

He had installed cupboard units and Baby Belling cookers on the top two floors, between the front and back rooms, in order to keep the lodgers out of the way in that part of the house. He put a small ad in the Gloucester *Citizen* offering double bedsits at £6 a week and found he could have filled them many times over.

The Wests were just getting on their feet around the time they picked Carol up outside the Gupshill Manor pub in Tewkesbury. But they – that is to say, he – had a way with the chat. Mouth almighty. He was good at putting a spin on things. And so the shabbiness was Carol's second disappointment. The cold lino and lumpy cushions. Bed springs that stuck in your back. It was just a rather lived-in house. It was quite tatty; nothing had been done. A little man trying to be a big man. That was Carol's verdict on the husband. All hat and no cattle.

And no mention had been made of lodgers. About the fact that lodgers had most of the rooms on the first and second floors, making them effectively out of bounds. The front downstairs room, Mrs Green's special room and the one where she had died, was Fred's and Rose's room. The door to the cellar was kept locked. Carol's movements were restricted to the room she shared with Anna-Marie, the eight-year-old who was all over her, and the small living room on the ground floor. But where else was she going? She'd left school at fifteen, and had no concentration and had done no exams. All she wanted to do was get away from home.

Fred West knew Cinderford. He'd grown up a few miles to the north, just over the county border in Herefordshire. His father was a farm labourer, and he had lived in and around farms all his life. As recently as five years earlier he had had a job that involved regular trips to Cinderford and the Forest of Dean. He drove a lorry around abattoirs, collecting hides and skins and offal. It was a night run and his route included Tredegar, Newport in Monmouthshire, Ross-on-Wye, and Ensor's in Cinderford. They used to kill late at Ensor's, which meant a wait. So he would pass the time sitting in the Telebar coffee bar at the bottom of the town. Carol used to get in there on occasions and, although she was only eleven or twelve and had no memory of ever seeing him, it is possible Fred West noticed her then.

Northwood Close, where Carol had gone back to living with Alf Harris and her mother and all her half-brothers and sisters, including the two sets of twins, Adrian and Angela and Richard and Robert, was at the opposite end of the High Street in Cinderford to the Telebar. The Wests had taken care to drop her off outside her door in Northwood Close the night they gave her a lift home from Tewkesbury. And they were back there in the grey Ford Popular a few days later to persuade Alf and Betty to let Carol come and be their live-in help. They brought the three children with them to meet Carol and they were given tea and biscuits and a nice Sunday afternoon tea.

A certain, not unhumorous, pageant of small talk and niceness was carried out. There was the Wests with their talk of 'nurseries' and 'nannies' and mortgage commitments, and Betty who was introduced to the Wests as 'Liz'. This was the name she had switched to when she changed her last name to 'Harris', following her marriage and her move from Gloucester to Cinderford a dozen years before. Carol, too, had told the Wests her name was 'Caroline', and this was true. But all she had ever got in Cinderford was 'Carol' and the even shorter 'Car'. Now she was embarking on a new phase of her life and she wanted 'Caroline' and the Wests seemed happy to go along. Alf, whose name Carol had always had difficulty pronouncing – it came out as 'Halfred 'Arrison', with the aitch in the wrong place – was still recovering from the heart attack that had brought Carol back from her Southsea jaunt. He came in from the shed just long enough to say hello.

Alf didn't say much, but it didn't matter. Fred West did enough talking for them all. He hadn't made any kind of effort for the occasion in terms of how he looked. Casually scruffy, you would have to say. But you wouldn't say he looked dirty when he visited Carol in Cinderford. He was just scruffy, that's all. The Wests didn't really stand out that bad, to Carol or her mother. As looking . . . rough. 'Nobody', Carol remembers, 'was that smart in them days.'

They had a cup of tea and biscuits and a chat, and they agreed. Caroline had moved in with the Wests within a few days.

Rose and Caroline would go shopping together, do the housework and cook together, and quickly settled into a harmonious routine. But, although there was only two years between them – Rose was nearly nineteen, Caroline coming up to seventeen – there wasn't a lot of common ground. Caroline had been to nightclubs and hitched all over the country and had loads of boyfriends and liked pop bands and fashionable clothes. And Rose was with a man twelve years her senior and had an eight-year-old stepdaughter and two babies and, as far as Caroline knew, no social life. She was quite a pretty girl. But she had a drippy voice on her. Quite annoying, that slow voice. And she dressed too old for her age.

Caroline had friends working in a café on Clarence Street in Gloucester, which was virtually around the corner. A chip bar plus restaurant in the main shopping centre. They were a couple of girls she had grown up with and gone to school with in Cinderford for a while. She would go to the café to see them, and now and then they'd go out round to the Dirty Duck off Southgate Street and have Ponies and Cherry Bs and lots of other sticky drinks in little bottles until they were sick. A Wicked Lady was brandy and Babycham. About four of them and you'd be throwing up.

There was a nightclub called Tracy's below the multi-storey car park on the bus station, another short walk away, and Caroline used to sneak in there sometimes. Very occasionally she'd hang around the bus station itself in her platforms and wide flares. She was still staying well away from the park. But most of the time the children kept her in or around the house in Cromwell Street, which she didn't regard as any kind of sentence at all. She wasn't often bored.

The room that Caroline shared with Anna-Marie was on the first floor at the back of the house. There was a bathroom and separate toilet opposite, and both of the rooms upstairs were filled with lodgers. Officially there were four of them. But from the amount of traffic on the stairs and the noises coming from the boys' rooms and the bathroom at night, you could obviously multiply that by several times. Caroline would lie there on red alert, trying to piece together in her mind what was going on.

All the first intake of lodgers were male; hippies or bikers, Hell's Angels types. A café on Southgate Street called the Pop-Inn was frequented by the Vampire motorcycle gang. Another gang, the Scorpions, mostly used the Talbot pub next door. Fred West, once the owner of a 1000 cc. Triumph, knew members of both gangs from being a Pop-Inn regular, and also from when he was living above the Rendezvous café in Newent, a popular biker haunt.

Eric, one of the first to have the top-floor front room at Cromwell Street, was a Scorpion. He was seventeen, had recently dropped out of school, had a bad drink problem, and needed somewhere to doss down. He moved into Cromwell Street with Wagg Jones, another Scorpion gang member, and a half-caste boy called Billy. There were a lot of parties. Endless parties. And a lot of drugs. From about eight in the morning, you'd have all the girls who were old enough to have jobs, the seventeen- and eighteen-year-olds, leaving to go to work. Then you got what Fred West called the 'teenyboppers', the fourteen- and fifteen-year-olds and younger, all the teenyboppers coming in for the day. They disappeared about half-past four or five, and all the other girls came back. There were comings and going at all hours of the night and day. And the people who owned the house never seemed to mind. There could be anything up to thirty people in the house at any one time. It was just a continuous flow going in and out all the time.

Caroline was aware that there were mattresses on the floor of the room that shared a landing with hers, where people could 'crash', but she never went in. When she wasn't with her own friends she was shy. She could appear tough and probably a bit brash, but that was only when she was with people she knew. At other times, she'd get nervous if people started chatting her up. It was only when she was with her mates that she got brave. With her mates and dancing. Otherwise she was pretty shy. During the day she spent all her time downstairs in the living room and the scullery, looking after the children and cleaning and generally helping out. There was an outside toilet between the scullery and an old garden shed the Greens had left behind, and she was happy to use that.

She was still seeing Tony Coates, her boyfriend in Tewkesbury. But now Tony was travelling to see her. He had to go to Gloscat one day a week as part of the apprenticeship he was on. And Gloscat – Gloucester College of Art and Technology – was on the next street over from Cromwell Street. Practically backed on to it. So Tony would bicycle over from Tewkesbury, a distance of about ten miles, and stay with Caroline the night before. The Wests were all for this. Very encouraging. They were very keen for Tony to come. So he started coming and staying one night a week, and the next morning he would get up and go to college.

Caroline was approaching her seventeenth birthday. She was going to be seventeen on 26 October 1972. She had stayed in touch with Steve 'Jimmy Riddle' Riddall, the sailor she'd met in Southsea. And Steve wrote to her at the new address she had given him in Gloucester saying that he would like to come and see her on her birthday. He asked if he could stay the night and again Fred and Rose were very keen. Caroline had told Rose about this old boyfriend she still wrote to, about how they had made love once before when she was living in Portsmouth and about her infatuation with him and him having a girl in every port. She confided her worries about two-timing Tony. But it was at Rose's suggestion that Caroline had written to Steve inviting him to stay the weekend.

She was very excited the day of her birthday and waited all day for Steve to turn up but he never came. However he did appear at Cromwell Street the next day. It was late. They got to the pub just before closing time and Caroline quickly got a few drinks inside herself. She always felt shy in front of Steve and so she needed that. When they got back, Fred and Rose were waiting up to tell them they had decided to let them use their room for the night, which had a double bed. They would sleep in her single upstairs.

It was the first time Caroline had had a bed that was big enough to roll around in, and they talked or made love all night. She experienced her first orgasm that night, although she wasn't clear at first that was what it was. She thought she was having palpitations and her legs went stiff and she felt her muscles ache after. When she told her sailor he laughed and informed her, 'That was an orgasm', so now she knew what all the fuss was about.

He left the next day instead of staying the whole weekend. After he had gone, she found a twenty-pound note just showing from behind the big mirror in the room. His birthday present to her, as she found out later. But she thought it must be the Wests' and so she took it and gave it to them.

Later, Rose asked Caroline how it had gone, her night with her sailor. And Caroline told her: it had been great. But then Rose had to go and tell this to Fred and Fred as usual had to know more. She had started to notice this tendency in him. His liking for smut. He liked talking about sex. He used to ask all sorts of personal questions about her sex life. What she did in bed with Tony, and so on. He brought every conversation around to sex in the end. He thought he was the expert on it to hear him talk.

There were two, sometimes three, men a few years older than Caroline living in the rear top-floor bedsit, immediately above her. They were hippies and they played loud music and smoked grass and she would talk to them when they met each other on the stairs or in the street and she took a fancy to this one called Ben. He was tall with long dark hair and a nice smile and he talked rather slowly on account of him always being stoned.

Ben Stanniland shared with Alan Davis, who was known as 'Dapper' and was short and skinny and not as hot in the looks department to Caroline's way of thinking as Ben. When the inevitable happened and the hippy lodgers invited her upstairs to their place for a drink one night, she went.

In the event, she wouldn't be able to remember whether she had a drink *and* a smoke, or just the smoke. Another new experience. It was her first attempt at dope. So there was druggy music and dope and she ended up having sex – 'nookie', she called it – with Ben on the floor. When it was over Ben got into his single bed and Caroline fell asleep where she was. When she woke up, the other one, the one known as 'Dapper', was on top of her, and she's like, 'Oh, get off.' Still not quite back on the planet. 'Leave me alone.' You wake up and somebody's messing you around and it's not the person you thought it was. Ben's telling him 'Get off her' and 'Leave it' but Ben's still out of his brain and Dapper Davis is going on being his usual horrible self: fucking this, fuck you, fucking that. 'Ahh, she wants it.' That one, of course. All this kind of stuff. And he did get off, but not until he'd finished. Then he gave her another load of verbal abuse.

The next day she felt horrible. She felt disgusted with herself. But there was nobody she could tell. She couldn't tell Tony because she had been with Ben as well and that was out of choice. She couldn't tell the Wests because she knew what he would say: 'Why didn't you stay away, they're druggies. I warned you to stay away.'

But Caroline's feeling was that Fred West had quickly found out what had gone on upstairs anyway, either through listening or watching (a possibility that didn't occur to her until a long time afterwards), or through being told. She was conscious that, from around the time of this incident, his sex talk and sexual innuendo started to become more and more crude. He grew increasingly bare-faced in his references to sex and kinky sex and the 'operations' he had performed.

What she didn't know was that the situation in which she had found herself that night was a virtual rerun of what had taken place on the night Ben Stanniland and Dapper Davis moved into Cromwell Street just two or three weeks before. The difference was that the woman involved then was Rose West and all the sex was consensual.

Fred West had invited them out for a drink with him and his wife on their first night. They had gone to the nearest pub, the Wellington, thirty yards away along 'little' Cromwell Street on the corner of Wellington Street, and call-me-Fred, the new landlord, had spelled out the broad-minded, free-and-easy, anything-goes attitude – what he would regard as the 'hippy' attitude – he took towards sex. To prove it, the door to their room opened and his wife climbed into bed with Ben Stanniland later that night. When she had finished with Ben, it was Dapper Davis's turn. They were dubious about what would happen the next time they saw Fred West, but the next time they saw him he just grinned.

An aspect of living at Cromwell Street that had immediately struck Caroline as strange was the fact that there were no locks on the bathroom and toilet doors. If she was in the toilet and there was the sound of somebody outside, this involved a lot of coughing to let them know that it was being used. She would get a foot to the door if that was possible.

Of course you couldn't do anything when you were in the bath apart from slide down into it a bit deeper if somebody walked in. Rose frequently used to come in the bathroom

61

when Caroline was in the bath. She would stand by the bath and stroke her hair. The crop growing out around the edges into feathery strands. Lift the damp hair away from her face and tell her how lovely it was. Rose was always telling Caroline she had beautiful eyes and if they sat next to each other on the sofa she would mess with her hair, just like Anna-Marie. But she never worried about it. She never saw it as leading to anywhere else.

It would have been just about understandable for anybody not up with the latest trends in fashion and popular music to misread the signs that Caroline was sending out. The big boots, the boyish hair, the high-waisted, tight-fitting trousers. That tough-nut attitude which was new. Fred West went around whistling the ancient Susan Maugham hit, 'I Want to be Bobby's Girl'. A record from his youth. He was a man who it is probably safe to say had never danced in his life. Rose West had gone to live with him more or less straight from school at the age of fifteen. But it was the year of David Bowie and *Ziggy Stardust* and *The Spiders from Mars*. And the way Caroline looked was only that: a look; a tribal thing; a fashion. She never thought it could be misread as a statement about her sexual preference. It had never occurred to her that it could be open to that kind of misinterpretation.

None of these things had occurred to her until an encounter that took place with a woman in Cromwell Street after she had been living there for two or three weeks. It started off quite hostile. Caroline was alone in the house and the woman accused her of stealing her job and replacing her as nanny to the West children. This was a big woman. Tall and bleached-blonde and very buxom. Very big and powerful-looking. Loud. About nineteen. But she was buxom. And things looked nasty for a while until Caroline explained that she didn't know anything about the woman – she never learned her name – and wasn't aware that she was taking any-body's job away from them.

They started chatting and this girl who used to babysit for Fred and Rose asked Caroline, 'Has Rose ever tried it on with you?' And Caroline said no, in quite an indignant way. What did she mean? Of course she knew what she meant but she wanted her to spell it out. 'You know, tried to get into your bed with you or have sex with you or anything like that? Because she did with me. You want to watch her. Didn't you know she's both ways?'

The blonde then went on to tell her about the time that she had brought a black bloke back to Cromwell Street one night and Rose had jumped in the bed with them. Caroline was starting to think now that maybe the girl was trying to scare her into leaving so that she could move back in and take over. But that was the first inkling she had had that Rose might be that way.

And then she ended up asking Caroline out on the day she visited. The big buxom piece asked Caroline to go to the local Jamaica Club with her. And, having nothing better to do, Caroline said OK. It wasn't her kind of place and she had never mixed with blacks before but she went anyway.

The only black people she knew in those days were on *The Black and White Minstrel Show* on television. She used to hate it, but Alf Harris used to make her sit down and watch it. There was one black man in the whole of the Forest of Dean, Big Joe, and he was a character and called them all 'honkies' and married a white woman in Cinderford.

Actually, Alf and Betty had a couple of friends who were black. Their main friends, the couple they went around with, were white, but *they* had black friends. And they all used to come through to Cinderford now and then for a drink. Afterwards they would come back to Alf's and Betty's after shut tap at the George or the Foresters for supper of a

ploughman's. Cheese and bread and pickled onions. Always
a ploughman's. Caroline was still little then, and if she saw
them it would either be because she got out of bed when
they came in, or she saw them going into the bathroom,
through her bedroom door. These were the only black people she had had any personal contact with, and she was
always a bit wary.

Most of her life Caroline grew up thinking that all black
faces washed off like the ones on the television and like Alf's
when he came home from the pit. Fred West also had a black
face for a lot of the time as a result of the job he did at the
factory. He would come home and go back out without
washing. He wouldn't wash to sit down and have his dinner,
or even to go to bed on many nights. He'd keep the oily black
face on all the time.

There had been a slowly growing West Indian community
in Gloucester since the mid-fifties. Today it is based mainly
around the Midland Road area on the other side of Gloucester Park. But in 1972 many Jamaicans lived in and around
Wellington Street and Cromwell Street, closer to the city centre. A Mr Joiner in Wellington Street was one of the first gro-
cers to supply Caribbean produce and, in the sixties, with the
help of a grant from the council, Jamaicans in Gloucester
opened their own social club.

The Jamaica Club was virtually empty on the afternoon
that Caroline visited with the former babysitter for the
Wests. There was just a band that had been rehearsing and
an old man. Caroline was nervous. She was still a bit leery.
Maybe it was because of that rumour there was about black
men. Black men are big boys.

The blonde girl disappeared after a while, to have sex, as
Caroline later discovered, with somebody outside in a van.
And then somebody else had decided they were going to have
sex with the girl as well. Later Caroline remembered a text-

book pursuit dream. A dream of being chased. But it wasn't a dream; she says it was real. 'After the blonde piece, they decided they were going to have me. I know I got a warning that if I didn't get out of there I'd be gang-banged. That was the intention of these blokes. So I did a runner. And I got chased by half-a-dozen of them. I had one left chasing me in the end, and that was the youngest of the crowd, and he's saying, "You're all right, you're all right . . ." Anyway I managed to get away from them and went back to the house.'

The most regular visitor to Cromwell Street during Caroline's time there was Frank Zygmunt, the elderly Pole who had advanced the Wests the money to buy the house. He would come about once a week and money would change hands. After a while Caroline became pretty sure that there was something going on between him and Rose.

The only other regular visitors were a number of West Indian men who Caroline was told came round to see Rose for a 'massage'. Even before what had happened at the Jamaica Club she was wary of these men. She didn't like being on her own in a room with them. But they turned out to be all right. One man in particular was very nice. He would come in the back room and chat with her while he was waiting for his time with Rose. He had met Fred and Rose in the Arthur, another local pub, and they had invited him back round to supper. Caroline liked him. His name was Roy. He never made any kind of move on her. He was very smiley. He reassured her.

The longer she went on living at Cromwell Street with the Wests, the more Caroline felt she needed reassurance. Fred was a bully. Anna-Marie, the oldest girl, was always quiet when Fred was around. She did what she was told when she was told without a murmur. And from time to time he would pick on Rose.

Rose wanted to please. Giving your man a good meal after

working hard all day was very important, was the kind of thing she would come out with to Caroline. It was what her mum had taught her. She was only nearly nineteen. That's how old-fashioned she was.

Caroline had never had a live-in relationship with anybody, but she had seen people. She had seen her mother with Alf Harris, and her mother with Michael Mahoney, the Irishman who was her real father, and it hadn't been like this. Not so strong and locked into each other. He was very sexual with her, and he liked talking about it. He was always grabbing hold of her. Grabbing out and touching no matter who was there, which was a bit embarrassing.

But he would suddenly turn on her. Caroline would try and stick up for Rose when that happened and he would tell her to mind her own business. And it was true. Rose seemed prepared to take it. Caroline didn't know what she was doing with him in the first place.

She wasn't getting on with Fred and hated it when he started telling her about the operations he could do. If you had anything wrong down below he'd put it right for you, and he knew different ways so you could get more pleasure from sex. He would brag about his sex life and tell Caroline if she ever got pregnant he could give her an abortion; he'd done them before. He was talking as if he had actually performed some sort of operations on women.

Caroline began to dread these conversations. At first she had suspected it was just lies. Then one day he was talking about sex yet again and he said that Anna-Marie wasn't a virgin. He told her that Anna-Marie, who was eight, had already lost her virginity. She was aware of him watching her carefully while he was telling her this, and when he observed how she reacted – she was upset and angry; repulsed by what she was having to hear – he said, 'She fell off her pushbike and hurt herself.' The saddle had come off Anna-Marie's bike and she had gone to sit on it without realizing and damaged herself.

Caroline wouldn't be able to remember for a long time how she had come to get away from Cromwell Street. She knew he'd said all this about operations and abortions and about Anna-Marie not being a virgin any more. But she couldn't remember about the nice Jamaican, who she now knows was called Roy Morgan, coming to the house one day and finding her hysterical and crying and begging him to help her because they were saying things to her and wanting her to take part in a 'sex circle'. She buried all this. How she left the house when she was living there.

Roy Morgan remembered where she came from, Cinderford. And he told her to get her things together and he drove her there. He took her all the way home to Northwood Close and met her mum and Alf and had one drink in a pub in Cinderford with them, wished them luck and went on his way.

But she blanked this for many years. Her memories were revived years later only by hearing Roy Morgan's account of what happened. And the reason she thinks she blanked it is because she made an inexplicable mistake and accepted a lift from the Wests again. She had had the warning but she still got into their car. She had been given the signal but she ignored it.

She reported what she believed was the abuse of an eight-year-old girl living at 25 Cromwell Street in Gloucester, but she didn't hear any more about it.

Caroline left Cromwell Street about two weeks after her seventeenth birthday. She had been there for six weeks altogether. She stayed shaken up for a few days, but soon she went back to her routine of going to see Tony three or four nights a week, thumbing it from Cinderford to Tewkesbury.

A month would pass until the night when Tony would leave her at their usual place across the road from the Gupshill Manor pub and she would be driven off to face the ordeal that some raw part of her had always been dreading. She knew even as it was beginning that this was the most terrible thing that had happened to her and that she would for ever be singled out by it.

6 December 1972 was a Wednesday. Caroline knows that from the police reports of what followed. But it could have been any day. They hadn't done anything special. She had met up with Tony and they had killed a few hours doing what they usually did, which was mooching about, wandering around town, sitting in cafés. They had spotted the Wests about nine thirty or ten. The main Gloucester Road forks as it enters Tewkesbury, and they had seen the Wests' Ford Popular going off the roundabout to take one part of the fork while they were on the other. They seemed to be riding around, cruising. They knew that Caroline would be hitchhiking home at her usual time, and when they saw the Wests, Caroline and Tony gathered that they were keeping an eye out for her. They had seen the Wests but they didn't think the Wests had seen them.

Caroline had been standing by the road for about ten minutes on her own when the grey car came to a stop beside her. She didn't know what was going to happen until it happened. She didn't have anything in her head to say, in spite of the advance warning. It was Rose who spoke first. 'Oh, we really missed you. The children really missed you.' All this. She was out of the car, standing on the roadside next to Caroline, being really nice. She chatted away. He was being really nice from inside the car as well. 'I'm sorry you left on bad feelings. I'm sorry we had a row.' De dah. She didn't know what was going to happen. They could have started a confrontation. And because she was so nice, and he was so nice, although she was

68

still a bit dubious about it, she got in the car. She didn't want to start the friendship off again, but out of relief partly, and partly out of embarrassment, she got in the car.

And Rose said, 'Oh, I'll get in the back with Caroline, so we can have a chat.' Her drippy voice. Slow and high. And that's what happened. She got in the back and she was all like nice again and chatting away about the kids and that. Girls' stuff. Nanny stuff. Rose sitting next to her, Fred in the front. Caroline was just trying to get home to Cinderford. It was when they got to Gloucester and had crossed the river and were starting along the Chepstow Road towards the Forest that some change occurred. Like a change in pressure, when your ears pop. It was as noticeable as that. Almost physical. Caroline could sense that there was something between them and that she wasn't quite in on this.

'Had sex with Tony tonight, then?' This was him speaking of course. Watching for her reaction in the mirror. 'Had sex with Tony tonight, then?' And then she started grinning at Caroline and laughing, edging closer, and Caroline was saying no. No! Unlike the time in the toilets when she couldn't get any sound to come. She heard her voice and it was loud in the car. No! *No!*

And, over Rose's laughing and Caroline's protests, he said, 'See if she has, Rose.' So Rose thrust her hands between Caroline's legs, grabbing. And then he said, 'What's her tits like?' Seeing her in terms of her parts. Breaking her down to her parts. Her head also disembodied and floating in the mirror. So she grabbed Caroline's breasts and kept grabbing, all the time laughing and grinning up close in her face. And an odd thought occurred to Caroline then: that Rose might have been nervous as well for all she knew. As scared as her. But no. Horrible laugh. Horrible grin. And him looking in the mirror all the time.

Caroline was still wrestling with Rose, who she found to be

strong, still trying to fight her off, when she felt the car moving over softer ground. Next she saw a five-bar gate brightly illuminated in the headlights. A farm gate opening into a field.

For Cinderford, you turn left at the first big roundabout out of Gloucester. This is Highnam. There's a big field and a five-bar gate there. Caroline knew the roundabout and the gate well, having used the road regularly from the age of five. Strange that she should recognize this gate, one gate out of so many, but she did. It gave her a bearing when the car came to a halt.

The gate was the last thing she saw before he knocked her out. As soon as they stopped, he turned around in his seat and punched her in the side of the head. She saw stars like in the cartoons. Black-framed flashes of light. She was knocked out as a result of the punches she took to the mouth and the head. She had started panicking. And that's why he did what he did; to quiet her. She was making noise and shouting and panicking. The main road was just behind them and it was quite busy. It was the going-home time of night. And then when she came round she found that she was tied up and they were putting some stuff around her head. They had forced her forward and tied her hands behind her back with her scarf. It was December, coming up to Christmas; it was cold nights and she had brought a scarf. He dragged her head up and, while she held her, he taped it all around, across her mouth and around the back of her hair so she could hardly breathe. And all the time they were laughing and threatening her and telling her to just shut up and things would be all right. The sound of the tape and the effort it took to get it off the roll. She could tell from his breathing it was effortful. The tape they used to gag her up was brown and very tough. Textured and gummy. Like parcel tape. Very sticky. And when it was on and she could only breathe through her nose, they pushed her down on to the back seat, bound and gagged, and Rose sat on top of her.

He turned the car around and set off back to Gloucester.

The way she was lying, she was able to see up. She could see all the street lights, the lamps lighting up the road signs, and she sensed they were travelling back towards Gloucester. She knew where she was going.

They took her back all tied up. But Rose had been her friend. She thought Rose was her friend. After that girl had told her what she had about Rose being both ways and liking other women, Caroline had thought that maybe she *was* a bit strange. But even if she was a bit strange and she fancied her, she had been sure Rose would never hurt her. She'd stuck up for her a few times in front of Fred when he'd had a go at her about anything.

And she had never seen them bundle anybody into the house, or seen strips of tape or anything. Never heard anybody. And they had tied her up with her scarf, which meant they obviously hadn't planned it. And the tape, she thought he'd just grabbed hold of that out of the car. It must have been in the car and he'd just used it. If they had planned it, it made sense that they would have brought something with them. The street lights kept going by like a stick against a railing.

Caroline has an idea now that he went in first to make sure the hallway was clear. One of them went in, then they all went in. They took her upstairs. Led her upstairs, one behind, one in front. Upstairs and left through a door. She couldn't remember ever being in that room before. It was the room on the first floor at the front of the house, overlooking Cromwell Street. She had been thinking if they were going to take her to a bedroom, it would be their bedroom just inside the front door, because there was much less risk of being spotted that way. But they ended up in the other room on the floor where she had shared a room with Anna-Marie, the bigger room with the mattresses in it for 'crashing'. Brian Fry's last bedroom when he was living in the house.

In addition to the mattresses, there was a sofa. They sat her on it. Then, when she was seated, Fred West brought out a knife. Of course she thought he was going to stab her and that at the time was the worst way to die as far as she was concerned. For a long time – for the remainder of her life; twenty-six years now – she would have nightmares, varying from seeing herself being used for sex by the Wests and their friends, and the different ways they killed her, to being buried alive and hearing people walking and talking as they passed over her grave on one of Gloucester's busiest corners. She is shouting for help, for somebody to come and get her, clawing the under part of the pavement, and nobody can hear her and she wakes up still shouting. Yet when they had her in their home that night she was too scared to shout out for help in case they killed her sooner in panic.

When he went to cut the tape from around her face and head she thought he was going to kill her then but he didn't. He did cut her, though. Nicked her face with the double-sided knife he used to cut away the packing-tape gag.

This made her more comfortable, but her comfort wasn't his main concern. Taking away the tape made her mouth available for his wife. And his wife sat down next to her on the sofa and began pleasuring herself, bearing down, touching and kissing. Caroline remained fully dressed at this point, and after a while Rose went and made them all cups of tea. Fred West untied Caroline's arms so that she could hold her tea, but as soon as she had finished they both started to undress her. When she was completely undressed they retied her hands and packed her mouth with cottonwool. While Rose West was taking her own clothes off, he told Caroline to lie on her back on the double mattress on the floor and he put a blindfold on her. Defaced her again before he started to probe in between her legs with his grimy fingers in a way that suggested he was preparing to perform one of his much-boasted-about operations. She felt Rose's longer-nailed fingers join his inside her and was terrified they were going to put something in her or operate or something. She heard them discussing the appearance of the 'lips' of her vagina and what could be done to them to increase her sexual pleasure. They were too fat and should be 'flattened', they decided. And a few moments later Caroline felt something strike her violently between the legs. The blindfold must have slipped, because she saw him whipping a wide leather belt, buckle end first, down on to her. Rose held her legs open while he hit her repeatedly with the belt. The next thing she was aware of was Rose crouched between her legs, exploring her with her tongue. It was the first time this had happened to Caroline. She had never had it done to her before Rose did it. She didn't respond even though she was scared Rose might get nasty.

He seemed to be happiest scaring and hitting, and then withdrawing to watch. But quite soon he took his clothes off and, while his wife was still crouched over with her back to him, had sex with her from behind. He spectated for a while, with a kind of excited detachment, and then he briefly took part himself, drunk on his wife's erotic drunkenness.

Unbelievably, they were able to sleep. Fresh tea was made. It was the middle of the night. And then quite soon they seemed to be fast asleep on the mattress on the floor. There were blankets. Caroline, still bound, was lying on the floor next to them. She was unable to sleep and only able to think about her mother – what her mother was going to be like when she didn't go home or if they didn't find her. Her poor mum's face and how heartbroken she would be if she never went home.

Some time in the night Caroline managed to make herself upright and got over to the window. Outside had become a place that seemed not even to exist. There was no way of opening the window with her hands bound behind her back.

She thought of throwing herself through it, but quickly dismissed that idea. So there she was. Her mouth was still filled with cottonwool. A figure at a window.

Very early in the morning, before it was light, there was a knock at the door and he jumped up and pulled on a sweater and his trousers and went to answer it. Caroline could hear voices and she knew that the door to the room where she was being kept had been left slightly open because light from the stairs was coming in through it. It was her chance to bring help by attempting to make some noise. She tried to yell out, but Rose immediately grabbed a pillow and smothered the yell with it. She pressed it down over her face very hard and went on pressing.

Caroline struggled with her but she could feel herself beginning to pass out and so she played dead. Rose didn't stop until Fred had got rid of the visitor. He took the pillow off her face and his face was twisted with anger. Now Caroline thought she really was going to die. They were both very angry. He shook her about and they were both cursing her and calling her bitch. Rose looked furious. Caroline thought she was going to get another beating, but instead he said something about keeping her in the cellar and letting their black friends use her and then burying her under the paving stones of Gloucester.

After that, Rose went to see to the children and Caroline was left alone with him. He stood over her as she lay crying on the mattress. He was speaking softly to her to hush, then he removed his trousers and raped her. It was all over in seconds. He raped her but he didn't ejaculate. He had done it while Rose was out of the room and it didn't even last long, just a few thrusts and it was over and suddenly Fred was crying and begging her not to tell Rose because she was there for Rose's pleasure, not his, and she would be angry with him. He pulled his trousers on and sat next to her down there on the mattress. She was sobbing. He looked at her with tears in his eyes and said he was so sorry for what they had done to her but that she mustn't tell Rose what he just did. He said that Rose was pregnant, she had just fallen, and that was the explanation for what had occurred. He said, 'When Rose gets pregnant her lesbian urges get stronger and she has to have a woman and she really wanted you.' He said, 'If you promise not to tell anybody what happened and come back, I know it will make Rose happy.' He said, 'Why don't you come back here to live and everything will be OK?' He was crying as he said all this. Caroline felt almost sorry for him now. She couldn't believe the change. She said, 'I promise I won't tell Rose if you don't kill me', and it was a deal.

Fred left her in the room alone, still gagged and bound, and went to pass on the good news to Rose. Minutes later they were both back happy and smiling. Rose was very happy that Caroline was going to move back in and gave her a hug.

She was allowed a bath. Rose helped her to get the gum from the taped gag out of her hair. Her hair had come out in handfuls when they had removed the tape and it was all floating in the bath. They changed the water and Caroline bathed a second time. Gum had stuck to the side of her face. It was sticking to the downy hair around her jaw. Her head was hurting from the punches she had taken to the side of the head when he knocked her out in the car. There was puffiness around her cheeks and some grazing. She had weals at the top of her inner thighs and bruising on her legs and arms. She had rope burns on her back. She couldn't remember but thought at one time she might have been tied to a chair.

When the light came, and the day began to take on the appearance of a normal day, Caroline behaved like nothing had happened and helped with the housework and the children and went with them to the laundryette on Eastgate Street nearly opposite Barton Baths.

By eleven thirty that morning she was walking. She started walking and kept walking and she didn't dare to look back. She avoided Eastgate Street and Westgate Street and the busy shopping area around the Cross and kept instead to the noisy main road along Bruton Way, past the main railway station at Gloucester, where there was less pedestrian traffic. Some memory of walking. She kept her head down and walked.

She had crossed Westgate Bridge and was heading in the direction of the roundabout at Highnam when she became aware of a car pulling up alongside her. Her heart was beating so fast. She kept staring ahead. At the ground and straight ahead. She was sure it must be Fred. She heard a man's voice offering her a lift. 'Carol, do you want a lift?' It wasn't a familiar voice but it wasn't Fred West either. She stopped and turned to see that it was a Mini and that the driver was the brother of a friend of hers from the Forest. She said, 'Yeh. I do. Thanks', and got in the car but hardly addressed another word to him after that. She didn't tell the man what had happened to her because she could hardly believe it herself.

One minute they were committing their perverted acts on her, the next bringing her mugs of tea. One minute she was convinced she was going to die in unbelievable, horrible circumstances, bringing shame as well as grief to her family, and the next she was helping to look after the babies, helping Anna-Marie get off to school, tidying around and hoovering the floor. It was while she was doing the hoovering that Ben Stanniland, the hippy lodger from upstairs, had looked into the room where all of it had gone on and where she now was with Rose. Afterwards, nobody would be able to understand why she hadn't grabbed this as her chance. Why she hadn't run to Ben and begged him to call the police. Even many years later she would have people asking her the same thing.

What they could never understand was how spaced and out of it Ben and the other lodgers there were.

Caroline might not have been a dopehead herself, but she knew dopeheads. She knew what they were like. *Whaaaaa'?* She had a dopehead brother. And she knew that if something had happened and her dopehead brother walked in and she told him she had been attacked, he'd be like: *Whaaaaa'?* And by that time you're dead.

Same with Ben and the other boys at Cromwell Street. They were so stoned. So laid back they were horizontal, was that what they used to say? She didn't have to imagine their reaction to her turning round and saying, 'Look, they've kept me here overnight, I've been raped, you've got to get me out.' She didn't have to imagine; she knew. She knew it wouldn't have been, 'Let's get her out of here!', like they do in the films. *Let's get you out of here!* It would have been: 'What you on about? What happened?' You would have had to have *explained* it all. And by that time you're dead.

One thing she knew: she had to rely on herself. She definitely had to rely on herself. Most of her life she had had that attitude around her: 'Oh, you can get on with it yourself.' She knew for a fact, if and when Alf found out what had happened to her, what his attitude was going to be: don't get the police involved; she'll get over it. He never wanted the police around. There had always been that attitude towards her anyway, all the way up through her life. 'Oh, just *get on* with it. Take no notice. You'll be all right.'

Fred helped get the bags of washing and the youngest two, Heather and baby May, into the car, and they drove to the laundryette opposite the Barton Street swimming pool. Barton Baths was part of the recently opened leisure centre. It was glass-sided and situated on a corner so that the swimmers were visible from the street. People up on the diving boards and children splashing and a nice light, high, openly designed place. The baths and the launderette were only a three-minute walk from Cromwell Street, but they had the washing and the children, so they took the car. It was only twelve hours since Caroline had been beaten and gagged in it, but she tried to keep that from her mind and having the children helped. All that was holding her together was the thought of getting out of the house.

When they got there he couldn't park up, so Rose and Caroline took the children and the bags of washing in alone. He drove off either to do a job or go and see somebody, leaving Caroline with Rose and Heather and May. She didn't want to alert Rose by just running away so she told her she would have to go home now and get her things and that she'd be back. She turned and walked out and pulled her collar up and kept walking. She didn't dare to look round in case Fred passed her in the car.

It was lunchtime when she got back to Cinderford. The friend's brother who had given her the lift dropped her at Northwood Close and she sneaked into the Bradleys' house at the bottom of the cul-de-sac.

It was now Thursday and Doreen Bradley was at home because she wasn't working. Five months had passed since their return from Portsmouth, and Caroline felt that Doreen was somebody she could go to because of the experiences they had lived through there together.

Not much was said. She was exhausted. She had been awake all night and was tired and confused. Mentally battered. She was stiff and aching. She was bothered by the idea that it must have been her own fault; that she must have done something to give them the wrong impression. Even with somebody who knew her as well as Doreen, she felt she was hiding a dirty little secret. Holding the dirty thing back. She felt ugly and ashamed.

She quite soon fell asleep and stayed in a deep sleep in

Doreen's room right through to the next day. The next day was Friday, and Caroline slipped into her own house a few doors away along the street when nobody was about. She knew that the details of what had happened to her would upset her mother, and she didn't want her to know what the full details were. She stayed in bed through the afternoon and into the evening, but then it couldn't be put off any longer. As soon as her mother saw the state of her, she called the police.

An episode in Caroline's childhood had brought home to her how determined Alf was not to get the police involved in their affairs. When she was aged about nine or ten she had gone into hospital to have her appendix removed, and a small girl she was sharing the room with had died. They had taken her away from the ward to be operated on and brought her back, and then suddenly there were nurses and doctors and a nurse pulled the curtains shut around Sarah's bed. Caroline had to watch the Gloucester Carnival parade, which was just then coming past their windows, the windows of the Gloucester Royal Infirmary where they were patients, from another room.

A few weeks later a man Caroline recognized as Sarah's father came to Cinderford to ask her some questions, and Alf Harris sent her to her room while the man explained why he was there. It seemed that he suspected that his daughter had been given something to eat before her operation in spite of the 'Nil by Mouth' sign over her bed. And Caroline told Alf that yes, that was right, Sarah had been screaming and yelling that she was hungry all night and the nurses in the end had given her some squash and a couple of biscuits to shut her up. She told Alf this up in her room – the room she shared with her mother and her two sisters – and he had said, no, to shut it, to tell the man nothing, he wasn't going to have the police coming round. He didn't want the police up there. And she had done what he said. She had gone down and told the man, who was very upset and angry, which scared her, that she had seen and heard nothing because she had been asleep at the time.

And, as Caroline had suspected, Alf took the same position again now. Don't get the police involved. She'll get over it. Meaning: she must have asked for it. She was asking for it hitch-hiking on her own. Betty usually gave way to Alf in these situations. Usually she sided with Alf. But not this time. She put her coat on and went down to the phone.

Fred West was arrested leaving work at Permali's at seven thirty on Saturday evening. Police Constable Kevan Price and Detective Sergeant John Pearce, two officers from Gloucester Central police station, had been around to Cromwell Street at lunchtime, but found nobody in. It was almost seventy-two hours since the Wests had picked up Caroline Raine hitching outside Tewkesbury when Price and Pearce intercepted him coming off the late shift at Permali's and cautioned him and took him for questioning down to Gloucester Central nick. It came as naturally to Fred West to call it this as to the two policemen, because he wasn't a stranger to the place. He was no stranger to Price and Pearce who, in addition to their other duties, functioned as the drug squad in Gloucester, and they were no strangers to him.

Of course he wasted no time in telling them about Caroline and the two lodgers. And Tony the boyfriend from Tewkesbury who slept with her at Cromwell Street once a week. And then there was the sailor who'd been and given her a good seeing to just a few weeks before. He denied the charges of indecent assault. She had stayed with him and Rose at their house on Wednesday night, but only at her own what's-her-name. You know. She had got stuck hitching through Gloucester and had come knocking at their door and asked to stay. Request. She had slept with them and left the next day. The three of them had slept together.

'Look, to put it right,' he said, 'I kicked her out 'cause the

80

blokes in the top flat was fucking her and I didn't want that in my house 'cause I was going to buy the place. That's why I told her to pack her bags and go. She's saying this now to get her own back on me and Rose.'

This was a lie of course, but there was a truth at the heart of it. It would have appeared a small truth then, if it was noticed at all. But it looks like a bigger truth now. Fred West was desperate to stay the owner of 25 Cromwell Street. He had worked a lot on the house in the three months they had been there and he was fiercely committed to it becoming their home. The abuse of Caroline Raine was the first exercise of the new freedoms it had brought him. In time to come it would become apparent that there were deeper-seated reasons than the house's practical advantages to explain its importance to him. And there were some hints now. Most of the questions were about what had been done to Caroline Raine. Many of his answers were about how she had become a threat to his ownership of the house.

'All I want is to buy the house and settle down' was his reply when he was asked whether it was true that his wife 'had sucked Carol Raine's breasts and private parts' after he had tied her up. He went on: 'Nothing like that happened. She is making it all up. The only thing is that some coloured blokes did it and she's trying to blame Rose and me.'

At ten forty-five that night, Price and Pearce, together with a woman officer, WPS Digweed, went to interview Rose West at Cromwell Street. Many years later, she would claim that Caroline Raine had been her first experience with a woman. 'With his persuasive nature, Fred did persuade me that Caroline had agreed to try it out. I told him I didn't believe Caroline was that way inclined, but still I allowed him to. He was acting as a middle-man between the two of us . . . He was just so good at talking, making excuses, making promises . . . I was a young girl. I realized I'd been conned into this. I wanted it over with . . . I knew it was wrong to force anybody to do anything.' Fred had been wanting to 'put her' with a woman and she had eventually caved in.

But 'Don't be fucking daft. What do you think I am?' Rose West said on the Saturday night in December 1972, when she was asked if the allegations made by Caroline Raine against her were true. When they asked if she had any objections if they searched the car or the house, she replied, 'Please your bloody self.'

When they searched the Ford Popular, which was parked between the church and the front door at the right side of the house, they found a button from Caroline's coat under the nearside door. They removed a partly used roll of parcel tape from the rear living room.

Caroline had been brought to Gloucester and interviewed and photographed at the Central police station earlier in the day. It was only after she was finished with the doctor, forensics, the photographer, etcetera, and she was walking across the car park to go home that she was asked by the policeman she was with if any penetration had occurred during her assault by Fred West. 'Oh yeh,' she said, 'but it was just a second. It didn't hurt.' She went back in and made another statement.

At nine o'clock the next morning, the Sunday, Kevan Price travelled out to Cinderford to re-interview her. PC Price was from New Zealand. Or South Africa. Somewhere. He had an accent. Caroline didn't take to him. His attitude from the beginning seemed to be that she was a scrubber who had asked for everything that had come her way. That's how it looked to her anyway. 'You knew the lodgers, didn't you? You were into it, weren't you? You were no innocent. You were into this. You just complained.' Price was saying it, but she knew it was what her stepfather, to name just one person in Cinderford, thought. That she had been a willing party to what happened and had decided to complain when it got a bit rough. Shagbag. Slut. She got this from her brother, Phillip, her full blood relation, when she saw him in pubs or whatever up the town. Under his breath and accompanied by a mean look.

'You like your sex, don't you? Don't tell me you weren't loving it.' He kept hitting the same note over and over. There was quite a lot in this vein from Kevan Price.

And it worked. Caroline was nervous about having to go to court because she knew that her mother would want to be with her and she didn't want her to hear the horrible details of what had gone on or the fact that she had had sex with so many men in such a short space of time. The Wests would each plead guilty to the two lesser charges of indecent assault and actual bodily harm if she dropped the more serious charge of rape. Their guilty pleas meant that she wouldn't have to be in court.

The case was heard by Gloucester magistrates on Friday, 12 January 1973. Fred West and Rose West were fined £25 on each count, a total of £100, and advised to seek psychiatric help. Fred West bowed to the bench and clasped his wife's hand. He was thirty-one. She was just over eighteen. It was her first conviction. She was pregnant for the third time. She just went on staring straight ahead.

An article appeared in the next day's Gloucester *Citizen*, with the headline 'City Pair Stripped and Assaulted Girl'. 'We were asked by the prosecution not to put the girl in the stands,' he was quoted saying, 'so we pleaded guilty.' The article was cut out by her and kept and became one of the first items in the archive of their life together which would be found many years later, boxed and stored in the attic at 25 Cromwell Street. Part of an obsessive, and more or less exhaustive, collection of holiday postcards, birthday cards, Mother's Day cards, hospital appointment cards, bills, idle scribblings, faded photographs, summonses, hire-purchase agreements, prison letters, love notes, receipts, dockets, brochures. A whole life – their life as a couple – preserved in scraps of paper. A museum of themselves.

Caroline would go on seeing the Wests in and around Gloucester over the years. She mostly saw Rose. And each time she saw her she seemed to have become heavier-bodied, with some of the reasons for that straggling behind the inevitable pram. She could have been born with her hands locked on to a buggy or a pram. She'd see her in the pedestrianized precinct or Eastgate market or crossing at the lights, shouting at one or other of them, clipping another, nondescriptly dressed, spreading, gradually growing into the done-down homebody of a woman she had always struck Caroline as being.

There were odd sightings that didn't fit into this picture. Pointers to her having another life. Out with a coachload on a hen night one night, Caroline spotted Rose in the vaulted bierkeller bar that ran under the Fleece. She was wearing jewellery and make-up and sitting in an elevated part of the pub with two men. Laughing and flirting with these men; and also with them joining in was Anna-Marie, who by then was thirteen or fourteen. And she turned to the friend who was nearest her in the crush and said, 'Oh my god, Anna's on the game.'

Caroline's friends, who knew the background and could see the effect this was having on her, quickly got her away. She actually followed Anna-Marie into the toilets at one point and they exchanged a few words. But five years had passed and a lot had happened and it was obvious Anna didn't know who she was. In any case she was pretty near totalled, she could see. She was very drunk. Caroline's friends got her coat and her bag and hustled her away.

Her life continued. She hadn't been crippled by her experience with the Wests. But she had been destabilized by it. Certainly that. She started to have doubts about whether her body was normal because of what they had said needed doing to it to put it right. She was ashamed of her body and ashamed of her past private live that had been disclosed to the police.

And then, after the way her stepfather and her brother and the policeman had reacted, and the outcome of the trial, which was no more than a slap, she believed herself to be worth even less than she had before. Although she did manage to have a few months' good relationship with her stepfather before he died, and was able to think of him as a dad instead of a stepdad, she still believed it was the way he had treated her all through her life that had made her feel she was trash and deserved all the bad things that had come along. If good things happen to good people, which is what she truly believed, what did that make her?

After the Wests, she started going out with younger boys – boys younger than herself. It seemed to give her a sense of being more in control. But she ended up ruining all her relationships with her insecurity and her jealousy tantrums. She'd be suspicious and possessive and if she thought that the boyfriend was getting fed up of her, she'd turn on them and hit them around. Kim, for instance. One night she was parked with Kim up in their usual spot in the woods and he was telling her it was all over and she was begging him to stay, and he was adamant, so she beat him up. Tried to force him to make love to her. She was desperate and like a madwoman. She'd always feel ashamed and sorry after but she couldn't help herself.

The low point came when she was twenty in 1975 and tried to commit suicide. She was working at the Rozel Hotel in Weston-Super-Mare and took an overdose of the antidepressants the doctor had just given her. She was rushed to hospital and had her stomach pumped.

After that, Kim and her mother did everything they could to get her to raise her opinion of herself. She entered for Miss Cinderford because of them and ended up riding through the streets on a camel, waving at the crowds and even appearing on the local television news that night. Then she got nervous about having to speak at functions, and for the rest of the year the girl who came second had to do that for her.

No matter how many people told her she was a pretty and lovely girl, she still didn't like herself. It wasn't until 1979 that she agreed to pose for a keen local amateur photographer. The pictures were nothing too glamorous but he told her she was photogenic and said she should advertise herself. An elderly man booked her for glamour shots wearing pretty underwear. She worked with him a few times, but the last time he got shaky and knocked over a lamp and that worried her, so she didn't work for him again.

Later on she worked with an Irish guy. He was very sarcastic towards her, but in a fun way, and eventually she agreed to go topless for him. They worked well together and they did a shot that he sent to Page Three at the *Sun*. The *Sun* was interested but it was at that point that Caroline discovered she was pregnant. Kelly was born in January 1980 and gave her back her interest in life. She never thought of suicide again.

She had a second daughter in 1988. Dylan, the father, was a member of the Desperadoes Outlaw Club, the local biker club, and had come to live in the Forest from Manchester. They lived next door to Mrs Maude Potter, the aunt of the writer Dennis Potter and a very strict old lady, and she babysat Kelly and the new baby when she arrived.

The baby's name was Shani-Jade. Shani, pronounced 'Shay-nee'. Caroline had liked the sound of it when she heard it on the news. A woman of this name had been found dead with her hands tied behind her back in a lake. She had cut her

lawn and had been taking the bags of grass for disposal somewhere when she disappeared. And, perhaps because of the
submerged, but never totally eradicated, conviction that she
would herself end up being famous for the wrong reasons one
day – famous for being a body; the logical outcome of the
self-destruction mission she seemed to be on – she took the
name of the woman whose body had been disposed of in a
lake and gave it to the baby that was on the way. There were
lots of investigations going on, and she heard the name Shani
pronounced 'Shay-nee' on the news, and she thought: Oh! I
like that! It had been going to be 'Shannon' but it ended up
'Shani'. Shani-Jade.

Afterwards, it would sometimes strike Caroline as ironic
that, during her time at Cromwell Street, she never once went
in Gloucester Park. That when she was out with the children
she would skirt the park rather than walk through it, and
always kept a distance between the toilets in the park and
herself. When all the time of course the danger was where
you would least expect it, in the safe, protected spaces of the
house. She had thought of it as being out there, when all the
time, without her knowing it, it was in here.

It would never occur to her, though, to think that she had
known murderers.

Chapter Four

He brought her a lace dress and a fur coat. The year was 1969. The year of Woodstock. *Easy Rider*. The acid counter-culture. TV pictures of violence and atrocities. Vietnam protests. Student protests and sit-ins. Charles Manson. Terrorist bombings. It was a Regency dandy look that year for pop stars. The fashions in the street reflected the ethnic look from Morocco, Turkey, Kashmir – kaftans, beads, fringe jackets. 'Youth' had been given the kingdom. Drugginess was mainstream.

And he brought her a lace dress and a fur coat. Symbols of everything everybody was apparently rebelling against. Straight life. It was his present to her. To mark their first date. A kind of nylon lace dress suitable for somebody double, even treble, her age, and this rabbit-fur coat. Fred's gift to Rose.

He had brought the parcel to the bread shop where she was working in the centre of Cheltenham. He was twenty-eight at this time. She was not quite sixteeen. Nearly, but not quite there. This man had walked in the shop, thrust the parcel at her and walked out. Told her to be at the Swallow at eight o'clock, and turned heel.

She had first encountered him on the bus from Cheltenham to Bishop's Cleeve, a village about three miles north of Cheltenham, where she lived. Where he also lived, or was living, as it turned out.

She had seen him at the bus stop and was conscious of his interest in her but had tried not to catch his eye. A gypsyish individual with a swarthy complexion and a prison build. Short and disproportionately big in the upper body. An impression of physical strength. Broad shoulders, powerful forearms. She hadn't returned his glances but there had been no avoiding him once they were on the bus. He made a bee line for her. He was in overalls and boots. The overalls were muddy. The boots had gas mud caked around them. He had startling pale blue eyes with a lot of light in them and a winning grin which also appeared wary at the same time. A wary cast to his eyes. A cheeky grin, though. He told her he lived in Cleeve and worked on the motorway. He said he was going home because of an accident. The digger he was driving had turned over and rolled down an embankment. He had just come back from a check-up at the hospital. Going for the sympathy vote.

Before she got off the bus he asked her out to a place she knew to be a rough pub in Cheltenham and she told him no. Then a couple of days later he was waiting for her at the bus stop when she arrived there from work. He asked her out again. Again to a place with a rough reputation. Again she said no. But he didn't take the hint, and soon after was in the shop, pushing the parcel at her and telling her to meet him at the Swallow at eight o'clock. The Swallow was a pub in the village just yards from her house so she thought it would be safe enough to go and see what this one was all about. If anything happened she could run home.

Rose was floating at this point. Her family had come apart and she wasn't connected to any part of it. She was fifteen and a half and had only just left school and was adrift in her life. And with his instincts he was able to spot a floater, any directionless or rudderless person. She had drifted into his radar, and he had locked on. For example, she hadn't told him where she worked, but he knew. She hadn't told him where she lived, but he obviously knew that as well, just along from the Swallow. (Not usually a bus user, he also knew where she caught her bus, and when. It's likely he had calculated that the knee-to-knee crush on the tea-time commuter bus to Bishop's Cleeve was a good way to approach her and have her as a captive audience. That invitation to a dirty world made with a cheeky grin.) For a man as directed and alert as him, giving the appearance of being haphazard but actually scrupulous in his methods, she hadn't been hard to find. For Rose Letts, 1969, the year she left school, had been a turbulent year.

At the beginning of the year, after being bullied and beaten by him all her married life, Rose's mother had finally drawn the line and walked out on her father for the first time. Bill and Daisy Letts had been married for twenty-seven years. The marriage was the kind of oppressive, brutal regime that appears to have been all too common then but which many women of Daisy Letts's generation accepted as their lot in life. Bill Letts had been in the Navy. He had signed up during the war as a radio operator and had volunteered to stay on after the war was over. He was a disciplinarian and a pathological bully. He would turn off the gas and electricity and then beat his wife for not having a meal ready on the table for him. He expected the house to be spotless and woke the children at dawn with their household duties for the day. Daisy, Rose's mother, put this down to him being 'Victorian'. 'Dad', as she always called him – he has been dead for twenty years, but she still calls him this – was very Victorian. *Very* Victorian.

He was probably a schizophrenic. He had been diagnosed as schizophrenic at an early stage of his life, but his family were told this only after he died. He pulled knives on his children for not eating their breakfasts and wielded hatchets. He fisted his young sons in the stomach if they came in a minute after he said they had to be in and threw his daughters bodily down stairs. Joyce, Rose's second-oldest sister, has retained a big dislike towards him for this very reason. He used to hit her around. She used to take really big hidings from him. After she went to work, he used to beat her black and blue, throw her down the stairs. Joyce was older and took a lot of the responsibility for running the house and she got a lot of the brunt of it. This was in the house. Outside, with strangers, he was easy-going, affable; a little stiff and formal, but reasonableness itself.

Daisy Letts had suffered a series of nervous breakdowns. She had had ECT treatment. (She was having ECT treatment while she was pregnant with Rose.) She had lived with Bill Letts for twenty-seven years and was preparing something nice for his birthday – he was going to be forty-eight – on the day she was finally pushed over the edge.

It was February, Rose was in her last term at Cleeve School, and she came home from school to find her mother making a cake. She had got Bill a present earlier in the day on her way home from work – she had a job at a café on the Promenade at Cheltenham – and now she was baking him a cake the way she always did. But she had forgotten some of the ingredients needed for it and she asked Rose to run down to the shops. There was a row of shops about thirty yards away, next to the Swallow, so she was there and back in a few minutes. She was soon back.

When she got back she couldn't believe what she saw. The house was smashed up. Her mother was battered and bleeding. There was blood everywhere, and mess. Broken furniture and spilled and broken things. Eggs and blood up the walls. Her mother said she was leaving and Rose was going with her. The Letts family fell into two halves, divided by age. The oldest four had already left home, driven out by their father. Rose and her mother took Graham, who was eleven, and Gordon, who was eight, and packed a few things and headed out to Rose's sister's place in Cheltenham.

Glenys was three years older than Rose. She was eighteen in 1969 and had recently married a car mechanic called Jim Tyler. He was from Gotherington, the next village north of Bishop's Cleeve. But they had moved into a small terraced house in Union Street in an old run-down part of Cheltenham, close to the town centre. Near by was the High Street and the Full Moon which had a reputation at the time as a drug pub, and was a place where Fred West used to like to hang around. He wasn't a drinker. He rarely drank more than a half of shandy. He wasn't a drug-user either. But he was interested in observing the effects drink and drugs, these kinds of disinhibitors, had on other people. He liked to sit in a corner of the bar separate from the druggies and the hippies and observe.

It had come as a surprise to her family that Glenys had ended up living in Union Street, married to Jim Tyler. Glenys was bright and they had always seen her as headed towards better things. She had had boyfriends who were college students. She could have had her pickings of anyone. And she had gone off with Jim Tyler.

He worked for the Volkswagen–Audi garage in Cheltenham as a general mechanic. But Jim and Glenys had another business that they ran together. They had a mobile transport café in a lay-by at Seven Springs on the Cirencester Road, just south of Cheltenham. Glenys usually looked after the snack bar while Jim was at work, but she was heavily pregnant with her first baby at the time that her mother and Rose and her two little brothers took refuge with her. They had been looking for another girl to tide them over. And with Rose being fifteen and a half and due to leave school in the Easter anyway, she got the job. It was decided that she could help out brewing the tea and selling the hot-dogs for a while.

Jim Tyler got up early every morning and towed the caravan from Union Street to its site by the gravel pit at Seven

Springs. He stopped at the cash-and-carry to buy bread rolls and fillings before going on to his mechanics job. Part of his job was to test-run cars, and at least once during the day he would take a route that brought him past the snack bar, and in that way he was able to keep a check on what was going on.

Rose had shown signs of being sexually precocious from the age of thirteen. At fifteen, she was still going around in knee-socks and other schoolgirl clothes. But while she was living at Union Street with the Tylers, she had relationships with a number of different men. One of these was Jim Tyler's brother, whose sexual inexperience Rose found amusing. Her brother-in-law, who was six years older than her, called her 'a hot-arsed little sod'.

Most of the people who pulled in to the lay-by at Seven Springs were lorry drivers and salesmen and reps. And on three or four occasions after Rose had taken over from Glenys at the counter, Jim arrived to find the shutters down, the caravan empty and Rose tumbling out of a lorry or a car. She would be in the cab of some lorry driver or off with one of the team laying gas pipes over the Cotswolds. Her clothes would be dishevelled and it would be obvious she had just been having sex, but her explanation would be that she had run out of bread or sausages for the hot-dogs and that the man, or men, whoever she happened to be with, had been giving her a lift. Her boast was that she took a lot more money at the site than Glenys ever had.

It was while she was helping out at the café that Rose arrived back at Union Street one day to find her mother, and her brothers, Graham and Gordon, all gone.

Once, while Glenys was away in hospital having her baby, Jim Tyler had heard odd moaning sounds coming from the room where Rose was sleeping downstairs. He had gone down and had found her sucking her thumb and groaning and rocking herself repeatedly backwards and forwards on the bed. This was a habit she had had since childhood but he had never seen it before. She wouldn't tell him what was wrong, but she put her arms around him and cried into his shoulder and dropped one hand and slid it along the inside of his thigh. According to Jim Tyler that was as far as it had gone. She had tried to touch him up and he had gone back to his own room upstairs. But Rose's brothers and sisters believe that their mother surprised Rose and Jim Tyler in bed together and that's what made her pack up and leave. Their mother still won't say, but that's what they believe.

She had packed her things and she hadn't gone back to Bill Letts in Bishop's Cleeve. Rose was very close to her younger brothers. And her mother and Graham and Gordon had disappeared and left her. 'Abandoned' was her word. Glenys had been given instructions not to tell Rose where they had gone. Just that they'd gone. They'd moved on.

The atmosphere among them was bad. Eventually Rose and Glen had a stand-up row. A fight really. It developed into that. Glenys told Rose that she had been left in charge and so from now on she would do as she said. It became physical. Glenys took back and swiped Rose across the head. And it all came down on her then. She'd left her father's house and she expected the support of her mother. Her mother had left her. She was on her own. She had been abandoned. She had left her father, her mother had left her, and now she had to start to look after herself. She made a fist and launched one right at Glen. Contact was made. She was used to defending Graham and Gordon against the bullies in Cleeve and had earned herself a reputation for being useful with her fists. She fisted up and hit her own sister. Jim Tyler watching all this, knowing he was not unimplicated in the bad turn of events between the sisters.

Half an hour later she was out of there and out on the

street with her bag. A schoolgirlish-looking solidly built girl, tramping the streets of Cheltenham with a bag. Dragging her life around with her in a soft-sided, cardboard-and-canvas case. She was a lumpish adolescent. How it had happened she couldn't exactly remember. She was walking the streets through a long day with nowhere to go. Cheltenham on a Sunday. Everything closed.

It was just starting to get dark when she realized that a car was moving slowly along behind her and that she was being kerb-crawled. The car came along very slowly, with the driver leaning over and saying something to her through the window. His left arm along the passenger seat and him craning his neck towards her the way they do. She stepped back into the shops and told him to clear off. He said, 'It's all right. I know your sister.' And when she looked close, although she didn't know him very well, she had seen him at Glen's and Jim's. An older man. Old to her. He was about thirty, twice her age.

He was being nice. Concerned and responsible. He told her she couldn't just wander around the town. Unless she told him the problem he would have to let the police know she was homeless and wandering around town on her own. He said he lived not far away and if she got in the car he would take her to his house and make her a cup of tea.

She was wary. Naturally she was wary. She had already been raped – what she considered to be rape – once that year; and she would be raped a second time within weeks of walking away from Glen's and Jim's.

The first time had been after a Christmas party in January. It was now April time. So about four months. She had gone to the party with a friend at the place where the friend's mother worked. She was aware of a man whose eyes had been hot on her all night. And at the end of the party her friend, who was supposed to be giving her a lift home, had gone off with a boy, and she was wandering around outside on her own when this man pulled up and said he would drive her back to Cleeve. The last bus had gone and she was wandering and so she got in. Bad move. Instead of turning off at Bishop's Cleeve, he went on past her home and on to the hills where she lived. Cleeve Hill, where she had played with Graham and Gordon and all her friends all her life. They stopped up on the golf course on Cleeve Hill and the situation had seemed very threatening to her. She had wondered whether he was going to kill her. She took her clothes off and got in the back seat as he had ordered her to do, and then he raped her. Afterwards, he drove her home and dropped her off outside the house. She didn't tell anybody about what had been done.

By her own account, the second rape in 1969 happened four or five months after this rape, just before her encounter with the man called Fred West. She was back by then living at the family home in Bishop's Cleeve and waiting for a bus out of Cheltenham at a stop on the Evesham road. The stop is close to the famous Pump Room, near the railings of Pittville Park. She has done her day's work and is waiting for a bus, and the memory of what happens then will be vivid for her even twenty-five years later. A man standing at the bus stop starts chatting to her. There's just the two of them, quite a lot of evening traffic passing on the busy road, and he starts chatting her up. She indicates that she isn't interested, but he is very forceful. Very strong. He is crowding her; grabbing her. He's a strong man. Then it gets out of hand. She panics. She gets frightened and runs away from him towards the park – Pittville Park overlooked by its ice-cream-coloured Georgian terraces, often known as Cheltenham Park. An up-market very green area on the edge of the town centre, between the main shopping streets and the race course. There is nobody around; no other pedestrians. And this man's gaining on her, pursuing her towards the park. There is a little gate set into the railings of the park. It's locked but he smashes the padlock off it; right off the gate like it's nothing. That's how strong. He drags her down by the lake under some trees, into the dark, and rapes her. Eventually she gets on board a bus when one comes and nobody notices anything, or says anything, and she goes home and tells nobody about this second rape of 1969.

Because of the chase followed by the rape in Pittville Park, she started to use the main bus station in the town centre after work. She stopped walking out to the stop along the Evesham Road. And it would be there, while waiting for a bus in the town-centre stand, that she would first become aware of Fred West.

But this man now, who was offering her a way out of her predicament, who said his name was Ken and who was a friend of Jim and Glenys, he seemed all right. So she did as he asked. She got her bag with all her belongings in it and got in the car. He was kind to her and listened to what she had to say, about the fight with Glenys and being dumped the way she had by her mother and her brothers. Ken was Irish and twice her age and they had sex together that night. Although, because he wasn't rough and didn't rush it and insisted on wearing protection, she thought of it as making love. He made love to her that night and told her there was a room for her there as long as she needed it. She could pay him rent and food money when she found a job.

She got a job with Sketchley's in Cheltenham, but it was dirty and low-paid work and she didn't last long. She left Sketchley's and, along with another woman she had met there, was taken on as a trainee seamstress at County Clothes, a high-class shop on the Promenade.

She went on living with the Irishman, Ken, and sleeping with him. But there were also other boyfriends around. She found out from her brother Andrew's girlfriend, Jacquie, whose family lived next door to the Tylers in Union Street, where her mother had gone. She had found work as a house-keeper–cleaner at a chicken farm in a village called Teddington, near Tewkesbury, and was living with Graham and Gordon in a small cottage that came with the job. Rose tracked them down and started going out to see them some-times, taking whatever boyfriend she had at the time. It was lovely countryside in the area and plenty of it where you could be private and alone. There was sex in the fields around Teddington that summer with a drink afterwards in a big old-fashioned pub there called the Royal Oak. Lots of the kind of high-class people who would shop at County Clothes. Ken always used a condom, which was a pointless precaution as far as Rose was concerned because she never bothered to with anybody else.

Teddington is a few miles north of Bishop's Cleeve. And, to the amazement of her mother and her older sisters and brothers who had all been browbeaten and damaged by him, Rose moved back in alone with her father in the house at 96 Tobyfield Road. There were days of silence followed by vio-lent eruptions. He was bullying and violent. You didn't dare look at him the wrong way. And she had moved back in to live with him – there was only going to be the two of them – out of choice. To put it mildly they were amazed. Before long, Daisy Letts and Graham and Gordon came home to Cleeve to live, and the pattern of unpredictable kickings and beatings, the black moods and silences, started all over again.

Rose was going to be sixteen in November 1969. It was only late summer. And the police started to come around to the bread shop in the centre of Cheltenham where she now worked. Every night when the time came for her to pack up work she'd look outside and see a uniformed policeman, occasionally two, waiting there. Every night she was taken to the police station and questioned about the many boyfriends she seemed to have. They were particularly interested in an older man at whose flat she had become a regular visitor. They showed particular interest in Ken and the fact that she was a minor and that therefore any sexual intercourse with her, as far as the law was concerned, was rape. She undertook to stop seeing Ken and then didn't. Undertook to stop seeing him and then didn't. Ken or the others. Ken or anybody else. And the next night there would be a plod pounding the pavement waiting for her after work. This was her attitude to the police then – to any kind of authority – and it would never change. Hello, Mr Plod. Cunt. Oh, already she had a mouth on her.

Bishop's Cleeve isn't a big place. It's a small, tightly knit village community with a large housing estate added on. Bill Letts worked for Smith's Industries. He was an electronics engineer working on flight simulators at the Smith's factory complex outside Cheltenham, and he lived in a Smith's house in Bishop's Cleeve. The company had built the estate for its workers, and the estate is known by everybody locally as 'Smith's Estate'. New model homes for the new post-war generation of workers. The verges are clipped; the 'No Ball Games' notice still fixed to the side of 96 Tobyfield Road, the Letts' house, weathered and worn. The atmosphere is watchful; the houses regular and neat. Little, particularly in those days, went unremarked.

The decamping of Daisy Letts with the younger children would have counted as a scandal. It would have caused talk. Word of Rose Letts's sexual shenanigans around Cheltenham would have quickly got back. Tongues would have wagged. And Fred West, a watcher and a prowler who was fly enough not to appear either of those things, would have heard them, or at least have got wind of them second hand. Rose was a subject of gossip around Bishop's Cleeve in those days. But then so was he. They both were. It is possible that neither was aware of the existence of the other before he made his move on the Cheltenham–Bishop's Cleeve bus that night, but it seems unlikely.

He had been living in Cleeve for just over a year by the middle of 1969. He was married to a woman called Rena, and they lived at the Lakehouse caravan site on the outskirts of Bishop's Cleeve with their two young children. They said they did at least, and it was in their interests that the authorities and others believed them.

But Rena West, who was twenty-five and had been born Catherine Costello, was a handful. She had a long history of borstal and prostitution, and more recent convictions for burglary, stealing, and actual bodily harm. She carried a cut-throat razor and another knife in her handbag, if her husband was to be believed. She liked drinking and having a good time; she still worked intermittently as a prostitute and would go off for long periods without any warning. Sometimes she was there and sometimes she wasn't. Sometimes the children were there and at other times they were being taken care of by foster parents. Rena would reappear and the children would come back to live at the Lakehouse site in the trailer. Then Rena would disappear again, and new fostering arrangements would have to be made for Anna-Marie and Charmaine. It was a shambolic existence.

Anna-Marie was five in 1969; Charmaine was a year older. Anna-Marie was Fred's and Rena's daughter. But Charmaine was Rena's daughter by another man. Her father was Asian, so she was half-Asian, and that was apparent from the colour of her skin. There weren't any Indian or Pakistani, or even Chinese, families living in Bishop's Cleeve at that time, and so she was noticed; she stood right out.

Rena's absences meant that Fred was constantly looking around for minders and babysitters and people to sit with the children. It gave him the excuse he needed to approach girls in the village and all around the surrounding area. He had a routine he developed of waiting in his van close to the gates of Cleeve School, sometimes with the children. And he was able to talk several girls from the school into going back to the caravan with him. The mess and conditions they found when they got there made them feel even sorrier for the two girls. But as soon as Anna-Marie and Charmaine were out of earshot or in bed, he would shift the conversation away from whatever they had been talking about to sex talk and abortion talk, and talking about the operations he could do on women. You know. The what's-her-name. The down-below areas. The curtains of the trailer would be pulled closed, and he would show them things – crude and rusty-looking tubes and rods – that he said he used for abortions. Vagina, isn't it what they call it? He had a set of black-and-white Polaroid pictures showing close-ups of women's vaginas, and he would bring them out. He would try to get the girls to pose for photographs, depending on what signals he felt they were giving him. He told them he could pimp for them like he pimped for his wife and like he had pimped for other women. Women were sitting on a goldmine but most of them didn't seem to know it. He told them how much money a girl could make on the streets of Cheltenham.

On the night of his drink with Rose, he rolled up in what she would remember as an old ice-cream van. It was actually a white camper van with a blue stripe on its side and a stolen tax disc on the windscreen. She was waiting outside. You could see her house from there. It was eight o'clock. She had the parcel he had delivered to her at the shop earlier under her arm. They went in the Swallow and sat for a long time over a single drink. He had his half a shandy. Always that. And for her maybe half a cider. Later she would drink Malibu and Coca-Cola. But Malibu wasn't around in those days.

So maybe a half a cider or a Bacardi and Coke. Drink would never play a significant part in anything that happened between them and they stuck to the one.

They had a drink and he told her he was married but his wife had left him two years earlier. He said he lived in a caravan on a site in Stoke Orchard with his two children. Stoke Orchard, which she knew very well. Just a short walk away on Stoke Road, at the point where Cleeve village turned into countryside again. He was always a good talker. She liked that. She wasn't. He was the sort of man who could talk the birds out of the trees. He had the gift of the gab.

He had worked around Bishop's Cleeve ten years earlier, when he was eighteen. He had delivered bread around Cleeve and the surrounding villages in a Sunblest van. He had been a seaman in those days, and Sunblest had just been a fill-in job. Only a sort of one-fling job. But he had a son in Bishop's Cleeve somewhere as a result of that round. The mother had the brightest ginger hair you've ever seen in your life, and she was clubbed, look. Lived off Tobyfield Road and had been put in the club by him. There was a woman next door to her had loads of children. She used to have something like four or five loaves of bread a day, and this ginger piece next door, the redhead, used to have a brown loaf now and again. Her mother and father worked in Smith's Industries. She didn't work. This particular day she asked him to bring a small brown in and he walked in and there's a big rug in front of the fire and she's starkers lying on it. She says: How about it, then? Well, you couldn't refuse. Couple of months went by, she come to the van one morning and said: Look at this, I'm pregnant, look. She was clubbed. He jacked the job there and then. He was gone. Didn't wait to finish the round. All this in 1959. Rose would have been five.

He had sea stories. He had been at sea. Six months as a deckhand fetching oil from Amsterdam and bringing it in to

Gloucester docks. You didn't pay tax or nothing, and you just signed on in any name. He went to Jamaica, the Far East. He went to Jamaica twice, for bananas, oranges, stuff like that. He went to Kenya once, that was on a safari trip, which was a hundred pounds and everything supplied. Bigger docks and bigger journeys. Girls just standing waiting on the docks by the dozens. It was gang-bang, thank you ma'am, and that was that story finished. He could remember times when he slept with three or four girls and went with each of them at least twice in a night. Just gone from one to the other and then gone back over them, look. In the same bed. He never paid for it in his life. Sailors' stories. Tales of the sea. Stories of his far-flung and manly life.

He was a story-telling cowboy. He yarned in the same way he would operate as a cowboy builder: adding and bodging, lagging and pointing, improvising until a story could seem upright and watertight, with the idea of not being around to watch it topple over. Whether telling or building, what mattered to him was that something looked sound, and not to worry about the qualities of straight and plumb, square and level, right and true. The mugs could look after all that.

And all the time the parcel that he had delivered to her at the bread shop earlier in the day sat beside them in the Swallow. He had brought her a lace dress and a fur coat, which she knew by now, because she had taken it home and had a look. They were nice, but she couldn't keep them. There was no way she could keep them because her mother or her father might find them and they would go really up the wall. Nylon lace. Rabbit fur.

Clothes – certain items of clothing – were to play an important part in their life together. Clothes as tokens of affection, as souvenirs and eroticized playthings. Clothes as fetish objects; clothes as bonds and restraints.

That first time, though, she told him that she couldn't take his present to her back to where her parents might ask questions, because she wasn't supposed to have boyfriends. Her original idea had been to bring it and return it to him as a bare statement of the fact that she had no intention of starting any sort of relationship with this stranger. That had been her intention. But now an hour or two had passed. Between them they decided that he would take the coat and the dress back home to the site where he lived and store them in the trailer. The unspoken promise being of course that she would wear them there for him. And sooner rather than later he did photograph her standing on a deserted road leading from nowhere to nowhere, striking obscene poses and dressed in nothing but a thin fur coat.

He brought her a lace dress and a fur coat. The first secret between them.

A day or two after their first date, Fred West and Rose Letts arranged to see each other again. They got in the camper van with the stolen tax disc on the windscreen and drove the few miles north of Bishop's Cleeve to Tewkesbury and a country pub there called the Odessa. The Odessa was the kind of place young couples like them would drive to for a quiet evening. It was a nice class of person that got in the Odessa, and she was pleased and impressed.

The year was just on the turn. They were going into autumn. And after a quiet and pleasant drink it was still warm enough to go for a walk. They set off on a short walk. And that was when he kissed her. He pulled her in towards the gate of a field and it was a romantic moment. Later, he remembered that moment as a turning point in his life. In both his and Rose's lives, he felt sure.

'We stood at that gate and something happened to us both,' he said years later. 'We clashed in to each other and just locked so solid in each other's minds, it was just unreal.

Rose knew that something had happened at that gate, and so did I. We weren't a hundred per cent sure what *had* gone on. And from that time we have absolutely been locked into each other's thoughts. We can virtually read each other's minds at all times.'

She wanted to commemorate the moment, he said, by taking the gate home; lifting it off its hinges and carting the gate away then and there: 'Rose always wanted that gate, a big farm gate. To have as an ornament at home. A big five-bar gate! It was a couple of years later before we went back there and the gateway was filled in and the gate was gone, and Rose actually stood there and cried. It was only a farm gate, you know, but it meant so much to her because she realized that was the start of our life together.'

Like the dress and the coat, which were the bearers of meanings they would have found it difficult to put into words, the gate, the crux of their second meeting, became part of the private language they started to evolve. A private and complex, and eventually almost subliminal, language of signals and cues.

They would make night-time visits to another five-bar gate outside the village of Minchinhampton, south of Gloucester, in the years to come. At her request, he would tie her to the gate and whip her and make love to her there. It was something she enjoyed doing with other men as well, and she would come home on those occasions with the marks of the crossbars from the gate on her body, as well as deep weals and cuts where she had been whipped and tied. A farm gate becoming lit up in their headlamps would be the signal for the restraining and gagging of Caroline Raine to begin.

But it is probably significant that Fred West attributed the sentimental, 'feminine' feelings about the gate near the Odessa in Tewkesbury to Rose, rather than to himself. All through his life he would invest his deepest and most complicated emotions

– all his most difficult and disturbing thoughts – not in people, but in things. Places and things. People *as* things.

He always preferred inanimate objects to breathing, responding – and therefore threateningly dangerous and unpredictable – people. The deadened and dehumanized over the alive and responding. That would be his choice every time.

Many years later, when Fred and Rose had a son, Stephen, and Stephen was old enough to go with his father on night-time bicycle-stealing raids around Gloucester and Tewkesbury and Cheltenham, his father would make a big point one night of showing him where he had met his mother at a bus stop in Cheltenham. There was a whole row of stands, wind traps set around in a circle, and he told Stephen he had first seen his mum when they were standing together at number 13.

They were driving around in the converted Group 4 security van, looking for bicycles to lift, and his father stopped the van and insisted that Stephen get out and come and stand with him at the exact spot where he first saw Rose. As if there was some magic or mystery or something around it. This bog-ordinary, prefabricated, pebble-finished stand; windowless where there should have been windows, and busted open in places so that the twisted metal of the interior support frame was exposed and showing; the insides showing out. They stood in this faintly rank and urine-smelling place, and his father tried to convey to Stephen the deep significance it had for him. These pavements. This bus stand which, as far as Stephen could tell, was just an old clapped-out pile of junk.

It was always objects over people. Activity over closeness. He could never be comfortable with what he called 'loving and cuddling'. It wasn't his thing. He could never feel easy and unselfconscious and comfortable when he was out on his own in public with Rose. He wouldn't know how to behave or what to say.

The hour or two they spent together in the Swallow and their night out at the Odessa in Tewkesbury would be more or less their only conventional nights out with each other in a relationship that lasted for twenty-four years. A more normal night out would involve a variety of sexual partners, elements of sadism and bondage and, in the later years, a video camera which he had bolted into the back of the van. He put carpet down in the van and even installed a little gas fire for the winter. One of Rose's men friends would come round and they would take some rope and a whip, some vibrators and a flask of tea and all go together off in the van. Some rough sex. Some new footage to add to a growing video collection. It was their idea of a good night out.

After those first two times in Bishop's Cleeve and Tewkesbury, on the few occasions they ever went out together after that, his attention was always elsewhere. On other men. He was always scouting for other men he wanted her to go with. They were usually black. Almost without exception black. In the end it was an obsession. Fred and his other men.

Chapter Five

Then it was one short street standing in the middle of nowhere. A donkey on a hill; some chickens or some kind of farm in the front. Big skies making it an exposed and wind-whipped place. Water in three directions: broad rivers to the east and north; the sea to the west. All of this water visible and within walking distance. Northam, the village in north Devon where Rose Letts grew up, is out on a limb and so a weather-blasted place. Baked in the summer months; windswept and apt to be wet throughout the rest of the year. Built on a hill sloping upwards from the sea.

Northam Burrows, standing between the village and the sea, is half water, half land. Thousands of tough, springy islets, micro-islands, which go on for miles and are dark and treacherous-looking. A dark, flat wilderness, intersected with dykes and mounds, with scattered horses feeding on it.

For all the drowning space, this is a part of the world that has a trapped and cornered feel. There is nowhere to go but back to Bideford in the direction in which you came. There is a bridge across the river at Bideford. A ferry in the season to Instow, a beach hamlet dominated by a white wedding-cake-style hotel, commodore class and not really the Letts's sort of place. Bill Letts's sort of place maybe; a place to walk his uniform of the Royal Navy. His summer whites. A smart-looking man. Immaculately turned out always. The rest of the family stayed on their side of the water where few holidaymakers came. Westward Ho! and Appledore were holiday destinations. Northam was apart and dislocated and slightly doomy like the Burrows. The village square remains a dark and unquaint place today, with the small council estate where the Letts used to live hidden away out of sight just off it, the stumpy tower blocks built on the decline of the hill to prevent their tops showing. Although then it was one short street standing in the middle of nowhere. A donkey on a hill; some chickens.

Rose Letts was the youngest of the Letts' four daughters. Pat was ten years older, Joyce was eight years older, Glenys was three years older, and Rose. She was born in 1953. She had one older brother, Andrew, and the two babies, Graham and Gordon. Her mother always called her Rosie. Rhymes with 'dozy'. So that's what she got and would probably have got whether the name fitted or not. It was a nickname she wore with pride and lived down to whenever she could. Rosie-proud-to-be-Dozy.

It seems that she probably wasn't really stupid. A teacher at Northam village school would remember her as being 'just like any other happy, ordinary little girl. She didn't excel at anything, neither was she a troublemaker.' 'Keen', 'steady', 'polite', 'sensible' are some of the things she would be called by other teachers over the years, right up to her last term at school in Bishop's Cleeve.

Academically she was never going to be brilliant. At Northam she would be made to wear a dunce's hat and stand in the corner. She would be kept back a year and made to squeeze into a seat that was biting and too small. She wasn't the full cup of tea in her brother Andrew's opinion. That was based partly on this habit she had of rocking. Andrew called it her 'wiggling'. In bed she was always wiggling. Lying asleep with her head rocking from side to side. Wherever in the house you were you could hear it. Rose rocking; the bed creaking hour on hour. But no sign of the glowering vindicatrix, the heavy-set prisoner, is yet discernible in the shiny-haired, olive-skinned schoolgirl, skipping along Morwenna Park Road to buy her mum a bag of sugar from the shop in the square.

Rosie could have been forgiven for wondering how she had ended up in this quiet, edge-of-the-earth place. But she never stirred herself to find out. She knew that her mother from time to time made trips back to visit her own family in Essex. But it never occurred to her to wonder how she had got from there to here.

The short answer was the war. Daisy Fuller, as she was, had left school when she was fourteen and made a life for herself. She had gone into service, and worked in pubs in the Brick Lane area of east London in the thirties before taking up domestic work for a local Jewish family in Wanstead. When the war came, they wanted to get their children away from London. And Daisy decided to stay with the Greens, as her employers were called, when they moved to north Devon. She went with them to live in Lime Grove in Bideford in Devon. And when they wanted electrical work done, Bill Letts was the man they got to do it. His mother and father were in Northam. They were Northam-born, and so was he. He had a daytime job working for an electrical shop in Bideford, and he'd go out again in the evening just to earn a few shillings, wiring up farmyards and farms. He came to the Greens' house where Daisy was working on several occasions. And although they were both shy and not in any way outgoing, they started going girlfriend and boyfriend together, the parlour maid and the electrician.

She had transplanted herself from Chadwell Heath, which is near Ilford and Romford in Essex, and found the shock of the changed way of life to be no shock at all. Her father was a Cambridgeshire man, and the Essex she grew up in was quite country-like, not factories and shopping centres; quiet and rural. As a girl, she used to run into the house when she saw the cows coming. They used to kill the cattle behind the shop then, and she used to run away when she saw the cows and the man coming behind them with a stick. So the pace of life and the way of life in Devon suited her quite nicely.

Bill Letts's father had been with the Yeomanry out in Australia in the First World War. His mother nursed the soldiers at the front in France. Then she did district nursing in north Devon. Mrs Letts – Bertha – was very well known around Bideford and Northam. What her husband – he was another Bill – did wasn't so easily described. Many years later, Graham, Rose's brother, would be told by both his father and his mother that his grandfather got by seeing to the needs of rich women in Devon. He was a paid companion and, more than that, a kind of gigolo. And he certainly remained spritely into his seventies and even eighties. Bill Letts's father would live with them in Bishop's Cleeve for periods in his later years, and Graham remembers him having relationships with local women. He was good to be with, he liked things tidy, liked his plants, a bit of gardening. He'd become their partner, really. There was a woman at the end of Tobyfield Road used to give Graham and Gordon cakes and treats on the way to school and their grandfather moved in with her. Graham used to see them on the way to school in the mornings: *Whoa, you should be slowing down at your age!* But he didn't. His grandfather kept on going. Graham's feeling was that his father never seemed comfortable when his own father was around, as if possibly he was a reminder of something.

Rose's mother and father got married in Ilford in 1942 and moved in with Bill Letts's parents in their small house in Castle Street in Northam. For the rest of the war, Daisy Letts divided her time between Essex and north Devon. Pat, their first child, was born in 1943; Joyce was born eighteen months later. Shortly after that, Bill Letts joined the Navy as a radio operator and, when the war ended in 1945, he volunteered to stay on. Although it meant that his oldest children grew up without him being there, he remained in the Navy until 1952.

Daisy Letts had four children and an established way of living by then. She had a council house and her routines, and they were thrown into total chaos when Bill tried to impose naval rules and practices on to them. Used to bulkheads and ships' galleys, he would bleach carpets and steam rooms in the house as if he was on a ship. He used to have a scrub-out, shutting himself in a room and cleaning it. Many carpets were ruined that way. Any room failing to meet his standards would have to be started on again and cleaned from top to bottom. Shoes would be inspected. Hair and nails. He could be really bloody-minded. The lavatory could be bleached as many as four times a day.

Mealtimes were an ordeal. All meals were to be eaten in absolute silence. The sound of a knife on a plate counted as breaking the silence. He would lash out. Just go berserk. Scalps were opened, eyes blackened. If they had been arguing he wouldn't give Daisy any wages, and when she somehow found money to put food on the table, he would throw the food away so they couldn't have it. They would be made to sit in silence and watch him breaking eggs into the dustbin and pouring out tea and sugar from their packets.

To get away, their mother would take the children on long walks across the Burrows to the sea and along the cliffs, or inland through the country. They would come back happy and exhausted, and then they would be made aware by the silence that he had one of his black moods on him. He was too controlled. He'd never oversleep in the mornings. He couldn't bear to be late for work. He'd go out and come home. He was ticking. Waiting for it to happen was worse than when it happened. It put them on edge. And then bang.

His wife was seen in the village with bruising and black eyes. There was an occasion when the police were brought, when he knocked her down the concrete steps at the front of the house and dragged her along the path by her hair. He was always looking for a reason to lock the children out. They only had to come home seconds after he told them to – his watch would be in his hand – and it didn't matter what the weather he would lock them out. He threw boiling water at his wife. He didn't just lose his temper. He used to flip. Blow. He would just blow.

Eventually Daisy, so compliant and submissive in character, a slave to his whims, broke down. She suffered a nervous collapse, and electro-convulsive therapy was prescribed. ECT. A very controversial treatment even now. She was given six treatments, the last of them being just before Rose was born at the Highfield Maternity Home in Northam, in November 1953.

Rose was four when her mother had Graham. And although she was closer in age to the next ones up, Andrew and Glenys, it was with Graham and his younger brother Gordon that she made a special bond. She always played with younger children. She would laugh at little things that they did. She would play with them like a young child, whooping and laughing. She was babyish herself.

Rose was always happy looking after her baby brothers. Then as they grew older the three of them became kind of her little gang. They shared a bed. The three of them became familiar figures in the more disreputable parts of Plymouth when the family moved there. Then in the non-tourist parts of Cheltenham. Graham was a child alcoholic. He started drinking heavily as a young teenager and would have drink and psychological problems all his life. He was drinking twelve pints of lager and a bottle of Scotch or vodka on almost a daily basis when he was fourteen. There were also drugs. He would be in and out of prison for burglary, theft and fraud. Gordon would put himself into care at the age of twelve. He would be in borstals, and then prisons and mental hospitals, all through his life. He would come to his father's funeral in 1979 handcuffed between two prison guards. Gordon was always very disturbed.

Rosie and Graham and Gordon. Rosie and the boys. It was as though they consciously cast themselves as outsiders. An undermining confederacy within this outwardly god-fearing and respectable house. A commitment to the sadness of being white trash. 'We just thought she was trying to make the little ones happy,' Rose's mother says now. 'But it's as if they couldn't cope with life. That's how I see them. Mind you, there's a lot of their father there. The big difference is that he always worked hard. But there's the same weakness of character. I always felt I upheld Dad in a lot of ways. I always felt he needed me as a leaning post. To blame me for everything. He would always put the money on me, for me to sort out. Bills. But Rosie and the boys, I'm almost frightened to talk about them. They don't seem to want to live how we live. I blame Dad really for most things that went on.'

Home from the Navy, Bill Letts got a job as a television engineer. He had his own van. But there weren't many televisions around then or even people who could afford to have electricity in their houses in Northam in the fifties. In Northam you were either a farmer or a fisherman and you made your own entertainment at night. So when Rose was eight, the family packed up and moved to south Devon where her father had found work in the Naval Dockyards at Plymouth. That lasted two years, and then they were on the move again, this time to Chipping Campden in what is known as the 'haute Cotswolds', near Stratford-on-Avon, where he had got a job as a cook in a private school. But this didn't last either and there was a brief stopover in a flat in Cheltenham before he landed the position with Smith's Industries and the house in Tobyfield Road on Smith's

Estate, in 1964. The job was low-ranking – he was an electronics engineer working on flight simulators – but it was top secret according to him.

He liked the job at Smith's. It was reasonably well paid, and he became fixated on his work. The only thing he ever talked to people who came to the house about was his work. Sometimes he would be gone so long that Daisy would have to send Andrew down to the factory at nights to bring him home. The security on the gate knew Andrew and they would let him in and his father would be there working all on his own. Totally tucked up in his work.

When he was sixteen, Andrew was taken on at Smith's himself. He was earning only apprentice money, £5 a week, which he was giving to his mother towards his keep. He had a fish-and-chip-shop job at nights in Bishop's Cleeve. All his life he had been taunted by his father. But it was as if Bill felt he had to ride Andrew more than ever once he was working at the same place. The particular incident that Andrew remembers happened on a Saturday morning after his father came to get him out of bed. 'He came into the bedroom. This was around nine. This was "lying in". He made me get up. Absolutely taunting me all the time. So I got some cereal. I took my time on purpose – that was the thing to get him going. If you took your time. I didn't want to get him going, but I'd had enough. He used to always strike us across the head. Our mum used to say she didn't mind him hitting us, as long as it was in the right place. I think I got the better of him. He pulled the knife out on me then. The kitchen knife. Cut me several places on my arm. I went to the police who treated it as just a domestic, more or less. Mum snuck my stuff out for me, and I went and got a job and a place in town then. It was mental and physical cruelty, all the time we were there. I have to say I was terrified of him. Scared to breathe.'

Their father was constantly on the look-out for reasons to

give one of them a beating. If he couldn't find any, he would make them up. He'd accuse them of things they hadn't done, like touching his radio. He'd pick Graham up by the ears and swing him until his ears turned blood red. He'd bang his head into the wall. He claimed once that a five-pound note had gone missing and made Graham and Gordon go up to their room every night for several nights and strip naked, then he thrashed them with a belt. He would use anything; sticks, belts. He would just flip.

Pretty soon, probably thinking that if he was going to get beaten he might as well get beaten for a reason, Gordon started stealing money from his mother's purse. Graham couldn't stand that. He told Gordon, who was three years younger, that if he was going to do that, he should do it out of the house, which had always been his own code. In his adult life, Graham's wife would send him out to do jobs: burglaries, shoplifting. But he had a code. 'I only used to do factories, not ordinary people.' Eventually he let even that go.

Graham and Gordon were in trouble with the police from a very young age. They started sleeping rough from being young, in toilets, derelict houses, fields. Graham was found asleep one night by a woman neighbour, covered in ice. But it was preferable to being beaten to a pulp when he got home. It was probably only the alcohol in his body that had kept him alive.

They used to go and stay in these terrible old dives. And their mother could never find them, no matter how hard she looked. She used to leave the door unlocked for them and sleep on the sofa waiting for them to come home. The police used to come in and wake her up and say, 'Mrs Letts, we've just caught Graham.' She was pretty sure Graham was involved with drugs. With bad people. But she didn't know how. She would look around her on her street and in her village, and she didn't see people who looked bad. She knew one family. There were three boys, and she was told two of these boys were housebreakers. The mum and dad didn't seem like a bad family. She went round their bungalow and the boys looked clean and smart; you would never believe these were bad boys.

Graham stole his father's car while he was still at school, something that was unheard of in those days. Went to the Smith's car park and took his father's Toyota and drove out on the motorway. Floored it on the motorway. The older part of the family just couldn't understand how the two halves of the family could have turned out so entirely different. Andrew used to go round to Jacquie's, his girlfriend in Cheltenham, and so was saved.

When Rose was fourteen, Graham was ten and Gordon was seven. And, when she could, she would come in as their protector, protecting them against their father. Andrew used to sleep in a bed with Graham and Gordon. But with Andrew gone, she could come in with them in their double bed. They would huddle together for comfort and protection, and the sexual activity among them started there. She started masturbating Graham and that led to them having full sex together. She had always bathed the boys from them being very young and would masturbate Gordon in the course of drying him although, at the age of six or seven, he was too young to know what was going on. Bathtime would always take a very long time.

In the late sixties, Daisy Letts took a cleaning job in a brewery. The work kept her out of the house in the afternoons and evenings, and Bill Letts never came home from Smith's until late. So, with both parents away from the house for long periods, Rose, as the eldest, was put in charge. They had the house to themselves and Rose started to walk around naked when her mother and father weren't there. She was never shy physically and, in addition to Graham and Gordon, some boys of her own age from school would sometimes be around. She would take off her clothes and invite the boys to what she knew was their first real feel of a girl. She liked holding these 'parties'. She used to barge her way into the bathroom when she knew Andrew was in there getting ready for the bath or something. He would hear the door open and go to shut it; it didn't shut easily; there was quite some force there. She had been inquisitive herself. Soon she was running about in her underwear regardless of whoever was in the house.

Shortly after Rose moved out of Tobyfield Road to live with Fred West, neighbours would start to complain about Gordon exposing himself at an upstairs window. He was aged about nine or ten and had already been caught stealing women's underwear from washing lines. He liked to wear the underwear and other items of women's clothing. He enjoyed cross-dressing and going around when it was just the three of them at home in Rose's clothes. Slipping into bed in lacy bikini briefs, shiny pants. It might partly explain why she didn't want to keep the dress and coat that Fred West had given her; it wouldn't suit her to have to share them. It possibly explains why she cut up the first grown-up underwear given to her by her mother. Her mother spent her last pennies getting Rose her first set of underwear that wasn't either home-made or hand-me-down. And she cut it all up with scissors. Just ripped it all up. But nothing unusual with Rose.

The heavily eroticized atmosphere in Tobyfield Road seems to have left only Mrs Letts untouched. Because Rose had been having a sexual relationship with her father for two years at least before leaving. Her father had started having sex with Rose when she was only thirteen.

After their drink at the Odessa in Tewkesbury, Fred West did what he frequently did with the girls he got in his van: he took Rose back to the Lakehouse caravan site to meet his children.

There was a lake at the site, as the name implied. And it would be landscaped one day. Dredged and filtered and given a pier and ducks and turned by the developers into a feature. Grandfathers and granddaughters feeding bread to the ducks from the pier. But then it didn't look like that. It was a grey and soupy and unlandscaped lake, and all around it were little rusting snailback caravans and bigger trailers. The trailers were flat-sided and raised on blocks. They were called 'mobile homes' but they weren't. They had travelled from the factory straight to the site – the first and last journey they were going to make. A number of the trailers had chicken-wire fences and low picket fences marking off their space. The roads on the site were unmade and there was quite a lot of car breaking and livestock rearing – chickens, geese, goats – as well as other backyard industries going on. A lot of noise from loud radios and the animals; bawling children. Mud in the winter and tattooed torsos in the summer. Fred had the name 'Rena' tattooed at the top of his left arm. Rena had scratched it in herself with a needle and ballpoint pen one night when she was drunk.

The sense of people living with a minimum of regulations was strong, and was something that was reflected in the ramshackle, backwoods atmosphere. Lakehouse didn't have a good reputation among local people. They hadn't wanted it and many parents warned their children against going there. For that reason the site had a fascination for teenagers of Rose Letts's age and explained why so many girls from her school before her had been prepared to go back when they were asked.

There was a fence around Fred West's trailer in bay 17. He had made a Wendy house for the children in the back of it and there were also acetylene and oxygen bottles and hoses and an acetylene cutter for a van he was cutting up inside the fenced-off area. Also a plastic-lined pond. On her first day-time visit Rose would see that he had put in a pond. But the pond was empty by then because Anna-Marie, the younger girl, had taken the fish that used to be in it and cut them up with a knife and he hadn't replaced them. There was still water in it but no fish or anything swimming; just rubbish lying on the bottom and oil on the surface and oily nuts and bolts.

Anna-Marie, named by her mother after a Jim Reeves song, was five in 1969. Charmaine, her half-sister, was six. Rose took to them. One so blonde, one so dark, in their little foldaway beds in their little nighties. They had both been born in Glasgow and it was quaint the way they still spoke with quite pronounced Scottish accents. They had been living in the south half their lives but there was still a strong Scottish twang to their voices. The accent was particularly notice-able with Charmaine because of the fact that she was half Asian.

Charmaine's story was a romantic and exotic one, if you believed Fred. Her father was a Pakistani shopkeeper and a Mr Big of the Gorbals. He drove a long limo with two flags flying from the back of him and slept in a round bed with a canopy over it draped in Indian silks. He owned his own ship and all types of shops. You couldn't turn a corner that he didn't own a shop. He had a knife, a beautiful knife about that long and the handle all done in red and white what's-her-names. Not diamonds. He was a beautiful knife, and he wasn't slow to use him. There was a gangster connection and protection money and a Glasgow gang-war tie-in. He was the big boy. Beautiful clothes. Massive bloke. The biggest Pakistani you've ever seen. And Rena was dressed in the fin-ery. She had it all. She was absolutely beautifully dressed. And Rena never ever wore the same clothes twice. She stripped and binned it. Threw it out and put on new. The satins and silks that he brought back aboard his own ship from the Orient.

If you believed Fred. Charmaine's father was an Asian bus conductor who had been based at the same depot in Glasgow as Rena. Away from the buses, Rena worked as a street prostitute around the stations and bars in the city centre.

Rena was the friend of a girl called Margaret Mackintosh Fred West had gone to school with in Much Marcle. The girls had met when they were in a borstal in Greenock on the Clyde. When she was released Rena had followed Margaret south and had got a job working with her in a café in Ledbury, in the High Street opposite the Ledbury cottage hospital. Margaret had introduced her to Freddie West from Marcle. And Fred, as soon as he was told that she was pregnant, had volunteered to get rid of Rena's baby for her. The father was a bus conductor from back in Glasgow and she didn't want it. He had learned to do abortions during his time in the 'Navy' and he offered to help her out.

Rena was a 'suicide' blonde (dyed from a bottle) and 'a fair picture'. She was eighteen the year she met Fred West, three years younger than him, fearless and up for anything. Feart of nobody and scared of nothing. Quite soon after Margaret Mackintosh had introduced them, Rena was lying in the open in a place called Dog Hill with Margaret standing as look-out one Sunday afternoon while he used his tools to try and perform an abortion. It didn't work. But the experience apparently taught them something useful about each other because they married soon afterwards, at the end of 1962. Charmaine was born undamaged in March 1963 and was registered under the name 'West'.

Seven years later, Fred West would show a dopehead and petty criminal he had offered a bed to for the night what he claimed was the close-up photograph of a woman's vagina during an abortion. He had a whole set of Polaroid pictures of what he said were the vaginas of the girls he had operated on. He had bumped into Terry Crick in the Full Moon, the 'drug pub' in Cheltenham, and back at the caravan on the Lakehouse site he also showed him the instruments he used for operating on women. The 'van was littered with what looked like machine parts and tools and children's toys and dirty clothing all jumbled up. And he said he used the rusty tubes and rods and corkscrew-like devices to carry out abortions. Pulled the curtains closed and gave them an imaginary demonstration. Crick and the girl. Crick was with a girl, and Fred told her to come and see him if she ever got herself in trouble.

When he asked Terry Crick to help him with his 'work', Crick went and reported it to the police. But the policeman he reported it to took the view that the pornographic snapshots were Fred's own business. The officer Terry Crick saw used Fred West as a 'grass' on other local villains. Very small-time stuff. Small beer, but useful. No further action was taken.

The second time Rose visited Fred in the trailer at Lakehouse he had prepared her a meal. He made her the one meal he could make, which was beans, sausage, egg, chips, slice of bread and margarine, tea. The girls liked Dad to cook their dinner because he made it as a face on their plate. He would put the chips as hair, sausage for the mouth, beans for a beard and two eggs as eyes. It is unlikely that he arranged Rose's dinner for her on her plate like this. But it's interesting he would make this physically mature but still poorly and schoolgirlishly dressed not-quite-sixteen-year-old the same meal he made six-year-old Charmaine and five-year-old Anna-Marie. She wore white knee-socks then and it was one of the idiosyncrasies of the way she dressed that she would wear them for the rest of her life.

Rose had walked to the trailer because she didn't want to

attract attention by somebody picking her up. He had sent the children to be looked after by a neighbour, and after they had eaten, they played some records and drank more tea. Nothing too unromantic or loud. He didn't like loud music. In the years to come, their favourite listening would be film background music. The music from porno movies. Feature-length hard core. That would be the soundtrack of their lives. Music like supermarket Muzak, if you ignored the panting and the snatches of German or Scandinavian dialogue and you weren't paying attention to the screen.

He had gone to see one of the top groups at the Barrowlands ballroom in Glasgow with Rena once, and he hadn't been able to stand the mayhem; he had had to leave. Everybody was on the floor screaming and in hysterics and he had turned to Rena and said, 'Let's get out of this, it ain't my idea of life.' So nothing too booming or raucous. Nothing too loud. 'Bobby's Girl'; 'Kiss an Angel in the Morning'; 'Crystal Chandelier'. That was his kind of taste. There was some kissing and she took her clothes off for him that night, her second time at the 'van, but nothing more. They played some more records and drank more tea until it was time for him to go with her along Stoke Road until she was almost home. Out of the dark of Stoke Road into the lights of the village and she was nearly home.

Before long, she wanted him to meet her mother and father. She had never done this with anybody before. She wanted to stop sneaking about and bring him back to where she lived. Show him off. So this is where the fight began.

He came to the house in some kind of tipper or digger. He was working for Costain's on the construction of a section of the M5 not far away, just a mile or two to the west of Bishop's Cleeve. And he turned up on some tipper thing with his overalls rigid with oil and dirt and his face smeared and blackened. He showed up looking like this for his introduction to

Rose's parents and instantly launched into one of his fantastical stories about being the owner of a big hotel and caravan site in Scotland. Digging hole after hole for himself. Throaty cackle. Maniacal grin. Making a roll-up between the thumb and thick fingers of one hand, a prison habit, as he talked. This owner of a string of hotels. Burying himself deeper and deeper. They hated him. The filthy state of him and the rubbish he was talking and where he was living and his age. It was sad, actually, was what it was. It was a disaster. As soon as he was gone they told her she had to stop seeing him. This filthy older man with two children. The thought of him on their doorstep. He never got any further than the back kitchen. He wasn't Dad's company. Dad was quite particular and clean. They were telling her; ordering her. Keep that lot out of here. No arguments. Filthy and living in that filthy place. The way he rolled a cigarette with one hand.

She stopped going to her job at the bread shop in Cheltenham and started staying all day down at his 'van. She never said anything. 'If anybody grumbled at her, she'd hold herself tight,' her mother says. 'She wouldn't make a conversation. She never had a lot to say, actually. She'd always hold herself.'

He gave her the three pounds a week she was used to giving her mother, and she took care of the children when he wasn't there. She would creep there across the fields in the mornings and meet him without anybody knowing. He threw in his job with Costain's and started working at a big sandpit, a sand and gravel site, by the Cheltenham North Rugby Club on the Stoke Road to give this arrangement a chance to succeed. That was the only reason he came to take that job. Because Rose was banned from seeing him. You've got to work things out.

There was a house at Lakehouse in addition to the lake, and he did maintenance work and odd jobs for the house's owner, Mrs Dukes, who was also the owner of the site. Whatever else he was doing, he always tried to have what is known around Gloucester as a 'cobble': a job on the side. And while he was at Lakehouse he worked as a maintenance man for Mrs Dukes. Completely self-taught. That was the reason he lived surrounded by his tools.

There were tools everywhere in the trailer, on the chairs, on the floors and counter tops, and even on the beds. Mallets, hammers, soldering irons, drill bits, jemmy bars, plumbing joints, monkey wrenches, power drills, angle files. Like everything else of any value there – the record-player, the television, the Polaroid camera – all the tools were stolen. The trailer had the appearance of being a work shed or a tool room with the basic domestic necessities like a sink and a bed and a hot plate just barely squeezed in.

Rose started to change that straightaway. Started to make inroads on the mess. Drew back the curtains so that she could see it. She didn't know that the tools were fetish objects that he had to keep near him in order to perform. He probably didn't know that was why he had them, and if he did, he didn't tell her; he probably hadn't admitted it to himself. Spanners, starting cranks, hacksaws, circular saws, electric cable, cold chisels, car jacks, planes. There was a shed on the site where they were supposed to be stored. And she kept gathering them up and putting them there. She was determined to make inroads into the mess that was the result of there being no woman around to look after things. But no matter how hard she worked, the tools would keep creeping back. All over, on every surface, even on the bed. He had stolen them and they were his trophies and he found it difficult to become sexually excited unless he knew they were somewhere near. Greasy spanners, blowtorch nozzles, spirit levels, pipe cutters, copper fittings, grease guns, jump leads.

All his life he would make the places where he lived look

like work places by filling them with these things. Rubble and sand and cement and tools. And all his life he would add carpets, mattresses and other domestic touches to his work vans to make them suitable places for Rose to have sex. Comfortable for Rose and her men. And comfortable for himself and Anna-Marie.

Once, in a different caravan in a different part of Gloucester, Rena's friend, Margaret Mackintosh, had seen him rubbing and sexually exciting Charmaine against his groin. Charmaine had been little more than a baby then and she had been naked. And he had lain there among the usual mess and rubble, grinning up at her wearing only his trousers and telling Margaret that if he carried on she would come.

He believed his children were his to do what he liked with. They were sex toys. Showing a daughter what sex was was 'a father's job'. Her virginity was his to take. He would force Anna-Marie to have sex with him on a regular basis from the age of eight to the age of fifteen, and most of the sex would take place among the pots of paint and bags of cement and work things in the back of his van. There in the back of the van or on building sites or at the houses where she would have gone to help her father, who she adored, with his work. Whenever she was with him in the van on their way to or from a job and the van stopped, she always knew what was going to happen next.

His favourite location for his voyeuristic activities with Rose would be the various 'rolling homes' and 'love wagons', carpeted and decorated by him to be used as a travelling bordello at night, but fitted out to be work vans in the day. The neighbours in Cromwell Street would often see them carrying lengths of wood and other building materials into the house when they returned from their late-night jaunts. The tools and building materials eventually removed by the police from 25 Cromwell Street would fill dozens of inventory pages and several vans. 'The first time I had sex with Rose was in a caravan,' he would blurt out and tell people for no apparent reason. Sex and work. Work and sex. The two mutually contaminating; continually cross-feeding. This constant two-way current, to the point where everything important in Fred West's life became sexualized. There was always this blurring. Always this confusion of uses between where he worked and where he lived. No matter how hard she worked at getting rid of them, the crowbars, the plumb lines, the sanders, the wheel braces, the lengths of hose and the drill bits kept creeping back. Tools for fixing things. Rusty tubes and rods and corkscrew-like devices. Tools for fixing women. All over, on every surface, even on the bed.

Her priority, though, top of her list of the things that had to go, weren't the things that couldn't argue or talk back, the greasy inanimate objects, but the things that could. Girls from Cleeve School still occasionally turned up at the trailer at Lakehouse looking for Fred. But Rose's school reputation for being somebody not to be messed with soon put a stop to that.

Next to go was a box she uncovered at the back of the trailer filled with girls' underwear and clothes. She took them and the other women's clothes that were strewn around and put them all in a tea-chest and said to him: 'Dump that.' The lace dress and fur coat that he had brought her as a present she left hanging alongside what she took to be Rena's clothes.

But the discovery that would certainly have done the most to stir her interest was one she made while she was clearing out the 'van with him. They had decided to gut it out and alter it a bit, and there was a stove that had never been used. And when he took the bottom out, it was full of letters. Packed full. Letters from customers of Rena's. There was a whole pack of them in there, and the ad from the paper that she had taken out. Rena had started to call herself by the working name of 'Mandy James', and she had paid for an advertisement in the local newspaper saying: 'Young, attractive lady looking for employment. Anything considered . . .' She had received a load of letters, many from people actually offering jobs. Which had given him a laugh. But most of them were from actual men. Punters. The punters used to pick her up in Stoke Road and she had had quite a round going on. And it was all hid underneath this stove. Which he claimed had come as a surprise to him, the twenty-eight-year-old opening the doors of the dirty world, the secret realm of thrills and concealment, to the not-quite-sixteen-year-old; although he almost certainly knew.

So his wife was a prostitute. He had black-and-white pornographic pictures of Rena – pictures of Rena in explicit poses. And some of the men who went with her were local men from Bishop's Cleeve. Men Rose knew by sight or to say hello to and who she never would have guessed were that type of man. Men with wives and families and jobs. Nice houses. Nice cars. Your kids aren't good enough for mine, my dogs are better bred than yours, we've got a bigger and better car kind of man. They were so bloody superior. The owner of the market garden about a hundred yards up the road from the Lakehouse site, who had turfed Rose's father's garden in Tobyfield Road. He was one of Rena's most regular clients. *Everybody's at it.* When she needed it, he used to lend Rena his car.

Sometimes Rena used to bring customers back to the 'van. And when she did, Fred used to listen or watch. Listen mostly. But when circumstances allowed it, and the punter was too drunk or into doing business with Rena to care, he would watch. What he enjoyed was to see how they were by themselves. When they allowed themselves to abandon themselves, that was what he found exciting. That's what he liked best – watching them lose control.

Rena was a goer. A wild woman when she wanted to be. A bottle a day was her medicine. Rena could drink. She had taken him to parties where it was no holds barred. Rena had taken him places and shown him things and now he would show Rose. She had taken him to a party where he had had to be blindfolded to be taken there. Rena and her bodyguard, a Greek, six foot tall and four foot across. Massive man this. Huge. They had gone down some steps and into the basement of a house, and when Rena took the blindfold off he still couldn't see. It was so dark. There were flashing lights, red, blue and yellow. It was full of black people and a smell of drugs. There were four small tables in two rooms with what looked like Christmas cakes made with Christmas paper on them. Two spotlights came on. The paper was ripped off. There was young girls in them. They were drugged. They were handed round to drugged and drunken men. They had stayed at the party for fourteen hours.

Slowly painting the portrait of Rena as a woman actively seeking her sexual pleasure and being rewarded rather than punished for it. An enticing idea for a guilt-ridden girl who has grown up in a household where sex is still something forbidden, furtive and never to be spoken about.

And, being the kind of combative character Rose was, we can guess that she would almost certainly feel the need to offer something back at this point. Something to tease and titillate him. Something that would give him the green light for further disclosure. The fact that she had sex with her brothers, perhaps. Or Gordon's cross-dressing. Or the story of her rape just a few months earlier by a powerful, hypermasculine man in Pittville Park. (Although there has to be a strong suspicion that this rape, never mentioned until their arrests in 1994, was something that happened after 1969; that it was the acting out of a sadomasochistic fantasy in which Fred West was the pursuer and she was only pretending that she was being coerced into sex.) Something anyway to indicate that she understood the game they were playing. Something to show that she was not quite the unformed girl that he supposed. That she could be, and was in fact on her way to becoming, a highly valued, sexually exciting woman and a worthy successor to Rena.

An indication of how little catching up Rose had to do, in spite of an age difference between them of ten years, is the fact that she had had a string of sexual encounters with lorry drivers and building labourers while running the mobile snack bar at Seven Springs for Glenys and Jim Tyler at the beginning of the year. And now, as it happened, just six months later, Rena, the wife of Fred West and the mother of Charmaine and Anna-Marie, was driving the catering Land-Rover that provided Costain's workers building the section of the M5 motorway near Tewkesbury with sandwiches and tea. Rena had moved in with the site foreman in his caravan in Gloucester, but she was continuing to offer her services as a prostitute to a number of Costain's men. She would be arrested for soliciting in Gloucester in early December 1969.

It's not hard to see how Rose would be excited and aroused by the things she was finding out, or why he would be excited and turned on by telling her. He enjoyed talking sex. Talking sex and watching sex. Increasingly rarely would he enjoy performing sex. To be what she wanted to be (to be what he needed her to be), what she needed from Fred West was yes. He was giving her permission to pursue her pleasure. Making a foundation for the nagging insupportable erotic excitement that would be the hallmark of their years together. It was exciting to them both. If she had to give up her friends and her family and her home to stay with him, she would. And that is exactly what she proceeded to do. Do as you like, Fred West was telling her, and she did.

She decided to have his baby. She was going to be sixteen on 29 November 1969 and she wanted to have his baby. The minute she was sixteen she would start trying for a baby with Fred. And one morning she slipped out of the house when it was still dark. It was very cold and there was a fine layer of snow on the ground. Frost or it might even have been snow on the fields she had to cross. Fred started work at the gravel pit at six, and she was waiting for him there at six when he turned up for work. The foreman took her into their cabin and gave her a cup of tea. It was late in the year. It was the tail end of the year. It was early in the morning and very cold. Fred was really surprised when he saw her. But when she told him what she was there for, he walked straight up to the foreman and said, 'I've jacked.' The foreman said, 'You can't.' But Fred said, 'Sorry, mate. I've jacked.'

They went back to the trailer together. Charmaine and Anna-Marie had been taken into care at this point and so the trailer was empty. They went back to the trailer through the dark and she would be sure that was when she got Heather. She would remember getting Heather.

But no matter how hard she worked in the trailer, the tools kept creeping back.

She wrote him a letter. 'Dear Fred,' she wrote. 'Last night made me realize we are two people, not two soft chairs to be sat on . . . I love you, Fred, but if anything goes wrong it will be the end of both of us for good. We will have to go far away where nobody knows us. I will always love you, Rose.'

Her father of course had gone berserk. A number of single men who worked at Smith's Industries lived on the Lakehouse site. And when word had got back to him through them what was going on, he flipped. He would just blow.

He waited for them outside the Swallow in Bishop's Cleeve one night and flew at Fred when they came out. He had a crash helmet on and was wanting to fight him. He landed a few punches but Fred turned and walked away. Another night her father went to the caravan and threatened to burn it down with Fred in it if he didn't stay away from Rose.

Fred spent three days in prison in the middle of November. He was arrested for the non-payment of two sets of fines that had been imposed on him earlier in the year for thieving, and given three days. When he came out he found that Social Services had contacted Rena, who had returned to the caravan at the Lakehouse site, and the children. Three days later, though, Rena went off on her travels again, and Charmaine and Anna-Marie were returned to care. They were put into a children's home, a big mansion with farm animals and massive grounds, not far away in a postcard village called Whitminster.

They spent that Christmas in a home. Rose spent it locked into her room at Tobyfield Road by her father. She wasn't allowed to give or be given any presents. She passed the time making rag dolls for Fred's girls, and then a few days into the New Year it was confirmed that she was pregnant. The balloon really did go up then. Her father told her either to forget that dirty gypsy and have an abortion or be bombed out of the family for ever. And that meant for ever. Forgotten about. If he saw them in the street he would pass them as if he had never seen them in his life. If he ever saw them in the street, he would knife them. Her and that gypsy.

Fred West had a reputation dating back to his childhood for being a runner; for being somebody who would always back away from trouble. And, nervous perhaps that Bill Letts might carry out one of his threats, he vacated the caravan in Bishop's Cleeve and moved to Cheltenham. He took a job at Cotswold Tyres in Cheltenham, and moved into a flat in a large house close to the city centre. The flat was a bedsit. Just one big room sharing a bathroom and toilet, and a sink in the corner. But Social Services allowed him to have the children back, and Rose moved in to look after them. And they lived there in a family situation until the police caught up with her and took her back to her parents and Tobyfield Road.

Not knowing what else to do with her, they put Rose in a home. They put her in a home in Cheltenham with little babies, to let them scream at her, in the hope of bringing her to her senses. This was a bad girls' home for girls like her who had got themselves in trouble. Bad girls who had got in with the wrong crowd and brought trouble down on their families. Her mother was telling her she was going to have to have an abortion. Her father was telling her she was going to have to have an abortion. There was no *way* she was going to have an abortion. She was beginning to show then, and she wanted her baby.

She was in the children's home for about three weeks. And then they let her out to go home on a Friday, on the understanding that she would go into hospital to have the pregnancy terminated on the Sunday. The termination would take place on the Monday but they wanted her in the night before.

The home was about a hundred yards from where Fred worked. She had been a hundred yards from him all the time and he didn't know. She went straight to where Fred was at Cotswold Tyres, and they hatched a plan. Her father was going to take her in on the Sunday night. Fred had a Vauxhall vx490 then, and he would be waiting, parked just around the corner. When they tried to take her, she would run for it and come to him and he'd burn it out for her. It was a twin-carb and it could move. He would lay some rubber. And then they would hide until she had the baby. They would head for Scotland with the girls.

In the end none of it was necessary. A reconciliation of sorts took place over the weekend between Rose and her family. On the Saturday night her father came up to her room

133

and told her she could go. They were letting her go, but on the understanding that she wasn't just walking out of the house if she went. She was walking out of their lives and out of the family.

'She came down the stairs with her little bits and pieces,' her mother remembers, 'and my sister who was staying with me then, she looked at Rosie and said, "You're not going, are you, Rose?" She laughed. "Yeah, I am." She looked lovely, her hair was lovely. And now when I see these horrible pictures of her, it doesn't look like Rosie. She looked so lovely on the day she left . . . So to listen to Rosie going into this sex world . . . She went straight from school to him.'

Fred had a night job at a pub called the Gamecock in Cheltenham. And on Saturday night Rose turned up looking for him there with her belongings packed up in a bag. His floozy or his bimbo, the landlady at the Gamecock called her. 'Your floozy's at the door,' she came in and told him. And that was enough for him. He gave her a mouthful and told her to stick her job and went. The pub was on Clarence Square, just around the corner from the flat, and they set off along the road to start again properly together.

Chapter Six

The freedom conferred by masks. The freedom conferred by cities. In the city the forbidden – what is most feared and desired – becomes possible. And Fred and Rose, both born in houses with uninterrupted views across open countryside to the horizon – light places, poking up in the light – had found themselves separately drawn to the dark recesses of urban life. Instead of fixed community and the slow turning of the seasons – pleasure, deviation, anonymity, disruption.

These were freedoms that Fred West made himself familiar with from an early age. A country boy from a long line of country people, he quickly became restless to break the line and escape from that way of living. He was naturally secretive and sly and there were no well-kept secrets in a community as small and closely knit as Much Marcle. He hated the fact that everybody knew what was going on in the village all the time. He especially disliked the postman, who always knew what was in every letter he brought. The postman, Jim Southers. The Marcle policeman, PC Rock. Mr John Rock, a personal friend of the family. Of every family in the village.

The postman used to bring the mail, and then he'd tell Fred's mother all the news of the village. Nosey-parkering. Fred couldn't stand that. And if you did anything wrong, you were reported. The policeman would come with your parents and give you a good lecture. The vicar would come, the headmaster would come if it was something out of the ordinary where it was touch and go whether they charged you or not.

Community strangles. Girls used to be run out of the village because of being pregnant. Their mothers ran them up the Marcle Straight, right out of the village. If a girl was expecting, then she wasn't wanted in the village. That was another thing that got him with village life: how hypocritical they could be. He had a strong inclination to be private and unobserved. Community throttles.

For his fifteenth birthday, his mother and father brought him to Gloucester and bought him a suit. It was brown, double-breasted, from Burton's up on the Cross. That was when the old tramlines used to be up there. A boxy British style, wide-lapelled and boxy, in the age of the Teddy Boy and narrow Italian-American fashions. Later he would remember wearing the suit to the local dance, and the attention it brought. To see a young lad in the country with a suit on was something very rarely ever seen. But it was sort of a family thing, a tradition among the Wests. One of many traditions and bits of lore rooted in the Wests' deep peasant background. When you were fourteen, you got a gun. A twelve-bore shotgun for rabbiting. Crows. Squirrels. At that time, you got sixpence or a shilling for the tails of squirrels. Grey squirrels, which were becoming a pest. The squirrel carcasses were usually chucked into the trees for the crows, then blam! It was a tradition. Everyone had a gun at that age. When you were fourteen, you got a gun. When you were fifteen, you got a suit.

As far as he could see it, village life meant you were programmed and wound up. You got up in the morning and you did the same routine. A key turned in your back like a toy. Moorcourt Cottage, tied to Moorcourt Farm, the cottage where he grew up, had no electricity or gas, and water came from a well in the yard. The toilet was a bucket which was emptied in a sewage pit. Bath night was waiting your turn for a tin bath in the hearth. Hygiene was basic.

As soon as they could walk, the West children would go

with their mother and father into the fields to help with the lambing, droving the cows, sheaving the corn. Whisky was a badger dog, then there was a fox dog, cattle dog, sheep dog. They all had different jobs. Whisky, Brandy, Ben, Lassie, Lad . . . By the time Freddie West got to Much Marcle school in 1946 he stunk of pigs. Reeked of pigs. But he didn't go to school a lot in the last. He was too busy farming, look, bringing home half-a-crown a week and keeping sixpence of it for himself. He was nine when he started driving a tractor. Your father used to take the tractor up and put him in the field. A little Fergie – a Massey-Ferguson. The pigs, the sheep. Feeding them, lambing them down. He could draw lambs when he was about eleven. Lambing ewes down, you always had your mother or father with you because they were strong. He used to drive the cattle through the bluebell woods just by them with his dad and his mam. Pigs, sheep, chickens, cows. That was their life. They were tied to the land. They didn't do anything else.

And then, as the seasons changed, you just did the same things. You didn't have to think. If it was haymaking, then you went and got the mowers out and you did the mowing and turned the hay. Stood by with sticks to brain the rabbits as they fled for cover, and then took them home to skin and make into pies or stew. Some used broken pickaxe handles, others walking-sticks. In the spring they would gather wild daffodils from the fields to sell at the side of the road. Coming up to Easter was the time to slaughter the family pig. It might have become a pet and acquired a pet name but it still had to go. The pig they killed was always kept at home and fed off the house scraps and it had usually been a 'nisgrow' – the runt. And of course that was fed up until it was bigger and you had got very attached to it, and it always had a name like 'Sally' or something like that. There would be tears, but it always had to go. The main thing was to get the blood out of the animal, or the meat was no good. Every spot of blood had to be got out. There was so much of the pig had to be used within days – liver, lights, belly fat, belly meat. So the local children used to come up when word got about. And when the pig was killed and hung up on the ladder to drain, then they made what they used to call fry-ups in those days. There used to be a fight over the bladder to make a football. Arthur Price, the local butcher, used to come around, and Fred used to help. He helped to kill the last pig at home when he was fifteen by cutting its throat and hanging it to drain. And then they made it that you had to have a humane killer; a gun. The pig would be salted and hung up to make bacon, which would be made to last for a year.

In the summer there was hop-picking and in the autumn apple-picking for Weston's cider factory at the crossroads in Much Marcle. Fred's father, Walter, helped to organize the day trip to Barry Island on the South Wales coast in May every year. And every year, on the last Saturday in August, there was the Much Marcle Fair. Walter West, a widower, had met Fred's mother, Daisy, there in 1939, and they had married at the beginning of the following year. A strapping, rather moon-faced girl from Cowleas, a tied cottage on Cow Lane near the cider works, minding the needlework stall. Most of the girls married and stayed in the village at that time. It was the tradition again. Everybody who knew him envisioned Freddie West walking behind a cow with a stick for the rest of his life. He left school barely able to read and unable to write even his name. All he knew was the seasons of the year. And yet before the age of fifteen he decided to cease being the boy he was; to break the line and start over again as some other boy instead.

They had their local blacksmith by the pub. Weston's garage with the showground at the back of it. You had the big pond where all the frogs used to be, then the village shop and Weston's garage and then the pub. Weston's cider works. Past the Wallwyn Arms and then you turned uphill for home. Peter Evans the blacksmith used to make all their shoes. He'd have the horse there and he'd be shoeing in there, and you'd sit on the what's-her-name and he'd make your boots and shoes. Herefordshire Hounds, Ledbury Hunt used to meet up at the Wallwyn Arms, then they'd move off into the woods. Anvil, was it? Fred liked the pomp that went with that, the horses and their dress. And the dogs theirselves. But he decided to turn away from all that. He wanted to be more adventurous, and get out and see what was about. He had always loved Gloucester from that day, the day of the suit.

The day he made the break with home, though, he didn't head for Gloucester but for Hereford, which was to the west. Gloucester was east and Hereford was west, and he started out in the Hereford direction on his old bike. If he had said he was going to leave there would have been one mass of tears. So he got up during the night and, saying nothing to nobody, just went. Much Marcle–Kempley–Upton Bishop–Ross-on-Wye–Howard End. Beyond the landscape he had explored on foot to the furthest point he had ever been alone. Along dark empty roads between big empty fields and into Hereford sleeping rough in hedgerows and woods, a ride of about two days.

He left in what he stood up in and in Hereford he found a job labouring on a building site. He stayed on late at the site and in order to save all he earned slept in a half-made house there when everybody had gone. Bedded down with his tools amid the rubble and, for a month or more, never bathed or washed. He put on layers of town dust in place of his custom-ary country dirt, never washing. Accumulated it like a veneer until he was like an African tribesman when he eventually stripped off. Black and matt. And, like a primitive, he returned home bearing gifts which he offered as evidence of the other life to be lived. He reappeared as abruptly as he had left them with gifts of watches all round. He bought his oldest brother John a wristwatch; his oldest sister, Little Daisy, a nurse's watch; his mother, Big Daisy, a locket watch that his brother Doug still has, and his father a pocket watch in a rubber case – one of those Ingersoll watches with the hands that glow in the dark, enough of an innovation to still be a talking point then.

It was to be a recurring pattern: Freddie returning to his Munchkin, place-based family in Much Marcle with evidence of the life being lived elsewhere. Sometimes it was consumer goods like motorbikes and watches. And sometimes it was city girls on high white shoes with fruity perfumes and piled-up or peroxided hair. Fresh city girls with drink and tobacco on their breath and loud, careless city ways.

Returning as a fifteen-year-old, though, in 1956, he was set about by his mother who had spent the weeks of his disappearance going around trying to get news of where he was. She used to wear a big thick leather belt with laces on and she whipped that off and gave him a good hiding as he came up the path. Then, when she was finished, she tied it back on and said, 'Welcome home, son – we're level.' The other thing about the time he pushbiked from Hereford back home was that when he stripped off, his body underneath was black.

Walter West, Fred's father, was an ugly man. Daisy, his mother, was also ugly. In pictures she looks like a snow shifter from Belorussia or the Russian steppes. A bandit chief. A very tough woman. Very big in the bones. Big all round. In Walter and Daisy, ugliness had come to ugliness for mutual support. The first child she had had was a girl, Mary, and she had died at birth. And Walter West had hit the drink over that. He took to drink and he was letting everything go, and Daisy had to step in and stop it. That was how Fred's mother had first come to take charge of the family, and she had stayed in charge ever since. From that day onward Mother was always boss. That's the way the family was run. 'A pillar of steel' was how Fred West described his mother. 'There was no messing. She'd sort anything out. Sixteen or sixty, didn't matter. No problem.' She would fly down to the village school the minute she heard the teacher had been strapping her Freddie. A formidable figure with jaw set and vast apron flapping. Nobody wanted to cross her.

There were other children. John, Little Daisy, Douglas, Kitty, Gwen. Five younger Wests in addition to Freddie. But Freddie remained his mammy's favourite. She doted on him. They were close. How close nobody now can really say. But almost certainly closer than they would have wanted anybody to know. There are rumours that he lost his virginity to his mother when he was twelve. 'You'll soon be ready to sleep with your mum' is something Fred West used to say to his own son, Stephen, when he got to that age. Incest was still common in rural communities like Much Marcle in the years after the war. Mother–son incest was less common than incest between fathers and daughters. Father–son incest was rarer still. But there are still rumours in the village that Fred West was abused by his father as well as his mother when he was living at home. If it's on offer, take it. That was what his father taught. Whatever you enjoy, do, only don't get caught doing it. Walter West took it for granted that it was his right to begin his daughters' sexual life. 'Boys don't do it properly,' Fred West would tell his own daughters when they were growing up. 'Dads know how to do it right.' He said that his father had done it to his sisters and made it clear that he intended doing the same to them. He'd say, 'Your first baby should be your Dad's.'

He found life at home after he came back from Hereford exceptionally slow. He was back working with his father on the farm, rising before dawn to do the milking and roll the urns up to the main road for collection. Then silage and mud and milking again at night. What you did yesterday, you did the next day. Changeless and monotonous. Five Woodbines and a pint of cider on a wall outside the Wallwyn Arms of a Saturday dinnertime was all the social life. His father had first told him that it was possible to have sex with a sheep by putting its rear legs down the front of your own wellington boots. A sheep tied to a tree in a field was the Much Marcle social club. That was the joke.

Fred's brother, John, was just a year younger and the two of them hung around together. At the Wallwyn Arms. Under the Market Hall, a Tudor structure raised on wooden columns in the centre of Ledbury sometimes at weekends. A seventeenth-century bus shelter open on all sides. Sons of the soil. Yokels. The big night out in Ledbury, all of five miles away. Any sex that happened came under the heading of horseplay and was hush-hush. They used to dive in the hay, take pot luck and go for it. They didn't have girlfriends and boyfriends in the sense of getting paired off. They were just one massive village gang, and whichever one you went with was the one you went with, and that was that. Nobody actually settled with anybody as such. Because you weren't allowed to do that in those days. You weren't allowed a girlfriend until you were twenty-one. Whenever the opportunity came up, in the woods, or anywhere quiet in a field, you just went with them and enjoyed yourself that time, and that was it finished until you met them again. And that was the whole village way of life.

In September 1957 Fred West bought himself a 98 cc. Bantam motorbike, registration number RVJ199. Something to quicken the pace of country life. The dead life. The slow movement of time.

His mother didn't like it. She wasn't happy. It took him out of her orbit and brought him closer to girls. She was possessive. Some people in the village would have said jealous. She wanted to keep a hold. Fred got a new job at Weston's cider factory, which paid more than farm labouring and allowed him to make the payments on his bike. He was also able to keep himself cleaner and he got a new girlfriend from along the Dymock road in the hamlet of Preston. Elsie Piner. Whose father, Art Piner, Daisy West had had an entanglement with when she was younger and in service in Ledbury. That had ended badly. And so of course it was: he's bad, she's bad. Daisy hated Elsie and used to give Fred some stick over her.

It was one night while he was coming home from visiting Elsie that he had the accident on a bend in the Dymock road that nearly killed him. He came off the bike and was splattered, to use his word, the word that for thirty years he would go on using. The Iron Duke motorbike suit he was wearing – a complete leather motorbike suit – didn't offer much protection. It was ripped open. His crash helmet was split straight down the middle. He opened the bike up and let go, and he came round a sharp bend on the Dymock road, hit a pushbike that had been laid there by his brother John's girlfriend, Pat Mann, and went through a nine-inch wall. Pat Mann had stopped to drop her knickers out of sight of the road. She was crouched down on the verge by a gate and her bike had sent him into orbit. Her front wheel had skyed him.

Over the years he would embroider around it, work it up into one of his yarns; one of the bits of conversational business he would use when starting a charm offensive with a young girl. His near-death experience; the one noteworthy experience of his life to then. He had had a metal plate put in his head as a result of the accident (false). He had been paralysed from the waist down for the twelve months following the accident (false). He had been lying in the ditch for eight

143

hours before anybody found him (false). He had been pronounced dead on arrival at the hospital and only the cold of the mortuary slab had shocked him back to life (a favourite lie). He was a story-telling cowboy.

He had been taken unconscious to Ledbury Cottage Hospital and then transferred immediately to Hereford Hospital, where he did lie unconscious for seven days. His nose was broken and he had a fracture and severe lacerations of the skull; his right leg was so severely broken that he was given metal callipers and told to wear a special metal shoe. From then on he always dropped one leg harder than the other when he walked. His right leg came back slightly shorter than the left one, and he walked with a slight but noticeable limp. You could always tell by the footfall that it was Fred who was coming after that.

His mother was waiting by the bed when he regained consciousness. She visited him every day while he was recovering from his injuries, and she took him with her back to Moorcourt Cottage when he was ready to go home. She had banned Elsie from seeing him when he was in hospital, and she wouldn't allow him to have Elsie to the house. So that broke up.

He stayed at home for twelve months getting the use of his legs back. He worked for a short while for Godfrey Brace, a small farm by the church in Much Marcle. And then he was gone. Once he got his strength back he was gone for about two years then. Off on his bracing, seafaring life.

In those days you used to have a board up outside the docks showing where the ships were going and what hands they wanted on them. You didn't pay tax or nothing and you just signed on in any name. Signed with an 'X' or other identifying mark if you couldn't sign. Already walking with a sailor's rolling walk because of the accident and the inactivity and the callipers, aged seventeen, nearly eighteen. Looked back over his shoulder and called his mother an old cunt as he went.

There may have been the trips to Kenya and Jamaica, as he said. Australia, the Pacific, Hong Kong. But he started short-haul. Portsmouth, Clydeside, Bristol. On the waste boats taking sludge out of Sharpness to the dumping grounds. On the oil boats down to the Bristol Channel. Blackface jobs shifting fertilizer and waste.

It was between jobs that he worked as a bread roundsman for Sunblest bakeries for a while, delivering around Bishop's Cleeve. He moved up from the Bantam to a 1000 cc. Triumph motorbike and lived above the Rendezvous café in Newent during his brief stopovers from the sea. The Rendezvous, between Ledbury and Gloucester, was popular with the motorcycle gangs. The Scorpions and the Vampires from Gloucester; the Wolves from Cheltenham; the Desperadoes and their closest allies the Cycletramps from the Forest of Dean; the Pariah and the Pagans from further afield.

Danny Knight, the landlord of the Bristol Hotel on Bristol Road in Gloucester, used to have the blue films on a Sunday. The stag films and the strippers in the blacked-out room in the afternoon. Part of a ritual folk tradition of the Gloucester male in the late-fifties. The gangs used to come in on motorbikes, and Fred West used to join them on his grey Triumph, his small body at full stretch astride the big frame and the massive tank.

With the gang but not of the gang. Aside from the ritual bonding. He was never a joiner. 'I enjoy my own company,' he admitted many years later. 'I don't like parties and things. I don't like being clammed up to people.'

Even now he was one who preferred to watch. At the stag afternoons liked to watch the watchers as much as the show. Watching sex was good. Watching the others get off on the sex without them realizing he was watching was better. That kind of giving yourself up to the moment which he could never do. These kinds of disinhibitors. It was important that they didn't know they were being watched. So he watched. A cat who walked by himself.

He was marking out new territories. Real maps and mental maps. Places to avoid and places he wanted to go. Because of his various jobs and the mobility that owning the bike had given him, he had gained a useful knowledge of the countryside and the roads around Worcester and Hereford and Gloucester. The patch around his home patch. When he went home at the end of 1960, after an absence of almost two years, he was able to place his family and Much Marcle into the bigger picture. He wasn't covered in building dirt this time. There was nothing so noticeable about him. No sign that the time away had changed him. No hint of any secrets he might be keeping. He fitted straight back into life at Moorcourt Cottage, returning to work in the fields with his father.

Then Fred passed his car driving test, and he and his brother John bought an old Ford Popular between them. Two months later, he was arrested for the first time, for theft. The items in question were women's items: two ladies' cigarette cases and a rolled-gold watch strap taken from Tilley and Son, a stationer's, and Dudfield and Gaynan's, a jeweller's, in Ledbury. 'Christ, these are nice,' Fred said to the friend he was with when he spotted the cigarette cases on a display card, and slipped them in his pocket. A week later, in April 1961, he pleaded guilty to two charges of theft at Ledbury Magistrates Court and was fined £4. It made three paragraphs on page 1 of the *Ledbury Reporter*.

His first court appearance at the age of nineteen. And three months later he would again be in trouble with the police. Serious trouble this time, of the kind it would take more than the vicar and the headmaster and the village policeman to drag him out of. His thirteen-year-old sister was pregnant, and they accused him of having had sex with her on a regular basis since his return home at Christmas. Well, of course he had. Wasn't that what her was there for? What did they think, that she was one of them lesbians? Of course he had. He didn't try to deny it. The case was set down for trial at Hereford Assizes in the coming November.

His mother and father wanted him out of the house. His father refused to go on working alongside him. He was sent to live with his mother's sister, Violet, and her husband Ernie at Daisy Cottage in Much Marcle, and he found a job on a building site at Newent. But he hadn't been there long when he was caught stealing tools and equipment. He was only bemused when his thieving was uncovered: he was doing nothing that the other builders weren't doing. He was found guilty at Newent Magistrates Court on 18 October 1961 and fined £20.

He appeared at Hereford Assizes three weeks later on the charge of 'having unlawful carnal knowledge' of his thirteen-year-old sister. His mother had agreed to give evidence in his defence. The other defence witness was the Wests' family doctor, Dr Hardy, who told the jury that the head injuries Fred West had sustained in the motorcycle accident three years earlier might mean that he was possibly an epileptic 'given to blackouts'. Although it wasn't mentioned, he had suffered a more recent serious injury to the head. Having apparently lunged at a girl on the fire escape outside the Ledbury Youth Club one night – he had been trying to get his hand up her skirt – he had toppled over the iron railing, falling ten feet and landing on his head. He stayed unconscious for twenty-four hours, but otherwise seems to have been more or less unhurt.

When the time came for his sister to go in the witness box

she refused to say anything incriminating against Fred. In fact she refused to speak, or even to write down, without speaking, the name of the father of her baby. The judge had no alternative but to dismiss the case against him. Because it had been dismissed, it did not appear on his criminal record: that still simply showed that he was a petty thief.

Quite soon after this, in early 1962, Fred West was giving a fifteen-year-old girlfriend a lift home through the Herefordshire countryside in the early evening when he suddenly stopped the car at a farm gate and got out. When the girl, a part-time waitress at the Rendezvous café in Newent, followed him, he forced her on to the grass bank by the gate and raped her. Then he fell over on to his back, she remembered, and seemed to be unwell. He apologized to her for what had happened and told her not to be frightened because he 'had blackouts'. She didn't tell anybody about the incident for more than thirty years.

Rena, born Catherine Costello in 1944 in Coatbridge outside Glasgow, followed her borstal pal Margaret Mackintosh to Ledbury to live in 1962. It was the summer and they waitressed together at the Milk Bar close to the Tudor Market Hall in the High Street in Ledbury and had a high time lodging together at the New Inn and ruining the furniture in their room there with hair lacquer. The day Rena lay down on Dog Hill and Margaret stood look-out for her while Fred West from Marcle tampered with her and tried to abort the baby she had found herself carrying probably didn't count in her eyes as much more than larking about. Having a lark. She was a bit of a girl, Rena. She was a goer. Shapely and blonde. She was up for anything.

It was an unusual start to a relationship. But there was no doubt in the minds of anybody who saw Fred and Rena together at that time that a relationship was what it was. He had taken a job with Ledbury Farmers by then, working as a lorry driver, delivering animal feed to farms all around the area. Cattle cake, pellets, turkey food. And Rena started riding in the lorry with him after work, travelling high up, along the narrow country lanes. The ride occasionally took them to the home farm in Much Marcle and, although he could have guessed the reaction, he eventually took Rena – pregnant, lipsticked, slum-born, blonde – in to meet his mother. His mother was affronted. She went mad about it. Called Rena a lot of names and so on after she had gone. Filthy. Common. Sanitation had improved at Moorcourt Cottage. They had an indoor toilet by then. And Fred's mother made a great performance of cleaning the seat after Rena had left the house. She hated Rena. Hated everything she stood for. So Fred asked Rena, eighteen to his twenty-one and expecting another man's baby, to marry him.

Fred's brother John was the only member of the West family to attend the perfunctory ceremony on 17 November 1962 at the Ledbury Register Office. There was no reception. John West brought a bottle of Bristol Cream sherry, and four of them – Fred, John, Rena and Rena's friend Margaret – stood outside in the street and drank it. Then they went back to work.

He had gone back to living at home after the dust surrounding the incest charge against him a few months earlier had settled. But now his mother, who had gone apple-picking on the day of the wedding, refused to have his new wife in the house and so he was homeless. They tried living in the tiny room Rena shared with Margaret at the New Inn in Ledbury but that was hopeless. All they could think of doing was to go back to the only place where Rena had friends, which was Glasgow. Back to the thrown-together kind of life that she had limped along in before her spell in the south. The life she had led between her many spells away in borstal. Her mother was gone. Her mother had left home when Rena was only young. Her first appearance at Coatbridge Juvenile Court had been in May 1955, when she was eleven, for thieving. But she still knew people in Scotland. John West drove them to Birmingham to catch the train.

At first they lived in Coatbridge: 46 Hospital Street, Coatbridge. Charmaine was born at the Alexander Hospital there in March 1963. Originally she was going to be 'Mary'. But by the time of her christening in September, she was Charmaine. Charmaine Carol Mary West. From then on they lived in Corporation-owned flats in Glasgow. Areas that were a mixture of industrial use and tenement living. One flat, in Savoy Street, was next door to a sweet factory. Another, in McLellan Street, was opposite the McLellan steel works. Closes along the whole of one side of this very long street, the steel works along the other.

It was town living at its most compressed and chaotic. So many people living so closely together, and yet there was a freedom in the chaos and closeness; a way of being private and unobserved. You could get lost in the crowd if that was what you chose to do. Dissolve into the crowd and draw no attention to yourself. The crowd was his element. And of course it was a boozy life. Glasgow was famous for it. For its slums and for the drinking life. Drink was Rena's medicine. She liked to drink and stayed at least halfway drunk a lot of the time. Always topping up. She liked a drink and so did her friends and Fred used to drink as well then. He was drunk the night she tattooed her name on to his arm with a darning needle. She was drunk the night he tattooed his name in a heart on to hers.

But he quite soon gave up drinking. Perhaps because he realized this gave him something over Rena and the others stewing around him. It was a way of acquiring the sort of knowledge about people he was always seeking. What they said and did when their guard was down and their tongues were loosened. He didn't mind Rena drinking. He encouraged it. 'It did actually change her nature, take her off her guard, 'cause she was very much on her guard all the time.' In later years he would claim that Rena was drunk on the occasion that Anna-Marie was conceived. 'She got drunk, or near as. That was after three bottles, I think. So anyway, going back home in the car, she started lyin' about and messin' about with me, so I stopped the car and sorted her out an' [throaty chuckle] put her in the family way.'

Rena tried to abort this baby using a knitting needle. But Anna-Marie was born in July 1964, delivered at home, so he would always maintain, by her father. Charmaine was then sixteen months old and he had never taken to her. He took no interest in her and for a long time had refused to register her birth. Only the threat of legal action in the end made him do it. People commented on how he didn't seem to care much for Charmaine. But Anna-Marie was his, and when she was still a baby he would take her around in his van with him. He'd got a job driving a Mr Whippy van which was rented from Wall's Ice-Cream, who had a main yard in Paisley. He made the baby a cot out of a wooden box and kept her on a shelf under the window he sold ice-creams from. He also had girls in the van, and it would be in character for him to use the baby as a lure. A girl magnet. Most of the drivers returned their vans to the depot by eleven or twelve at night, but he was out in his until three or four. He would be away all hours. He'd talk to the girls and, in the words of somebody who knew him then, 'fanny about'.

The honeymoon period with Rena started to show signs of being over around this time. He started to hit her. He would come in in the middle of the night and pull her out of bed and knock her around. He would use his feet and leave marks on her face and body where it showed. He started taking swipes at

Charmaine. Yelling at the little girl and treating her roughly. He brought in a regime for the two children which was intended to keep them caged up. There were two sets of bunk beds and he wanted Charmaine and Anna-Marie kept penned up in the bottom parts of them. He improvised bars between the upper and lower bunks and gave instructions that he wanted them kept there: fed and changed and forced to play there, as well as sleep. One of the people he gave these instructions to was a friend of Rena's, a woman called Isa, who had started helping out as a 'nanny'. But as soon as his van turned the corner she would lift the children out of their 'jail' and let them play.

There were allotments at the end of McLellan Street and Fred West took one of these. It had a shed where he kept a collection of tools, and he spent a lot of time in the shed when he wasn't selling ice-cream around the poorer districts of Glasgow from the van. Rena didn't see much of him. If he wasn't at the allotment he was out in the van. When she did see him there was the risk that he might beat her. He saw her through the window of their downstair neighbour's flat one day and he burst in and flew at her. She was sitting having some drinks with her neighbour and another man when they saw a face at the street window watching them. He dragged her upstairs and kicked and battered her. They could hear it going on above them.

The other man's name was John McLachlan. He used Telky's bookmaker's next to their close in McLellan Street and he was sweet on Rena. She liked him and, although he was married, they started seeing one another. They would sometimes go into Kinning Park and one night they were kissing in the park when Fred came up on them from behind. He lunged at Rena and threw a punch at her. John McLachlan set about Fred, and Fred slashed his stomach with a knife or some other sharp object, drawing blood. McLachlan had tattooed her name on to his left forearm, just above the wrist, or maybe she had done it to him just the way she had done it to Fred. In small letters: R–e–n–a. They were always fighting over Rena.

Fred West had been living in Glasgow for nearly three years when, in October 1965, Ian Brady and Myra Hindley were arrested for what were to become known as the Moors Murders. Brady was a Glasgow boy. He had been brought up in the Gorbals and then on an estate in Pollok. Winter arrived early that year and the papers were filled with macabre pictures of police activity on Saddleworth Moor near Manchester where a number of children's bodies had been found in shallow graves. Many people saw it as the dark side – even the consequence – of the permissive, 'swinging' years that Britain had been having and grim pictures of Brady and Hindley were all over the papers.

Brady and Hindley appeared at a preliminary hearing on Thursday, 21 October 1965, charged with the murders of two children. The same day the police discovered the body of a third child on Saddleworth Moor. The case continued to dominate the radio and television news and the front pages of the newspapers. On 4 November 1965, two Thursdays later, and a week before Brady and Hindley were remanded on a charge of multiple murder, Fred West killed a child, apparently by accident.

At ten past three in the afternoon he backed over a three-year-old boy in a cul-de-sac in Castlemilk and killed him with the ice-cream van. He knew the boy. He had bought him a ball and had promised him a firework to play with – it was the day before Guy Fawkes' – if he came back that afternoon. The boy's ball rolled under a hedge and he went after it to retrieve it. It was a four-tonne van. It had a heavy engine in the back for making ice-cream. Fred West reversed it about three feet, and he said he drove over the boy without seeing him. There was a loud bang and he got out of the van to find him lying under the back axle. He said he fainted then and fell straight over the top of a fence into a garden. The man whose garden it was took him in and had to protect him from the child's father and a mob that had quickly gathered. Feelings were running high because of the horrific headlines and the bloody details being reported from the magistrates' hearings against Ian Brady and Myra Hindley and a crowd outside was baying for him. He was taken to Glasgow Royal Infirmary, where he was put under sedation.

In his prison jottings, made in the last months of his life, Fred West would claim that he had loved this little boy 'as a son'. He had no son of his own at that time and he wanted one and he had thought of the little boy as an adopted son. He spoke in the same way about another boy who would die in peculiar circumstances fifteen months later.

Robin Holt wasn't a child. He was fifteen, and Fred West described him as 'nice looking'. Helluva nice lad. Tall. He had first encountered Robin Holt, he said, sitting on a gate close to the caravan site in Gloucester where he was then living. He was sitting on the gate and he was crying. He stopped and invited him to the 'van, and after that the boy started going with him places in the lorry. He was working for Clenches then, going around slaughterhouses late at night picking up hides and skins and offal. It was a night run and his route included Tredegar, Newport in Monmouthshire, Ross-on-Wye, and Ensor's in Cinderford, and Robin Holt started going with him. When he changed jobs towards the end of 1966, leaving the slaughterhouse and turning instead to driving a sewage lorry, emptying septic tanks, the boy continued sometimes going with him. He got to know Rena and the children, and Fred would take him with him sometimes to Moorcourt Cottage. He was at Moorcourt Cottage one day in February 1967 and was seen there by Fred's sister and other members of his family. And then, two days later, on 22 February, Robin Holt disappeared. On 3 March his body was discovered by a farm worker while he was looking for firewood at the old cowshed next to the Longford Inn on the Tewkesbury road near Gloucester, less than a mile from the Sandhurst Lane caravan site where Fred West was living. He was half naked and hanging by a rope from a beam and, according to the pathologist who inspected the body, had been dead for about ten days. Spread out on a manger underneath him were pornographic pictures of women. Each woman had a biro marking around her neck in the form of a noose. A verdict of suicide was recorded, but local people would always be suspicious about the official reason given for Robin Holt's death.

After running the little boy over with his van on Guy Fawkes' in 1965, Fred West said he couldn't face going back on the round. The Wall's people came to ask if he would consider going out with the van again at night. There had been blood all over the wheel, and they had scrubbed the wheels and repainted them. But he couldn't go near the van. So he got a job driving a timber lorry, hauling timber, instead. Still, though, he couldn't shake off the feeling that, as a result of the death of the little boy, people in Glasgow were out to get him. He stayed away from the flat in McLellan Street and stopped with friends for a while because, he told them, he was frightened the parents were going to come and get him. And then there was Rena's boyfriend, the man she had taken up with, John McLachlan. He was a member of a motorcycle gang called the Skulls, and he had come home to find Rena 'starkers' in bed one night with McLachlan and other members of the Skulls. Rena had become a member of this gang and he was on the books to be killed. Rena was quite capable of killing. Carried a cut-throat razor and a knife in her bag. She was certainly mixed up with the right crowd.

All these stories, made up many years later, to explain why, at the end of 1965, he was feeling himself being drawn back to his mother and his father and his familiar family circle in Much Marcle.

The departure itself he would build up into a drama – a dramatic getaway with Rena throwing baby clothes and the baby Anna-Marie in through the window of his Vauxhall Viva. A tyre-screaming chase, shooting the lights with desperadoes on their tail. In fact he simply told Rena and her friend, Isa McNeill, who was still living with them as a baby-minder, of his decision to go home and the fact that he had already contacted the Corporation to say he was ready to give up the keys. He would take both of the children with him and then, when he had found his feet, found a job and a place for them to live, he would come back and collect her. Them. Isa as well if she wanted to go.

By mid-December he was back living at Moorcourt Cottage with his parents and Charmaine and Anna-Marie. Daisy, his mother, was very happy to have Anna-Marie who looked so like Fred and her own Hill side of the family. Big tawny moon face. Strong features. But she wasn't happy having Charmaine living with her, no blood relation and a child of mixed race. She was prepared to look after Anna-Marie while Fred went out working but she wasn't prepared to look after Charmaine. Because she was Indian. Old country people were a bit funny about that. His mother wanted him to put Charmaine in a home and she'd bring Anna-Marie up as her own. Those were her conditions. His conditions were that she had neither of them or both. Fred against his mother, by this time a mountainous woman. And his mother won. On 29 December 1965 both Charmaine and Anna-Marie, at the ages of a little over two and a half and just eighteen months, were taken into care by the Herefordshire Children's Department at their father's request. An officer of the Department found them to be 'in a deplorable state'.

It was six weeks before he got up to Glasgow to collect Rena and Isa McNeill. He arrived in the small hours of the morning and they were waiting. He wanted to do a quick turnaround and he found that there were three women to bring back with him, not two. Ann McFall was another pal of Isa's and Rena's who had sometimes sat the children. She was younger than them, not quite seventeen, with nothing to hold her in Glasgow and she had decided to give it a go in the south. He had driven up in his works wagon and he started to pile their stuff in the back. It was the wagon he used to transport hides and skins for Clenches Field Farm in Longford. Their few belongings. There wasn't much. And the three girls piled in among the untrimmed skins and animal leftovers and the rank animal stench, sitting on their bags. The van he used to tour the abattoirs. Painting by Otto Dix or George Grosz. There is an actual painting. In fact a drawing by Grosz: *Just Half a Pound*, 1928. A drawing of a 'real' butcher's shop which specializes in carving up and selling female carcasses. A Hausfrau buying meat from a butcher who has human carcasses hanging up in the shop behind him; dismembered bodies and knives. A drawing to illustrate the fact that the German language uses the same word – *Fleisch* – for living matter and dead matter; for flesh and meat. Women's bodies are positioned as pure victims, as nothing more than *Fleisch* (both 'meat' and 'flesh') that has been slaughtered and put out for display. People who were subjects have become objects, corpses. They are no longer anything. The ability to perceive subjects as mere objects – to turn people into things – is something that Fred West had to a murderous degree.

Just two months before he went up to collect his special load in Glasgow, he had gone with his brother John to visit John's fiancée in hospital. She had been standing in front of a fire in her nightdress and her nightdress had caught fire and she was in a critical condition in the burns unit of a hospital in Birmingham. They had to fight to get in to see her. The doctors didn't want them to see her. She had suffered burns over most of her body and she was lying in an oxygen tent wearing only dressings. Kitty, a village girl soon to be John's wife. And Fred had turned to his brother and said to him – and she heard him say this; she would be able to repeat it later; it was imprinted on her brain – he said, 'Christ, you're not going to marry that, are you?'

The cattle market in Gloucester used to be close to Cromwell Street, in the centre, where the bus station now is. But when Fred West was sixteen, in 1957, it moved to a new site away from the congestion of the city centre. The old tree-shaded market was replaced by a series of buildings based on a style of architecture made popular during the Festival of Britain. Fred West was a regular attender at the cattle market. He also became a familiar figure at Gloucester's 'Private Shop' – its one licensed outlet for sex aids and pornography and so on. The Private Shop also used to be close to Cromwell Street. It used to be on Barton Street for several years. But the pressure of public opinion eventually pushed it to the outskirts of the city. The move was resisted by Darker Enterprises, the shop's owners. But in 1987 they finally gave in and moved to a premises on St Oswald's Road, part of the South Wales–Birmingham ring road, well away from the town centre. The Private Shop now occupies a cabin in the cattle market. A unit in the Trade Exhibits block which is surrounded by agricultural wholesalers and butchers' shops and men moving around sheep and cow carcasses on their shoulders; meat and feed and holding pens. The customers are fairly average-looking men – and a few women – who pull in off the ring road. Pull in, make their purchase and go. But on livestock days the sex shop, which is still Gloucester's only sex shop, inevitably attracts cowhands and farm workers and men with blood over their aprons and white coats.

The noises made by penned-in and panicked animals and the auctioneer calling in the bidding ring – 'What grand heifers they are . . . Two super heifers there, gentlemen, right the way off the top of the Cotswolds . . . Good bulling heifers, look at those' – and slaughterhousemen and butchers thumbing through magazines showing women opening themselves for display and doing difficult, unnatural things. Painting by Otto Dix or George Grosz.

Fred West's pet name for Rose was 'cow'. He constantly referred to her as his cow. He called her this for many years. He was always talking about wanting to put her with a bull. 'I, Rosemary West, known as Fred's cow . . .' one document recovered from the attic in Cromwell Street begins. And it ends: 'I must always dress and try to act like a cow for Fred, also to bathe and wash when I am told. Signed Mrs R. P. West.' Fred would do some cow paintings for Rose, oil-paintings of Jerseys and Frieslans, varnish and frame them and hang them in her bedroom. Paintings of cows hanging on the wall at the end of her bed so that every morning, right up to the morning she was arrested on suspicion of murder, they would be the first things she would see.

Two of the three women Fred West delivered to Gloucester from Glasgow in his abattoir lorry would be murdered by him. Decapitated and dismembered by him and buried in the fields he had worked as a boy in Much Marcle. There were flat fields and valleyed ones. Letterbox Field was a valleyed one, and he had gone there on his occasional trips down from Glasgow with Rena. It was his favourite place in Much Marcle. A place to sit on the bridge and watch badgers come down to the stream to drink. Badgers. Foxes. Various animals in the dusk. There was a coppice. The steeple of Marcle Church in the distance. You can't see Moorcourt Cottage from Letterbox Field because it's valleyed, and you can't be seen. It was romantic and it was their place. And it would be to this place that he would bring Rena on the night he killed her.

It was one night at the end of August 1971, a full five years after he had brought her south with Ann and Isa in the meat wagon. He murdered her. Nobody will know how. He removed her head. He removed her legs at the hip, twisting her thighs out of their sockets. He dug a hole. The ground was rock hard. It was the middle of summer. The field was planted with corn. He dug a hole under the canopy of a tree where the grain wouldn't grow. Using a pickaxe and a spade he made a hole and he put Rena's remains – her legs, her head, her torso – in it. He removed a kneecap and several of her fingers and toes and carried them away with him. He would always do this. He would do it with every girl he murdered. It was part of his method; his need. A man who couldn't write. It was a part of his 'signature'.

It was a small hole. Two and a half feet by a foot and a half across, and not quite four feet deep. Vertical rather than horizontal. A small, deep, well-dug hole. A vertical shaft. He pressed what remained of Rena into the ground, and fitted her legs in around her.

There was one tree in that field; a marker in the hedge. And he buried Rena under it. Rena, his first wife. It's the only tree there.

'I had a special load on last night. Three girls in the back.' You can hear him saying this. It's what he said. He was a boaster. A braggart. Nobody believed him. He was a romancer. He was a bullshitting liar.

Sandhurst Lane caravan site, which is where he took Rena and her friends Ann and Isa on the day he brought them in the abattoir lorry from Glasgow, was, as it happened, close to the cattle market in Gloucester. The site and the market were near-neighbours on a water meadow adjacent to the east channel of the river Severn. The cattle standings and the sale-ring block were visible from The Willows, which is what Sandhurst Lane was officially called.

A caravan is not what they had been expecting. He had got word back to them that he had found a house which had plenty room for all of them, plus the children. A lot of space and a new start. But he had bought a caravan with the help of one of his sisters. He had gone to his mother first and asked her if they would guarantee a hire-purchase agreement that would allow him to buy a 'van for £600, but his mother had told him no. She knew Fred. Not much about him that she didn't know. After some persuasion, though, his sister Daisy and her husband Frank had agreed to act as guarantors. He had given his blue Vauxhall Viva in part-exchange for a new caravan. It was brown and cream; a four-berth. He liked a 'van. Something about the restricted space and the thin shell seemed to appeal to him. A room, the simplest form of shelter. And he had arranged to have it delivered to the Sandhurst Lane site close to a reservoir and a tar works and a loop of the river on the edge of Gloucester.

It wasn't much. But it was enough for the authorities to let them have the children back again living with them. Fred and Rena had a partitioned-off part to themselves at one end. Charmaine and Anna-Marie slept in put-away beds that dropped out of the wall in a small room in the middle. There was a built-in table with padded benches going round it in the shape of a U. Isa slept on the bench on one side, and Ann slept on the other. Ann and Isa were good friends. They had worked at a knitwear factory together, sewing the necks on to polo-neck jerseys at the same table. And Ann, because of her age they supposed – she wasn't quite seventeen – was infatuated with Fred West, who was eight years older.

Ann hadn't had a happy life. In truth, it had been a bleak,

horrible existence. A miserable life blighted by drink and poverty and violence. Tommy McFall, her father, wasn't married to her mother. He kept a wife and a second family in another part of Glasgow. He would come and go, making demands, arriving drunk, being violent. Jeannie, Ann's mother, was a cleaner and a chronic alcoholic. She cleaned people's houses and lived in stripped-out, almost empty rooms surrounded by bottles. No electric, no gas very often, just chaos and filthy lino and tins and bottles. Tommy McFall beat her. She was beaten by a son who had acquired the nickname 'Scarface' McFall. Ann's brother. He beat Ann as well. Came out of prison and took anything that was worth taking from her and beat her. All this in a close in Malcolm Street, just by Parkhead, the Celtic stadium. Tommy McFall was an attendant at the Parkhead Baths in addition to working as a street-corner bookie.

Ann had been placed in care in Nazareth House, a Catholic children's home in Aberdeen, when she was ten. She had returned to living in Malcolm Street when she was fifteen and by then her mother, who couldn't be considered an old woman, was already failing. She wouldn't eat. She liked the drink and eating took the edge off. Eating kept her from getting where she wanted to go and so she didn't like eating. Ann used to try to make her but it was useless trying. When she eventually died of malnutrition in 1969 a tin of beans would be the only food anywhere in the house. That was it. Just a small tin of beans.

Ann had a boyfriend. Duncan McLeish, nickname 'Kelly'. She had his nickname tattooed on her arm. But a short time before she left Malcolm Street to begin her new life in Gloucester, her boyfriend was killed in an accident at work, electrocuted while climbing into the cabin of a crane. One less thing to hold her there. Another reason for leaving.

Life among them in the caravan on The Willows site at first

must have been fun. The three lively girls and the two attractive children and the breadwinner with his suggestive stories and his cheeky cackle and his rabid imagination in this all-female household. Ann, really little more than a child herself and recently out of care, playing with the children who were out of care now, babysitting other children on the site for smokes and pocket money, and flirting with Fred West. 'Flaunting herself' at him, as Isa would say later. A slight girl with waist-length shiny brown hair. He called her a 'dainty little piece'. Fun before the pattern of her other life came down and re-imposed itself on them. The oppressiveness and the restrictions; the violence and the beatings. It was true she wasn't the target of the outbursts and the beatings. This was Fred beating Rena. But it was all so close to what she must have thought she had got away from and left behind and it was happening more or less on top of her because of the close conditions. Every intimate sound. Every kick and bruising. Even when you took the children to a neighbour's 'van to protect them from hearing and seeing the sound still carried. The cursing and swearing. The smashing. The sound of something dully hitting against metal.

Before long they came to feel like prisoners. He laid down rules and conditions and he expected them to be followed. No trips into town was one. They were perhaps a twenty-minute walk from the centre of Gloucester, the big shops at the Cross. But visiting Gloucester was not allowed. Leaving the site was not allowed unless he said they could do it. Leaving the caravan some days, depending on how the mood took him. And he would check. He would come by in the slaughterhouse wagon during the day just to make sure that they were doing what he was telling them and that they hadn't strayed. Trying to catch them. He would come home from work covered in blood and smelling of the job and demand his dinner. Acting the big man. Throwing it about. Slapping

Rena. Smacking the children. If Rena tried to stop him hitting Charmaine he would turn it on Rena and Ann and Isa would take the children out into the site until it seemed safe to return. Welcome to The Willows.

After about six weeks Isa had had enough. Both Isa and Rena, who had come in the first place only to try and get her children back off him. She had been happy in Glasgow with John McLachlan. Happy enough. Things had been turning over. He had his name on her arm. Isa had been going with a friend of John McLachlan's, a man called John Trotter. The two Johns. Neither of them small men. So Isa and Rena worked out a plan, a way to remove Ann and themselves from this Willows.

There was a phone by the main gate opening off Sandhurst Lane. And Isa went down there one day and phoned the Victoria café in Glasgow, one of the two Johns' regular haunts. All of them used to meet up there before their move south. She left a message for John McLachlan telling him to phone her at that number at a certain time. When he did, she asked him to come and collect her and Rena and the children, Ann and the children, really all of them, as soon as he could. She told him a day and a time when she knew Fred would be at work and went back to the caravan and waited. When the day came – it was by now towards the end of April in 1966 – the two Johns turned up at Sandhurst Lane in a rented car and hurriedly packed the women's belongings in it. Only Ann seemed to be dragging her feet. Dawdling and not seeming to feel the same sense of urgency as them. Hanging on to Anna-Marie. Hanging back in the 'van. Of course she had told him. Told Fred what they were planning. That they were thinking of bolting. It was an infatuation. And here he came, looking very pleased and knowing. He wasn't at work where he should have been, but back at the site and coming towards them. He made a grab for Charmaine. That was the first thing he did. Scooped her up and held her and used her as a human shield. John McLachlan punched him in the stomach anyway but he didn't let go. Ann had Anna-Marie and he had Charmaine. Rena tried to pull Charmaine off him but he pulled back. He had a firm grip on her. He was determined. There was a scene developing. Nothing new at The Willows and a diversion on a weekday afternoon. A small crowd spectating. A lot of shouting. Rena crying and shouting and demanding to have her children back. John McLachlan gave him a slapping and punched him in the stomach again. Punched him low. Then Ann was shaking her head and saying she wasn't going. She was stopping. She was staying to look after the children. Be a nanny. A shouting match going on among them. And then a policeman on a bike showed up and it went very quiet. Pedalling down the track that connected the 'van site to Sandhurst Lane. Rena and Isa got in the back of the Mini. John McLachlan and John Trotter got in the front. Isa would say later that Rena had cried all the way back to Scotland. Isa, whose family lived in the same street as Jeannie, Ann's mother, would read cards and letters that Ann sent to her mother telling her how well she was doing and about the lovely children and the beautiful big house and the successful man. The tremendous man. Jeannie would call her over and she would look at the letters, written in a neat hand. But the cards and letters would stop arriving after a year or so. Isa would go ahead and marry John Trotter but she would never see her friend Ann again.

Back in Glasgow Rena got a job working on the buses and shared what they called a room-and-kitchen flat with Isa McNeill. But then Isa started going about with John Trotter who she was marrying and Rena started doing it for drinks and money in closes and back alleys with a lot of different men and John McLachlan dropped out of the picture. She got herself in with a rough crowd and didn't turn up at Isa's wedding in July and, like her previous best friend Ann McFall had, drifted away out of Isa's life.

By July Rena was in Gloucester once again, living with Fred and Charmaine and Anna-Marie in the caravan at Sandhurst Lane. Rena was back and Ann McFall was out. Ann was farmed out to a neighbour on the site until Rena took off on her travels again. Rena had this thing in her where she couldn't live with one person for any length of time. She had to go on her way. She would go off living with different men and come back to him in between times. It would go on like that for a year. Rena back, Ann out. The kids are calling different ladies mummy and nobody really knows where they are. Ann back, Rena out. Ann would come and stay. Then Rena would come back and just chuck Ann out. It could be five, half-past five in the morning. She'd be well oiled. Oh, she was a goer, Rena. 'Right you, out.'

Rena, the kind of girl who would let a man she had just met, a stranger, introduce things into her body in a public place in an attempt to abort the baby she didn't want. 'Anything considered.' He had black-and-white pornographic pictures of Rena – Rena in explicit poses. Rena had an extensive repertoire of sexual numbers. She didn't particularly care where she did them or who with. Straight, oral, anal, sadomasochistic. And she let him watch. He was a peeper. He could be there in a so-called security capacity as her protector or her pimp. Standing guard. Looking out. When really he was just looking. Such an appetite he had for looking.

If he took the children to a safari park he would stop the van to watch animals mating. The children would get bored and didn't know anything about it but he could get excited watching animals having sex. Go on about their testicles. How long they could keep at it. The size of their parts. To them it was weird sex stuff, and meant nothing. They wanted to get moving. Get going. But he wouldn't move.

Whoever was with Rose in their early years together, he would usually stay while the man was undressing 'to see that Rose was all right'. Only to go off and watch secretly though a peep-hole in the door.

Rena let him look. She was the first. Rena was his whore. So Ann could be his madonna. His angel. His temple of perfection. 'Ann was not hard; she was gentle, kind and pleasant,' as he once said. 'She was my angel. Rena could be the devil if she wanted to be.' *I Was Loved by an Angel* was the name he gave to the saccharine prison scribblings which describe his brief time with Ann McFall. 'Ann [he actually refers to her as 'Anna'] was happy and contented and joyful . . . I got out my guitar and sat on the step of the van. Ann sat by me. I played and sang to Ann . . . "Kiss an angel good, good, morning" . . . We always had tears in our eyes, tears of happiness and love. Ann would wipe the tear from my eyes and I would from her eyes . . . I said to Ann, "Can I comb your hair?" I was combing her hair for two hours . . . her smile lit up the heavens.' And endlessly on in this vein.

In an unintentionally revealing passage he claims that they slept in separate berths in the trailer for the first one or two weeks after Rena had gone, presumably because Ann was too 'angelic' to be besmirched. A temple of perfection. She had to make the first move: 'I said "good night" to Ann and Ann said "good night". My bed was made up by Ann. I undressed and lay on the bed. The moon was shining in the window . . . It was about eighteen months. I had not made love to my wife. She was always too drunk or gone. I was in love with Ann, but was Ann in love with me? It was twelve thirty now . . . Ann's bedroom door opened. Ann stood in the doorway. She had on a black négligé nightdress . . . and said, "Do you like it?" I said, "Yes . . . But I am married." Ann said, "Is that what you call it?" I pulled back the bed covering and said, "Get in."'

Ann McFall was seventeen. Robin Holt, the boy who would be found hanging by his neck in a cowshed with a semi-circle of pornographic pictures at his feet, was a fifteen-year-old. These were Fred West's companions in 1966. His acolytes. His audience. Robin Holt would be dead, apparently a suicide, by February the following year. Ann would be dead by the summer. And meanwhile the caravan, delivered new from the factory only eight months earlier, was filling up with spanners, starting cranks, hacksaws, circular saws, electric cable, cold chisels, oily rags and rubble. The caravan was becoming dilapidated. It was turning into a filthy tip, the usual thing with him.

On August Bank Holiday Monday in 1966, in an effort to throw Rena off the trail, he towed the caravan to another site called Watermead, six miles away in Brockworth right on the other side of Gloucester. At the same time he changed jobs, moving from the abattoir lorry to emptying septic tanks in order to make it doubly difficult for Rena to track down him and her children. She kept wanting to grab Charmaine and take her, and leave Anna-Marie. Once they were settled he changed jobs for a third time, moving from the sewage lorry to a grain tanker which impressed his father with its size. His father couldn't get over the size of the tanker he was driving.

Unusually, his mother took to a girl he had brought home to meet her. She liked Ann and even took her into her front room. Rena had never been in the front room. You had to be special for his mother to let you in there. It was the first girl he had had his mother took to and he felt wonderful about it. The additional good news was that Ann was pregnant. He didn't think it was fair to Ann to have his children and not have one of her own. And now she was going to have his baby and she had told him it was going to look just like him and she was going to call him Fred Junior. His father went out and came back with a bottle of home-made wine and they all got a glassful, and the two girls. His mother said a toast to Ann being pregnant. Ann looked at him and smiled. He smiled back. They both had tears in their eyes.

Rena found them. It couldn't have been difficult. Social Services had to know the whereabouts of the children and she was their mother so all she had to do was go to them. He always claimed to be frightened of Rena and it was probably true. Ann's pregnancy was still too early to be showing and Rena kicked her out of the caravan and he allowed it to go on. He transferred Ann to the other site many miles away at Sandhurst Lane. He rented her a small 'van and put her in it and spent the time while Rena was around shuttling from site to site between them. He'd spend part of the evening with Ann in the smaller caravan at Sandhurst Lane and part of it with Rena and the two girls at Watermead.

It was a hard one. It was difficult. Fortunately the untamed part of Rena came to his rescue. At the beginning of October she burgled another caravan on the site at Watermead then took off for Glasgow in an attempt to escape the police. By 29 November 1966 she was standing in front of Gloucester magistrates charged with housebreaking and theft. She had been arrested in Glasgow in mid-November and a WPC had been sent to collect her and bring her back to face trial. Her counsel made a plea for leniency on the grounds that her offences were 'the actions of a jealous woman', adding that if she was sent to prison 'her children must go into care'. Fred West appeared before the court himself, admitting his relationship with Ann McFall. The pleas for leniency succeeded. Rena was placed on probation, but she didn't return to look after the children. She went back up to Scotland and Ann again moved from Sandhurst Lane to Watermead, ready to resume her life with Fred West.

It was a life that it is hard to recognize from the soft-focus version memorialized by him in *I Was Loved by an Angel* twenty-eight years later. The 'van was cramped and filthy and the children were fractious and giving concern to their social worker who disclosed in a report that Ann, the young woman who was looking after them, had told her that Fred had planned to 'artificially inseminate' her if she didn't fall pregnant quickly, but that there had been no need.

It was a mark of her naïvety that Ann would say such a thing to a person who had authority over them. And it is easy to guess that the signs of her youth and inexperience – the things that had made her attractive to him in the first place – would begin to grate with Fred. Her submissiveness and dependence. They were gratifying but they were not exciting. And he was looking for things to excite and fire him, that he found sexually exciting, all the time at this time. There were eight violent sexual assaults against girls and young women in the Gloucester area during the time that he was living at Sandhurst Lane and Watermead with Ann McFall. And after he was dead a string of middle-aged women would come forward to identify Fred West as the man who attacked and sexually assaulted them – terrified and in some cases physically injured them – when they were waiting at bus stops or on the way home from school or trying to get home at night when they were still young girls.

It seems that the eroticized excitement that had always formed the basis of his relationship with Rena probably wasn't there with Ann McFall. The danger and the voyeurism and the deviant sex. The straight kinky sex, as he called it. The delirium of dangerous pleasure. And that if the time ever came for him to choose between whore and angel the choice was not going to be a hard one for him to make. He was conscious of being compelled to do things that were secretive and risky and of not feeling sinful and wicked. In fact the opposite. He felt elated. He felt different and brave for what he was doing rather than perverted and ashamed.

In the meantime though he was proud to show off his pregnant young girlfriend at Moorcourt Cottage and at Bush Cottage in Much Marcle where his brother John lived with his own baby daughter and his wife. Kitty West couldn't stand him because of what she had heard him say eighteen months earlier while she was lying in the burns unit in hospital believing herself to be close to death. And although they were close, there had always been a strong competitive element in his relationship with John. For Fred his brother had always been 'too forward' when it came to girls: 'hand on the bottom . . . kiss 'em before he even knew their name'. John was always top monkey. He had gone out with Rena's pal, Margaret Mackintosh, and therefore had been the one responsible for Fred meeting Rena. They had gone around as a foursome for a while in the black Ford Popular John shared with Fred. He couldn't do anything but he had plenty of talk. Now they were older Fred liked to stop round every so often and show John the latest goody he had collected on his travels. Incite John's jealousy with the latest catch.

Fred and John were alike in having daughters, although both were hoping for sons. When his daughter Amanda was born in September 1966 and he had gone to see the baby in hospital, John had made it plain that he had wanted a boy and was not happy with a girl. He caused such a fuss that the hospital staff in the end had asked him to go. He had been thrown out of the hospital. All through her pregnancy Kitty West had been having problems in her marriage with John's behaviour towards her which was very stressful. During the period she was away having the baby she believed John was having an affair with another woman. Rose West would claim that on the day she came home with May, her second baby, she went next door and found Fred in bed with Mrs Agius, a neighbour. So Fred and John had these and many other things in common. John had been the only family member present

when Fred married Rena. He would be the only member of
the family present when Fred married Rose. You couldn't discount the element of competition and rivalry between them
but Fred and John were close.

Little Amanda West was six or seven months old in spring
1967. Anna-Marie was nearly three, Charmaine was four.
And Ann McFall was pregnant. Only three years out of
Nazareth House, the Catholic children's home in Aberdeen,
and already expecting a baby of her own. The baby was due
in September and because she was such a small girl she was
starting to show. Ann was only a little tiny girl while Rena
was big. She was pretty. She might have been very pretty but
for the fact that her teeth protruded slightly. That was made
up for by her hair. She had beautiful hair, as everybody who
met her remarked. It was hair of the kind young girls used to
iron on a board under brown paper with an electric iron in
those days. She had pretty hair and she was quiet and pretty
and in her own way full of presence. And Fred's mother even
took her into her front room and you had to be special for his
mother to let you in there.

Fred sometimes stopped round to see John at Bush Cottage
when he was in the area. He would call in with Ann and the
children and Ann was already pregnant in spring 1967, the
first time they met her. He stopped round once or twice as the
pregnancy progressed in the first half of 1967. And there was
only a month or two of the pregnancy to go by July, the last
time they remembered seeing Ann.

A few weeks, perhaps as much as two months, had passed
since the last time they had seen her when John's mother
came up to Bush Cottage to find them and tell them that Fred
had killed the girl and buried her in Kempley woods. Kitty
West had never seen her mother-in-law cry before. But she
was sitting at the kitchen table and crying and telling them
this about Fred and the girl. It was possibly late August; one

evening. And John and Kitty went and sat down with her in the kitchen and she then broke down and was very upset and distraught. 'Freddie's killed the girl and buried her in Kempley woods.' Which as of course they knew was near by. It was very close. Of course they were stunned. John told his mother not to be so stupid. Kitty made a cup of tea and John was talking to his mother. She stayed for about an hour and had calmed down, she wasn't crying anyway, by the time she left. Kitty remembers asking John did his mother mean the girl who was pregnant. John told her Fred had thrown her out after she had packed her bags. Kitty kept on to John about it – who did his mother mean and why would she say that. But John wouldn't discuss it. He would never discuss it. Mrs West, his mother, never mentioned the matter again and nobody else in the family mentioned it. It was never talked about.

When Ann McFall's remains were disinterred from Fingerpost Field in Much Marcle in June 1994, twenty-seven years after Fred West had put them there, two plastic bags were recovered with them. One bag contained blue-coloured pieces of curtains or sheets and a flower-patterned quilt. In the other bag was a round-necked, long-sleeved cardigan. He claimed that Ann used to be waiting for him in bed at her caravan every night wearing only a cardigan. The contents of the bags suggest that Ann McFall was murdered in the caravan at Sandhurst Lane and brought by Fred West to Much Marcle to be buried, although 'disposed of' is closer to the truth of what he did.

It was a small hole. Two and a half feet by a foot and a half across, and not quite four feet deep. Vertical rather than horizontal. A small, deep, well-dug hole. A vertical shaft. He pressed what remained of Ann into the ground, and fitted her legs in around her.

It was brutal and savage and what we would call psychopathic but not panicked. A set of horizontal marks on the thigh bone, the femur, would show that a sharp knife had been used for dismemberment and that the work had been even and methodical. The work of somebody assured in what they were doing.

Ann McFall's may have been the first known murder that Fred West committed, but already the signs of what would become a perverse ritual are apparent: the decapitation; the dismemberment of the legs at the hips; the carrying away of the kneecaps and of a number of fingers and toes (thirty-six of an expected seventy-six toe- and finger-joints were missing); the digging of a narrow shaft. And, with Ann McFall, something else that would become recognized as part of the signature of these murders: a ligature or binding. In this case a length of rope or what could have been a dressing-gown cord, tied around her hands and twisted around her arms almost certainly as a restraint.

He dug a hole. The ground was rock hard. It was the middle of summer. Using a pickaxe and a spade he made a hole close to a cattle ramp where the ground would be considerably softer. A concrete ramp he had poured and made with his father. He dug a hole where the water ran over into the field and where the cattle trod it night and morning, and he put Ann's remains – her legs, her head, her torso – in it. Also the eight-month-old foetus that Ann was carrying whose tiny bones would survive for more than a quarter of a century in the ground. A child conceived on concrete, at the place he called 'our heaven', a concrete bunker that lay just above the Watermead caravan site. Conceived on top of a concrete bunker in the country and buried in open country under a concrete ramp.

It was the cruelty of the man who looked after animals. A cruelty that the writer V. S. Naipaul, who lived in a house in

Gloucester for a period in the eighties, came to recognize: 'Not absolute cruelty; more a casualness, the attitude of a man who looked after lesser, dependent creatures, superintending the entire cycle of their lives; capable of tenderness, yet living easily with the knowledge that though a cow might have produced so many calves and given so much milk, it would one day have to be dispatched to the slaughterhouse in a covered trailer.'

Fred West was unable to understand the difference between killing a farmyard animal and killing a human being. To him there was no difference. He would remember the names of almost none of the people he murdered. They weren't flesh-and-bones people with memories and stories who were hurtable and capable of feeling pain, but 'Newent Girl'; 'Worcester Girl One', 'Worcester Girl Two'; 'the one with the crinkly hair'. Carcasses to be disposed of once their usefulness to him had finished.

In his many weeks of police interviews after his arrest in 1994, he would repeatedly refer to the body of a murdered person as 'it' and to inanimate objects and materials and pieces of equipment – a cattle ramp, a paddling pool, a patio slab – as 'him'. 'As the end of the slab sunk, you put more soil under, or gravel, to level him. As the body sinks, then the slab was tipping . . . Pea gravel.'

Although he would admit to many murders he would never admit that he had murdered Ann McFall. He preferred to talk about the concrete ramp for the cows that he had poured at the site of her murder with his father. The cattle ramp and how they had done it and what with. It was a tactic to take them away from the subject of murder and mutilation and to give himself time to think. A tactic he would use over and over. But it was also an obsession. Buckets of lime. Sacks of cement. Sewer pipes. Shovels. Back axles. Ice knives. Rakes. The sheath knife that he always carried on his belt. An actual dagger, used for laying felt.

Making and constructing. Working and making. Activities that always held more meaning for him than unmaking a person.

After he had disposed of Ann McFall he sluiced his arms and chest in the field's cattle trough and went back to the caravan at Watermead in Brockworth where Rena was once again installed. It was going to be four years before he buried Rena in Letterbox Field in his village. Fingerpost Field was the next field over. And the following day he was back there looking for his father. He went to his father and told him what had happened and asked him to go up to Fingerpost Field with him because he couldn't go up there on his own. And his father went with him to the field where Fred had started driving a tractor when he was nine. Your father used to take the tractor up and put him in the field. A little Fergie – a Massey-Ferguson. They stood at the spot where they had poured concrete on a farm field many years earlier and he told his father what he had done.

His mother died suddenly in February 1968, six months after he had murdered Ann McFall. She had a heart attack and died at the age of forty-four. The funeral was held at St Bathelomew's, the Much Marcle parish church. And it was the subject of much comment afterwards that Fred was the only one of them who didn't mark their mother's passing with tears. Then back at the house when it was all over he upset the others by wanting to talk about selling his mother's clothes. This was shocking.

The death of his mother effectively ended Fred West's association with the continuities of rural living and with that kind of settled country life. Countryside in the years ahead for him would increasingly mean a place to let the children out for a few hours on a Sunday afternoon. He'd take them there and let them run around and video them. They would go to a play area in the Forest where there were wooden bridges and climbing frames and a stream. Then he'd herd them into the back of the converted Group 4 Ford transit van with its blacked-out windows and welded security vents and put them back under lock and key at home.

The country had become an alien environment in which things proliferated and grew and flourished and bloomed and constantly threatened to run out of control. He was attracted to the margins and the dark recesses of urban life where you could cease being the man you were and start over again as some other man instead.

Almost his first act on taking possession of 25 Cromwell Street would be to uproot Mrs Green's pear and apple trees in the back garden. Dig out what Mrs Green liked to think of as her orchard, demolish her raised beds and throw out her hen run. He was a town dweller by then and what he had in mind wasn't a patch that needed cultivating but an urban garden. No more fruit trees with their blossom and shade. No more chicken coops and cinder paths and border plants. He wouldn't achieve his objective overnight. But gradually over the years he introduced a barbecue pit, a climbing frame, a Wendy house (it was called a Wendy house, but it was actually a cycle shed), a fishpond, a paddling pool made from engineering bricks, plastic decorative lions, patio furniture, pink-and-white chequer-board-pattern patio paving over half and then all over the garden area. And at the same time the house was being steadily pushed out into the garden. The garden was slabbed over and extended into until there was no green left and there wasn't a garden. No shrubs or trees. Only a stand of Leyland pines. *Cypress leylandii*. Which were hardly trees at all but things planted by people forced to live together in towns and used by them as screens to protect their privacy. Trees planted not for being pleasing to the eye but for shutting out the light and aggravating the neighbours.

Trees as offensive weapons. Britain's most common tree.

By the time he had been in Cromwell Street for a few years, more or less the only signs of Fred West's country beginnings would be the horseshoes nailed up over the front and back doors. Peter Evans the blacksmith used to make all their shoes. He'd have the horse there and he'd be shoeing in there, and you'd sit on the what's-her-name and he'd make your boots and shoes. Mementoes of a world that was a dozen miles and already a lifetime away. Rusting horseshoes from Peter Evans's forge. Small threshold gods.

Among all their children, the oldest, Heather, would be the one who showed the fiercest longing for the countryside. Heather, who they had fought so hard to keep and who they would murder and bury under the patio paving a few weeks after she left school in 1987.

FODIWL. This was something that turned up inked on to all Heather's belongings. On her books and her schoolbooks and her records. Heather's private promise to herself written on nearly everything she owned. FODIWL. They didn't know what it meant and she wouldn't tell them. They kept asking her but she wouldn't say.

Then they murdered her and put her in a dustbin and put her under the patio by the Leyland pines. FODIWL. Forest Of Dean I Will Live. Somewhere far removed from the torments of her city life. Heather's private promise to herself.

Chapter Seven

The house that she moved into with Fred in Clarence Road in Cheltenham was well known to the police. Costa, the Greek Cypriot who owned it, was also well known to them in his own right. Bikers lived there. And when you had the bikers you always had the runaways coming round. The runaways. The potheads. The drop-outs and schoolgirl alcoholics. The pill-poppers. The pushers.

When the police were looking for runaways and missing persons, 9 Clarence Road would be one of the first places they would look. You had a frantic mother on your hands pleading with you to bring her daughter back, you went round there. And nine out of ten times you would find her. Rose had been found there herself only weeks before and returned to her parents, who had promptly placed her in a home. Fred had to call the law on a girl from Bishop's Cleeve School who had followed him to Clarence Road. She stood outside all day shouting and followed him to his job at Cotswold Tyres and stood outside there shouting and he had her removed for her own safety because he knew what Rose could do.

The house that Rose moved into with Fred, where she was living in one room with him and trying to bring up his two daughters, was well known for being a place where you could crash. You could crash there and you could score. Not bad blow. Decent five-pound deals. It was a whole scene there in the centre of Cheltenham. All these kinds of words that they were hearing all around them for the first time, coming out of a new way of living that Fred and Rose were intimidated and attracted by at the same time. In 1970 the wild behaviour was still new. The dropping of inhibitions. The kids going crazy. Bikers, druggies, drongos, pseuds, freaks and students. Pretty good shit. Bad mother. Outtasite. Bummer, man.

Not many of the bikers living at Clarence Road worked. But those who did almost without exception worked at the Wall's sausage factory butchering pigs. For many years their natural enemy had been the wearers of long hair – beatniks and poncy art-college students and so on. At every end-of-term party, Cheltenham Art College students used to be set upon by the rockers from the town who used to come in with razorblades between their fingers and chains and lay into all these middle-class art-student poseurs.

But by 1970 many of those tribal divisions had faded away. Bikers and hippies had come to realize that they were generally speaking for and against the same things. They were for pleasurable anarchy and the carnivalesque aspects of life, and against the rigid, routinized order of the official, public city. The drugs squad in Cheltenham consisted of one person. It was still possible to feel that by taking drugs and living in a certain fashion you were being an outlaw against society. If you were somebody who had been on the road, somebody who was a bit lost and drifting, a set-up like the one at 9 Clarence Road could be like a security. There were many people around who wanted to belong to a house like that; to join an extended family.

Fred and Rose looked pretty straight. But she was only sixteen and pregnant and living with a man who was twelve years older. So she passed for those reasons. And she was Fred's old lady. Rose could appear disapproving of these drop-outs. She was probably strange and unsure and it came out as disapproving. She was keen to play the little mother, making dresses for Charmaine and Anna-Marie and cooking for them. She would take an old dress apart, using the pieces as a pattern, cutting them one size bigger and putting it altogether. She had a sewing-machine and she could get remnants of material quite cheap. It worked quite well. And at least they looked tidy to go to school. She was looking for the approval of the welfare. The Welfare were still keeping a check on the children and it was important to her to prove that she could cope. That she was capable. She loved to give them a bath. Charmaine's hair was beautiful, a lovely raven black and it was long down to her waist. How it would shine. They had only a Baby Belling cooker. It wasn't very big but she managed to get some pretty good meals cooked on it. On a Sunday she could get a full roast dinner cooked on that little cooker and pudding. The little mother. Out around the town people would take them for sisters. Charmaine was seven and Anna-Marie nearly six. Rose was sixteen. She was trying to be a homemaker and to the drop outs and heads she could seem like she was on this other trip. The schoolgirl mum. She could seem disapproving.

But Fred seemed to revel in all the upheaval. The police coming was just a joke to him. He didn't care whether they came or not. Fred was cool about drugs and drunkenness and crazy bombed-out behaviour. He was a familiar figure at the Full Moon, the drug pub in the High Street in Cheltenham. Fred seemed to like it in there and he seemed very much at home at Clarence Road. The noise at night and the falling around. The raids. The busts. Completely comfortable with that kind of out-of-it, anarchic atmosphere. He would remember it and try to re-create it when he had his own house at 25 Cromwell Street a couple of years into the future.

The one thing there weren't any of at Clarence Road were black people. There were no spades. It was very rare to see a black person anywhere in Cheltenham. Cheltenham was old and straight and down on any kind of non-conformist behaviour. There was a lot of animosity towards hippies and homosexuals and unmarried mothers and a great deal of animosity towards blacks. More than twenty years later the selection of a black barrister as Conservative candidate for Cheltenham in the 1992 General Election would lead to a mass defection of the Tory faithful which would cost the party a previously safe seat.

Gloucester, on the other hand, whose eastern suburbs were starting to join up with the western suburbs of Cheltenham in those days and join up completely with them now, is a working-class city with a strong industrial and manufacturing base. Somewhere where the people 'only care about fairgrounds and fish and chips' according to a former Cheltenham lord mayor. Gloucester and Cheltenham are two cultures united by a common antipathy, as somebody once perceptively said. The cathedral and its closeness to Cheltenham and the fact that it mainly sells itself as a touring centre for the Cotswolds obscure the fact that most people who live in Gloucester work in foundries and factories and – this was truer in the seventies than it is now – the docks. Most of the West Indians who were drawn to Gloucester in the years straight after the war were drawn there by the availability of menial and labouring jobs which they were very often over-qualified to do. Foundry jobs and dirty jobs in factories where aircraft and railway carriages and motorbikes and matches were made. Gloucester Aircraft Company. Gloucester Wagon Works. England's Glory matches.

Most of the immigrants who settled in Gloucester came from a handful of neighbouring parishes, mainly the parishes of St Ann and St Catherine, in Jamaica. It was a strange and often hostile environment with colour-bar policies and quota policies in operation in clubs and pubs and other public places. In Gloucester as in the rest of the country there were serious problems with housing, many men having to share rooms in a house, sleeping on the floor, sharing a kitchen, toilet and bathroom (if there was one). It was not unknown for ten or twelve to be sharing rooms in a house. With so much shiftwork some would be resting while others were working. In pooling finances through 'pardners' many were able to put a deposit down on their own home when their 'hand' became due. Hard work, sometimes to the point of holding down more than one job at a time, was, and still is, part of the immigrants' creed.

Fred West's reasons for moving to Gloucester from Cheltenham in April 1970 were in many ways what the immigrants' reasons had been half a generation earlier. He was an unskilled but hard worker looking for work to support a growing family; he had a third child on the way. He had difficulties with the language; with reading and writing. And he was adrift in a strange and what to him must have still seemed an alien culture. It has often been argued that the differences between the agricultural South and the industrial North for the hundreds of thousands of American Negroes who made the trek north in the early decades of the century were even greater than the differences between the white and black races. And his poor country background was one of many things Fred West had in common with the members of Gloucester's small Jamaican population. His children would find it funny when they went back to visit his father and his brothers in Much Marcle and they had tea bags hanging out for drying and reusing. All his life Fred would come in from work and pick up an onion and start eating it as if it was an apple, or lift a lump of lard out of the chip pan and eat it on bread. He would retrieve things that Rose had thrown in the bin as being too good to throw away. Retrieve them and eat them. His children couldn't believe what he would eat. Still a hillbilly mesmerized by the pace and possibilities of the city.

Frank Zygmunt, an elderly immigrant Pole with very poor

English, was one of the few landlords in Gloucester who was prepared to let to Jamaicans. Most of his houses were occupied by Irish, Poles and Jamaicans. Fred West and his family were given a flat by Mr Zygmunt. Fred stayed working as a tyre-fitter and earning extra money by being on call to Frank Zygmunt as a jobbing builder. And his ability as an odd-job man and builder spread by word of mouth from Zygmunt's tenants into the wider West Indian community. He became well known for being reliable and personable and very reasonably priced. A laugh and a joke and a cheeky grin. And there was another reason. He took every opportunity to encourage the black men he met to consider having sex with Rose, not least because he was obsessed with the idea of them having 'larger ones' than white men. 'Rose only had big fucking blokes,' he said. 'She didn't want little worms playing about with her.' She didn't like 'some little thing wriggling about' in her. The bigger the better. The bigger and the blacker the better for Rose, Fred decided.

Fred West had an obsession with size. 'Big', 'huge' and 'massive' were his most frequently used words. Big this. Massive that. Used equally of people and things. The following exchange would take place when he was being interviewed by the police after his arrest in 1994:

QUESTION   . . . you find [Rose] so perfect for your needs, and the fear of losing her is beyond belief to you?

FRED WEST   Yes . . . Yes.

QUESTION   Because for all those years, as you say, you've trained her, down to letters and commands, and she's complied, and she's got a very wide and open . . .

[The questioner is about to say 'attitude to sexual matters' here. It is a woman officer, WDC Hazel Savage. But before she can finish, he says:]

FRED WEST   . . . vagina, isn't it what they call it?

SAVAGE   And that all pleases you?

FRED WEST   Yep.

SAVAGE   And that has taken a lot of years for you to perfect?

FRED WEST   Yep.

'Rose didn't want the gentle part of it,' he would say in the last months of his life. 'She wanted some big nigger to throw her down and fucking bang on top of her, and treat her like a dog . . . that was sex to Rose. "I don't want any of that soppy shit," she said. "I want fucking. Not fucking about with. Or chatting up" . . . She'd been fucked all day, and I'd come home from work and she'd sit deliberately on the edge of the settee with her legs wide open and . . . say, "Look at that . . . I bet you wish you had something that could fill that" . . . It never stopped. It didn't stop at all. There was no let-up.'

Fred was a masochist in this way. He pushed Rose out to go with the black men he had picked for her. Or he had the black men in so he could listen and watch. After so many years he would be able to tell the regulars what he wanted of them. Keep her with you for this long, give her this to drink, she likes this done to her, etcetera. In the end he had them like robots. And he would want to hear her version of it afterwards, whether they had done what he said. His mind was filled with fantasies of Rose with other men. On and on about going with other men. They were usually black. Almost without exception black. And the black men were well aware that in having sex with Rose they were doing Fred a favour. They brought her presents sometimes, a bottle of Malibu, a toy for the children, sexual accessories, some Bacardi rum. But never money. They never paid. Only the white men paid. If Rose ever did go out with Fred it was with Fred and the black men and it was to make sure that she was put to bed with them. He was always touting. The one who had the obsession with the sexual potency of black men was not Rose but him.

She had a red and black book in which, at his insistence, she would keep all their statistics – penis size, performance marks out of ten, what they liked to do to her, what she liked to do to them and all the names. There were about seventy names. They also had an album of close-up pictures of men's erect penises which was kept locked in a briefcase in Rose's 'special' room. It was one of his rules that both the diary and the album had to be available for him to consult at any time. Eventually he even installed a two-way mirror in the upstairs toilet at 25 Cromwell Street so that he could see for himself the size of some of the men Rose was going with. Also what they did in those intimate moments when they thought they were alone. He would creep up the stairs after them to peer through the mirror while they were standing at the bowl. Trying to catch reality offguard.

Fred West was interested only in parts of people – usually their depersonalized genitals – rather than in whole, integrated human beings. This ability he had to perceive subjects as mere objects. He had started at an early age to build up a collection of photographs of vaginas. And he had a set of pictures that he had taken of Rose's vagina in various states of engorgement. Rose holding herself open to his gaze. He showed these around as 'tasters' to men he met on jobs or in pubs in the days when he was still using pubs and trying to get people to go back home with him and give Rose a 'seeing to'. 'Meat shots.' 'Hamburger shots', in the jargon of the world of home-made pornography and contact magazines with which they would become increasingly involved as the years went on. Catalogues, contact books, subscription clubs, coded small ads in privately circulated magazines. Magazines dedicated to the worship of parts.

By definition he saw black men as sexual savages and potential superstud figures like 'Shaft'. Intrinsically wild, dangerous, rough, 'untamed' in every sense of the word. King Dicks. In touch with some primal, sexual energy. The classic stereotype. The faces, the heads and, by extension, the minds and experiences of Rose's black 'clients' were not as important as the close-up pictures of their genitals he liked to take. Zooming in. Coming up close. Always this obsession with fitting large things into small holes. This fixation. This obsession with size and dimension and the sexual superiority of his Jamaican neighbours. Black men are big boys.

They built up an enormous collection of dildos and vibrators and other prostheses and sex aids and some of the sex equipment they had was huge. Rose learned to bring bigger and bigger objects inside herself and he liked to watch this, and later film it. They amassed more and more and bigger and bigger sexual accessories and vibrators. They kept them in drawers. Under the beds. In a big black trunk in Rose's special room. He had special names for some of them. The Eiffel Tower. The Exocet. And his favourite, a fourteen-inch black rubber phallus that he christened the 'cunt-buster' and was always telling his older children, when they were still children, that they could borrow if they liked. There were pictures of Rose wearing this black dildo strapped around her in her special room, and also pictures on display of Rose having sex with some of the black men who regularly came around.

The first house they moved to in Gloucester was what Rose regarded as a 'coloureds' house'. After only a few weeks in Clarence Road in Cheltenham, they moved to a house that Frank Zygmunt had offered them overlooking Gloucester Park. In April 1970, Fred and Rose and Charmaine and Anna-Marie moved into 10 Midland Road in Gloucester which it didn't please Rose to discover was full of the blacks. Jamaican immigrants and their families. Thought of by Rose, who had never met a black person in her life before let alone lived close to one, as 'the blacks'. She didn't know Jamaicans then and she didn't know Gloucester and she was too young to know if it was a good or bad place.

In 1970 West Indian men still far outnumbered West Indian women in Gloucester. But the imbalance was nothing like it had been twenty years earlier before the women came over in numbers to join their husbands and boyfriends and fathers and keep them in order. By 1970 the women were firmly and domestically dug in and the golden age of the Jamaican male on the rampage was over. The numbers in the congregations of the many mainly black churches were swelled by women. The New Testament Church of God, to take one example, had its beginnings in the living room of a Mr Wright in Howard Street, one of the many small streets running into Midland Road. He started to have prayer meetings at his house and there were only seven people then. Then they managed to get a little hall in Park Road which was rented on Wednesday and Sunday nights. The congregation grew and they bought a church building in Cromwell Street and painted it a happy blue. From there they expanded into the present home of the flourishing New Testament Church of God in Stroud Road.

At the beginning, many Jamaicans had lived in and around Wellington Street and Cromwell Street, closer to the city centre. But gradually the heart of the black community shifted to the Midland Road area on the other side of Gloucester Park. And this is where Fred came with Rose and the children in spring 1970. What he didn't tell her was that they were moving into a coloureds' house. She didn't know what a Jamaican looked like close up and all of a sudden they're moving into a house full of them. It was so alien to her. Different ways of cooking, unfamiliar smells and such a job to understand what they were saying. Fred said it wouldn't be long, and they did have two rooms, a shared kitchen and use of a garden for the girls. The bathroom was on the first floor, and afterwards she would remember that the young Jamaican who lived in the flat up there had tried it on with her. She was four months pregnant with Heather at the time and he forced her into a corner and started to force himself on her and she had to fight him off. But after a couple of months they were on the move to another of Frank Zygmunt's properties not far away, in fact only the next main street over, on Parkend Road, still near the park.

This was better. It was the middle flat in the house and St Paul's, the school where Charmaine and Anna-Marie were about to start going, was just around the corner at the top of a narrow terraced street like Coronation Street. The brook that runs along the southern edge of the park was near by and it was somewhere Charmaine and Anna-Marie liked to go. Being right close to the park was good. But Fred was getting on very friendly terms with Mr Zygmunt who seemed a lonely sort of a man, for what reason they could never understand. Fred was still working at Cotswold Tyres in Cheltenham during the day, then coming home and doing odd jobs and building and emergency patching-up work for Frank Zygmunt at night. More and more work for Mr Zygmunt, who was buying up houses and wanting them filled as quickly as possible, and coming home later and later. Coming home black and staying black. Black from the tyre works and black from the building and staying black and rarely washing. Then one night Fred brought Mr Zygmunt around to meet Rose and he said he would find them a better place and one with a garden, Fred being such a good worker and so useful to him. So back they went to Midland Road, only to number 25 not number 10, and Fred said they would settle for a bit longer this time. Mr Zygmunt gave them his own flat occupying the ground floor at Midland Road and left behind a few scraps of furniture such as chairs and a sofa for them, but they were living carpetless on bare boards. The houses had been villas and many had servants' entrances. But like every other area this close to the city centre, Midland Road and the many smaller streets running into it had deteriorated over the years. They had a front room which was their bedroom, a middle dining room which the children used to sleep in and a kitchen all going off a long corridor running from front to back. They had to share a bathroom on the first floor.

You could see the park out of the window at the front of the house. The front room of their house was raised several feet above pavement level and you could see the park and the black and white timbered café at the centre of it, the people coming and going from there; the black and white lavatory building and the dog walkers and the tennis courts. Cromwell Street, their eventual destination, was diagonally across to the right from here. But a number of obstacles came in between the park and Midland Road. There was the busy main road carrying traffic out of Gloucester to Bristol and the south. And there was the raised railway embankment which, at that time, brought trains right past the front of the house. Big goods trains rumbling past just yards away in the night causing vibration and a din, plus the traffic. Where they were looked out on the park which was really a field, open and full of light. But Anna-Marie's adult memories of the flat in Midland Road, where they would spend three summers, was that it was a dark place. The curtains were always closed or perhaps it was a blanket that was hung at the window. She would remember it as being dark in that flat and always cold. Dark and cold with the windows rattling from the wind and the trains rattling by. 'The witches are trying to get in,' the girls would tell each other and hang on to one another giggling under the blankets.

Since she had left home three or four months earlier, Rose

had had no contact with her mother and father or that life in Bishop's Cleeve. She was there on her own, a young girl who was pregnant and having to look after somebody else's children. She was on her own and she was sixteen and she was frightened. Because she didn't know how to look after a child of six and seven. She was trying to get some sort of regime. Some sort of balance. Trying to be a mother figure. A little mother. Trying to show that she could cope when she couldn't.

Charmaine and Anna-Marie had been in and out of local-authority homes and foster homes ever since they left Scotland, a total of four years. Sometimes they were kept together and other times they lived apart. Sometimes Rena went to visit them and sometimes she didn't. When she did she had a tendency to take Charmaine out with her and leave Anna-Marie behind. When their father had them there were always different women around to call mummy and they didn't know who they were. They would get to know them and then, like Ann McFall, they would disappear. There was always a lot of trouble with social workers telling him he had to get some stability into the situation or they would take the children and keep them permanently in care.

The children were stubborn. It didn't surprise anybody that they were disturbed. Charmaine wouldn't do anything Rose told her to do because Rose wasn't her real mother and her real mother was coming back to get her any day. 'You're not my mum. So no.' That was Charmaine. Char. She would go out of her way to antagonize and aggravate Rose. And never cry. Rose or anybody could do anything to her and she would never cry. Anna-Marie was very much Daddy's girl. At this age and even when she was older she used to tell her dad that she was going to marry him. Her and her dad were always together. There was a competitive element entering the relationship between Anna-Marie and Rose involving the father of one of them and the boyfriend of the other. Anna-Marie used to call her 'Rose', but her father told her off. 'That's your mum now. You've got to call her mum.' Which she was very reluctant to do. Six plays sixteen.

The crux of the problem was that Fred was never there. He had a new job delivering milk for Model Dairies which saw him leaving the house when some people were just going to bed. Three o'clock was the middle of the night. A new job to add to the job he already had at Cotswold Tyres. Then it would be home from work at night, have something to eat and straight back out. He would do up people's cars for them or be out working with Frank. Rewiring. Roofing. Whatever. Widening his circle of West Indian friends. He just worked. It was even a problem for her to get him to bed at night. They had been a couple for under six months at this point and she never saw him. The children never saw their father. She never saw him. He just worked. Even one morning when she left the paraffin heater tilted on a carpet and paraffin spilled and the children's bedroom caught fire, it wasn't enough to drag him away from work. 'You'll have to get on with it. I'm not leaving work.' The fire brigade came. She phoned him but he wouldn't come.

The children were stubborn and always pushing her. They seemed to go out of their way to antagonize and aggravate her. Not so much Anna-Marie. Anna-Marie was Charmaine's shadow. But it frustrated Rose that she couldn't curb and control Charmaine the way she wanted. Her father's way of expressing his domination of his children had been by assigning them jobs to do. The morning duty rota followed by his inspection, followed, almost invariably, by one of his violent lashings out, hitting whoever was closest with whatever was at hand. He used to flip. He would just blow. And Rose would flip and lash out at Charmaine and Anna-Marie with no warning. Give them the back of her hand for not stirring the gravy in the right way or not mashing the potatoes properly. 'Your fucking fault. You should have done it properly.' Anna-Marie was taken to the hospital one morning to have stitches put in her scalp. The cause given was a household accident. The accident involved Rose hitting Anna-Marie in the head with a breakfast bowl because she was taking too long at the kitchen sink. They each had to wash their bowl when they finished their cereal and Anna-Marie was waiting for Charmaine to wash hers when Rose, who she refused to call mum, let her have it with a bowl. She was a tomboy and falling off things and all sorts. She had to have a number of stitches to her head wound as a consequence of her 'fall'.

One morning Tracy, the little girl from upstairs, burst into their kitchen to see if she could borrow some milk. She knocked and went in without waiting for an answer and found Charmaine, her first best friend Char, standing on an old wooden chair with her hands held behind her by a buckled leather belt and Char's mother, the lady who lived with Char's father, with her hand took back and ready to hit her with a long wooden spoon. 'I'm going with my mammy shortly,' Charmaine would tell her, 'so I'm not taking no orders off you.'

The children had jobs to do. Rose made them do most of the household chores and if they didn't do them right she'd erupt. Vacuuming, cleaning, dusting, washing up. They would set and prepare the table for meals, help with the cooking, wash up, tidy their rooms and the rest of the house and do most of the washing and ironing. Charmaine was made to do more because she was more resentful. They were not allowed to play. Apart from Tracy from upstairs, the upstairs neighbours' daughter, they had no friends at all. Tracy was different. She was already in the house. But they weren't allowed to bring anybody home. They'd be locked in their bedroom. Sometimes they'd be tied together. They weren't allowed to communicate much. They weren't allowed to talk. If they wanted to talk they had to whisper. They'd be in trouble for talking. A slap on the face or a wet belt across the legs. A broom across the head. Their mouths were taped so if they were hit people couldn't hear them; there were people upstairs. Then she would carry on with what she was doing as if nothing had happened.

Rose made no attempt to hide her cruel streak. And on the rare occasions when their father was there he didn't seem to care anyway. 'Your mum is doing that because she loves you. It's for your own good.' She didn't try to hide the beatings. If anything she did the opposite. She seemed to enjoy lashing out and clipping them and hurling things at them in front of their father. It was rare for him to lose his temper with them or hit them himself but he never objected to Rose doing the 'disciplining' as he called it. A kindly word from Fred was often followed by a thump from Rose. 'Make sure you hit them where it doesn't show,' he would tell her, a phrase often spoken by her own mother in Rose's own, still very recent childhood. And there would be a look then that flashed briefly between them that said there was something between them and nobody else was quite in on this.

Rose started to feel Heather coming on a Friday in October. No pains, just uncomfortable. Friday, 16 October 1970. Heather was born on the Saturday morning at a quarter to three. No problems, just a couple of stitches. Six weeks before Rose turned seventeen. When she got home Fred had the cradle all ready, the pram was put together and polished and the girls were really excited. So, a new way of life. It was hard work being up with Heather and then up with Fred and then up with the girls, seeing them off to school. But she soon got used to it and made up for lost sleep during the day.

But Heather was an awkward baby. And it was the dark

nights. It was dark in the morning and nearly dark again by four. She had to get up to Heather in the night. Sometimes three or four times a night. Sixteen, still not quite seventeen yet, and Heather was fractious. Crabby, whatever you want to call it. Fractious. And to Charmaine and Anna-Marie just pure nastiness. If you were cleaning or dusting you were always conscious that she was there watching you. Because it was very much with Rose her way was the right way. And if she's putting herself out to show you how to do it properly, you should be grateful and learn to do it that way. After a while, you learned to get it right quite quick. And if not, look out. Because she could kick you, punch you. It got to the point where she would twist you at the throat and you can't breathe, which is a horrible feeling. She had a look that she would look at you, and it would literally paralyse you. Frighten you. Who could know where such anger would come from. When Rose was angry she would literally froth at the mouth.

Being beaten up by Rose was like going ten rounds with Frank Bruno but without the laughs later, Anna-Marie would one day say. Rose pulling their hair, dragging them by the hair, kicking, swearing, shouting. Rose in an ecstasy of anger like a performance. Like she would soon perform sex. Bellowing and screaming with the windows open so that the neighbours could hear and the children were ashamed to go out in the street. The notorious caravan holiday one year in a year soon coming up when they would leave the windows open so the sounds of her pleasure – she would scream all the things she had learned from the porno films like 'Fuck me harder' and 'I'm going to come . . . *I'm coming!*' at the top of her voice – would carry across the site at night. The caravan would shake and people would come out of their own caravans to see what was happening and Rose would go on screaming and carrying on. She would carry on and the children would hide and pretend that they weren't with her. There was a performance aspect to the sex as there was to the violence she unleashed in the flat at Midland Road against Fred's children, Charmaine and Anna-Marie. A strong suggestion that she was using the children to test the boundaries. That they were testing each other's boundaries and using the children as the means by which to do it. Rose out to impress Fred by her audacity as a performer. Fred out to impress Rose by his impassivity as an audience. His disregard. His excited detachment. She would drag them into the bedroom and tape up their mouths. Tear a piece of tape off and tape it across their mouths. She would tie them up, sometimes together, sometimes on the bed. She would use very much whatever she could get hold of. For dusters Rose used to always rip up old sheets. Sometimes she'd rip them in strips. Sometimes she'd put old sheet in their mouths as a gag to keep them quiet. Or pull them really tight across it. Like a 'bit', isn't it? Like a horse's mouth. Like a bridle on a horse. Or she would use them to tie their arms or legs. Strips of sheet or washing line. Straps. Tie their hands behind their backs or sometimes tightly in front of them. They might be tied to the bed with their legs spreadeagled or bound together. Anything. The abuse and the violent assaults against his young daughters. The things he was prepared to be a spectator to.

Rose didn't have a washing-machine so she used to boil the nappies in a galvanized bucket on top of the stove. Everybody used to ask her how she kept them so white. There was a Polish lady who had the ground floor flat next door, name of Jaruga. Mrs Jaruga who lived at 24 Midland Road the same time as Rose and Fred and the girls were next door at 25. She had a little girl. And she said to her as she was hanging out her washing one day, 'How do you keep your clothes so clean?' and Rose told her. The Polish neighbour said she was very good for one so young. She felt very proud. Because of this she liked the Polish lady, whose name was Kay. She passed on a lot of good advice about babies and Rose liked her telling her how the Polish people lived. Good recipes, wine punch, boiled puddings wrapped in cloths and what was good for babies. The Polish lady's husband grew tomatoes and she would give her some straight from the garden. Great.

And then Fred gets arrested for tax discs on cars. Rose had only been home two weeks with Heather when Fred was arrested for 'swapping' a tax disc from one of Frank Zygmunt's vans to his own and changing the details. Two weeks later he was arrested again, this time for the theft of four tyres from his employers at Cotswold Tyres. He was sacked from his job as a tyre-fitter but him and Frank Zygmunt got on great together and he went to work for his landlord every day after he had come home from the milk round. Always a cobble on.

On 4 December 1970 he was fined £50 and sentenced to three months' imprisonment for the theft of the tyres and the road-fund disc. It was a conviction that breached the suspended sentence he had been given the previous August in Cheltenham for the theft of some fencing, and that brought him a further six months' imprisonment.

Their first Christmas together was going to be spent apart. Rose was going to spend it on her own in a damp flat with bare floors and minimum furniture and poor metered heating with two hostile children who she had no money to buy presents for and a new baby. Fred spent it not far away across the park in Gloucester Prison. On New Year's Eve he was back in court again to receive a further one-month sentence for another theft, which brought his total sentence to ten months. He was to spend the next six months and three weeks in prison, first in Gloucester and then at Leyhill Open Prison twenty miles away in Wotton-under-Edge. He would be in Leyhill from 27 January to 24 June 1971, making models out of matchsticks, rolling his own, painfully putting down his feelings of love for Rose in illiterate and all but illegible letters decorated with tattoo-style crosses and love hearts ('Our family of Love . . . Mr and Mrs West for Ever'). While Rose sat it out at Midland Road without even the distraction of a television. The two girls spent a lot of the time locked in their room and were not allowed out even to go to the toilet. They would use a bucket and sometimes when they went to pick it up to empty it Rose would kick it over on to the floor, and so they had to pick that up. The television packed up early in the New Year and she didn't have any money to fix it. No money and no television and a flat that smelled of urine. Dettol and wee. This was the life she had run away to; the life she had chosen for herself when she went straight from school to him.

Letter from 25 Midland Road, 4 May 1971:

To My Darling,

What was you on about at the beginning of your letter. I just can't make it out for trying. Hey love that's great, just three more visits, it'll take up half the time I've got to wait for you. Blinking base people get's on my nerves. Darling, about Char. I think she likes to be handled rough. But darling, why do I have to be the one to do it. I would keep her for her own sake, if it wasn't for the rest of the children. You can see Char coming out in Anna now and I hate it.

Love, I don't think God wan'ted me to go to that dance. Because I didn't go after all. Darling, I think from now on I'm going to let God guide me. It always ends up that way anyway (As you may know) Ha! Ha! Oh! Love! About our son. I'll see the doctor about the pill. And then we'll be safe to decide about it when you come home.

Well, Love, keep happy, Longing for the 18th.
Your ever worshipping wife, Rose

Rose had drawn a heart at the top and written the words 'From now until forever' and 'That ring that means so much' in the top right-hand corner.

Letter from HM Prison, Leyhill, 14 May 1971:

To My Darling Wife Rose,
Darling be at home on Tuesday for your table Will be cuming so be at home all day until thy cum it will be in the morning if thy do cum then cum see me but dont cum till thy cum Darling.

Darling you for got to write agen. Darling your caravan is at the prison gate for you. I have put your assisted visits form for the 18th or 19th and for the 15th of June. Will, it wont be long for the 24 now Darling so get the pill if you want it or will be a mum for son or to son Darling. I love you darling for ever my love. Your has you say for now untill for ever. Darling. Will, Darling, Untill I see you. All my love I sind to you. Your Ever Worshipping Husband Fred.

Fred then decorated the letter with the words 'for Heather', 'ANNA', 'CHAR', 'for Rose' and a number of crosses representing kisses. Then he wrote:

And more, 100 more
Mr and Mrs R West for ever

The caravan he refers to is a gypsy caravan he had made out of matchsticks which opened up to make a jewellery box. A wooden heart suspended from the front by a chain was inscribed 'To Rose Love Fred'. The table was a heart-shaped table he had made in the prison workshop.

To My Dearest Lover,

Darling, I am sorry I upset you in my previous letters I didn't mean it (NO joking). I know you love me darling. It just seems queer that anyone should think so much of me. I LOVE You. Love I don't mind what you make me, because I know it will turn out beautifull. Darling I would like to get a horse for our caravan & put it in a showcase. We've got a lot of things to do darling in the next couple of years. And we'll do it just loving each other. Well Love, see you on the 31st, Better not write to much incase I go putting my big foot in it. (Ha! Ha!) Sending all my love & heart your worshipping Wife, Rose.

P.S. Love I've got the wireless on and it's playing some lovly romantic music. Oh! how I wish you were hear beside me. Still remembering your love & warmth, Rose.

At the top of the letter she had written 'From Now Untill Forever' with a heart.

Letters that would be found twenty-three years later, boxed and stored in the attic at 25 Cromwell Street. The archive of their life together. A whole life – their life as a couple – preserved in scraps of paper. A graveyard at the bottom of the house. Bodies taken apart and roughly buried in bits by the drains in the cellar and left to decompose. A museum at the top of the house. The scraps of their lives carefully kept and preserved. A museum of themselves.

A week after her eighth birthday in March 1971, Charmaine was taken to the casualty department of Gloucester Royal Hospital shortly before seven one evening and treated for a 'puncture wound' to her left ankle. The 'accident', which had possibly involved a knife, had happened at the flat in Midland Road where she was living with Rose and Anna-Marie and the new baby. Fred was still in prison. The incident with the breakfast bowl which resulted in Anna-Marie having stitches in her scalp also happened around this time when Fred was away.

Charmaine was a bedwetter. This meant more work every day for Rose and did nothing to improve her mood. She was on a short fuse. There was the money to get sorted out with the Social and bills to pay and food to put on the table. They lived on chips and bread and butter. She had to feed the meter. She was still making them things herself, school dresses, play clothes. She was on a short fuse.

While Rose lived and slept in the big room at the front of the house looking out over the park with Heather, her baby by Fred, the children of Fred's other marriage were frequently kept out of sight at the back of the house; locked up and shut away. Charmaine on the narrow bed under the window; Anna-Marie on the narrow bed against the wall. Rose adored children until they were about one year old, Anna-Marie would remember. She loved the helplessness of them and she loved to do things for them. But the moment children developed signs of independence, such as crawling, walking or talking, things changed. Then they became a nuisance and would feel the sharp end of her tongue and her temper.

She was unpredictable. Sometimes your legs were tied open, and sometimes your hands were tied behind your back. She'd lock the door behind her when she came in. Make you strip off, push you back on the bed. Perhaps the rope was on the bed all the time, under the spring. Plastic washing line. Strips of sheet. Perhaps they were there all the time under the mattress. It might have always been there. Sometimes tie your hands around your back and tie you to the bed. It depended.

It depended sometimes on whether she was going shopping or something like that. This was their hope. In the end in a way they were quite happy being tied up, because it meant she would leave them alone.

Some time before she saw Charmaine for the last time Anna-Marie opened the door to the bedroom at Midland Road and saw Charmaine naked, tied to the bed, lying on a piece of waterproof sheet. Her eyes looked frightened. She looked like she had been perspiring or crying and she never cried. Her fringe – her fringe or her forehead – looked wet.

One day in that summer when she had her seventh birthday Anna-Marie came home from school and was told that Charmaine was gone. She was gone with her mother. And although Anna-Marie wondered why their mother wanted just one of them not both, she was pleased for Charmaine. She was settled and content to stay with her dad. But Char had always wanted to be with her mum and so she was pleased. She had no clear picture of which one was her mother. All of her life she would remain unclear about which of the many foster mothers and carers and baby-minders coming and going, passing through, had been her. Rena. The Rena one. But if Charmaine was with her she was happy. Happy for Charmaine. Anna-Marie was told by her father that Char had gone to Scotland with her mother. Rose told Anna-Marie that Char had gone off to London with her real mum. All the same place to her. Scotland. London. But if Charmaine was happy. She didn't know where these places were.

Rena was here and there. She was here and then she was gone. She stuck to this pattern – or it seems was compelled to live by this pattern – all her life. She was a good mother when she was with them. She looked after them well when she was there. When they were together Fred and Rena could be quite happy together without any problem. But Rena had this thing in her where she would just disappear for a month. For you didn't know how long. She had to go on her way. He was always trying to get Rena to settle with them or get out of the way completely and let him get somebody else to take her place. And he would get somebody else and then Rena would reappear. And it would be 'Right you, out.' This went on from the day they went to Scotland. When she had been drinking Rena could have a loose mouth. He had a quick temper. The boot would go in. He wouldn't hesitate to use his feet. The fists would fly and the feet would go in and that would be Rena off again.

She had been with him when Ann McFall disappeared. She had been living with Fred and the children on the Watermead site at Brockworth and Ann had been living covertly in a little caravan at Sandhurst Lane on the other side of Gloucester when he told Rena that Ann had packed her bags and gone. She had been with him when he was being chased between Sandhurst Lane and Watermead by the hire-purchase people who he hadn't been paying and who were about to repossess his 'van. She had been with him six weeks after he had murdered Ann and buried her remains in Fingerpost Field in Much Marcle in August 1967 and they had moved to the Lakehouse site at Bishop's Cleeve in October that year. She had been with him when his mother died in February 1968. And Fred and Rena had been in one of their together periods when a fifteen-year-old girl called Mary Bastholm had gone missing just prior to his mother's death: they had been in a VW beetle that Rena had borrowed from one of her 'clients' when they were stopped and questioned about Mary Bastholm's disappearance during a random police check at Westgate Bridge in Gloucester.

Fred West would never admit that he murdered Mary Bastholm. (It can only be assumed that she was murdered:

her body has never been found.) But there are many things that connect him to Mary Bastholm's death. In common with several of the girls whose bodies would be recovered from 25 Cromwell Street, she was last seen standing at a bus stop on the night that she disappeared. She was on her way to visit her boyfriend who lived on the outskirts in Quedgeley and she was waiting for a bus just outside Gloucester city centre at a spot where the Bristol Road runs parallel with the Sharpness canal. She was seen there shortly after seven o'clock on 6 January 1968. It was a Saturday night in winter, frosty and sleeting, she was carrying a game of Monopoly in a plastic carrier bag and wearing a navy-blue twinset and matching shoes and gloves, and she was never seen again.

Mary Bastholm helped in the kitchen at the Pop-Inn, a café near the docks in Southgate Street in Gloucester where Fred West used to go; he had done some work on the drains in the yard there towards the end of 1967. His most usual reason for being in the Pop-Inn, though, was his friendship with a petty crook called Frank Stephens and Frank Stephens's dealings with the owner of the café who was a well-known fence for stolen goods. Pornography changed hands in the Pop-Inn, among other under-the-table transactions. Frank Stephens was to become a regular lodger at 25 Cromwell Street between his periods 'away'. A key link between Fred West and Mary Bastholm, although it was one that it wasn't possible to make at the time, was that a watch with a strap identical to the one Mary Bastholm had been wearing when she went missing was found in Tobyfield Road in Bishop's Cleeve. Fred West was living on the Lakehouse caravan site close by. Rose Letts was living at 96 Tobyfield Road and going to Cleeve School. She was fourteen. The watch was handed in to the local police station about a week after Mary disappeared but it provided no new lead.

After their move to Bishop's Cleeve, Rena went on being

what he liked her to be and what she had learned to be, which was somebody who gave sex for money in a boozy, rough and ready, semi-professional way. She gradually built up her list of regulars from the lanes and villages and around and about. And then she started going with the men who were building a new section of the M5 motorway near Tewkesbury. To start with she drove the mobile canteen which provided Costain's workers with sandwiches and tea. Charmaine and Anna-Marie were being looked after by a Mrs Nock, one of Fred's old bread-round customers, near by at Stoke Orchard. And Fred was working on the motorway extension himself, driving a digger, digging a drainage channel. But nobody made a connection between him and the bottle blonde bringing teas around in the Land-Rover canteen. There was no contact between them and nobody ever made any connection, certainly not that they were man and wife. It was the kind of private knowledge Fred liked to have and the sort of wool-pulling he enjoyed. It gave him the edge to know who had been with Rena and sometimes to watch. He was stealthy and sly and it put him in a position of power to know something intimate about them that they didn't know. There was a high turnover of manual staff because the motorway was hard work, but Fred was always there. After a time the foreman noticed that one man was always there.

He still had the schoolgirls coming around to the trailer after school and it probably suited Fred when Rena went off on her travels again some time in 1969. It had been one of their longest unbroken spells together in their seven years of unconventional married life. And Rena finally broke it by going off to live with the Costain's site foreman in his caravan at Sandhurst Lane in Gloucester, the place where Ann McFall had last been seen. The foreman, whose name was James, went up to Glasgow with Rena for Christmas and then Rena followed him to Reading when he went to work on the M4 near there at the beginning of 1970. He had been at Reading about a month when Catherine, as he called Rena, which was her real name, turned up at his lodgings totally unexpected. It was a Friday night. On Saturday morning he put her on the train back to Gloucester telling her it was all over and giving no reason, although it was probably the drink and the repetitive patterns of behaviour that go with being drunk. Her being on the game and the drink.

About two months later when the site was set up at Reading with all the Portakabins and canteen facilities, he was amazed one day to find Catherine working in the canteen. Her hair was dyed black now and she was calling herself Mandy and using his surname. There could be no doubt it was Catherine. Mandy James. She continued to work there for another four or six weeks before she left. She told him she had come to Reading because Fred, who he still didn't know was the little digger driver from the M5 at Tewkesbury, had a girlfriend. 'Young, attractive lady looking for employment. Anything considered . . .' She had received a load of letters, many from people actually offering jobs. Which had given Fred a laugh. Letters addressed to Van 17, Lakehouse, Stoke Road, Bishop's Cleeve, made out to Miss Mandy James.

The move to Clarence Road in Cheltenham might have been another attempt to get away from Rena, as well as escape the threats being made against him by Rose's dad. But Rena tracked him down to Clarence Road and she tracked him to Midland Road in Gloucester when he moved on to there. Rena had form in Gloucester. She had been done for soliciting in 1969 and for burglary the year before that. And many years later Fred would claim that in 1971 Rena was 'working for some Irish blokes in Gloucester – prostituting'. Alternatively he would claim that she was working for a Jamaican pimp from the White City estate called Rolf, who Rose would certainly remember working on cars with Fred outside the flat in Midland Road. 'I can't get the idea out of my head that you are going with someone else,' Rose had written to Fred just a few months earlier, when she was still living with her mother and father in Tobyfield Road. 'You told my aunt about Rena. But what about telling me the whole story even if it takes all day. I love you, Fred.'

Rose West still maintains that she never once in her life met Rena. That on the day Charmaine was collected from the flat by Rena, she had taken Anna-Marie over to Bishop's Cleeve to keep out of the way. Rena could be vicious, Fred had told her. That was a vicious woman. She was a nice-looking woman but, boy, you upset her and it was best if she kept out of the way. Rena always used a knife. All prostitutes carry knives. You didn't mess with that woman at all. That woman fought like a man.

When the children were in care and Rena visited them she had always had a tendency to take Charmaine out with her and leave Anna-Marie behind. And Rose on her visits to Fred in Leyhill Prison told him about the stories she was hearing that Rena was meeting up with Charmaine on her way to school. She was hanging around and meeting her and taking her away with her for the day some days. Just the odd day.

He would start forcing Anna-Marie to have sex with him within a year of coming out of Leyhill, when she was eight. But Anna-Marie's coaching and conditioning by her father would almost certainly have started some time before that. A long time before. Abusing her. Creating fears. Reassuring her that it's what all daddies do with their little girls. Fun. A game. They choose the children. They have the children or they select. That's about vulnerability and being available. They initiate that contact. They overcome the victim's resistance by seduction. They condition the victim to accept that what is being done is normal. If they can get the victim to agree that this is normal and OK, they're safe. He'd say: 'Shut up. It's going to help you in later life.' He'd say: 'This will make sure you get a husband when you're older.' He'd say: 'It's a normal thing, so stop carrying on.' They trap and control.

He had started abusing Charmaine when she was just a baby. Rena's friend Margaret Mackintosh had seen that. And the abuse had almost certainly continued up to their time in Midland Road. It was to be an unwritten house rule among future West children: no girl was to be on her own with their dad.

They have to control the environment. They have to be aware of other people. They have at some level to control those other people, because those people can tell. And then they have to overcome the victim's resistance. Because they don't want the victim to tell either. But he was in prison. And Charmaine was out and probably seeing Rena. And Rena was open with her mouth. When she had been drinking Rena could have a very loose mouth. Various members of the West family saw her in the fields close to Moorcourt Cottage one afternoon in August, talking to Walter, Fred's father. Rena walked down to the fields where Walter was working and the two of them stayed in conversation for several hours. Within weeks of Fred being released from Leyhill Prison at the end of June 1971 both Charmaine and Rena were dead. 'I had too many people to watch at once,' he said more than twenty years later. 'That's what went wrong.'

Rena was decapitated and dismembered and pressed into a narrow hole in Letterbox Field. Buried with her was a little red boomerang with 'Boomerang Woomerang' printed on the side. A boomerang from a Rice Krispies packet. Charmaine was murdered on the same night as Rena. Fred West gave many conflicting versions of these murders. But in the most believable – the least incredible – version he said he had arranged to meet Rena in a pub called the East End Tavern in Barton Street in Gloucester one night in August. When he got there at about nine thirty she was, as he knew she would be, already very drunk. She was with a group of Irishmen. It was the school holidays and she had Charmaine with her and she was falling-down drunk. Charmaine had also been given things to drink and was drinking something alcoholic, lager or something, from a bottle through a straw. He stayed long enough to let Rena get even more drunk and then poured her into the car. He put Rena in the front seat, Charmaine in the back and drove out to what had been his and Rena's favourite spot in Much Marcle at Letterbox Field. Rena was unconscious by the time they got there. She was 'absolutely paralytic'. Charmaine was also sleeping soundly in the back. He hauled Rena bodily out of the car and knocked her unconscious against the gate. 'I just smashed her against the gate.' He dragged her into the field and down to the tree that was a marker in the hedge. Using a 'massive' Jamaican sabre knife, a two-and-a-half-feet-long sugar beet scythe that somebody had given him once for chopping nettles, he took off her legs and her head and jammed the trunk of her body into the ground. Using the sheath knife that he always carried on his belt, he removed a kneecap and a number of toes and fingers and set them aside to bring away. An actual dagger, used for laying felt. He washed his chest and his arms in a cattle trough and then took Rena's clothes and bundled them and threw them over into an adjoining field where there were fires going. It was a country custom in Much Marcle and the villages around about for villagers to wheel barrowloads of household rubbish down to the cornfields in the summer and tip them into the burning corn stubble and burn them. It was that time of year with the field fires smoking and he threw Rena's clothes there and burned them. He said he remembered Charmaine only when he got back to the car and saw her lying on the back seat sleeping. 'There was Charmaine in the back of it. I thought, What am I going to do now? . . . So anyway I strangled her while she was sleeping 'cause there's no way I could have touched her in any other way and wrapped her up in the back and drove back to Midland Road.'

Charmaine was in the back and he was in the front and he turned around in the driver's seat and held her by the throat until she stopped breathing. 'The pressure's in my thumbs. I mean, I can undo three-quarter nuts without a spanner – just lock 'em on, turn 'em like that, an' I can do 'em . . . I'm strong in the hands because of the job I do. When you're using big spanners an' things like that, you get strong in the arms.' Making and constructing. Working and making. Activities that always held more meaning for him than unmaking a person.

Charmaine was discarded in the coal house under the kitchen in Midland Road where her body lay undisturbed until it was disinterred and reburied deep in the core of the building by Fred West many years later. He took it and placed it in one of the concrete footings when he was part of a small team helping to turn the three flats at Midland Road into six flats for Frank Zygmunt. Police diggers would have to go down through three layers of infill and mesh to a depth of nine feet in 1994 in order to recover the remains. Both kneecaps were missing in addition to a number of fingers and toes. The legs were not in the position they should have been in if the body had been buried in one piece.

The register at St James's School where Charmaine was a pupil in 1971 was marked 'Moved away'. She wouldn't be starting the autumn term a message reached them because her real mum had come to claim her and she had gone away to be with her real mum. 'She's gone to live with her mother, and bloody good riddance,' was Rose's reply to anybody who knew the trouble she had been having with Charmaine and who wondered where Charmaine had gone.

*

Heather had been born in October 1970. By August the following year Rose was pregnant again, this time with May. A gap of ten months. Fred was in prison for six of the ten months and having sex with men was something Rose could do for Fred while he was away. Do it and tell him about it on her visits to Leyhill. She started having sex with a bus driver on Gloucester buses and that led to introductions to other crews based at the central bus garage. Men who drank at the Busmen's Club. These men and other men. She was thin and she was tired and she was even sometimes hungry but she was never too tired or too hungry for a session of sex. Group sex. Serial sex. One-on-one. She was never satisfied and always hungry. Rose's gift to Fred.

When he came home from prison Fred started to offer Rose around. He offered her to a friend in return for work carried out on his van. Mrs Jaruga, the Polish lady who had the ground-floor flat next door, had heard rumours that Frank Zygmunt was very friendly with Rose, in particular during the time that this woman's husband was in jail and that sexual favours were given instead of the rent to Frank. She could also corroborate this as Frank Zygmunt tried to proposition her if she experienced a difficulty in paying her rent to which she had hit him in the face. She was also aware from other female residents that he had tried it on with them. Women were sitting on a fortune. The trouble was they didn't seem to know it. Fred had no hesitation in putting Rose with Mr Zygmunt. Old Frank. Of course he took Frank up on his offer on Rose's behalf.

Rose's willing submissiveness to Fred – her eager and dedicated dependence on him – was something that was going to turn into a fulltime occupation as her life progressed. Her masochistic submissions to her husband her badges of triumph. A whole life used up, bit by bit.

He made small holes. He drilled holes in the wall between

the front and back bedrooms at Midland Road and watched her with other men. So this was why he no longer needed Rena. Rose also gave him this. Rose was young and pretty and sexually audacious. Quite a performer. She was young and keen to experiment sexually. She looked fourteen. And she let him look. Loved him to look. Did what she did not only or even mainly because she wanted to do it but because she knew he wanted to see what she did. The intensive desire to look as an erotic activity. Feeding his eyes. And their understanding in those early years was that he got to go with her when the other man had gone. As soon as the other man had gone. Mixing his sperm with the other man's sperm. Coating himself with the other man's sperm in order (he said) to defer his orgasm. He was habitually prone to premature ejaculation and this was the solution he had come up with to deal with that problem. A problem to which he would never admit. He would claim that one of the reasons he started getting after her to go with coloured men was because of the superior lubricating qualities of the sperm of the coloured man. That was his reason. Just one of the assortment of reasons he gave. She was a very young girl and she couldn't just dedicate herself to cleaning and bringing up children. She'd miss her young life. And that was the beginning of his push to get her to go with black men. He could be very persuasive. On and on. Do it for me. Do it for the marriage. (Although they weren't yet married.) Just as she thought he was getting the message that she wasn't doing it, he would come back twice as bad. You've got to play your part in this marriage. It was a daily thing to be talked about. Here is how it began.

One day they became married. They formalized their union, which is something she wanted very badly. One night Rose and Fred had gone to bed and made love and then got back up again. They used to do that now and again and eat boiled eggs but this night he had asked her to marry him. She said 'Yes' and they went back to bed and made love again. It was January 1972. The beginning of a new year. Last New Year, which should have been their first New Year together, he'd spent in jail. Rose bought a new dress for her wedding morning and wore baby buds here and there in her hair. She was five months pregnant with May. Fred wore oily overalls and oil smeared over his face until the last minute. He had been changing an engine on a car at the White City estate and he was still wearing work clothes and oil on his face at five to eleven. They were booked into the register office for eleven o'clock.

None of the Letts family came to the wedding. Fred's brother John acted as a witness along with a small-time criminal associate of Fred's who signed in one name then crossed it out and signed in the name he happened to be using at the time. Just the four of them. Fred didn't like parties and being clammed up to people. He described himself on the wedding certificate as a bachelor and they both signed. John had bought a bottle of wine and some bottles of beer. Fred had one drink and then said he had to go out to a job. Just one drink and then he dived off back to work. Mr and Mrs West for Ever.

Just before they were married a rare thing had happened. Fred had shown an interest in another woman. A woman as a person, that is, rather than in terms of how she looked and her appearance. Rather than as a collection of body parts. Although his interest in Liz Agius was inevitably sexual. Somebody to do a three in a bed with. Somebody to be developed in that direction.

He introduced himself to Liz Agius by performing the act of a considerate neighbour. He saw her struggling with a pram on the steps of her house one day and offered to help. They were steep steps on the houses at Midland Road and she had moved into the next house. He quickly extracted from her the fact that she was a new arrival and that, for the time being, she was living on her own. She was married to a Maltese man who was still living where she had just come from, in Malta. She appreciated his friendliness and quite soon accepted his invitation to come in for a cup of tea with his wife, who turned out to be a pale girl looking young enough to be his daughter. Liz Agius was only nineteen herself.

Rose had a baby and Liz had a baby. Rose also had Anna-Marie, a seven-year-old from Fred's previous marriage, and a second baby on the way. So it was babies and children and cups of tea. How did she get her nappies so white. Baby talk. With Fred coming and going, hovering, on a scent, waiting for his chance.

He took his chance, according to Liz Agius, one night when she had been babysitting Heather and Anna-Marie. They came back late. It was the early hours of the morning. And when she asked them if they had had a good time he told her that they had been driving around for hours looking for young girls, fifteen-to-seventeen-year-old girls, virgins and runaways, to put on the game. He said they would drive as far as London looking and that the best place to find them was Bristol. Bristol bus station where teenagers passing through on their way to London would do anything for money. You could get more money for a virgin. He enjoyed talking sex. He was a boaster. A braggart. Teasing and titillating. He was a romancer. Putting down lures. Trying to snag her. Nobody believed him.

From then on he was always trying to persuade Liz Agius to have sex with him. He had taken Rose places and shown her things and now he would show Liz. She could do anything she wanted with him. Tie him up. Stub lighted cigarettes out on him. Anything she wanted with him. And Rose told Liz it was true. He wanted to do three in a bed and he gave Rose the task of talking Liz round. Girl/girl. Straight kinky sex. Rose told Liz that she was working as a prostitute. She was five months pregnant but she was still bringing men home to Midland Road with her and Fred watched them through a hole in the wall. A special hole he had made. If he couldn't be there she told him what had happened when he came home. Mad things. Crazy stories. Stories invented for the purpose of bringing her in. But she had to wonder. Rose showed her the condoms. Showed her the special pills shaped like sugar cubes that might have been a stash of LSD that he was storing but which she said were meant to stop her catching VD. 'Oh, what I could do to you,' he said to her. She had to think.

She had to think that they must have drugged her. That's all she could think. They'd given her a cup of tea and that was the last thing she could remember. They must have laced it or something because the next thing she remembered was waking up naked in bed with Fred and Rose. They were both naked and he told her that he had raped her while she was out. This heavily pregnant woman and her chuckling husband and she had been raped.

May West was born three months after they were married, on the first of June 1972. She had been due in late May and she had been born in June and that's what they christened her: May June. It was a straightforward delivery but all through the pregnancy Rose had been depressed. Ten days after giving birth she was still in hospital and refusing to budge until Fred came and took her home. But he didn't come. He kept not coming. And in the end she had to gather May together and her belongings and take a bus home on the tenth day.

Arriving at Midland Road she found Anna-Marie dirty and neglected and on her own. She was very clinging. She clung to Rose. Heather was in the cot. Dirty, messy nappy on. She was a mess. She put the baby in the front room and went to look to see where Fred was. He was next door at Liz Agius's in case she didn't know. She found the front door open at number 24 and went up the stairs. Liz Agius lived on the top floor. Rose had a white-hot temper. She was furious. She was very angry banging on the door, bellowing Liz! – Fred! Getting no answer. *Liz! Fred!* In a fury. Getting louder and louder. Until after a while Liz's bedroom door opened and they both walked out. Flushed and hussled like they were in a hurry and he dived off a bit quick down the stairs and out of there. A cheeky grin though.

Rose had come to Fred pregnant. She had been pregnant with Heather virtually up to the time he went into prison. Three months after he came out of prison she was pregnant again with May. And he didn't like women when they were pregnant. They weren't sexy. He said the bump in their belly wasn't sexy and turned him off. May was born in June 1972 and by November Rose would be pregnant again with Stephen. Their first son and the first of their babies to be conceived in Cromwell Street.

May June. Cromwell Street came up in July a few weeks later. Across the tracks and across the park. A snug harbour. Home at last. This narrow aspect opening on to so much space.

Chapter Eight

Traces of the life that Mrs Green had led in the house were still visible. Mrs Green had lived there for thirty-six years, from 1935 to 1971, in the last years alone with her grandson Brian, son of Eddie, 'Gloucester's Midget Strongman'. And they inherited many of Mrs Green's wallpapers and linos with their wear marks and dated patterns. Some of the wallpapers were buckling and not to their taste. They were not what Rose would have chosen. But they had to live with them. The wallpapers and linos and some of the other things Mrs Green had left behind. They had no choice. For a period before they left Midland Road the gas and electricity had been cut off. They had all been living in the one room with a paraffin heater and candles. Huddled around the heater like a travelling family. Like travellers. Like gypsies. Candles in bottle-tops and on saucers. In that case, what were Mrs Green's age patches and stains? A poor family existing on bread soaked in warm milk. Weak watery tea-coloured Bovril. Snouts. They were scratching about for money. Scraping and scratching. And yet mystifyingly, thanks to the intervention of Frank Zygmunt, they were miraculously about to become home-owners. Old Frank, their friend and a lonely sort of a man who had decided to look out for them. Real owners of a real house. Three storeys, not including attic and basement.

Traces of the former life of the street were still in evidence. The red-brick buildings of Tommy Rich's school were abandoned but still standing. The Seventh-day Adventists' church in Cromwell Street in 1972 was still leaking noise. It was contested noise. It had to compete with the human and the electronic and mechanical and all the other noises of a scrappy central city street. Random, mobile noise. Always bad neighbourhoods were linked with noise. And this was one. It had gone down. But the church building was still more or less a shanty building standing on the piece of spare ground between 25 and 27 Cromwell Street. The church was still only really a hut constructed out of scrap and sheets of corrugated iron and tar pitch over simple tar paper. Built on to here and there as the need had arisen and pushed into an irregular casual shape. And the sounds of the piano and the almost 100-per-cent Jamaican congregation singing from *The Seventh-day Adventists' Hymnal* still leaked out through the very many gaps and cracks over the building and the spaces where frames and joists didn't meet.

Behind the church, at the bottom of what was going to be Fred's and Rose's back garden, was another slightly leaning, knocked-together building. In it was a man who made his living dealing in cars and dogs. He ran a car-repair business and also sold pedigree Alsatians which turned out not to be pedigree and led to him being periodically sent away. Ducking in, ducking out.

That piece of land between the back of Cromwell Street and St Michael's Square had once been full of sheds and huts and makeshift buildings when the allotments were there. Now in 1972 there was only the car repairer and the church. The last examples of an unregulated way of building in which poor materials were put together in a resourceful way and given a new use. Basic shelter for poor people. A peasant tradition adapted to life in towns. It was a tradition in which Fred had grown up and one that he would keep going in his twenty-plus years at Cromwell Street.

He hated anything official. He had a phobia about the

police, the welfare, the planning people, teachers, even mid-wives and doctors. Anybody in authority. And he brought his children up to hate them. They were brought up believing they would only do them harm. Inside was safe and outside was full of dangers. People in uniform and briefcase-carrying nosey-parkers. He hated officialdom of any kind. Anybody in a pen-pushing capacity.

And so he would go about adding on to his house without asking for or being given permission; with stealth and in a piecemeal, sly way. He would extend the house incrementally over a period of years, putting up what was really a series of interlinking lean-tos and sheds. One-storey outbuildings. Flimsy envelopes of space tacked on to the main walls of the house at the side and the back. Jerry-built and screened off from the street so as to draw no attention to themselves. And in this way he combined two of the things that gave him the most pleasure. Making and constructing. And making a monkey of. Pulling the wool over. Putting one over on. The chisel. The blag.

His house would exist in a state of becoming which would last not just for two or three years but for nearly twenty years. All his life in this house. Constant digging, demolition, excavation. The house was a building site. Always Fred did the work. Fred alone or Fred working with somebody else. When he wasn't at work he was working on the house. Rewiring, replumbing, roofing, digging up floors, pouring new footings. New roof. New windows. He painted the out-side. Cladding. Skimming. Decorating inside. Always rubble and noise. Rose was always happy when she knew he had done things for her – a new bathroom suite, put swings up for the kids. He had a preference for trial and error over the fol-lowing of directions. The casual approach and improvisation. He was learning from Mr Zygmunt and practising on the house. Alone or with somebody else. He just worked.

Every penny they had for many years went into the house. And what they couldn't afford to buy he stole. Almost everything in the house was stolen. The sand and cement that kept it standing and the beams that held the roof up were stolen. When he needed wood or sand or cement for the house he would go out at night and lift it. Electric cable. Water mains. Beds and lino. Copper pipes. The incredible thieving machine, his son Stephen would grow up calling him. If he got his hands on some jungle-green paint the whole house would be done up with it. The floor in the hall and in some of the bedrooms was covered in sample squares of carpet. Uneven textures, shaggy and clipped and clashing patterns. He stole tools from his workmates and often stole ladders and tools from his neighbours. He rewired the telephone and rerouted the electricity. He'd drive out to building sites at midnight and pinch things for the extension he was building.

After Rose – perhaps even before Rose – the house was his most precious possession. He invested everything he was and had in it. He had an impoverished, perverted and murkily complex interior life. And whether he intended it or not 25 Cromwell Street would in time grow into the fullest expression of it. He loved the house. He was so proud of what he had achieved that he would strike up conversations with strangers in the street and invite them in for a guided tour of it. It didn't matter to him what kind of people they were, whether they were drunks and down-and-outs. Mental patients from Coney Hill hospital. He would waylay them and give them the tour. He liked people to say what a nice home he had. He would even show them the children's rooms. He would sit on the wall outside and wait and invite them in. Towards the end of his life, when he was in custody and being questioned about what the press had started calling the 'House of Horror', he would lose his composure only four or five times, and two of those times were when he was forced to face the facts of what was happening at his house. The police were digging and finding bodies in the cellar and in the garden. But that wasn't what agitated him. He was given two diazepam to calm him on the second full day of questioning and that seemed to produce a hallucination. 'I don't know what happened,' he said. 'When I walked in here and sat down there, I could feel my head like lifting up, and I was going into space. And I could see diggers and everything all ploughing round and ripping the house up and tearing floorboards up and bulldozing the house down and it was all weird and . . . I could see it all in me mind and everything had gone wrong.' With Stephen he cried when he talked about all the work he had done on the house, which was now all going to go to nothing. He seemed genuinely upset and agitated, but only about the house. Other murderers claim that they are being visited by the spirits of the people they have murdered. They see apparitions. They hear voices. Faces and voices. With him it was bricks and mortar. The changes in temperature and acoustics in remembered spaces. A building. He loved his house. Hallucinating himself back to his house. Nobody was to touch it. It was in a constant state of becoming.

The selling price had been £7000. Frank Zygmunt was letting them have it for that. He advanced them £500 as a loan and organized a local-authority mortgage with the council. Mortgages for poor people. One week's money was your mortgage, one week's money was your food and stuff, which they did then. Optional or summat. Looking out for them and for himself. Frank took it upon himself to do that. He had tried multi-occupation in the house for a year and it had been trouble. He had had students in and it hadn't worked. With Fred and Rose in he had live-in caretakers and that was the arrangement for the first six months. They would take lodgers to guarantee his loan and then, when it was paid off, or mostly paid off, they would buy. The house would be theirs. In that way also he had a reason to remain a regular caller and the opportunities to continue having sex with Rose in place of the rent. Which was all right with Rose. The sex with Frank Zygmunt she didn't mind. He was a nice old chap. It was the other part of the arrangement, which involved turning the top half of the house over to lodgers, that didn't appeal. Rose could see it was going to be her responsibility to put her foot down and maintain order and she didn't want it. Mr Zygmunt was Polish but in the Russian *domrabotnitza*: a woman you hire to keep your home in order. She didn't want it.

But Fred put the Baby Belling cookers on the landings and placed his two-line advertisement in the evening paper and word of mouth did the rest. He said they needed the money and it was the only way they could keep things turning over. Word soon got around among the Vampire motorcycle gang who used the Pop-Inn café on Southgate Street and the Scorpions who mostly used the Talbot pub next door and among the regulars at the Jamaican café/record shop in Barton Street and the chip bar plus restaurant in Clarence Street in the main shopping centre only a hundred yards or so away. All the first intake of lodgers were male; hippies or bikers, Hell's Angels types. And when you had the bikers you had the runaways coming around. The hellers. The misfits who were of two different sorts: ones who caused trouble and ones who merely had trouble. That wild runaway element. Soon the house was what Fred called a bloody communial centre. He let it to bedsits. But it was drug addicts. An address that started getting handed around as a place where you could crash. Where the landlord was cool. No questions. There were many people around who wanted to belong to a house like that; to join an extended family.

But it was all right for Fred. Fred never had to hear them. He was working at the Permali's factory on Bristol Road as a fibreglass-presser on permanent nights and jobbing for Frank Zygmunt during the day. Out on an emergency for Frank or shut away down in the cellar well out of the druggy music and the drugs and the drop-outs looking for somewhere to use as a hang-out free of charge. They'd come very smoothly dressed, the first week's rent money in their hand. Then once they moved in they moved all the furniture out of the room, put mattresses on the floors, stripped the wallpaper, painted it all black and purple and green and all psychedelic colours. Called each other 'man'. 'Man' and things like that. 'Hey, man, what you working so hard for, man?' 'Man' if you were a man or a girl, it didn't matter. When they turned up for the interviews, all dressed in nice suits, that was the last you ever seen of the suits and they were drug addicts. How could it work, Rose wanted to know from Fred. They were keeping them. But Fred didn't want to know. Rose realized but Fred didn't seem to realize how disruptive these boys were going to be. Dirty drop-outs. Didn't care about looking after other people's property. And soon there was the problem of the drug squad raiding the house regularly. The police came up to the house two or three times and smashed the doors off, arrested anybody who stood in the way and proceeded to rip the rooms apart. At one time they were raiding regularly and almost every day. If one policeman wanted to get in touch with another policeman, they radioed to Cromwell Street, because that's where they usually were. There were a lot of parties. Endless parties. And a lot of drugs. There could be anything up to thirty people in the house at any one time. It was just a continuous flow going in and out all the time. Going and coming. People staying and then going. A bloody communial centre. They got raided solid for years by the police. Mr Castle and Mr Price. There was so many drug-pushers and drug-takers coming there. And Fred thought it was all great. A joke.

Even the police coming was just a joke to him. He didn't care whether they came or not. The fuzz. Rose wanted the lodgers out. She told him. She said she didn't want them in the house. She wanted her part of the house kept separate but he wouldn't listen. He wouldn't hear of that. Fred seemed to revel in all the upheaval and misrule. Doors banging and constant digging, demolition, excavation. When he wasn't working on the house he was always up with the lodgers, never downstairs with his family. He would spend a lot of time with the tenants. She would cook his dinner and she could never find him to come and eat it. He made them part of their life whether she liked it or not and it sparked rows. They started to fall out over it. Started to have violent arguments on the subject of the hippy drop-out lodgers. The dirty junkies upstairs. And he started to show his violent side. He was vicious when he got angry. His eyes would roll and he would be livid. He didn't flip very often, but when he did go he was like a madman. He snapped very quickly. And when Rose got on at him about the lodgers he started punching and kicking. Coming after her with his fists and his feet. He held her tightly around the throat. He lost it. Wouldn't stop twisting her clothes around her throat until she took the words back. He was saying, 'Take them back or I'll kill you.' Snatched at a cup of hot tea and threw it over her. And one Sunday about two months after they moved into the house she got Heather and baby May together and packed them in the pram and went. He had sensed something brewing when she didn't get her regular weekend shop in on the Friday. And on the Sunday morning she got up early and said, 'I'm going out for the day.' Which came as a great surprise to him who knew Sunday dinner was always something really special. Their one blow-out meal. When she didn't come back by five o'clock, he decided to take Anna-Marie and go and find her. And he knew exactly where to start looking.

One night quite soon before Heather was born, which made it one night in September or October 1970, five or six months after she had walked away from Bishop's Cleeve, there had been a knock on the door at Midland Road. And when she had gone to answer it, there was her father. Her father with her mother, as it happened. The two of them. But it was coming to the door and finding her father on the doorstep – her father who had threatened to stab Fred or set his 'van on fire – that started the alarms ringing. They had found out where Rose was living from one of her sisters and here they were. Rose didn't know what to do and so she asked them to wait and white as a sheet went and told Fred. 'Mum and Dad's at the door.' Eight months pregnant and deathly pale. Fred went to the door himself and told them if they had come to make trouble then forget it. If they had come to make trouble he would give them more trouble than any they could bring him. Making a cigarette in his chipped working fingers, a prison habit. But they had said no – really no – and he had let them in. They saw terrible mess and the squalor in which Rose was living. Cigarette burns in the furniture and car jacks and chisels and unwashed plates. Rose saw Fred and Fred's children and her own little family and went to bring the cups that she considered her best china and made them tea. Anyway they had a nice chat. It was really nice. And when they went they said they would call again.

And they did. They had. But every time they had gone over there after that Rosie would be on her own. She always said Fred was working. But they never got any more out of her than that because she had always been crying. Rosie on her own with romantic radio music and dirty nappies and red-rimmed eyes.

Fred wasn't Dad's company. Dad was quite particular and clean. Dad used to say: Keep that lot out of here, when Fred used to turn up at their kitchen door at Tobyfield Road. But after that first visit he had started to turn up regularly at Fred's and Rose's flat by the railway line in Gloucester. Once the ice had been broken he had become a regular visitor. It seems probable that the pattern of his visits became established while Fred was serving his sentence in Leyhill and continued with Fred's encouragement and connivance after his release. Rose once again sleeping with her father as well as the men from the bus garage and whatever other men Fred brought home for her. 'He was bloody everlasting there after that,' Fred was to say of Bill Letts, Rose's father. Bill on his own.

In the period between Heather being born in October 1970 and the move to 25 Cromwell Street just under two years later Bill Letts and Rose and Fred had started to make up a regular threesome. Rose and her husband and her father driving around; driving out into the countryside for a drink. And sometimes Rose would go off for driving lessons with her father on her own. 'Driving lessons' with the nudge implied when this was said by Fred. A nudge and a cackle. He never knew that Rose was ever abused. Rose never told him that her father had ever abused her. 'Whenever I seen her with him she was more than willing to get them off, and having a good time at it,' he said, and it would have been surprising if he hadn't said it: a man who believed it was every father's right to 'break in' his daughters; that every woman was 'begging for it', especially from him. 'He was fucking her regular . . . I actually caught them in bed. He was well in.'

Caught them in bed. And joined them in bed on at least one occasion. Fred and Rose and her father in bed together. An incestuous triangle. A second triangle. Fred and Rose and Anna-Marie. Fred and Rose and Rose's father. Two daughters and two fathers and an incestuous chain that would be completed when Rose started to force Anna-Marie to have sex with her and Bill Letts started to sleep with Anna-Marie at Cromwell Street when she was twelve. Bill Letts – 'Grampy' to Anna-Marie – would by then have moved into one of the lodgers' rooms at 25 Cromwell Street at the invitation of Fred.

Of course he was right about where Rose had run to. Nothing about Rose Fred didn't know. She had got on the bus to Cleeve to be with her mother and her father. Rosie back home and united with her mam and her dad. Back to being a daughter instead of a worn-down mother.

So he gets there and he jumps out of the van because you had to go across the green to her place in Tobyfield Road and he crosses the green. By the time he gets to the door her father's standing there protecting his daughter, and he says, 'Rose has left you.' Even twenty years later the idea would make Fred laugh. So he says, 'What's the crack then? What's wrong?' And her father says, 'You treat her like a child.' No mention of the lodgers or none of that. Drugs and police raids. And Fred says, 'Right, tell you what. Tell Rose I'm going to sit in the van out the front there for ten minutes and if she ain't there there'll be somebody else in her bed tonight.' And with that he walks back across the small green verge outside the Letts' house and climbs in his van.

'Somebody else in her bed' meaning Liz Agius. Their neighbour from Midland Road who Fred had offered one of the rooms at Cromwell Street to on condition that she left her husband. Liz who Fred had put handcuffs on one day in the kitchen at Midland Road until Rose had shouted, 'Get them off her!' And within four minutes Rose is in the van with him with May and Heather and her father's following and he's saying to Rose, 'Oh, he's only kidding, he's only kidding.' And Rose turns round and says, 'I know him, you don't, so shut up, Dad.'

Which is what she had said to her mother on the doorstep as she was getting everything together. Dashing around getting her things together and the children: 'You don't know him. You don't know him. There's nothing he wouldn't do, even murder.' Which they put it down to being the words of a highly strung girl. And so they went back home and they sorted it out. And from then on, that was where Rose had always had the say in the house, and he had had the say outside, with work, his work and everything. After that day, slowly but definitely, Rose came to be in charge of everything.

He agreed to stop treating her like a schoolgirl which a lot of this had been about and which he admitted was how he had been treating her – as sort of Anna-Marie's schoolgirl mate; as the schoolgirl part of that marriage. As for Liz Agius, she faded from the picture. Liz Agius stayed on the other side of the park on the other side of the tracks and was never mentioned. Not seen and not mentioned. And Rose even started to look secure and self-confident. She was in fact confident that her family was not going to fall apart. No longer afraid that Fred would leave her for anybody else.

Still her mother so hated her being with him. The only thing you could say was that they had their own place to live in. Yes, they had that, for what it was.

As proof that he no longer regarded her as a schoolgirl but as an equal, Fred started handing his pay packet over at the end of every week unopened. He preferred stealing anyway and going about with his eyes in the gutter looking for money. He would never wear new clothes when old were available and enjoyed going foraging on tips for clothes and whatever else was available to bring home. He would never wear clothes that Rose bought for him. He liked to wear clothes he found while out working.

To mark the new balance they had established in their marriage Rose at last agreed to go the extra mile for him. She would do what he had been asking her to do since coming out of Leyhill Prison. Since he met her, effectively. But more insistently since the previous summer. She would go with some of his black men friends, who, he had been assuring her, were massive. His black men.

In the brief time they had been in Cromwell Street, Rose had been hopping in and out of bed with the lodgers – Ben Stanniland, Dapper Davis, David Evans, Charlie Knight and others. Going to bunnyland, Fred called it. She had slept with Ben and Dapper on the night they moved in, Ben first and then Dapper in their room on the top floor. But for her convenience – and more importantly to make it easier for Fred to watch and listen, which even over and above Rose's enjoyment was always the point of it all – Rose was given her own room and, before long, her own bell on the front door. From that point on there would always be one bell for Rose's visitors and one for general callers. Two bells. One for the house and one for 'Mandy'. 'Mandy Mouse'. This was Rose. 'Mandy James'. This had been Rena.

The room they settled on was Mrs Green's old 'best' front room, her special room immediately on the left in the hall as you came in the front door. The door to the living room was on the right directly opposite; and the stairs and the door to the cellar were in the middle, facing. The front street-level room is where Rose would receive her visitors and Fred went enthusiastically to work getting it in shape for her. Top priority was the bed and he put in a double bed, a double divan with a headboard of synthetic walnut, and surrounded it with satinized wallpaper and lots of pictures: a naked lady with a horse in a blond-wood frame; an oil-painting that he had done in prison of Rose – a ground of rose-red and Rose outlined in dense black silhouette against it. There were light shades on the candelabras on the walls, then a main light. A rubber plant that used to stand up into the corner. A big thing. Big leaves on it. With a synthetic-walnut vanity unit and an artex ceiling as the finishing touches. Her room, her private domain.

'Rose's Room' painted by him in yellow on a wooden plaque. And hidden under the plaque a wooden plug with screw threads on it so it could be unscrewed and removed. A one-and-a-half-inch hole drilled into the door at just above waist-level – about level with the bed, giving a sideways-on view of the bed – where he could come when she had taken a coloured man in there with her and crouch and watch. He was a small man and he had placed the hole to give a sightline that was of maximum comfort to himself and he would hover there only slightly bent over and listen and watch. 'Rose's Room' written in joined-up letters in yellow on jungle green on the plaque which he would fit back afterwards.

From such a semi-public exhibition or performance – he encouraged her to make a lot of noise, to keep it noisy, and she obliged – it was a short step to get Rose to stop wearing knickers when she was in the house, something that was to become a lifetime habit. It would be a source of embarrassment all through their lives for her children, and it would embarrass many visitors. But her answer was always the same whenever Heather or Stephen or one of the others dared to go near the subject of her aggressively exposing herself: 'If they don't like what they see they shouldn't be fucking looking.' It didn't matter who was there, Rose would just sit with nothing on under her skirt and her legs open. 'Don't bring her fucking round again if she doesn't like it.' And from there it was only a further short step for him to get Rose to go knickerless in public. She had never been shy and she started turning up on her own at the Prince Arthur public house, which was just a short two-minute stroll away along 'little' Cromwell Street. The Wellington on Wellington Street and then the Arthur. The Arthur was a pub that in the early seventies was a popular meeting place with West Indians, and she would sit on her own at a table or on a stool at the bar with no underwear on and her legs open. Drinking halves of lager and appearing shy and at the same time showing herself. She would always sit alone and would talk only if somebody joined her. The next stage in her willing fetishization of her body would be to invite a black man or men home for sex while Fred watched through the peep-hole in the door or watch with Fred while she demonstrated the use of dildos and giant vibrators.

Fred's face would often still be black on these occasions from the shift (sometimes several shifts) at Permali's and his on-the-side car repair work and jobbing. And he would wear his black face like a mask – 'De Dad' as he would be called by one of his half-caste children who he in turn called 'De Moses' (her real name was Tara) in a parody of minstrel speak. Rose was to have three children with black fathers; their 'love children' as Fred called them. 'De Da!' 'De Mo!' Fred burlesqueing as black, his grubby palms pantomiming either side of his smearily blacked-out face like a performer from *The Black and White Minstrel Show*. His darky routine. The rolling whites of the eyes; the deep red of the inner lips. Like the parts left exposed by a hood mask or a knitted mask. His blackface mask. The freedom conferred by masks.

Pornographic pictures of Rose with her black lovers started to be passed around in the Arthur, the Vauxhall (where Rose had worked for a short time), the Raglan Arms and other Barton Street area pubs. Fred would show the same pictures to men at work, never failing to comment on the 'massiveness' of the man and the pleasure it gave him to watch another man 'giving a good seeing to' to his wife. One of the Jamaicans who was becoming a regular visitor to Cromwell Street told the story of going there one night when Fred was supposed to be in Cornwall and waking up with Fred in the bed between him and Rose, and drinkers in the Arthur would have a chuckle over that.

Before long Rose was going down to the Jamaica Club in

the afternoons with two of the girls who had become Crom-well Street regulars and having sex with some of the club members in a dusty small room behind the stage. One of the girls was known as 'Run-Around Sue', 'Yankee-Doodle Sue' and 'Sue Sparrow'. She was heavily tattooed and wore a black biker jacket. She had a professional tattoo on her stom-ach which was in the shape of a heart. The other girl was tall and blonde and was almost certainly the 'big buxom piece' who took Caroline Raine to the Jamaica Club after accusing her of stealing her job working as a live-in nanny for Rose and Fred. Having somebody to live in and help with the chil-dren was part of Fred's and Rose's new understanding with each other. If he wanted her to go with other men then she needed help in the house. She had other men to keep her busy and if she had any spare time she would help with repairs to the house. If he wanted these other men he was going to have to act half civilized or he could forget it. She needed a mother's help or – the word Rose preferred – a 'nanny'. The blonde was the one who asked Caroline had Rose ever tried it on with her. 'You know, tried to get into your bed with you or have sex with you or anything like that? Because she did with me. You want to watch her. Didn't you know she's both ways?' That had been the first inkling Caroline had had that Rose might be that way.

It was an encounter that took place not long after Caroline started living at Cromwell Street in October 1972, just over two months after Rose and Fred and the three children had started living there themselves. She left at the beginning of November and on 6 December was subjected to what a jury twenty-three years into the future would decide had been a 'dry run' for the abduction, rape, torture and murder of seven other women and young girls.

But when they appeared before Gloucester magistrates on Friday, 12 January 1973, to plead guilty to indecently assaulting and causing actual bodily harm to Caroline Raine, Fred West and Rose West were fined £25 on each count, a total of £100, and advised to seek psychiatric help. A hundred pounds wasn't a punishing amount of money even in those days. The defence had suggested that a degree of 'passive co-operation' had been involved on Caroline's part and the magistrates were apparently persuaded that this was the case. It was a light fine which amounted more or less to an acquittal. A verdict that would have shored up Fred West's idea of himself as being invulnerable. Confirmed his faith in his powers; his feeling of immunity. He was thirty-one and had already committed three murders. He had raped his sister and made her pregnant and he had walked away from that as well. He was special. Entitled to that which was forbidden to everybody else. Invulnerable. Fred bowed to the bench and clasped his wife's hand. Rose was just over eighteen and pregnant and receiving her first conviction.

'City Pair Stripped and Assaulted Girl' was the headline that appeared on page 9 of the following day's Gloucester *Citizen*, dated 13 January 1973. Three months later they would sexually brutalize and murder a seventeen-year-old called Lynda Gough and bury her mutilated body at the back of the house. In the two years between April 1973 and April 1975 they would murder five other girls and bury them roughly in a circle under the cellar in Cromwell Street, clockwise in the order of their deaths.

Real owners of a real house.

The foundations were exposed in the cellar. The foundations were buried underground with earth behind them. The house stood over a cellar. It was the cellar where for many years Mr Cook the coalman came once a fortnight on a Friday and dropped four hundredweight of coal. The coal tipped through the wooden trapdoor under the living-room window into the back part of the cellar, and Brian Fry's train layout was in the part of the cellar nearest the street. A small 060 truck and *The Duchess of Atholl* going around the big chipboard trestle measuring four feet by eight that Brian's uncle Ray had made him. The sounds of his grandmother moving about in the house over him and sometimes on Saturdays, the Seventh-day Adventists' sabbath, the sounds of hymn-singing coming in from the church next door. 'Amazing love!'

There was no window, only a narrow vent let into the wall by the church. The walls were brick and there were crude timber beams running from front to back. The floor was brick. But it was as if the bricks had been laid and then something had happened – some settling, a small shifting – to cause the bricks to lift a little and the ground to become uneven. The cellar was a damp place. Windowless and damp. Dank. You could sense dampness in the air there but there was no water. Not water as such. It wasn't wet in a way that would require wellingtons or special boots. Mrs Green wouldn't have kept her coal there if that had been the case. Brian Fry wouldn't have run the risk of floor-level electric points. And he is unshakeable on this fact: the cellar never flooded in all his years there. Never when he was there. No flooding or even minor seepage. No water.

And so there is a small mystery: why the cellar at Cromwell Street filled up with subterranean water and sewage in Fred's and Rose's first weeks there. Or why Fred said it had if it hadn't. As usual he had a story ready and it was a story that, after he was arrested, he would tell to the police. 'What you got round Cromwell Street used to be the moat round Gloucester. Gloucester used to have a moat round it. The moat was filled in, so you've got a very high water table.' There were embellishments touching on the soil pipe, the storm drains and a hidden underground spring. A small lesson in local history. And the cellar would gain a reputation among

Rose and the others in the house for being like a cold wet dark cave. It was gloomy and dark. The floor felt wet under your feet and the atmosphere was wet and gloomy. Water just used to ooze up through the floor. Something to do with the storm drains. The dark entity of the house. And it is certainly the case that when Heather and May and Stephen were still little and being sent down to the cellar to sleep, it would sometimes flood: they would wake up and find themselves surrounded by water in the morning and get in a wooden toy box and paddle from their beds to the stairs.

As a consequence Fred didn't allow anybody down in the cellar in the beginning, only himself. It was no fit place for a pregnant woman or small children. He'd just lock off the doors and do what he was doing. He'd just bolt them shut and they would hear the sound of work being carried out. For years he would say he was going down to see to the drains in the basement to stop this water coming up. A preoccupation that started in the weeks before and the months immediately after moving into Cromwell Street. From the beginning the many possibilities of the cellar excited him. He was going to have it as a bar with card schools. He talked a lot about making films in it – bringing in prostitutes from Birmingham and elsewhere and making home-made pornographic movies. It would be a children's room – a playroom for the children when they had parties. Or he could make it his torture chamber he joked to Liz Agius when he was showing her around the house when he was still working on it the summer before they moved in. He told one of his new lodgers in the first weeks of 1973 about his plans to convert the cellar 'into a dungeon'. The Caroline Raine court case had brought him 'loads of kinky letters' which had convinced him there was an appetite for 'parties'.

In the last years of his life Fred West was on twenty-four-hour call as a general handyman at a home for the autistic in

Minchinhampton just outside Gloucester. Stroud Court was an old and rambling building with an underground network of passages, corridors and cellars. And Fred would use any excuse to drive there late at night – to drive there even in the middle of the night – perhaps to see to a light bulb that needed changing. He would often be discovered wandering the narrow passageways and underworkings at Stroud Court apparently locked in some kind of reverie. He could stay down there for hours just wandering and never offer an explanation or feel the need to offer one. A break in the sewer pipe that ran under the house and a rise in the water table were the reasons he gave for the powerful attachment that became evident between Fred and the cellar at Cromwell Street. He could stay down there for hours apparently trying to work out a way to stem the rise of thick murky water that had reached ankle height and was relentlessly rising. To repel the inrush of the sewage – the thick, consistent water – that all the time now in their new home was threatening to engulf them.

Not difficult to see from this how the cellar represented the unconscious for the psychoanalyst C. G. Jung. Jung compared the rationality of the roof to the irrationality of the cellar. Up near the roof all our thoughts are clear. In the attic it is a pleasure to see the bare rafters of the strong framework. In the cellar darkness prevails both day and night, and even when we are carrying a lighted candle we see shadows dancing on the dark walls. In the attic rats and mice can make considerable noise but they are easily frightened into returning to the silence of their holes. The creatures moving about in the cellar are slower, less scampering, more mysterious.

They took possession of the house in Cromwell Street in July 1972 and moved in towards the end of August. There was a light at the very top of the stairs leading down to the cellar, but apart from that nothing. By the end of the year

Fred had managed to make the cellar habitable. He divided it into three interconnecting rooms including a room where his tools could live. He kept his tools in the back room nearest the garden. He began work on converting the front room into a playroom for the children. The narrow middle room, where the stairs came down from the hallway, for the time being he left empty. He would work down there all day after grabbing an hour or two's sleep after his job at Permali's, sometimes bolting the door from the hallway behind him. He worked. He just worked. He was a what's-her-name. He was a workaholic. It was even a problem for Rose to get him to bed at night.

He started working doing odd jobs and repairs for his neighbours in Cromwell Street and the other streets crowded in between the school playground and the park. In addition to working for Frank Zygmunt, he started taking on jobs for a West Indian called Alex Palmer who let out bedsits in several houses in Cromwell Street. It was an arrangement that suited Fred because it gave him access to the homes and the lives of many of his neighbours and he was an inquisitive person. He was a snoop. He was nosy. But his casual, self-effacing manner disguised the pleasure that nosing about in other people's business gave him. He was the kind of neighbour who needs to know everybody's business but fiercely protects his own. He seems to have set himself the task of quickly getting to know the territory after moving in. Twenty-two years is a very long time but, as his police interviews show, he never tired of gathering information in that time and making himself familiar with the most intimate details of many of his neighbours' lives. He was able to tell the police who was living where with whom and when. He was able to tell them who was an alcoholic and who was a child-molester. Whose daughter was taking drugs and who a lesbian and who was having an affair with whose wife.

The hitman hired to murder two lovers at Barrow Wake beauty spot, for example, lived at 1 Cromwell Street and was called Norman White. He had worked with Fred on the renovations at 25 Midland Road when he had used it as an opportunity to rebury Charmaine's body. The purpose of this interview was to investigate the murder of Charmaine. But he couldn't resist going off on digressions intended to show his inside knowledge of Norman White, who is a Jamaican, and the White family. 'He worked with me in Midland Road, putting up ceilings. When I did the six flats there. Me an' him got on great together. He was a great guy, till he got on that ganja . . . He always treated me like a gentleman. Still does to this day. Always called me Mister West. If anyone said anything about me . . . He thought the world of me . . . I've known his sisters since years. I mean, Marcia's about the same age as Anna. Very big fat girl she is, ever so pleasant . . . Lives there on her own. I know why, an' all. [Her father] potted two of his daughters. One was shipped off to America. The other daughter lost the baby in the bathroom of that house, on the floor . . . I did the whole of that house inside, decorated it some years back when Euan got married, married a Welsh girl . . .'

A long-term tenant directly opposite at 26 Cromwell Street was known for interfering with children. Also at number 26 was a girlfriend of Alex Palmer's and a good friend of Rose's who used to live with 'a short black-haired kid, always had a black dog with him. She lived with him for years. Bit of a headcase. "The screwball" we used to call him. Used to do demolition work and that . . . She had been in Coney Hill for a nervous breakdown and she was hooked on – what's that stuff I had the other night? – valium.'

Fred was beaten up by the boyfriend of a girl who was living in a bedsit at number 19 in the mid-eighties. The boy came in and found Fred West with his face pressed up against the glass shower cubicle where the girl, Carol, was showering. He had the keys to the house where he was always doing odd jobs, and he had let himself in. About a year later, towards the end of 1985, when she had moved away from Cromwell Street, Carol and her cousin Hayley were trying to trace a third girl in Gloucester. Their search took them to the Wests at number 25 and he was very friendly and welcoming and invited them in. He didn't seem to recognize her from when she had lived in the street and he brought them in and before they could say anything took them on a tour of the house. It seemed a strange thing to do but he appeared proud of the place and led them through to the kitchen at the rear where his wife was sitting surrounded by a lot of young children. It was tea-time and there was a pornographic video being shown on the television and the woman and the children were watching it. He took them to a bedroom on the ground floor at the front of the house where there was a big camera mounted on a stand at the bottom of the bed. He opened a wooden trunk and a wicker basket which Carol saw were full of videotapes. On the walls of the room were Polaroid photographs of naked men and women in various poses. She could see from the satin-finish wallpaper in the background that the photographs had been taken in that room. He showed them all of these things as if to impress them but they just felt embarrassed and uncomfortable and said that they had to leave.

On another occasion when he was helping to move a fridge for a girl who was living in a bedsit at 4 Cromwell Street he casually mentioned that he knew her mother and that he had had sex with her and so she could be his daughter. When she asked her, her mother told her that Fred was not her father but that he had raped her when she was fifteen years old. The girl's only contact with Fred after that was when she went to the house with her boyfriend to borrow pornographic videos from him which he kept all over the house.

The police investigation of 1994 succeeded in tracing a hundred and fifty people who had lived in the house at one time or another, some for a night or two, others for longer. Fred West would remember many of them for something unattractive about the way they looked or for something unpleasant that they did. But he would remember a surprising number of them. 'She was a little tiny piece . . . She was a massive big fat piece . . . She was a little fat bird with straggly hair . . . She was the biggest, tallest girl I think I've ever seen. Strong; solid-built . . . She had tattoos. Her father worked at the same place I worked at, Cotswold Tyres . . . She's a copper's daughter. CID's daughter. She lives across the back here. I know her mam. Her mam's a little short woman . . . The mother was a little skinny piece. The daughter was the most disgusting animal you ever seen in your life . . . She was heavy into drugs. Anything . . . [She was] some duchess's daughter or summat. She had a chauffeur-driven Roller. Her daughter was a big fat girl and [the police] come and dragged her out one mornin'. There was one almighty gang-bang going on . . . She was there with them and the drugs. That's what she was there for. *All* the girls was there for the same reason . . . It was just like a meeting house for . . . I mean, Rose used to go crackers at me to get rid of them.'

Not a lot that they did – very little that they did – got past him. During the years that they had the lodgers in Fred was constantly on the prowl. It wasn't a big house. The one room back and front on each of the three floors was separated by a simple wooden staircase. The cellar was kept locked. But he would roam the house at all times of the day and night. On the nights when he wasn't at work and she couldn't find him, Rose knew what he would be doing. He would be roaming the house but she would be too tired to get up and argue with him. He was doing the house up and there was always something to be done. He was buying second-hand furniture and bringing it home. Stealing beds and miscellaneous odd items of furniture and installing them in the rooms. He could always come up with a reason to take him into their rooms. He would get to know them by holding them in conversation in their rooms or wherever he could grab them. In the bedrooms or coming out of the bathroom or on the stairs. There was no lock on the lodgers' toilet door and no lock on the tiny bathroom. It would become standard in the house: no locks on any of the doors except the door into the cellar and the door of Rose's special room. It was almost impossible not to walk in on somebody using the toilet or the bathroom on the first floor but the lodgers and the space cadets who hung around with the lodgers were mostly too out of it to care. They were going in and out of the door all night long. And he made it his business to know who was coming and going when and which room they were going up to and for how long and to do what and with whom.

But he had the knack of doing it not in a proprietorial or a heavy-handed way, but in a discreet way. He was old enough to be most of these girls' father but he didn't act like that. He didn't present himself in that light. The hippy trail led to Cromwell Street. And although he might look pretty straight and *was* straight – he didn't touch drugs or drink himself – he was anxious to let them know that he was relaxed about all that. He was also especially keen to impress on them the broad-minded, free-and-easy, anything-goes attitude he took towards sex. He was obsessed with sex. You could never get away from sex. He saw sex in everything. Driving to work he would say a girl had run at him waving her knickers in the air to try and stop him. Or that a hitch-hiker he had picked up had hitched her skirt right up to her waist while he was steaming along in the van. Or that some high-class people who owned the house where he was working had invited him to an orgy in London that weekend. If he crossed the park he would see people at it on park benches. And having the lodgers in meant that within the four walls of his own home he was able to let his imagination run riot. They were taking drugs and having orgies. Gang-bangs and bombed-out orgies. What did they think, that he was stupid? All the girls, all the blokes. There were girls on the run from local homes; boys who had nowhere to go for the night. Endless parties. He smelled the smells. He heard the noises. They burned that what's-her-name but he smelled through that. They played their loud music but he knew what they were doing. These little junky birds coming and going, they didn't care who they did it with. They did it with anybody. Floaters and drifters. Floating and drifting. They were anybody's.

And he asked them the questions nobody ever asked. Questions about what it felt like and what they liked and about size. Who was the biggest? Who was the best? 'Had sex with Tony tonight then?' Smutty talk. Talking dirty to these little birds. The things nobody ever said. The questions nobody ever asked them. Rose considered Fred was advanced in his thinking when it came to sex. He would tell them things. And sometimes they might tell him things back. Startling disclosures about the sexual experiences they had had. Startling to him who considered himself an expert on the hidden insides of women's bodies and the workings of the womb. He was fascinated with the interior of the female body – the insides, the mysterious organs of sexuality and reproduction. A fascinating territory. What it all does and how it all works. A voyeuristic fantasy of peering and prying. Opening up. And they would tell him, 'Nobody has ever asked me about this before', and he would look modest and examine the tip of his roll-up and say, 'Well, yeah.'

He spent a lot of time with the lodgers and the girls who

hung around – hung out, is it what they say? – with the lodgers. Giving them lifts to places. Running them out to places and coming back afterwards to pick them up. Decorating their rooms. If they wanted to run somewhere, he would take them. They were never slow in coming forward if they needed anything or were in any kind of trouble. Fred would just drop what he was doing and run and that went for everybody in the street as well. Always something. Always round and about with them and willing. Willing to take them and willing to wait. Casually pumping these little birds about their backgrounds and families. Making mental notes about their degrees of vulnerability and rebelliousness and isolation. Weighing the odds. And always trying to bring the conversation around to sex. Back around to sex if by some chance it had happened to drift away from it. He was obsessed with sex. 'All the girls I got on great with,' Fred said. 'I used to talk fucking dirty to them and they used to talk dirty back.'

Rose had slept with Ben Stanniland and Dapper Davis, top floor back. She had slept with David Evans and Charlie Knight, top floor front. She was the landlady but she came up there now and again because she liked sex. Caroline Raine had gone with Ben and Dapper. Ben was a long-haired hippy. He was tall with long dark hair and a nice smile and he talked rather slowly on account of him always being stoned. Caroline liked Ben. He was a dopehead but she liked him. And it seems so did a lot of other girls. He never seems to have had any problems in that department. Ben was a chick magnet and able to pull. It was through Ben, who she met in a café, that Lynda Gough started coming to the house.

Lynda was unusual in that she lived at home in Gloucester with her parents. Her father was a fireman and her mother worked for the council and Lynda was the oldest of John and June Gough's four children. She was from an unbroken family. In 1973 Lynda was nineteen and had a job working as a seamstress for the Co-op on the corner of Brunswick and Eastgate Streets, a short walk away from Cromwell Street. She could wake up in Cromwell Street and, by taking the shortcut across the playground at Tommy Rich's, be at work five minutes later. 'Seamstress': an old-fashioned word for an old-fashioned job in a place where they still clock-watched and counted the minutes. Two girls and a senior, Mrs Ford. Whereas Lynda was breaking away. She wore 'granny glasses'; a version of the wire-frame National Health glasses John Lennon had made popular even with people who had nothing wrong with their eyes. Lynda had prescription lenses in hers and she wore them with a long fall of hair in the Julie Felix folk-singer style. Both things counting as small rebellions in the house she came from; signs that she had broken off from her parents' way of looking at things and was ready to go with the flow.

Lynda became part of what appears to have been a regular pattern at Cromwell Street. She started off with Ben as his girlfriend and then after a while passed on to the friend he shared with, Dapper Davis. Over a period of probably a couple of months Lynda also slept with David Evans and several of the other lodgers at Cromwell Street, always coming and going and never living there herself on a permanent basis. In her fashion glasses and her folk-singer hair. She had an ankle-length black maxi-coat. Hanging out. The Oval, where Lynda's family lived, was close enough to the city centre for June, her mother, to go home for lunch. And one lunchtime around the middle of April 1973, June Gough returned home to find a note on the kitchen table from Lynda. 'Dear Mum and Dad, Please don't worry about me. I have got a flat and I will come and see you some time. Love Lyn.' Naturally Mrs Gough did worry, not only because the money she was earning at the Co-op wasn't enough for Lynda to be able to afford a flat. Lynda had had a patchy history at school. She had gone to the local Calton Primary and then to the Longford School for children with learning difficulties. (Many years later the Longford School was to become Stroud Court, the home for autistic people whose labyrinth of cellar corridors Fred West would roam.) Lynda had completed her education at a private girls' school in Midland Road run by a couple of elderly spinsters and left when she was sixteen with no GCEs or any other academic qualifications. So to find this note and all her belongings gone. 19 April 1973, a Thursday. Their first reaction was to go out and find her. Their second was to let her have her head for a bit and she'd be back. She had rebelled against their advice like a lot of teenagers in those days and today. So, OK, she'll be back.

When they hadn't had a visit from Lynda or heard from her after about ten days June Gough paid a call on Mrs Ford in the workroom at the Co-op where Lynda had worked since leaving school. Mrs Ford had trained Lynda and watched her come on. The conversation with Mrs Ford led Lynda's mother to the house at 25 Cromwell Street which really was very near. Turn left out of the Co-op, left again down the alley between Limbars discount cash-and-carry and Jennings the printer, take the first right off the school playground and you were there. That was how close. She wanted to know if Lynda was happy. If she was all right.

It was a Saturday and a lot of people were using Cromwell Street to park in while they went to the shops. Mrs Gough walked past Mr Miles's rose beds and the church and turned in up the alley-like path between the house and the church. Her knock brought a man and a woman to the door. Mrs Gough thought she recognized the woman as somebody who had come to collect Lynda to go for a drink with her shortly before she left home. But the couple denied having any knowledge of Lynda. They had never met Lynda, they didn't know

Lynda and they didn't know where she was. But then Mrs Gough recognized the slippers the woman had on as Lynda's slippers. They were the slippers Lynda had been wearing when she left. And there were other things. The woman was wearing a blouse or a cardigan of Lynda's and there were further items of Lynda's clothing hanging in the garden on a line.

Now the lady who was wearing Lynda's slippers and who one day very many years in the future would stand in court and deny that she had ever been that kind of person at all – 'I'm not the sort of person who would wear anybody else's things. I'm rather proud that way' – now the lady said that Lynda had gone. She remembered now yes, and she had gone. She had been there but she said she had gone and said something about going to Weston-Super-Mare. The couple thought Weston but they said they weren't sure. Lynda's mother and father were feeling very hurt that Lynda had gone and hadn't contacted them. They felt abandoned was the word. They cared, that's the point. They *cared*. Lynda's mother said all this but she got no feedback. There was nothing coming back, and so she turned and went.

Lynda's mother and father went to Weston to try and find Lynda but everywhere they looked they drew blanks. Although they appreciated that she was nearly twenty and therefore was not considered vulnerable, they reported her disappearance to a neighbour who was a policeman, contacted the Salvation Army and wrote to the DSS. But nothing. There was no trace.

Lynda's remains were found at twenty-five past two on a Monday afternoon in March 1994 under the floor of the ground-floor bathroom area of 25 Cromwell Street, the eighth set of remains to be found at the address. Forensic evidence established that her body had been buried there for nearly twenty-one years.

Many bones were missing, particularly from the feet and

hands. Several fingers and toes and wrist bones had been taken away. Her head was separate and the legs had been dislocated at the hip. The kneecaps were not there. There were no buttons or zips or anything to suggest that Lynda had been wearing clothes when she was killed. Apart from her bones the only items recovered from the hole where she had been buried were a length of string, a disintegrated fragment of fabric and a packing-tape gag similar to the one that Caroline Raine had described being wound around her head in the Wests' car just four months before Lynda Gough was last seen. It was a ring mask or gag, two inches wide and fifteen inches in circumference, brown in colour and containing brittle fragments of hair. The circular mask of tape had been excavated close to the skull, embedded in the pit wall.

Rose was five months pregnant with Stephen when Lynda Gough was murdered. She had just started on this pregnancy when the assault on Caroline Raine occurred and Fred told Caroline that 'When Rose gets pregnant her lesbian urges get stronger and she has to have a woman and she really wanted you.' 'When Rose was pregnant she was always extra sexy,' he would claim to the police many years later.

May was nearly a year old, Heather was two and a half, and Anna-Marie was nearly nine in April 1973. Lynda had done some babysitting for Fred and Rose but that had stopped when she started hitting Anna-Marie. This anyway is what Rose told Dave Evans and some of the other lodgers when she went upstairs at breakfast time one morning to explain Lynda's sudden disappearance from the house and why she wouldn't be coming round to the house again.

Major building work started at the beginning of the summer on the Seventh-day Adventists' church next door. They tore down the old tin and tar-paper building and started to put up an extensive new brick building in its place. The new church was several times bigger than the old one. It came forward to meet the pavement at the front and extended to the edge of the Wests' property all along the left-hand side. In order to construct the church's south-facing wall, which as it happened was the wall where the altar was going to be, they had to put scaffolding in the Wests' garden for what they said would be weeks but turned out to be several months. There was scaffolding in the back garden all summer and cement dust and brick dust. It was a hot summer and it was dirty and dusty and Fred decided to use the opportunity of the dust and confusion to do some building work himself.

Rose's special room was on the left as you came in the front door. On the right as you came in was another room of a similar size, with a window facing the garden. In the far left-hand corner of that room was a door leading down three steps into the kitchen, which was housed in a narrow, single-storey brick building jutting out into the garden. Just outside the kitchen was an outdoor toilet. And on the other side of the toilet was a potting shed with shingle walls and a corrugated metal roof and a window which had given a view of the apple and pear trees of Mrs Green's 'orchard'. And with three children and a fourth on the way and the lodgers monopolizing the upstairs, Fred decided to steal some extra space for the family by dropping the shed and turning the place where it had stood into a second bathroom. He would turn the toilet into a shower, add a combination toilet–bathroom, and house them all in one twelve-foot extension the same width (or narrowness) as the kitchen. He got some of the boys from the top floor to help with the shed and, when he needed her to, Rose helped him with the building. A workmate of Fred's would remember coming round one night and seeing Rose up on a roof applying tar from a bucket. Men he worked with at Permali's were regular visitors at this time, either to borrow pornography or to have sex with Rose. 'It would be easier if people asked me who Rose didn't have sex with, not who she did,' Fred said. 'When I was in Permali's, the blokes were taking an hour off and going up and fucking Rose. I never thought nothing of it.' Rose was up on the roof extension wearing a heavy coat and wellington boots. She was obviously pregnant and working under light from a tilley lamp and applying tar from a bucket. The roof looked to be unsafe and was supported only by one wall and a telegraph pole and Fred's friend from work found it to be comical. But he would also remember that visit for another reason. Anna-Marie was nine and Fred accused her of screwing in the park when she came in and this struck the man as strange.

Fred West buried Lynda Gough under the dirt floor of Mrs Green's shed, although he would choose to describe it as the 'inspection pit' of a garage. The implications of both, however, are the same. they were grave-size and grave-shaped and obviously suggested themselves to him as graves. But for this to make sense Lynda's body would have to have been intact when he put it in the hole and we know that this wasn't the case. There were cut marks on the femurs, or thigh bones, consistent with her legs having been severed at the hip, and her head had been removed. In other words, he had the space to bury Lynda's body without mutilating it if he chose to do it. That he didn't do it but dismembered her body instead shows that the dismemberment wasn't done for time reasons or convenience, as he always claimed, but for compulsive and obsessive reasons and for the pleasure it brought. The arousal and the pleasure.

He put plastic membrane over the hole when the cover of the shed was gone and mixed concrete and poured it and erected a structure with a bath and a toilet in it which he referred to from then on as his conference room or his office. He would sit on the toilet with his feet adjacent to the pit where Lynda Gough was buried and call out to one of his children to come and see him in his office. They would have to sit on the stolen bath and talk to him while he sat with his trousers around his ankles on the stolen toilet. Sit on the edge of the bath and talk to him across the space of a dead girl's body.

The bathroom extension was completed in time for Stephen's arrival in August 1973. Their first son. The son they had always wanted. Fred brought in Rose a massive big bunch of flowers and the biggest box of All Gold she had ever seen.

By the standards of Cromwell Street in the seventies, which contained the whole inventory of urban anarchy, the people living at number 25 seemed a model family. Father with a steady job and a commitment to home improvement; hard-working young mother who still managed to keep herself presentable and attractive; a baby and three young children who were polite, quiet and well turned out. She would see him off with a kiss at the door when he left for work in the evening and there would always be a breakfast waiting for him on the table in the morning. And soon Fred fixed a sign to the outside of the house that was almost a badge of their standing and a declaration of their respectability.

First, he coated the house in a suburban, biscuit-coloured cladding. Next he put up a suburban wrought-iron plaque with '25 Cromwell Street' spelled out in white-painted metal letters framed in fancy metal scrolling. Everybody did their little perks at the factory where he was working and the 'Cromwell Street' sign was one of his. The man on the next machine did it for him. Drew it up on a piece of paper and cut out the letters with a computerized burner. Burnt it out in metal when the foreman wasn't watching with a profile machine.

This sign, the sign of his stability and respectability. The murderer posing as unremarkable father and working man.

And a second sign, identical in every detail, the sign of his drives and perversions, which he fixed to a bed that he made. Using a lathe at work he made the pieces of a dark oak four-poster and assembled the pieces when he got them back to Cromwell Street. He got the whole family to help him fix the corner posts to the bed base and lastly the heavy oak canopy around the top. And after construction came decoration: four bulls, one on top of each bedpost; and on the side a bull and a cow – a toy bull and a toy cow; farmyard animals from a toyshop – stuck together as though they were having sex. The wrought-iron sign he had made went on the bed's front pelmet and it said 'Cunt'. In the same letters and to the same dimensions as the sign on the front of the house, framed in fancy scrolling and for their eyes only, it said just that: 'Cunt.'

After Rose – perhaps even before Rose – his most precious possession was his house. So he had two signs made. Two bells and two signs. Had the lettering burnt out for him and turned the scrolling and welded it together himself. One sign – '25 Cromwell Street' – he put up by the entrance to his house. The second sign – 'Cunt' – he put up over the entrance to his wife. This obsession he had with entrances and thresholds. He would dedicate the remainder of his life to his lust to look and his need to explore orifices and holes. Holes in his house which he packed with the headless and legless torsos of girls and young women: he said he 'always wanted the body to fit the hole'. And the bodily holes of his wife and other women and girls. He tried to take internal pictures of Rose using a torch and a zoom lens and, in later years, a video camera. Zooming in. Coming up close. He really wanted to get inside them. Such an appetite he had for looking. His ambition was to own a pencil camera of the kind used with pregnant women. He wanted to come as close as he could.

This was something even his children knew about Fred.

'He had a thing about women's bodies – he was into internal bits . . . He'd think, "I wonder what that looks like" and have a look,' Stephen said. 'He wanted to go right into the body and look at the internal organs,' May said.

He had two pictures of Rose that always fascinated him. One was of Rose sitting on a gearstick in a car. The other was a picture of Rose taken when she was pregnant. She was sitting back with her feet far apart and her legs open in the stirrup position and on her stomach she had written the words 'My black hole', intended as a message for Fred. A message written in lipstick with an arrow pointing to between her legs for Fred who was behind the camera.

What it all does and how it all works. The opening to a strange and secret place. This *unheimlich* place which is the entrance to the former home of all human beings. The place where Fred lived once upon a time and in the beginning. A place of unaccounted secrets and horrors.

'We've found another hole,' Mr Bennett, the policeman in charge of the search for bodies inside 25 Cromwell Street would say whenever another body was found.

Chapter Nine

Fred was going to be as famous as Elvis Presley. One day. He told this to his workmates at the wagon works. Bullshitter Fred. It was semi-skilled work. Repetitive, terrible, boring work, bending the same job or drilling the same job all day. Minute after minute; hour after hour. And a piece of Fred's bullshit, some of his bull, could lighten the day. The Elvis Presley crack. The stories about bringing a couple of prostitutes in from Birmingham to go three-in-a-bed lesbian with his wife. This. That. That little lisp. That chipped front tooth. A likeable kind of a bullshitter is what he was.

He had left Permali's on the Bristol Road with an anti-testimonial or reference. 'Do not re-employ this man. If anybody thinks of re-employing this man, do not.' The personnel officer of Permali's was a magistrate. A JP and a woman. He was in court for a few different things then, and that's how that came about when he left. She met him in the corridor and had a right old go at him. He went to get his cards and she flew at him. Massive big fat woman she was. She had done her worst but he had come out of Permali's and walked straight into another job.

In 1974 in the summer he moved to a job that he was going to keep longer than any job. He started at Gloucester Wagon Works that summer and he would stay there for the next ten years. From the ages of thirty-three to forty-three he worked in the machine shop at the wagon works, formerly Gloucester Wagon and Carriage Company, a canal-side firm with a hundred-year history, a ten-minute walk away from Cromwell

Street directly across the park. It was a noisy shop and it was dirty work. The wagon works was where they made the shells for railway carriages and trains for the London Underground. Panel plates for dumpers, diggers, earth-moving equipment, rolling stock. In the early eighties they would repair all the vehicles that came back from the Falklands War – diggers from the landing strips, transporters with their wheels blown off. It was a patriotic job. Dumpers and diggers with the dirt of the Falklands still on them straight off the television news. It was heavy, dirty work. And it was noisy. Heavy machines, big brake-presses, welders, drills, you name it, all running round you. Overhead cranes bombing over your head.

But they were a good group of men grafting in a relaxed and happy atmosphere that was down to the foreman Ronnie Cooper, who was Gloucester born and bred. A fur-and-feather man and a skittler. A good old Gloucester boy. It was too noisy to talk even during breaktimes which were usually taken at your bench. It was a seven-thirty start with a break at ten for what was known as the morning lunch. But there were ways of communicating that didn't involve shouting above the noise, visual signals and jokes, comical signs, and that was the atmosphere there. There were men who didn't take to Fred's boasts and jokes. He boasted so much to everybody that they didn't want to know. Men who used to call him the biggest bastard liar out. All he ever talked about was women. Work and women. If he'd had one woman he'd say he'd had a hundred. Bullshit city. But there were others who would regularly go to his house and he would go to theirs. They borrowed tools from one another, small chainsaws and rotavators, and did each other small favours in return. Colin Price, who helped Fred guillotine the metal for his house sign, kept cold-water fish and so did Fred. Fred had a tank, Colin had a pond and they traded ornamental fish. In after-work hours, though, he wasn't a joiner. Being near the docks there was a high concentration of pubs around the works which occupied a massive piece of land between Southgate Street and the docks. And the rest of Ronnie Cooper's men would go drinking together regularly but Fred never wanted to go. He wouldn't mix with anybody. Good worker, mind. Brilliant worker. He became known for moving large sheets of metal manually rather than wait for the crane to move them. He was very strong and wouldn't wait because he was on piecework. Always at work. He'd work all the hours God sends. But he wouldn't mix. He wouldn't drink. He never drank. He wouldn't go to a pub at all and always said he was too busy if they asked him. Said he had too much to do. But he was a good worker to Ronnie Cooper – he did his job – and that's all Ronnie Cooper as foreman bothered about.

All in all it was a good working atmosphere, as was proved by the length of service of most of the men there. Ronnie Cooper had already been at the wagon works for more than twenty years when Fred joined in 1974, and there were many among the men who worked under him who could come close to that. Close to a hundred men all with good service records. And there were perks. Everybody did their little perks. Wall brackets, hanging-basket brackets, fireguards, shelf supports, garden gates if they could get them out. And as long as it was within reason and done using what they called swarf and scraps, during the lunch hour or in break-time, Ronnie turned a blind eye.

When Fred West was in Winson Green Prison in Birmingham many years later facing trial on twelve charges of murder and had come to the decision to kill himself, he would go about it in a typically devious, thorough and concentrated way. He volunteered to mend the shirts of the other prisoners at Winson Green. And having volunteered he started cutting off and collecting tapes from the laundry bags the shirts arrived in. At the same time he was also stealing narrow strips of material from the hems of his prison blankets and twisting and sewing them together to make a noose. A ligature measuring eighty-eight inches by seven-and-a-half inches thick when he finished, put together from slyly snipped-off, scavenged, stored and plaited bits. Innocuous pieces and fragments collected and concealed over days and probably weeks and made into the means by which to take his own life.

And when he decided to build contraptions and devices on which to fasten and sexually brutalize his eight-year-old daughter he went about it using offcuts and bits of discarded metal from work in the same kind of obsessive, scheming way; with the same level of stealth and concealment.

The high front gates at the entrance to the house and the sign outside the house with '25 Cromwell Street' written on it were both constructed from the same basic components: straight pieces of metal and pieces of metal bent into florets and curved into S-shapes then welded into patterns. An attempt to make hard metal look softer and like something it wasn't. Like something organic or plant-like. Like tendrils. Clinging creeper or tendrils which contrasted forcibly with the house's slab-sided and unornamented flatness.

With the church building finished there was now a solid wall down the right side of the path going to the house rather than the old wooden fence. And he didn't waste any time in using the church wall as an anchor for one of a pair of arched gates that he brought out of the wagon works piece by piece and welded together when he got the pieces home. They were gates that Anna-Marie and Heather and May and Stephen and the five younger children when they came along would all be kept securely locked behind. He fixed a heavy silver lock to the tall silver gates and told them repeatedly all through their lives that they were better off behind them. He would tell them repeatedly that it was for their own good that they were kept shut up behind them and that it was safer. 'We don't want to have anything to do with people outside,' he said. 'We don't need them . . . You're with people who will protect you.' They weren't allowed to have friends to stay overnight and they weren't allowed to stay with friends. They wanted the family kept really tight. They wanted the family kept a vacuum. The gate was fixed at one side to the wall of the house and at the other to the wall of the church. A double gate with two opening parts to it and only its height perhaps – it was head height – alluding to a bleaker purpose.

He took the bells off the door and attached them to the gate when it was in position. One bell for general callers at the house and a second for Rose's visitors who knew that they had reached the right house when they saw the mock suburban sign. A different ringing bell for 'Mummy's friends'. Fred had started advertising for partners for Rose in contact magazines and he would remain in the room while 'Mandy's' visitors removed their clothes to make sure, he said, that she was all right. Rose was also having female visitors – what Fred called 'lemons', like the seventeen-year-old who many years later would remember having a mechanical dildo pushed into her which seemed to appear from nowhere. She hadn't been aware of its existence until she felt it move in her: 'She did it so quick it hurt me a lot and she held it up there inside me. I had to ask her to take it out because it was hurting so much.' People were also being directed to the Wests' house by the Private Shop, Gloucester's only sex shop, which in those days was still in Barton Street, not far away.

Garden gates were a perk that a lot of the men did; a lot of the men at the wagon works had made house signs in that style. Things that could be put together and taken apart again. The brackets for hanging baskets, the fireguards, the filigree shelf supports, the just a little bit elevated house signs

– elevated above the neighbours'. But neither Colin Price, Derek Clayton, Roger Kelly nor any of them could have guessed to what uses the pieces of bent and straight metal that they helped Fred with were going to be put. They watched the flame-cutting machine follow the dark path of the pencil and they didn't know.

The circumstances he found himself working in at the wagon works would allow him to refine the contraptions to which Anna-Marie was going to be subjected. But a few months earlier, while he was still employed at Permali's, he had come in with a metal object that instantly made Anna-Marie, who was eight, feel unnerved. She didn't know why because he said he'd made it as a toy for the children. And Heather and May would sit in the middle of this curved bar and sort of rock on it. It was a metal bar shaped like a U with two protruding handles. Two wings. And for reasons that were unknown to her, while the younger children played with it and rocked on it, Anna-Marie tried not to pay too much attention to this contraption or device. In time it found its way down to the front part of the cellar which was becoming a children's play area. And that was where Anna-Marie next saw it. The first time she saw it was when he brought it in and she had seen it in the living room rocking and she had thought it might be some kind of rocking-horse toy with other bits still to come. The second time was when she saw it in the cellar and even more so seeing it in that dimly lit place she suspected it had a sinister purpose straightaway.

She was told they wanted her in the cellar. There had been some whispering between them and some quiet laughing and then they came to her and ordered her down there. She was very apprehensive but she did as she was told. And when she was halfway down she saw this object against the wall. She wanted to go back up but Rose was behind her on the stairs. They were leading her one behind and one in front into the cellar playroom which they usually got to by using the old coal hatch at the back. They had been in the house only a few weeks. It was late 1972. Perhaps they had been in the house as little as a month. And in those weeks the door leading down to the cellar from the front of the house had been kept locked. Anna had been in the playroom section before but she had never actually played there. She was kept too busy doing the housework for that. The playroom section was at the front. The section that her father kept his tools in was at the back. And when they were through the door that was generally kept bolted in the hall, Rose turned and bolted it at their backs.

On the floor there was a Pyrex bowl and a cloth, a vibrator and tape. A smooth white vibrator – of course being still a child then she didn't know what it was – and a roll of strong black tape. Anna was very frightened. She didn't know what was happening. There was a thin single mattress and the bent metal device or contraption or whatever you could call it standing against the wall. She was asking what are these things for and there was nothing coming back. There was no answer. As the three of them stood at the bottom of the stairs she suddenly began to get nervous. All of a sudden there was an atmosphere she couldn't fathom or work out. There was something between them and she wasn't quite in on this. Then she had her clothes removed. She was crying. Asking what's going on? What's happening? And she was told that she should be very grateful and lucky that she had such caring parents. That when she got married she would be able to satisfy her husband. What they were doing would mean that she would be able to keep her husband. Struggling. She had her legs crossed. Screaming and crying. Her dad said, 'Just do as you're told. Take your clothes off and put them on the floor. Go on. Get on with it.' She didn't understand but she started to do it anyway. But she obviously wasn't quick enough for Rose. Almost in one movement Rose ripped her thin summer dress right off. And all the time they were laughing and threatening her and telling her to just shut up and things would be all right. Stop being silly. They were doing it to her because they loved her. It was for her own good. Ripped her dress as she tore it off her and threw it on the floor. Then they pinned her to the thin foam mattress and tied her hands and ankles to the metal frame. The ugly U-shaped metal frame. She was eight years old and had no understanding of what was about to happen to her but she knew it was something awful and that it was going to hurt. Her father used the strong black tape to secure her ankles and her feet. Rose used thin strips of torn sheeting to tie her hands and arms to the wings of the metal contraption either side of her head. Above and to the side. Rose sat on her face. She had started panicking. She was making noise and shouting and panicking. And so Rose sat on her head and face. She had a gag put over her mouth by Rose who was laughing and then Rose squatted on her face. It was something that had to be done and other families were doing exactly the same sort of thing. Her father forcing her legs open. And because she was struggling so much she had her hands bound and she was gagged. Trussed up. She couldn't see what was happening with Rose sat across her. Her private parts exposed in the centre of the frame. And she felt excruciating pain. She screamed out very loud and Rose sat on her head again because she was screaming. Gagged by Rose with some material. Like a 'bit', isn't it? Like a horse's mouth. Like a bridle on a horse. A white smooth vibrator and redness in a bowl. Red things had been taken out from inside her. She was terrified. It frightened her. But she also felt she shouldn't be so ungrateful. She was led to believe that all loving parents were acting the same. There was a buzzing noise that she didn't understand. Her stepmother grabbing her breasts and scratching and making them bleed. It seemed to go on for a long time. 'If you don't lose your virginity young, then the older you get the more it will send you mental.' This was her father who was now on top of her. Raping her while her stepmother watched. Rose smirking and joining in and telling her to stop being silly. And then it stopped and they went away leaving her crying and cold. And then they came back and it started again. She waited for their shadows to show on the wall and finally she saw them and all of it started over again.

Fred West was desperate to stay the owner of 25 Cromwell Street. He had worked a lot on the house in the weeks they had been there and he was fiercely committed to it becoming their home. The abuse of Caroline Raine was the first exercise of the new freedoms it had brought him. Or maybe, as seems likely, the first exercise of these new freedoms was the abuse of Anna-Marie. The binding and raping of Anna-Marie. One day when she was living with them he had told Caroline Raine that Anna-Marie wasn't a virgin. He had told her in September that Anna-Marie, who was eight, had already lost her virginity. Caroline had been aware of him watching her carefully while he was telling her this, and when he observed how she reacted – she was upset and angry; repulsed by what she was having to hear – he said, 'She fell off her pushbike and hurt herself.' The saddle had come off Anna-Marie's Chopper bike and she had gone to sit on it without realizing and damaged herself. He was a story-telling cowboy. He was a bastard liar. Bullshitter Fred.

He had murdered Anna-Marie's mother and her sister a year earlier. It was almost exactly a year. He had got away with that. He stood at the centre of a magic circle swathed in a cloak of immunity. He had got away with that and he would get away with this. Making themselves familiar with the freedoms the house was bringing them. Shoring up Fred

West's idea of himself as being invulnerable. Confirming his faith in his powers.

Afterwards Rose was really nice to her. When she had completed her ordeal and there was no more fun to be had from her, Anna-Marie was allowed upstairs to wash and Rose was really nice then. Rose used to run a bath and put salt in it, say it would sting but it would make it feel better and heal it. She was so kind to her. Got her a sanitary towel and helped her clean herself up. 'Our family were aware of our bodies because my stepmother and my father would touch each other and would kiss and cuddle in front of us children,' Anna-Marie said. Rose would be standing up at the sink wearing no knickers and Fred would walk in and put his hand straight up her skirt. He would smell his fingers and then put his fingers under the children's noses for them to smell. He would always grope Rose in front of them. She only minded if his hands were dirty. It was just their way. 'Smell that, that's your mother.' In the summer she would just wear an apron. They were told at a young age what sanitary towels were for.

The second device Fred was able to make with the help of his workmates during his break periods at the wagon works, although they were unaware that they were helping to make them, was a more sophisticated device altogether. It was a metal cup object. Anna-Marie, who had to wear it, described it as 'a bit like an egg cup with two handles'. An egg cup constructed from ribs of soldered metal so it looked more like a cage. A battery-operated vibrator fitted loosely inside it and Anna-Marie was made to wear both of these objects under her clothes. It used to pinch. It used to hurt. The vibrator inside her; the metal object which was fixed to her by a belt around her waist holding the vibrator in place. She had to walk around the house with it held inside her and the buzzing noise. For some years she was forced to walk around the house doing the dusting and other jobs while wearing this. This hurting cage contraption barely covered by a little mini--skirt. They were doing it to her because they loved her. It was for her own good. It was a normal situation in families. Everybody does it to every girl. It's something everybody does but nobody talks about. It's a father's job. Rose would get a real kick out of it and if Fred came home from work and found Anna in it he would just laugh along. The two of them laughing. Anna was warned not to tell anybody what happened. Rose couldn't wait for Fred to come home and see the humiliation of his daughter so she could have a good gloat.

Fred saw himself as being experimental; an experimenter. He cast himself in the role of scientist, investigator and sociological note-taker. And in this and many other ways he was closer to the Victorians than to the 'permissive' times going on in his house all around him and which he would so like to have felt himself a part of.

The sexual torture of women, masquerading as social or moral hygiene, was a practice advanced by many Victorian social reformers and investigators. The Contagious Diseases Acts of the late-nineteenth century, for example, were meant as sanitary measures to control the spread of venereal disease. What they meant in practice was that any prostitute or 'fallen' woman could be made to submit to a gynaecological inspection which involved her being forcibly strapped down and 'speculumed'.

The black market for virgins in Victorian times – a market that Fred West claimed to Liz Agius and others that he was supplying in the West Country in the seventies – stimulated a medical sideline in the certification of virgins by midwives and doctors. The ritualized degradation that this involved, the voyeurism and the violation of women's bodies, was something Fred West would inflict on his own daughters and other young women and girls. His lifelong obsession with the insides of bodies, with the 'dark centre' and the mysterious organs of sexuality and reproduction, was something that Heather and May and Fred's and Rose's younger daughters would come to know at first hand.

He wanted to know every detail of their periods and at what time of the month they occurred. He would call it rag week. 'I see Harry Wragg's riding in the two thirty.' That was his way of saying you had your period. They always wondered how he knew, but he did. He kept the details in a little black book. When it was their 'time' they weren't allowed to ride their bikes, play games, run or go to the fairground. If any of the girls were irritable around that time, he would say, 'You need a man to knock that out of you.' He taunted them and told the other children not to go near them. He was fascinated with 'women's problems'. May had thrush once and he made her tell him all about it – the symptoms and everything. Anything May said to her mother would get back to him and he would want to talk her through it and show her pictures. May was reading a pamphlet on cystitis and he completely took it over and went through it all with her because there was a diagram of a woman's insides.

The 'instrumental rape' that nineteenth-century doctors inflicted on prostitutes and the virgins who were being supplied to Victorian brothels is something Fred West also inflicted on women with a metal speculum which he claimed had been left behind by a midwife after a visit to the house. 'We put it in her, look in with a torch and things like that, and try to film inside as well,' he told the police. 'It shows the womb, like, inside.' The anatomist's cruel disinterest. Anatomy: a science of seeing, and therefore of knowing and controlling the body. Penetrating through the skin surface down to tendons, veins, arteries, and bones. Bending back the joints until they break and separate. A voyeuristic fantasy of peering and prying.

Fred West's fascination with the possibilities of the speculum eerily echo those of the speculum's inventors in the mid-nineteenth century. The American gynaecologist Marion Sims, for instance, experienced himself as a 'colonizing and conquering hero'. 'I saw everything as no man had ever seen before . . . I felt like an explorer in medicine who first views a new and important territory.' And the metal contraptions Fred dreamed up at the wagon works for his children bear a striking resemblance to the inventions of another Victorian doctor, the German child-rearing zealot Daniel Schreber. Inventions like the *Geradehalter*, a portable, T-shaped metal contraption that could be screwed on to any desk at school or at home, and was for preventing slumping while doing homework. By pressing hard against the child's crotch, the vertical bar of the *Geradehalter* discouraged leg-crossing and thigh-pressing and other acts of moral degeneracy. The *Kopfhalter*, or head holder, prevented the child's head from falling forwards or sideways. The 'abominal' head-pressing machine did what its name suggested. Both resembled the head cage that Stephen West would be forced to wear as he grew older. Made of ribs of metal, it was closed around Stephen's head and hooked over the back of the settee and he would be made to watch filmed pornography in it without any sign of blinking. If he blinked or attempted to move his mother would hit him in the face with a shoe or an ashtray or whatever was closest. Smash him in the face. Stare him out. The West children, like the Schreber children, were chained or strapped or handcuffed to their beds at night so that all body movement was rendered impossible. During the day under the Schreber regime the lower part of the child's body could be locked into metal contraptions that served as underwear. It was not uncommon for children to be sexually stimulated by their governesses and then bound up in leather straps or chains or metal underwear to ensure that they would not masturbate.

It is probable – virtually certain – that Fred West had never heard of Dr Schreber. He couldn't read. But the central library and reference library are only yards from Cromwell Street and he might have seen illustrations. The central library and reference library are only one street over and he might have gone in there and looked at pictures. Looked at drawings and illustrations of the hundred-year-old Schreber devices; the *Geradehalter* and the *Kopfhalter* and the literature of social purity and anti-vice groups, and misinterpreted them. Inverted them. Let his imagination run riot. In any case it would have tickled him to take contraptions that were intended to purge children of 'unnatural' passions and use them to incite aberrant sexual feelings in children. Pervert and corrupt them and make them compliant to his own wishes. Growing up in a world where wrong was right and up was down. An upside-down universe with little in it that was straight and plumb, square and level, right and true, only warpedness and deviation. Inversion and deviation. What was confusing was that Mum was a really nice mum if she wasn't being nasty. And if Fred hadn't been abusing them he would have been a really good dad. But he used to grab their hands and put them up their mother's skirt and then push them in their faces. 'Smell that, that's your mother.' He would get nasty and really aggressive if they told him to leave them alone and pushed him away. 'What sort of girl is it that won't let their dad touch them?' he'd say. 'Every girl should let their dad touch them.'

He would take tapes and narrow strips of blanket and turn them into the noose with which he was going to hang himself. And he took belts and turned them into a cat-o'-nine-tails and restraining harnesses. His scavenging eye. A large number of sexual harnesses of varying sizes and strengths would be recovered from Cromwell Street. He made the cat-o'-nine-tails for their messing about. His and Rose's.

266

Leather belts and plastic belts. He had an eye for spotting use in something that had been discarded by everybody else as useless. It was something he made for their life.

At one time Rose wore a weightlifter's belt. It made her look butch and powerful. It was broad at the back, narrow and buckled in front. It was broad, cinched. At all times she liked to wear a belt under her clothes and so was like Fred's mother in that habit. Big, thick, black, leather, powerful. She liked to use the belt to give you a thrashing. And she used to like to wet it first. Wet leather stings. Still not yet twenty and still not fat. In fact she was a nice slim girl. She was a smart girl. Ronnie Cooper and other men from the wagon works found her that way. Ronnie often wondered what she saw in Fred at the time. When he was dolled up, mind, Fred was smart. But few and far you saw Fred dolled up. Fred just stayed dirt black.

Rose was smart and slim but showing signs to those who knew her of the vocational humiliator and vindicatrix now. Rose made no attempt to hide her cruel streak. She didn't try to hide the beatings she doled out to Anna-Marie. In those days Heather and May never got it and of course Stephen was only a baby. They were too young to get it. Only just under two and three. There was only Anna-Marie. Rose pulling her hair, dragging her by the hair, kicking, swearing, shouting. She would drag her into the bedroom and tape up her mouth. Tear a piece of tape off and tape it across her mouth. Strips of sheet or washing line. Straps. Tie her hands behind her back or sometimes tightly in front of her. She might be tied to the bed with her legs spreadeagled or bound together. Anything. She was unpredictable. Sometimes your legs were tied open, and sometimes your hands were tied behind your back. And once you were trussed up and unable to move the assault would begin. Apart from the belts she had canes and whips including the cat-o'-nine-tails Fred had made for their life.

Rose in an ecstasy of anger like a performance. Once you realized you were in for it it was difficult to get away. Often she had stripped you naked in an instant and there was nowhere to run. Rose felt Anna-Marie was her father's favourite and perhaps to some extent she was. And for that she was always going to pay.

Rose would grab Anna-Marie's hand and plunge it in boiling water. Or photograph her alone and naked against the bedroom wall. On one occasion she grabbed her and plunged her bodily into a boiling bath. You would see a coolness transforming Rose's face. Then her eyes would disconnect. Internal and external doors were locked including the gates that led to the street to indicate the onset of a major rage. She never said why she did it and you knew never to ask. You never knew what brought on one of Rose's moods. Rose just loved to be the boss.

Of all the humiliations that happened to Anna-Marie – just one big joke to Rose – something that happened when she was aged about ten is the one she will never forget. Rose stripped her naked and got Heather and May to paint pictures on her with fingerpaints; they used pink ones, the kind of paints you can buy in Mothercare and children love making a mess with. Heather and May were having fun and although Anna didn't like it she could cope. But then Rose joined in. She made Anna get on all fours and, using black paint, she wrote 'black hole' on her bottom and an arrow. She had to stay like that all afternoon until Fred came home. When he did Rose said to him, 'I've been doing some painting, love', and laughed. Fred laughed when he saw what she'd done. They both laughed and Heather and May laughed seeing Fred and Rose so happy although they were too young to know what for. When she was given permission to wash it off Anna sat on the floor of the bathroom where Lynda Gough had recently been buried on the concrete and cold lino and cried. All this was all on her body and she was shamed and humiliated and she cried.

Fred got on with the machine he was put to work on at the wagon works very well. He picked it up very quick. It was a partnership and they were going to be together for ten years. The job description was 'driller'. And that was the job: drilling. He took to it within half an hour. Bringing the drill bit down and just drilling holes. Big holes. Small holes. It was an Asquith drill. A big radial drill with a capability of drilling up to six-inch holes. Small holes. Big holes. Minute after minute; hour after hour. And with an imagination like his. A mind like his. One track. Into the hole and out of the hole. Out and in. Poke, pole, pork, pump, prod. All day every day. Repetitive, terrible, boring work. All day drilling the same job. Boring. Drilling. The big drill going into the hole. Bringing it down and penetrating the plate. Plunging the drill through the metal and pulling out. Blinding worker. Always at work.

He'd come home from work and she'd sit deliberately on the edge of the settee with her legs wide open and say, 'Look at that . . . I bet you wish you had something that could fill that . . . ' It never stopped. It didn't stop at all. There was no let up. *Fuck me harder!* and all this she had picked up from the porno films. *Fill me up!*

Minute after minute. In and out. Day after day. Out and in. It was a noisy shop and it was dirty work. Heavy machines, big brake-presses, welders, drills, you name it, all running round you. Overhead cranes bombing over your head. Penetrating. Entering. Staying tight.

Bringing things into holes. Pushing things down in holes. A small, deep, well-dug hole. Vertical rather than horizontal. A narrow shaft. Preparing shafts. Peering into holes. Peering and prying. Black holes. *Fuck me harder!* Tight fits. Narrow shafts.

V.W.E. in the shorthand of the contact magazines. Very Well Endowed. Sexy housewife needs it deep and hard from V.W.E. male. Husband likes to watch.

Fred would set up the camera and Rose would often perform alone in a room for him so that he could watch it in his own time later. Rose bringing bigger and bigger objects inside herself and holding herself open to his gaze. A pint glass. A large orange. A whisky tumbler. A lager can. They amassed more and more and bigger and bigger sexual accessories and vibrators. They kept them in drawers. Under the beds. In a big black trunk in Rose's special room. The bigger the better. The bigger and the blacker the better for Rose, Fred decided.

Rose knew what Fred wanted. Rose knew what Fred wanted to see. She knew what he wanted to hear.

The following exchange tailored for Fred's listening took place between Rose and one of her 'visitors' and was videoed by Fred. He set up the camera, adjusted the lighting (it was daytime; sun was striping the bed through the Venetian blind, top floor back), and left the room to listen downstairs.

ROSE   Fuckin' hell . . . It's fucked me for the night. You have an' all.

MAN   [laughing] I can't help it, can I?

ROSE   It's massive that . . . Is it classified as a dangerous weapon?

MAN   [laughing] Dunno. I wouldn't have thought so.

ROSE   I should register it if I was you.

Feeding Fred's eyes. Feeding Fred's ears. Rose then steered the conversation in a different but connected direction. Pillow talk intended for Fred. The kind of talk Rose knew Fred liked to hear.

ROSE They tore our road to bits, mind. Putting a new
sewer in . . . Bloody filth and mess off of that.

MAN I bet it was. That's deep as well, innit.

ROSE I tell you what, they've gone so deep in places,
'cause they've put about three manholes in it . . .

MAN . . . Fuckin' manholes are deep, I know that. Ever so
deep, aren't they? They go down a long way.

ROSE Well, this bugger must've gone down twelve foot . . .
It was fuckin' gigantic down in there . . . Why do they
want the manholes so deep then? 'Cause the pipes don't go
down that fuckin' deep. The pipe goes six or seven feet in.

MAN That's to shift all the shit, I suppose. All the rubbish
. . . I 'spect the pipe they put in was about six inches or
summat.

ROSE What?! . . .They were great big ones. [She illustrates
with a loop of her arms. Rose and the man are still lying
naked on the bed.]

MAN Oh. Two-footers, are they?

ROSE Yeh. Sounds about right. They're big buggers. Huge.

MAN [examining himself in the convex mirror in the ceiling over the bed] And the manholes, are they fuckin' as
big again?

ROSE Oh, fuck me, they're massive. Gigantic. Fuckin' hell.

MAN They'd have to dig some big holes for them. They're
big.

ROSE . . . There won't be any water come up in our basement now, look. We used to have water come up in our
basements this side of the road. Used to come up six foot

one time. We got it right down to a dribble. Now it won't come up at all.

The name of Fred's machine at the wagon works and his companion of ten years was Power Thrust. He took his break on his bench at the machine. His morning lunch. And then it was just drilling holes all day. The big drill forcing the hole and going into the hole. Bringing it down and penetrating the plate. Plunging the drill through the metal and pulling out. Minute after minute. In and out. Day after day. Out and in. POWER THRUST. It was written on the side in polished letters; polished steel on drill-hall green. And then in smaller letters: 'Asquith–Archdale – Standard Machine Tools – 6PT – 1972 – Made in Birmingham.'

Asked to choose between friendly human presences and the companionship of objects there was never any doubting which Fred was going to choose. He always preferred objects to people. The deadened and dehumanized over the alive and responding. That would be his choice every time.

Ten years just drilling holes.

It never stopped. It didn't stop at all. There was no let-up.

He was obsessed with sex. You could never get away from sex. He saw sex in everything. Entering. Penetrating. Fitting tight. The big thruster. The Exocet. The Eiffel Tower. Power Thrust. Massive piece of equipment, mind.

If he couldn't think about sex he couldn't think at all.

Chapter Ten

Four months after they murdered Lynda Gough they had a holiday. Three weeks after they poured concrete and erected a bathroom over Lynda Gough's remains they set off on holiday with Rose's father.

It was 1973 in the summer and it was hot and dusty. The scaffolding for the Sabbath Church was still on the garden and it was brick dust and cement dust and they decided to go off to Westward Ho! near Rose's childhood home in Northam in north Devon with Rose's father. Even Fred who hated holidays. He had no time for holidays. He was too busy working. Bill and Fred took turns with the driving and Anna-Marie, who worshipped her father, passed the time making roll-ups for her dad.

It was a caravan holiday – one caravan for all of them. And since Rose's mother did not want to live in such a close way with this man, she stayed at home. Daisy Letts had not undergone the same thaw in respect of her relationship with Fred West as her husband. She didn't like him. Didn't trust him. She had never been happy with the explanation given for the disappearance of Charmaine, who she had considered a lovely, happy little girl. On one visit up to see Rose, Charmaine had been there and the next visit she was gone. Mrs Letts used to sneak up to see Rose because she wouldn't tell Rose's father that she was going round. The odd times Fred was home when she called round there, Rosie would say, 'Fred'll give you a lift home, Mum', but she always said no. She always got the bus. He stopped on the odd occasion and asked if she wanted a lift when he saw her waiting at a bus stop in Cleeve or in town, but she always said no.

Rose had closed off to her family. When she had come to the decision to go with Fred she had shut that other part of her life down. She had had the bust-up with her sister Glenys over Glenys's husband, Jim Tyler, when she had told Glenys she couldn't keep a man. 'You couldn't keep a man. You don't know how to keep a man satisfied.' Made a fist and launched one right at Glen. Fisted up and hit her own sister. Then Pat, her ten-years-older sister, had come round to Midland Road and sat there among the dirty nappies and tut-tutted and she had told her where to get right off an' all. Fucking cheek of it. High and fucking mighty. What right did she have? Fucking nerve. Joyce, the second oldest, was domineering and well out of order and she had found God. Andrew, the oldest of Rose's brothers, was naïve. He thought so himself. 'Daft Andrew' the others always called him. His mother and the rest. Although he wasn't unintelligent, just trusting and naïve. 'That way I might be taking after our mum,' Andrew says. He didn't see Rose for a few years and when he did he had to remind himself that this was Rose. She let him in at Cromwell Street and it was hard for him to believe what he saw. 'She came to the door in a see-through blouse, forty-inch bust, skirt round her arse, white socks, no decorum.' When she came to the door you could see what she was. Andrew could see what she was but he wasn't ready to believe what he was seeing. Even when there was a ring at the door and she went off for half an hour in mid-conversation leaving him sitting there to take a client, he couldn't quite take it in. It was bloody queer. 'I think she's on the bloody game, Andrew,' Glenys said the next time he saw her, and Andrew had to agree. She had her brains in her knickers, if you wanted to know what Andrew thought. It was a right show-up. He wrote Rose off after that.

Graham and Gordon, her little brothers, had always been

close to Rose. Rose would come in as their protector, protecting them against their father. They would huddle in bed together for comfort and protection, and the sexual activity among them had started there. So Graham and Gordon resented the rest of the family telling them that they weren't supposed to see Rose; that they were cutting her off. And when he was fifteen and sixteen and drinking heavily and probably already an alcoholic Graham started sneaking round. He started turning up at Cromwell Street to see Rose but only after he had phoned to let Rose know he was coming first. You always had to phone and let her know and you always had to phone between certain times. If you phoned outside those times she went mad. 'When I say before five I mean before five!' And she did. It wasn't an empty warning. With Rose she meant it. That's the way Rose was. She hardened up. Oh did she.

In 1972, the year they moved into Cromwell Street, Rose's baby brother Gordon had asked to have himself put in a home. He was twelve years old and stealing women's underthings from washing lines and wearing them and being ground down by the violence and constant sniping between his parents and he volunteered to go into a home in an attempt to right his life. He went into a home, and then after only a couple of months he started to reject it. 'All I wanted was to be happy at home and see my parents happy at home. None of us got that,' he says. 'In the end, I gave up. That was me giving up when I was younger. It was that I personally couldn't take it.'

Gordon ran away from where he was and moved in with Rose and her family for a while. But he robbed them and took seventy pounds and so Rose never had him in the house again. It was your family this and your family that. Fred went up the wall and gave her hell for a week. From then on Gordon would be in borstals, and then prisons and mental hospitals, all his life. At one time he tried to settle down with a girl called Karen. They had a baby called Michael. But Karen had her problems and Gordon had his problems and when Michael was aged eight months they woke up one morning to find him dead. They were living in Drybrook at that time in the Forest of Dean and Gordon was arrested and kept in custody for several days on suspicion of murder. What had happened was that Michael suffered from eczema on his face and they had put cream on it to soothe it when they put him to bed and the cream had adhered to the sheet which was made of bri-nylon. Gordon kept telling the police this but they didn't believe him and kept telling him that he had murdered Michael and they were going to prove it and they were going to charge him. After three nights and four days they released him without any charges being brought. But Karen didn't want to see him again. Karen was in hospital and didn't recognize him. Karen's parents didn't want to see him again and after the funeral Gordon sat on Michael's grave like a grieving dog for a week. At the end of a week he walked into town and into a pet shop and bought himself a puppy complete with new collar and new lead. But the collar was too big and the puppy wriggled out of it as they came out of the shop and ran out into the road under the wheels of a lorry. 'They broke me. They done me completely. They done me here,' Gordon says, indicating his head. 'It took more than three-quarters off my life. I still have blackouts and things.' The next time Rose was to see her little brother was when he turned up handcuffed between two prison guards at their father's funeral in 1978 and the policemen refused to take the handcuffs off him in spite of her mother's pleading with them. Gordon was crying and they wouldn't let Rose or her mother or anybody get near to comfort him. It's as if they couldn't cope with life. That's how their mother sees them. Rosie and the boys didn't seem to want to live how normal people live. She's almost frightened to talk about them.

Just as Gordon would be in borstals and other custodial institutions all his life, Rose's other brother Graham was headed for a future of woman-beating and detoxification units and crack-ups and jail. The times Rose and Fred were going to be called on to haul Graham out of the latest mess he'd got himself in, whether it was because of messing about with somebody else's wife or being hounded out of the district where he was living for robbing his neighbours. Graham and his family would have to be kept moving on because he burgled so many of the neighbours the neighbours were out to get him. The times they would be called on to save his neck. They would have to take Graham's wife in and give her protection when he was beating her up. For a period they were moving Barbara Letts from refuge to refuge to keep her away from Graham. They went over to where Graham and Barbara were living in Bishop's Cleeve one time and found he had smashed the whole house up. He was only little; you wouldn't think he was capable of such strength. It was the middle of the night. But he had ripped the kitchen units off the wall, turned the freezer over, even smashed the family photographs and the budgie cage. Barbara and the children weren't there. They had gone; fled to friends. They made a cup of tea and tried to tell Graham where he was going wrong. But of course with Graham and Gordon as much as you might think they had listened, they hadn't at all. Once Barbara was at Cromwell Street and Graham was outside shouting and shaking the gates and Fred went out to quieten him and he told Fred to fuck off. That did it then. Fred's eyes started staring; his body went rigid and shaking. He opened the gates and unusually for him laid one on Graham who was a thin, emaciated-looking individual. An alcoholic and drug-user. Ferret-faced and thin. When he was younger he had this charming talk and people would fall for it at the time. Next thing you knew he'd done the dirty on you. What a sad bastard. Fred sent him in the gutter and started Graham crying.

They were the responsible people. They were the ones who were careful and capable. They were responsible and capable and hemmed in by all this social wreckage. Rose and Fred were making their way and surrounded by so many people who wouldn't or couldn't. So many people lost and adrift in their lives and unable to cope. Floaters and drifters. Floating and drifting. They were like a magnet for these kinds of people. For the young girls flowing in and out of the house Rose was becoming like a young mum cum big sister. There were girls on the run from local homes; boys who had nowhere to go for the night. Endless parties. Fred spent a lot of time with the lodgers and the girls who hung around with the lodgers. Giving them lifts to places. Running them out to places and coming back afterwards to pick them up. Decorating their rooms. If they wanted to run somewhere, he would take them. Fred would just drop what he was doing and run and that went for everybody in the street as well. Always something. Always round and about with them and willing. Willing to take them and willing to wait. Casually pumping these little birds about their backgrounds and families. Making mental notes about their degrees of vulnerability and rebelliousness and isolation. Weighing the odds. In the seventies people drifted all over the place. They were anybody's.

When they got back from their holiday in Westward Ho! in the summer of 1973 there was a message that another of life's casualties was trying to get in touch with them and firing flares in their direction. Margaret McAvoy was somebody Fred had had a fling with when he was living in Scotland. He had taken her out in the ice-cream van and potted her, as he liked to put it. And that baby, whose name was Steven, was now eight years old. Steven was eight and Margaret McAvoy had brought him up by herself without any help from Fred in all those years. But now life had taken a turn for the worse and brought her close to a breakdown and she was appealing to him to take Steven off her hands for a while at least until she was able to pull her life out of the pit it was sinking in.

Their own Stephen was only a few weeks old that summer. Heather was nearly three, May was a year and Anna-Marie was just turned nine. For the past six months, ever since the terrifying day in the cellar when she had had horrible things done to her while she was strapped helpless to the U-shaped frame, Anna-Marie had been made to have sex with her father on a regular basis. Most of the sex took place among the pots of paint and bags of cement and work things in the back of his van where Anna-Marie was going to be forced to have sex with her father for the next eight years. There in the back of the van or on building sites or at the houses where she would have gone to help her father with his work. Whenever she was with him in the van on their way to or from a job and a little purple light came on in the van and the van stopped, she always knew what was going to happen next. But it was the only kind of love she knew from her father or really from anybody, and so she never complained. She didn't mind keeping it a secret from Rose. In a way it was something Anna had over her – something Anna knew and Rose didn't. Something to have over Rose. He would ask her not to tell Rose and give her a few pounds to buy sweets. Some make-up or powder or some sweets.

Quite soon after the first attack on her in the cellar had happened Rose had asked Anna to go again in the cellar and tidy up the toys. She was very apprehensive but she did as she was told and again there was this object against the wall. She wanted to go back up but Rose was behind her on the stairs. She felt frightened because her dad wasn't there. She was told to undress. She didn't want to but Rose got agitated. And then she was strapped to the contraption, the instrument, whatever you could call it. The instrument. No need to ask this time what was going on; what was happening. She was tied to it. She was frightened. She was completely naked. Her legs also were open. She was gagged. She started screaming. She was screaming in her head. She was trying to scream where she was with Rose in that room where little of the larger world was allowed to enter.

However near the prisoner the torturer stands, the distance between their physical realities is colossal, for the prisoner is in overwhelming physical pain while the torturer is utterly without pain; he is free of any pain originating in his own body; he is also free of the pain originating in the agonized body so near him. He is so without any human recognition of or identification with the pain that he is not only able to bear its presence but able to bring it continually into the present, inflict it, sustain it, minute after minute, hour after hour. The distance separating the two is probably the greatest distance that can separate two human beings. The larger the prisoner's pain, the larger the torturer's world.

Rose lifted her skirt up and she had a belt on and a vibrator in the top. She started hitting Anna with fists and hands and swearing at her, calling her names. Anna was gagged. She started screaming. She was screaming in her head. Rose raped her. And then Anna remembered her father being there and he had his work overalls on. She remembered pleading with him with her eyes. Her father raped her. She presumed it was his lunch hour. She was warned not to tell anybody what happened. She was told that she wasn't to say anything to anybody. And then he went.

On 6 July, ten days before her ninth birthday, Anna-Marie had fainted at the swimming baths when she was there with her school and had been taken to Gloucester Royal Hospital where they kept her in overnight for observation. The staff noticed small cuts and bruises on her chest and breasts but she was a tomboy and always falling off things and they had accepted her explanation that the marks on her body had happened as the result of an accident.

Just over a month later Stephen had been born. And then they had gone on holiday with Grampy Letts in a caravan in Devon. And then soon after that they had gone off with Grampy Letts in his car and brought Anna back a new brother. Another Steven. Another new brother but not a baby – one who was almost as old as herself this time. Fred went with Rose's father up to Preston to collect Steven McAvoy who had dark hair and dark skin and bore an unmistakable resemblance to Fred who that day was seeing him for the first time. He was like a duplicate picture. Because she had designed him like that – designed his hairstyle and his thick black hair to look as much as possible like Fred. Fred could see that. Anybody could see it, Fred thought. Fred and Margaret had worked together on the Mr Whippy van. She didn't have many friends. She was a lonely sort of a girl, really. But she thought the world of Fred. And when she got his son, that was her life made. She wouldn't let another man touch her. She wanted Fred to again, but he said no, once was enough. But now she was on the verge of a nervous breakdown, that was the whole problem.

Preston had been settled on as a pick-up point because it was roughly halfway between Gloucester and Glasgow, a route that held memories for Fred. They drove in Bill Letts's new Mazda which was a good deal more reliable than Fred's old A35 van. Rose's father replaced his car every year with a new one. Toyota. Mazda. Simca. He had a renewal thing with the garage that allowed him to do that. But it was at the root of most of the arguments between him and his wife: why he had to have a top-of-the-range TV or stereo; how they were going to pay for the new car. He lost his temper quick. She got annoyed because he used to like to buy things new. Went off fishing with the bosses from work. They weren't really flash sort of cars. Just cars that Rose's mother thought at the time he couldn't afford. The main thing he liked was to have a nice car.

They drove up to Preston and met Margaret McAvoy and a man who was with her in a car park and brought Steven back with them. 'If the boy's yours' is all Rose had said. She was all for it. Rose had been in complete agreement with this development. That is until she realized that although he was eight Steven was used to being hand-fed and was still wearing nappies. She had a six-week-old baby in nappies and an eight-year-old who still needed nappies and Fred had already started buying Sanatogen wine for her because she was run-down and feeling drained and on a short fuse. And now Anna had an ally; a co-conspirator.

All the West children would grow up knowing they weren't supposed to talk to anybody outside the house. Fred and Rose never wanted anybody to spend time with any of the children unless one of them was present. They didn't even like the children to talk or laugh among themselves when they were together playing. As soon as the children had a laugh themselves, that was it, Rose would step in with a slapping. 'Stop bloody giggling.' One night when Stephen was about five, Stephen and May and Heather were dragged out of their beds in the cellar where they were sleeping and bundled out into the garden. It was winter and wet and freezing and they were kept out in the garden clinging to each other for quarter of an hour before being allowed back in. Their crime was talking when they should have been sleeping, and being thrown outside into the cold was the punishment.

Steven McAvoy started the autumn 1973 term at St Paul's Juniors in New Street with Anna and he went about a lot with Anna and she was very proud of him, both of them looking so much like their father. They got on great with each other and liked drawing and playing and could never understand why this would send Rose into a rage every time she saw them. And there were other things that Steven didn't understand that were different from the home he came from in Scotland. The fact that there were no locks on the bathroom and toilet doors, for instance, and how this would lead to embarrassing incidents. Quite soon after arriving he walked in when Rose was using the toilet and he was flustered and embarrassed but Rose wasn't. In fact she made him stand there by her and watch her. She was completely naked but she made him wait and watch until she was finished. Another time he got up in the night to go to the toilet which was through the living room where his father and his father's wife as he called her were sleeping. When he walked in it was obvious they were having sex with each other but again he was made to stay and see everything and they laughed and seemed to enjoy him watching.

At the beginning Steven used to call his father's wife 'step-mum'. But she would hit him when he did this and tell him to call her mum. She would hit him often and it seemed to Steven not for any good reason. She would punch and kick them – him and Anna – and drag them around the living room by their hair. One day they were on the floor playing with his grandfather's coin collection that he had brought with him from Scotland when Rose found them and screwed her foot in his face. She was wearing stiletto heels and the sharp heel caught him close to one eye and opened a wound that when it healed was going to leave a permanent scar.

She thought nothing of kicking you. Feet were nothing. She'd hit one of them and then she'd want to hit them all because she was in the mood. She could seem impervious to pain and seemed to expect the same of everybody else. She

283

could be quite seriously physically injured and not even flinch. One evening in August 1974 when she was still only twenty she was admitted to Gloucester Hospital via the Accident Unit with a laceration across the ring and little fingers of the right hand. Both flexor tendons of these fingers were found divided. Which in layman's language means both fingers were virtually severed and hanging off. It had started as a game with Fred. Fred had come home from work and found her in the kitchen stirring something on the cooker and he began poking her with his finger and jumping back out of the way. Poking her and jumping out of the way. Poking and giggling and prodding although she was warning him to stop. A prod and a punch. 'Watch it, boy, just watch it look or I'll fucking have you.' Poking and prodding and punching and laughing until he eventually went a punch too far. She swung round and snatched up the carving knife and chased him out of the kitchen and across the living room and up the three stairs that led to a door. He slammed the door straight in her face and the knife came bang straight in the door. Straight through the door and he heard a scream on the other side. When he opened it one of Rose's fingers was hanging down and the other one was hanging off but she wasn't crying. 'Right, feller, you've got to take me down to the hospital,' she said, but she wasn't crying. Her fingers were hanging off by the tendons and almost severed but she wasn't crying. She went into the kitchen and wrapped a tea towel around her hand to prepare for the hospital but she didn't cry.

When she got her temper up Rose grabbed whatever was handy. A rolling-pin was one of her favourites. But if it was a knife it was a knife. She was constantly on the look-out for reasons to give one of them a beating. If she couldn't find any, she would make them up. She'd accuse them of things they hadn't done. For some reason she picked on May one tea-time and came at her with a knife. May was still little then and sitting on the top step in the living room and she suddenly lunged at her with a knife. May was screaming. She was crying and telling her no. No! *No!* She kept slashing the knife at her and there were little nicks all over her ribcage by the end. All up under her vest. She was only wearing a vest and pants. You never knew what Rose was going to do next. She would use anything; knives, belts. The house itself – walls, ceilings, windows, doors – could be a weapon. Fred always said that he brought in the money and everything else was down to Rose. He worked and the rest was Rose. If the kids were doing something they shouldn't in front of him he'd say, 'Rose, take care of that.' She would go then. She didn't care how loud or how violent or who heard her in the street. She would go. She would lose it. She would just flip.

When the time came and his mother wanted him back with her in Scotland they wouldn't let Steven McAvoy go. The Social Services contacted them and said that Steven's mother had recovered and she was wanting Steven back home now but they weren't keen to let Steven go. Letters from Glasgow were left to go unanswered. But the Social Services persisted. Pen-pushers and briefcase-carrying nosey-parkers busy-bodying and nosey-parkering around. Buzzing at the door. Standing at the door. Steven's mother was pining and the briefcases were bothering. His mother had somehow been able to drop back into her life and the authorities were noticing them. The authorities were becoming aware of them. They were being noticed and they had to let him go. Steven had come in the autumn of 1973. It was now the early spring of 1974. Two more women had been murdered and buried underground at 25 Cromwell Street in that time. By the spring of 1975 they would have murdered three more. Altogether five girls and young women murdered and mutilated and buried underground in Cromwell Street in the space of eighteen months. Sexually brutalized and murdered and buried roughly in a circle in narrow shafts opened in the floor of the cellar in the order of their deaths.

By November 1973 they had been living in the house a little over a year. The builders were still working on the church next door and the finishing touches were still being put to the bathroom extension like tar and sealant to keep the winter out. They called it an extension but it was really an outbuilding; a heat-leaking, flimsy envelope of space. So add dirt and treaded mud to the lodgers and their noise, and the runaways and misfits coming round and the dealers, and with the dealers the busts and the Bill, and you had what many of them living there at the time called pandom. Pandom, short for pandemonium. Beautiful pandom. Some would look back on their days at Cromwell Street as the happiest time of their lives.

The busts were getting ridiculous. The busts were getting out of hand. The lodgers had always been out of hand in Rose's opinion. And now you had the police raids to prove it. The police were raiding them once, sometimes twice a week. At one time they were raiding regularly and almost every day. If one policeman wanted to get in touch with another policeman, they radioed to Cromwell Street, because that's where they usually were. They pulled out cupboards, ripped up carpets and lino, took up floorboards and vacuumed everything. But always only in the upstairs lodgers' part of the house. Always in the lodgers' rooms on the first and second floors and never in Fred's and Rose's part of the house, which consisted of the two ground-floor rooms and the cellar. Which gave rise to suspicions that Fred was on the payroll as an informant, which would have surprised nobody about Fred. The whispering grass. In addition to the lodgers and their friends, and the friends of friends of friends, the house was also a haven for a number of convicts and recidivist petty criminals. Before the ground-floor room at the front of the house became Rose's room, Rose shared it with Fred and a small-time crook who was a friend of Fred's called Frank Stephens. Sometimes she shared a bed with Fred and sometimes she shared a bed with Frank Stephens. Fred would have liked it to have been the three of them in the same bed and he suggested this, but Frank Stephens – so he maintained – wasn't prepared to go as far as that.

On a number of occasions when Stephens was arrested on suspicion of theft and handling stolen goods he was staying at 25 Cromwell Street. He was involved in break-ins at Jason Tool Hire and West Midland Farmers among others and stored chainsaws, garden implements and other stolen property, mainly tools, with Fred's permission in the cellar. It was using the cellar for hiding things in without telling Fred that that's what he was doing that would lead to a major bust-up between them in 1979. Frank Stephens would be able to say that once Fred West found out that he had been alone in his cellar with regard to stolen property he had put there, he went absolutely mad. He didn't lose his temper very often but when he did it wasn't like normal anger: his eyes started staring; his body went rigid and shaking. The final parting of the ways between Fred and Frank Stephens would happen the following year when five stolen tape recorders and a number of tape cassettes were found hidden in a wardrobe at Cromwell Street. The contents of one of the tapes was judged to be so shocking that when Fred West eventually came to trial for receiving, the contents were not read out in open court. Instead, the jury was simply handed a transcript. He had got into the habit of lending around tapes of Rose's lovemaking to some of the men at work. And this one had been made during one of their nights out in the back of the van he had domesticated with a little gas fire and a carpet and a mattress, and it featured Rose and one of Fred's black men friends. They would take some rope and a whip, some vibrators and a flask of tea and all go off together in the van. In future years, when video cassettes had superseded audio cassettes and he was building up a video rather than a sound library, Fred would take out some of the old sound tapes he had made of Rose and her partners and play them as a soundtrack to whatever solo act she might be in the process of performing for his camera. Rose panting and moaning in present time and Rose howling in ecstasy or talking dirty from another time in the past. Fred escaped with a £50 fine but Frank Stephens was never allowed in the house again.

By the early seventies there were always a lot of people milling around and going up and down Cromwell Street late at night. The Ebony Club had opened in the old school buildings at Tommy Rich's and that drew a lot of complaints from the older neighbours on account of the loud reggae music and the persistent heavy bass. Maxi's was another club around the corner at the park end of the street where people from number 25 would come and go. It drew a rough crowd: one night a boy got up on his seat and fired bullets from a 12-bore shotgun into the ceiling above the bar. Tracy's on the bus station was safer and more mainstream, with bouncers and visiting DJs and a liberal, but if necessary enforceable, dress code. Caroline Raine still hitched in from Cinderford to go to Tracy's some nights. The brother of a fifteen-year-old from a local children's home who would become involved with Fred and Rose worked on the door. Liz Parry, one of the long-term tenants at Cromwell Street, was a barmaid at Tracy's; and Rose was even sometimes seen in the club in the early years of her marriage to Fred.

Rose West's diary entry for Thursday, 24 February 1977:

Went to Tracy's with Anna[-Marie, then aged thirteen] Meet two fellas

Not much good
Not feeling to good . . .
12 o'clock Got home. Hopeless!
Fella not a lot of good
12.30 o'clock with Fred. That's better. Got a little
cuddle.

Tracy's was under the multi-storey car park that had been
built when the bus station moved to the site of the old cattle
market, close to the centre of Gloucester. And Fred was frequently seen with his work van hanging around in the bus station late at night chatting to these little teenyboppers as he
liked to call them. These little teenybopper birds out of it on
drugs or drink; without money; perhaps in need of friendship
and somewhere to stay. Girls having what he was always
telling Rose she should be having. Girls having their young life.

Nobody will ever know whether Carol Cooper, known to
her friends as 'Caz', was part of the traffic passing though 25
Cromwell Street in the final months of 1973. But she was the
kind of age and living the kind of life being lived by many of
the girls who were regular or casual visitors to the house at
that time. Carol Cooper was friendly with one or two bikers,
members of the Scorpions who had dossed at Cromwell Street
in the year or so that Fred West had been letting out rooms
there. She was last seen getting on a bus in Worcester just after
nine o'clock one night in November 1973. She was fifteen,
and 10 November was the Saturday of the first weekend she
had officially been allowed to sleep away from the Pines Children's Home where she had been living since she was thirteen.
It was the first official time and she was going to spend the
Saturday night as she had spent Friday night, at her grandmother's in Warndon. But there had been several unofficial
occasions when, instead of going back to the Pines, Carol had
spent the night sleeping rough or in some abandoned railway

carriages with some of the bikers she had got to know. She wore a jean jacket and the gang's 'patches' and had used Indian ink and a needle to tattoo 'Caz' on her left forearm and a pattern of dots across the knuckles of her left hand. Physically she was tall and strong and she was regarded as being 'outward' as a person. Her parents had separated when she was four, and her mother had died when Carol was eight. She had made an attempt at living with her father and his new wife but that hadn't worked out. She was effectively without a family and rebelling. She had been caught shoplifting. She was devil-may-care and a rebel. She was a regular absconder from her local-authority home. On Bonfire Night in 1973, a few nights before she went missing, a firework had gone off in Carol's hand. That was a Monday. Her left hand was still bandaged on the Saturday when she met her boyfriend of the time, Andrew Jones, and a large group of friends to go to the Odeon in Worcester. When they came out of the pictures they went to a local fish-and-chip shop and sat on the steps of another cinema, the Scala, to eat them. It wasn't late when Carol and Andrew went their separate ways: it was quarter past nine. But it was later than Carol had intended because she had had a small spat with Andrew and she hadn't wanted to get on the bus without making up with him and that had taken time. But he gave her money for her fare and she got on the bus and nobody who knew her ever saw her again.

It isn't known how Carol came to get off the bus without returning to her grandmother, but it is known she ended up in Cromwell Street. Carol was certainly there because on 8 March 1994, just after seven in the evening, her remains were found under the cellar floor at 25 Cromwell Street, the ninth set of remains to be found at the address. They were in the rear part of the cellar, a short distance from the wall and adjacent to a washbasin which was installed some years after her death when that part of the cellar was made into a bedroom for Stephen. As in the case of Lynda Gough, many bones were missing, particularly from the feet and hands. Several fingers and toes and wrist bones had been taken away. The skull had been struck from the spine, and the bones had been chopped so that the remains could be forced into a small hole no bigger than three feet deep and two feet square. Again there was a ring mask or gag, this one made of elasticated surgical tape wound around itself several times to cover the jaws and lower face as well as the back of the head. There was also some hair remaining, some loops of fabric and a length of woven cord, doubtless all that remained of at least part of the binding that held her. The black discoloration of the soil around the area where the remains were found was a result of decomposed body tissue and demonstrated that the dismembered body rotted where it lay underground in Cromwell Street. There was nothing to suggest that Carol had been wearing clothes when she died.

Six weeks after Carol Cooper was murdered, Lucy Partington, a twenty-one-year-old third-year undergraduate at the University of Exeter, studying medieval history and English, became the second woman to be buried under the cellar in Cromwell Street. Her parents were divorced: her father Roger was a research scientist with ICI on Teesside; her mother Margaret worked in an architect's office in Cheltenham. She was a member of the university's medieval music group and had visited Much Marcle Church and the nearby Kempley Parish Church among other places to make notes on the medieval art works and paintings. Lucy Partington wore the same wire-framed glasses as Lynda Gough and wore her long hair in the same casual way. She had converted to Roman Catholicism only a few weeks before she disappeared after taking instruction from a priest in Exeter.

She had spent Christmas with her mother in Gretton, the

small village where she had grown up, just outside Cheltenham. Christmas Day in 1973 had fallen on a Tuesday. On
the Friday, Lucy was due to go and stay with her father in the
north of England. On Thursday night she paid a visit to a
close friend called Helen Render who was seriously disabled
and largely confined to a wheelchair. She arrived at Helen's
house around eight and spent a couple of hours there, mainly
composing an application letter to do an MA in medieval art
at the Courtauld Institute in London. She left Helen Render's
house just before a quarter past ten in something of a rush to
catch the last bus, known as the grey bus and cheaper than
the standard service, her letter to the Courtauld in her hand.
The old Kersey bus was half the price of the normal bus and
most people used to catch the Kersey. It was sleeting but the
bus stop was only a three-minute walk away on the main
A435 trunk road between Cheltenham and Evesham. A man
out walking his dog saw Lucy hurrying between Culross
Close and the bus stop. He would identify her from the
description: 'Dressed in rust-coloured raincoat, pink jeans,
red mittens, carrying faded brown canvas satchel. Gold-
rimmed specs. Was last seen in Albemarle Gate, Pittville,
Cheltenham.' It was a description that would go on the
'Missing' posters that would start to appear in shop windows
and on lamp-posts in the coming weeks. The grey bus was
ten minutes late that night and the streets were underlit and
in some cases not lit at all because of the fuel crisis and the
three-day week, and Lucy was never seen again.

Everybody who knew her agreed that Lucy Partington was
too sensible to accept a lift at night from a man, or even a
man and a woman, who she didn't know. (Graham Letts's
mother-in-law, Ellen White, claims to know that Fred and
Rose had Stephen, who was only a four-month-old baby, in
the van with them on the night they picked Lucy Partington
up, which could certainly have been a factor, but Mrs White

is unwilling to say how she knows.) She would not have got into the van voluntarily unless it was somebody she recognized or knew.

There is every possibility that Fred West had had a passing acquaintance with Lucy Partington at the very least since she was a child. As a bread-roundsman in Bishop's Cleeve and the surrounding villages in the late-fifties he had got to know, for instance, many of the families who lived in a hamlet called Stoke Orchard (population 312). One of these families was the Whites and in particular Mrs White whose daughter Barbara was going to marry Rose's brother, Graham. Fred would tell Barbara that he remembered her as a pretty child, and Ellen White, Barbara's mother, would remember Fred as somebody who would give you his last penny in those days and anybody in the village would tell you the same. The Whites lived where they still live, at 5 Cleeve View, a short terrace of forties brick council houses facing the main road in Stoke Orchard. Rose's sister Glenys and her husband Jim Tyler lived next door to Mrs White at 4 Cleeve View for several years. (It was through his sister that Graham met, and eventually married, Barbara White.) Mrs Nock at 1 Cleeve View, another of Fred West's bread-round customers, would look after Charmaine and Anna-Marie for him a decade later. Stoke Orchard was close to the M5 extension, and he would leave the children with Mrs Nock on his way to work on the motorway in 1968 and 1969, and collect them on his way back home to the trailer at night.

Jim Tyler was a farmer's son from Gotherington, the next village north of Bishop's Cleeve: Tobyfield Road, where the Letts family lived, very soon becomes Gotherington Lane; and the lane, going east out of Gotherington village, becomes the road to Gretton, the village where Lucy Partington grew up and where her mother was still living in 1973. It was Gretton that Lucy was trying to get back to on the night she disappeared. Lucy Partington was a year older than Rose Letts. She was six years older than Barbara White. Although he wouldn't see her for ten years, Fred West remembered Barbara as a child. So it is possible – more than possible – that he remembered Lucy Partington as a seven- or eight-year-old girl. The bread that he delivered was baked in Gotherington, the next village along the road from where Lucy was growing up. He delivered to Gretton and all the other villages around and about. He was well liked and attractive and friendly: Mrs White thought so. He was also devious and vigilant and patient. A shrewd, proud lout.

Lucy Partington went to Pates Grammar School for Girls in Cheltenham from 1963 to 1970. Pates is situated immediately behind the Pump Room made famous in the days of George III, on the A435, the main Cheltenham–Evesham road. At the end of the day she would come out of school and walk through the Pump Room straight to her bus stop on the other side of the Evesham road by the railings of Pittville Park. It was the grey bus to Bishop's Cleeve and Gretton. The same bus that Rose would take when she was working in the cake shop in Cheltenham in 1968 and 1969. The bus on which Fred West would approach her when she wasn't yet sixteen and ask her to go out with him for the first time. He was living on the Lakehouse site in Bishop's Cleeve from 1967 to the end of 1969 – years in which every day after school Lucy Partington would be waiting at her bus stop opposite the Pump Room. 9 Clarence Road, the first address that Fred and Rose shared and where he moved in 1969, was very close by. Did he remember her as a seven and eight year old from when he was delivering bread round Gretton? He was devious and vigilant and patient. Did she remember him? Did he stop and offer her a lift in the old white camper van with a blue stripe on its side which had become so familiar to the girls of Cleeve School? This man parked close to the school with the two scruffy but pretty little daughters sitting up in the front beside him. Even after they had moved to Gloucester he would drive the children over to Cheltenham on some Sundays to play in Pittville Park. Did she ever get in?

By coincidence, the bus stop closest to Lucy Partington's friend Helen Render's house, the stop where Lucy was waiting on the night she disappeared, was the stop she had used all through her time at school. The bus stop just at the top of that brow there. That's the top of the Evesham road almost up towards the race-course roundabout. Lucy had written a poem about it and the many wet and cold afternoons she had stood by it waiting for a bus, the park at her back and the Pump Room directly opposite, her school beyond that, giving the poem the title 'Bus Stop'. This is not the stop that Fred West invested with so much significance the night he made Stephen get out of the van and stand on the spot where his mother and father first met. As if there were some magic or mystery or something around it. These pavements. This bus stop. That bus stop was back in the centre of town.

But the bus stop where Lucy Partington waited every day and wrote about and which she was hurrying towards when she was last seen *is* the stop that Rose West claimed she had been standing at and been chased from and pursued into Pittville Park and raped there when she was fifteen. 'I was waiting for a bus when a man approached me,' she said. 'He was chatting me up, I resisted his advances, I wasn't interested in men at that time, but he was very forcible, very strong, because he was grabbing me, then it got out of hand. I got frightened and I ran away from him. I ran towards the park in Cheltenham. There was nobody around, this man's gaining on me, pursuing me towards the park . . . There was a little gate to the entrance of the park. He smashed the padlock off it as if it was nothing, and dragged me down by the lake under some trees and raped me.' Afterwards she went back to the bus stop, she said, and got on a bus when one came and went home.

If this was something that happened it was something that Rose West kept to herself for twenty-five years. It is strongly reminiscent of the chase-and-rape scenarios that are a staple of many full-length, hard-core pornographic features of the kind the Wests watched together and Fred West kept and lent out from Cromwell Street. What is interesting is the location of the bus stop – which Rose claimed she was too frightened ever to stand at again – and the part of Pittville Park closest to the bus stop on the Evesham road. Places played an important part in their private mythology: the five-bar gate near the Odessa in Tewkesbury; the disused airfield near Stoke Orchard where they liked to go at nights for rough sex and taping sessions in the van; the hunting stile close to where Rena was buried in Letterbox Field; the house that they built with their bare hands together at 25 Cromwell Street. Although they were interviewed separately and were unable to confer with each other – all communication between them ended after their arrest in February 1994; Rose withheld her co-operation almost entirely from the police, answering 'no comment' to all their questions to her for weeks – they both made references to the bus stop that Rose had been raped from and Lucy Partington had travelled home from school from and was hurrying towards on the night she disappeared, and to the part of the park adjacent to where the bus stop still stands. The old Kersey bus was half the price of the normal bus and most people used to catch the Kersey.

Fred West told the police that he had had sex with Rose at the place close to the lake in Pittville Park where she claimed to have been raped. He had been spotted there with Rose by Andrew, her brother, and it was this that had got him barred from seeing her: 'Because her brother walked that road at all hours of the day and night, going to see his girlfriend in Cheltenham.' Grotesquely, but instructively because of what it reveals about the transferences and distortions that fed his fantasy life, he also claimed to have had sex with Lucy Partington in that same part of the park. They had agreed to meet in the park, he claimed, because of the danger of being spotted by Andrew Letts or some other member of Rose's family: 'The last thing I wanted them to do was to go and tell Rose I was meeting another girl in Cheltenham.' He said that he 'used to park in Pittville Park and wait for her', keeping the van out of sight. 'I met Lucy . . . in the park one day. On the boating lake there when I was with the kids and I got going with her after. It was all secret hush hush . . . I took the children home and I arranged to meet her back at night, and I came and met her on that hill and we had a bit of a sex romp and that, and that was it. Most of the time I met her was in the dark . . . [The murder – he claimed to have strangled her when "she come the loving racket" and was threatening to tell Rose about their affair] must have been about when I was taking her back to the bus stop. She used to get the bus at the top of . . . er, where the peacocks are. Pittville Pump Rooms or summat there by the side of it . . . I used to bring her back to there and drop her to get the bus.'

All through his life Fred West would invest his deepest and most complicated emotions – all his most difficult and disturbing thoughts – not in people, but in things. Places and things. And it is possible to detect signs in the parallel but separate accounts that Rose and Fred West gave of events related to the abduction and murder of Lucy Partington that that bus stop on the Evesham road and the part of the park that fell within its force field was such a place. He spun a fantasy around it involving sex and murder. Her fantasy focused on coercion and rape. It is a location that appears to have assumed an importance for them retrospectively because of what happened there on the night of 27 December 1973, the details of which only one living person knows.

Lucy Partington's remains were found in the cellar of 25 Cromwell Street at nine o'clock on Sunday morning, 6 March 1994. Her body had been dismembered, decapitated and many of the bones from her toes and fingers had been taken away. Pieces of cord and rope were recovered from the hole where she had been roughly buried – a sewer pipe running through the hole had made the process unusually difficult – together with a mask or gag made out of strong plastic-backed tape. But in this case another item – a knife – was also excavated from the grave. It was a kitchen knife, black-handled and mass-produced in Sheffield, with an eight-inch blade which had been sharpened to a point. It begins to look almost certain that this was the knife used to dismember Lucy Partington's body when a fact is mentioned alongside the discovery of the knife. At 00.25 on the morning of 3 January 1974, which was seven days after Lucy's disappearance, Fred West presented himself at Gloucester Royal Hospital for emergency medical treatment on a laceration of his right hand. The significance of this would be spelled out many years later by the prosecuting counsel at Rose West's trial: it indicated that, once taken, Lucy Partington had been not only bound and gagged but almost certainly kept alive but helpless 'for whatever hideous purpose' for some days. There were no clothes found with the jumbled parts of her body or remains of clothes.

Lucy Partington was buried in the part of the cellar that was immediately under the front door at Cromwell Street; under the front hall. Her remains were found in what the police diggers called 'the nursery alcove' on account of the children's drawings that had been made straight on to the plaster of the walls. Shirley Hubbard, another of the Wests' victims, would be buried against what became known as the

'Marilyn Monroe wall'. She was murdered eleven months after Lucy Partington and buried in the front cellar room at Cromwell Street, the one nearest the street. Fred West then created a false chimney-breast around where she was buried in the floor and some time afterwards decorated it and the walls around it and adjacent to it with wallpaper bearing the image of Marilyn Monroe – silver foil-backed paper with popular images of Marilyn Monroe repeating in a shiny pattern across it. There were four images from four films, and the juxtaposition of the tinselly glamour with the depravity and inhuman cruelty with which the cellar had quickly become associated disturbed everybody who saw it. The excavated hole filled with liquid mud and the black slurry of decomposed body tissue surrounded by shiny images of Hollywood glamour was disturbing and very shocking. In addition to the pin-up poses the pattern of the paper included the titles of the films from which they had been taken. They were *Niagara, The Seven Year Itch, The Misfits* and *Bus Stop*.

Like Carol Cooper, Shirley Hubbard had last been seen by her boyfriend getting on a bus in the centre of Worcester. Carol Cooper and Shirley Hubbard both boarded buses at The Trinity in the centre of Worcester and were never seen again. Mary Bastholm was last seen waiting at a bus stop on Bristol Road in Gloucester. Lucy Partington of course disappeared from a bus stop on the Evesham road. She had written a poem called 'Bus Stop' and Rose had been 'raped' after being chased from the same bus stop and Fred would take Stephen and introduce him to the bus stop where he had met his mother as if it was a shrine. As if he thought it was part of history, as Stephen would say. And now here were these two words blocked out in silver against black – 'Bus STOP' – the first thing you saw as you came down into the cellar, all over the fireplace wall.

When money worries were less pressing and they had

cleared out the lodgers, Fred West would turn the first-floor front room at Cromwell Street into a bar. Paste up a mural of the Canary Islands foregrounded with spiky orange strelitzia flowers and put in a sofa and a video-player and a tiger-pattern rug and a chandelier and the dark-oak, hand-crafted, four-posted 'Black Magic' bar. It gave the name in painted letters complete with a palm-tree motif – 'Black Magic' – on a sign above the bar. On the pelmet above the bar in the same position as the 'Cunt' sign was on the pelmet of the dark-oak, hand-crafted four-poster bed in the room immediately overhead. On the one hand it was a reference to the brand of chocolates Rose liked best. On the other it was a reference to the black male visitors, pictures of whose naked bodies and erections she put up around the frame of the bar. Part of the private language Fred and Rose had evolved. A private and complex, and by that time almost subliminal, language of signals and cues. 'Black Magic'. 'My Black Hole'. 'Cunt'.

Another of the little secrets they had between them, and one of Fred's most prized possessions, was his Roses Chocolates jar. Rose didn't wear knickers at home, he told the police, she 'only wore them to go out for sex'. One of the rituals he evolved was that when she came in after having sex, she had to put her soiled knickers in a glass storage jar. She had to put her knickers in the glass jar as soon as she got home 'as souvenirs of her sex life', and date them in ink. 'At the end of an era, at the end of the passion, when it faded out,' Fred said, 'then they'd be burned and put in another jar.' The charred remains of Rose's underthings were kept in tiny pots on the mantelpiece in her special room and in the Black Magic bar. 'The idea was that in years to come we could say – well, that represents so-and-so, and that represents so-and-so . . . It was just something we thought up between us – to have these knickers in these jars – and then when you're sixty or seventy years old, like, you could say, "Well, there's twenty in there" . . . They were nice pots, and the tops were sealed on, glued on.'

Rose's black men. Rose's chocolates. 'Roses Chocolates'. Fred's most prized jar. The jar containing the semen-soaked knickers from Rose's encounters with her Jamaican men. 'Black Magic'. A private and complex, and by that time almost subliminal, language of signals and cues. A private language between them and nobody else quite in on this.

Not one of the many bones that Fred West took away from the women they murdered – kneecaps, a collarbone, dozens and probably hundreds of ankle and toe and finger bones – has ever been recovered. One of the biggest mysteries he left when he killed himself was why these bones and not other bones and where these totems and horrible trophies, as he obviously saw them, were hoarded and stored.

The indirect language of codes and signals that operated inside 25 Cromwell Street offers a possible clue. Among all the layered meanings of the Black Magic bar it is perhaps possible to peel another one away. 'That Ol' Black Magic' is a song that has been recorded by many people. Marilyn Monroe is one of them. She sang it in one of her films and the film was *Bus Stop*.

Another trail that seems to lead us from Gloucester to Cheltenham and away from the centre of Cheltenham and once again out to Pittville Park and almost up towards the race-course roundabout along the Evesham road.

Fred West became skilled at indirection. Tortuousness and indirection. Talking palaver while apparently talking the truth. Laying out and simultaneously covering up. Very little of what he said or did was ever straightforward. None of it could be assumed to be what it seemed. Only once in the 151 interviews he did with the police after his arrest did he come

301

close to admitting this fundamental truth about himself. 'What happens is', he said, 'I'm talking away to them . . . and suddenly it comes into my mind, shit, I'm telling them the truth – you know, what's been going on . . . So then I shove something in there . . . to get away from it.'

It would be in character for Fred West to want to take his oldest son and expose him to a place that was so heavily charged with meaning for him. Their first son and the first of their babies to be conceived in Cromwell Street. It would also be in character, when it came to it, for him to back away from full disclosure; to retreat to what in the end turned out to be only a near boast – a near confession. There were two bus stops, both places charged with a strong past event, but from which the event itself was absent. And he took Stephen to the one in the centre of Cheltenham when it came to it. They stood in this faintly rank and urine-smelling place, and his father tried to convey to Stephen the deep significance it had for him. This prefabricated, pebble-finished stand. Wind traps set around in a circle. This stop and not the other stop which, according to Graham Letts's mother-in-law, Mrs White, Stephen drove up to in their van with them on the night they abducted Lucy Partington when he was aged just four months. As if it was a shrine. As if he thought it was part of history, as Stephen would say.

Seventy-two of Lucy Partington's bones were found to be missing when her remains were recovered from underneath the cellar in Cromwell Street. The forensic pathologist Bernard Knight ruled out everything except deliberate dismemberment as an explanation for how this could have happened when he appeared as an expert witness at Rose West's trial in 1995. The bones were not missing as a result of degeneration (the bones that had survived, especially those under the cellar, were in very good condition) or as a result of a failure to excavate properly (he had witnessed the excavation himself) or because the bodies had at some time been moved from one burial site to another and some bones had fallen off in the process: the black soil that surrounded the remains proved that there had been a substantial quantity of soft tissue present, which meant that the limbs must have been whole when buried, that is to say with flesh and the strong ligaments and tendons still intact. The only way the bones could have gone missing is if they had been removed as a result of deliberate dismemberment and mutilation. 'Fingers and toes are very easy to remove,' Knight said, 'and a kneecap is quite possible to remove with a sharp knife.'

In common with the remains of everybody murdered by Fred West, a number of Lucy Partington's fingers and toes were amputated and taken away. It was part of his method. It was a part of his 'signature'. Part of his perverse ritual. Her left kneecap was also missing and so were three of her ribs. A shoulderblade, Bernard Knight pointed out, is a large and very difficult part of the body to remove. It would take time and a degree of expertise to do it. But Lucy Partington's right shoulderblade was missing and, like all the bones taken from all the bodies, has never been found.

People tend to bury bodies near their homes or other places they know well. He buried bodies under his feet in the back garden. He buried bodies under his house in the cellar. He put bodies in the fields as close to his childhood home in Much Marcle as he could get away with. That was about feeling safe and secure. It was also about control and possession. About staying in a position of ownership and power, not only over his 'girls' but over the people who couldn't see who he was and what he was doing. Having one over on the rest of the world who he was running rings around and making a monkey of and fooling and tricking.

People tend to bury bodies and other things they might want to find again in a physically recognizable place rather than in the middle of nowhere. And like a tree in a field – the tree standing by itself in Letterbox Field, for example, marking the site of Rena's grave – a bus stop is an urban marker. Lucy had written a poem about it. The bus stop just at the top of that brow there. Written about the many wet and cold afternoons she had stood by it waiting for a bus, the park at her back and the Pump Room directly opposite, her school beyond that, giving the poem the title 'Bus Stop'. It was a stop charged with a strong past event: a girl had disappeared while waiting for a bus there during the Christmas holiday of 1973 and was never seen again. But it was also a stop that crowds of people surged past in their thousands several times a year, separating from each other like water around a boulder and joining up again without having their attention snagged by anything they are passing.

On big race days – and Cheltenham Gold Cup Day is one of the biggest days in the international racing calendar – racegoers are disgorged from the hotels and pubs in the centre of Cheltenham and course on foot in their thousands along the Evesham road towards the races. Cheltenham race course is a ten-minute walk north of Pittville Park at the foot of Cleeve Hill, and on the three-day National Hunt Festival in March forty thousand people every day descend on it. It is one of those events that every year features on the local television news and in the newspapers. Thousands of people surging past the bus stop from where Lucy Partington disappeared and from which Rose Letts claimed to have been chased and raped and that part of the park that so clearly resonated for Rose and Fred and where perhaps – maybe – Fred West's terrible collection of bones and body pieces, his ossuary, lies buried. The pleasure of a secret is enhanced by the heightened possibility of discovery. So many people coming so close to it and yet staying so far away.

Is it a place that Fred and Rose would visit? ('The idea was that in years to come we could say – well, that represents so-and-so, and that represents so-and-so . . . It was just something we thought up between us.') Or where they would all go together as a family and play and picnic together and the look would pass between Fred and Rose because of the secret that they shared and, like Ian Brady and Myra Hindley who made recreational visits to the graves of the children they had murdered on Saddleworth Moor complete with flasks and cameras, were literally sitting on?

In the years after they had murdered Heather and he had buried her in the back garden Fred West used to go out there at night and sit for hours on a stool just by where Heather was buried. There was a stool put there by him and he was just sat alone in the dark. Rose would be upstairs doing something and he just used to walk out there, take the dogs out, sit with the dogs. And before the dogs, the cats. Topper and Potter and all them. He used to sit out there with them. Whenever it got on his mind too much. He would get up in the night and go out there at night and stand by her. Nobody ever saw him.

When the floor of the cellar had been filled up with bodies and concreted over and made into a bedroom for the children, he would spend many hours sitting on the edge of their beds drinking tea and talking. Talking if there was anybody with him but sitting for hour after hour down there anyway where five bodies were buried and the floor came a foot and more higher up the walls than it had when they moved in because of the volume of concrete that had been poured. The height between the bottom of the beams to the floor had been more than seven feet when they moved in to the house. But by the time it was being used as a bedroom for the children the ceiling in the cellar was probably no more than five foot nine. It was very low and towards the front where Heather and May slept two notches had been cut into the top of two of the beams that the children, unaware of any sinister purpose, looped strong nylon ropes through and used the ropes for hauling themselves up with and swinging on.

The park was a contemplative place, so quiet and yet so close to the world rushing by on the other side of the railings. So many people so close and yet so far away. The cellar was a quiet place where little of the larger world was allowed to enter. Only the muffled sound of footsteps and traffic and intermittent radio noise and the congregation and choir of the next-door Seventh-day Adventists' church on a Saturday morning, which is their sabbath, milling and chattering, unaware of how close they were to defiled and desecrated human remains and worse – a bound and gagged and helpless and struggling human being.

Thérèse Siegenthaler was also bespectacled and also a student and she also was murdered by the Wests three months after they had murdered Lucy Partington, during the Easter holiday of 1974, Fred West's next holiday from work.

Thérèse Siegenthaler was twenty-one and was studying sociology at Woolwich College and living in lodgings in Deptford in south-east London when she disappeared. She had been born and brought up in Switzerland, where her family still lived, and possibly through that connection had got a part-time job at the Bally shoe shop in the Swiss Centre on Leicester Square, in the heart of London's West End. She had set out to hitch-hike to Holyhead to catch a ferry to Ireland where she had arranged to meet up with a priest friend in April 1974. They had a shared interest in the politics of South Africa. She was going to be away for only a week because she had tickets for the theatre in London on her return. She didn't go to the theatre. One of her friends warned her about the perils of hitch-hiking. She assured her that she could look after herself because she had trained in judo. If she was hitch-hiking across the country to Fishguard or Holyhead she could well have been picked up around Gloucester. She was never seen again.

Her body was buried adjacent to Lucy Partington's body, on the other side of 'the nursery alcove' in the cellar at Cromwell Street, the third body in five months to be buried there. Again it was the same pattern of finger and toe and ankle and wrist bones missing; a great many of these bones missing altogether. Again also the evidence of dismemberment and decapitation and the circular, silencing mask or gag, although this time made of a rolled and looped scarf square tied in a bow that could be undone, but not by Thérèse Siegenthaler whose hands, like her feet, certainly would have been bound. The bones had been chopped and compressed into a roughly cubical area about two to three feet in each direction. There were no clothes although some hair remained.

The floor in the cellar wasn't even. The floor was red brick. It was a brick floor which you could just pull out whenever you wanted to. He'd just lock off the doors and do what he was doing. He'd just bolt them shut and they would hear the sound of work being carried out. For years he would say he was going down to see to the drains in the basement to stop this water coming up. Doors banging and constant digging, demolition, excavation. Then they had a massive thunderstorm, and the basement filled half up with water, the sewers couldn't take it. And it just busted the floor – he just lifted up and broke up. From the beginning the many possibilities of the cellar excited him.

Carol Cooper's body was buried in the back part of the cellar near the garden. The heavy wooden trapdoor was still there and the stone steps leading up into the garden, with the new high brick wall of the church on one side and the long low pier of the kitchen-plus-bathroom extension on the other giving excellent cover. It was possible to back a van in along the side of the house and unload things through the trapdoor entrance to the cellar, as Mr Cook the coalman had, without attracting any attention, especially at night.

He could lift bricks out of the cellar floor and stack them and dig a hole and put the bricks back down again when the hole had been filled. The excess soil could be carried away through the old coal hatch and thrown on the garden. It was mud really. Solid clay. So it was dug out in spits. Blocks. Then he put it back in with his hands. The level of the garden had been raised by about two feet after Mrs Green's orchard trees had been uprooted and her hen house levelled. Lorryloads of soil had been brought in so it was easy to throw on any new dirt and soil – the solid clay that he had broken up with his hands – and incorporate it into the garden.

The shaft in which the jumbled parts of Carol Cooper's body had been buried was towards the middle of the room in a direct line with the coal-hole stairs. Down the coal-hole stairs and straight ahead. He was using the rear cellar room as a place to store his tools at that time and the walls were piled with pickaxes and mallets and shovels and sacks of cement and other building materials. And so he made a hole away from the walls towards the centre.

Between the rear room, which he was using as a tool room, and the front room, which he had begun work on converting into a playroom for the children, was a narrow middle room, the same width as the staircase that went up through the centre of the house. There was a cupboard under the flight of wooden stairs that came down from the hall into the cellar and it was in there that Frank Stephens would store his chainsaws, garden implements and other 'hot' and stolen items. The nursery alcove where Lucy Partington was buried was also in this narrow middle room, and Thérèse Siegenthaler was buried on the left side of the children's playroom just beyond it. The playroom was also the burial place of Shirley Hubbard, whose grave would be marked by the false fireplace wall covered in shiny foil images of Marilyn Monroe. The expression 'the Marilyn Monroe wall' would become a shorthand used to identify the site of the most horrifying of the many bleak Cromwell Street discoveries.

The packing-tape masks, which would survive in the graves of all the people who were murdered, were partial masks – lengths of tape wound around the face and hair and occasionally around the top of the head and under the chin and therefore only partially obliterating; cruel and brutal but not wholly dehumanizing. But the mask that was wrapped around Shirley Hubbard's face while she was still alive obliterated her whole face and mummified her. It covered her hair and mouth and nose and eyes and she was kept breathing and alive with the aid of two plastic tubes which were forced through holes in the brown plastic mask and up into her nostrils. Repellent white semi-opaque plastic tubes that Fred West said had been used as part of a piece of home-brewing equipment but of the kind used by him all his life for stealing and siphoning off petrol. There was all manner of things in the basement.

Shirley Hubbard had been born Shirley Lloyd in 1959, which made her fifteen. She was from a broken home and from when she was two until she was six she lived with one parent or another and in children's homes. In 1965 she was fostered by a council worker called Jim Hubbard and his wife, Linda, in Droitwich in the Midlands and had established the kind of settled relationship with the Hubbards where she wanted to use their name. But in October 1974 she ran away from home and was found a few days later with a soldier camping in a field about five miles outside Worcester. She had tattooed herself on the left forearm with 'SHIRL' in one-inch-high capital letters. Not long after this she met an eighteen-year-old called Dan Davies at a fair at the Worcester Racecourse grounds and he became her regular boyfriend. Danny's brother Alan, who worked on the fair, had once gone out with Carol Cooper, but it seems that is just one of the several coincidences that now link Shirley Hubbard and Carol Cooper who almost certainly never knew each other. In the middle of her final term at Droitwich High School in November 1974, Shirley got a work-experience job on the make-up counter at Debenhams in Worcester. Danny Davies worked at a branch of John Collier the tailor's in Worcester and they spent the afternoon of 14 November together around the town, eating chips on the banks of the Severn, and later at the Davies's house with Danny's brother and sisters. Shortly before eight thirty in the evening, they wandered back into the centre and he put Shirley – he thought – on the bus to Droitwich. What he didn't know was that she had packed a few things and taken them into work with her that morning. She never returned to Droitwich and Linda Hubbard and her husband never heard of or from Shirley again. Somehow Shirley Hubbard made her way, or was taken, to Cromwell Street, where she was kept in secret, murdered, and buried in secret until her remains were excavated from underneath the cellar at ten to three on the afternoon of Saturday, 5 March 1994, the fifth set of remains to be discovered. A number of toes and fingers had been amputated and taken away. She had been decapitated and her thighs had been twisted out of their sockets. The bones showed many cut marks in the region of the neck of the hip bone. Her skull was still encased in the frightening hood mask. One of the plastic tubes that had been used to keep her alive had come loose and was adrift in the hole. The other was still poking into the mask at nostril-level and curved upwards over the dome of her skull, discoloured brown after twenty years in the ground. The slurry around it was cleared and it was lifted out carefully and photographed and logged as having been found close to the Marilyn Monroe wall.

Thérèse Siegenthaler was murdered in April 1974. Shirley Hubbard was murdered in November 1974. It was in the summer of 1974 at the midpoint between these two murders that Fred West started working as a driller/borer on the big Asquith drill at the wagon works. And he quickly made it clear to the men he was working with at the wagon works, as he had made it clear to the men he worked with at Permali's and other places, that he was in charge of a household where an open attitude to sex was not only welcomed but expected, and where his wife in particular was anybody's. She was going out a lot, putting out with other men and was particularly interested in black men and other women, but she was anybody's, 'So if you want sortin' out.' He had a load of audio tapes of himself and Rose and others having sex and he would bring these to work with him in a carrier bag and lend them out. He had home cine movies as well and he would bring these in in a carrier bag. Home porn. He had both types in fact: he had your run-of-the-mill under-the-counter jobs – American- and Scandinavian-made black-and-white stag films; and he had 8 mm. home movies of his wife performing alone and with others although the others never included Fred. They were open about it in this way. They were quite open about it. It was an open lifestyle.

   In the televisionless days twenty years earlier when the door to his grandmother's house – to virtually all the houses in Cromwell Street – had always been open and you'd walk up the alleyway and straight in, Brian Fry had put on film shows in the back living room on Sunday evenings and the whole family had come. There were a lot of sons and daughters, cousins, aunts and uncles and, for the Greens as a family, number 25 was the main meeting point. And on Sundays after tea as many of them as had come would squeeze into the tiny back living room to watch the newsreels that Brian's perk from his job as a rewind boy at the Ritz in Barton Street had allowed him to slip home. For a screen he used a bit of cardboard painted up with a professional-looking black border. But the equipment he showed it on was professional standard – he had a Pathé H camera and a Pathé Son sound projector – and through the miracle of advanced technology they would be able to watch Derek Ibbotson recapturing the mile record in 1957, the swearing-in of President Kennedy in 1961 and other world happenings only a week or so after they had taken place. The lights would go off and the projector would start up and the voice of Bob Danvers-Walker would come on explaining what they were seeing and the world would be brought into their living room, which Brian's grandmother was old enough to still find thrilling. There were two film buffs in the family: Brian was the rewind boy at the Ritz in Barton Street and his uncle Raymond was the projectionist at the little fleapit cinema in Lydney in the Forest of Dean. It was Ray who had bought Brian his first camera and it had become more than a hobby; it had become a passion. Brian was a railway buff: he followed the steam. But he picked up an interest in photography and cameras at an early age and it got into his system. He lived it. He lived and died films. Photography and cameras. There is a word for it – scopophilia: 'love of looking'.

Polaroid cameras were the perfect kind of camera for the kind of pictures Fred West liked taking. They were fast – virtually instant; and, more important, the film didn't need to be taken for processing by somebody else. He stole an early Polaroid camera and started taking close-up photographs of vaginas when he was in his early twenties; there would be an album of these pictures still in Cromwell Street as late as

1992. Throughout their twenty-five years together he took numerous pictures of Rose on her own and with other men. There was the album of close-up pictures of men's erect penises kept locked in a briefcase in Rose's special room and the still photographs and home-movie footage and eventually videotapes of Rose holding herself open and being explored clinically and forensically by him; being gazed into in a fixated, insatiable, obsessive way.

Around the time he started at the wagon works he acquired an 8 mm. movie camera. And he would go round the factory on a Friday or Saturday and ask the other drillers and welders and brake-press and grindstone operators if they wanted to come round to his house on Sunday and watch some pornographic movies which he had on super-eight film. This was before the days of video recorders and he would show the films from midday to early evening in the cellar, getting as many people in there as possible. He had a makeshift bar down there and would charge for the drinks he supplied as well as a small entrance fee. He would occasionally say he'd been over to France and got a couple of new ones in. It was mostly the single men who were interested and the most regular white attender was a man called Robert Jackson whose nickname was 'the Honey Monster'. He worked in the time clerk's office at the wagon works and was regarded as a bit weird because he used to talk a lot about witchcraft and covens and sacrificing lambs. Jackson, who was also known as 'Peardrop' because of his size and his shape, was always a good source of pornographic magazines, which he said he had got from abroad. He claimed he had contacts in the modelling world and could get photographs done. And he persuaded at least one girl to pose topless for him at a friend's house. He carried the Polaroids of her around in his pocket.

They were a close-knit gang of men at Wingate's, as the wagon works was sometimes called. Fred would get to work at seven in the morning and was starting to do his work by quarter past although the official clocking-on time was seven thirty. He would take any overtime that was going and got on well with his chargehand, Ronnie Cooper. Ronnie was Gloucester man and boy and, although he had grown up in Coney Hill, a rough part of the city, he had lived for many years in Apperley, a village on the river Severn near Tewkesbury, and now was more country than Fred. His house was on a hill at the bottom of the village, near the river, and there hadn't been a month of the year that he hadn't seen the road to his house flooded. When that happened he would get in a boat and row over hedges and five-bar gates to the high point where he had parked his car the night before. Then he'd tie the boat to a tree and at night-time make the same journey in reverse with the help of the house lights and a torch. It was an operation that involved waterproofs and waders and God knows what else and Fred loved that. Hearing the stories of how Ron had had to bloody swim to work. It was the kind of thing Fred liked. Fred was having a running battle with the underground water that was constantly threatening to flood *his* house – constantly carrying out running repairs to stop this water coming up; to stem the rise of thick murky water. What you got round Cromwell Street used to be the moat round Gloucester. Gloucester used to have a moat round it. The moat was filled in, so you've got a very high water table. A small lesson in local history from Fred. Ronnie learned to take a lot of what Fred told him with shovelfuls of salt and Fred and Ronnie got on great. Fred was up to Ronnie's house in Gabb Lane at Apperley all the time. And when Ronnie had to go into hospital for a week Fred insisted on staying out at Apperley every night to make sure that Ronnie's wife was all right. He'd drive out every night in the caravanette he was driving at the time. A bloody blue thing. A bloody old thing. An old Trojan caravanette. And he'd park up in the orchard below the patio and spend the night. 'I'll look after your wife, look. I'll keep an eye on the wife.' The nearest neighbour was half a mile away down there. Being mates, Ronnie thought it was bloody good of him, like. In the mornings Fred used to drive to work in the 'van.

Fred was always there at Gabb Lane. And Ronnie got into the habit of going to Cromwell Street on a dinnertime nearly every day with Fred. How it happened was one day when it was hot and they were sitting outside in Bristol Road, Fred just said, 'C'mon.' Ten minutes' walk across the park and into Fred's house. They'd sit in the back room. There was a spy-hole in the side door. You couldn't get in there. And there were Polaroids in the bathroom of Fred's wife. Kinky pictures stuck to the wall of a woman who was obviously Rose who would always be in the scullery off the living room making tea for them when they arrived. Didn't talk really a lot. But if the two of them were talking, laughing and joking, she wouldn't half stare at Fred sometimes. Glare. Give him that glare. Half an hour a day, four or five days a week for five or six years and Ronnie never suspected a thing. He took his sandwiches with him and supped his tea and he never suspected nothing. Fred told him she was a model and offered him home movies of his missus. Took him and showed him where the cameras were. Ronnie never told his wife about any of this or about the kinky pictures or the spy-hole in the door. It's how men talk. And at over fifty years of age he believed he was way too old for that kind of thing himself. He was bloody fifty-odd then. What interest did he have in that? That was the end of the conversation as far as Ron was concerned. Oh, bloody yeah.

Fred's total obsession with decorating was the only thing Ronnie thought was slightly strange. The house was like a building site. It was never not like that. Decorating, building, DIY. As a result he was always black and never clean. Black hands. Black face. It was a noisy shop and it was dirty work. It was heavy, dirty work. And he would go home off one shift and come back for the next shift on the next day and it was obvious he hadn't washed. Forget a bath. He hadn't washed. Some of the men who worked with him moaned that every time they went near him he always smelled. Black face. Black hands. Boilersuit stiff and the jeans and shirt under it stiff with grease and dirt. Turning up day after day in the same flared jeans and dirty shirt. Working at home and working at work and presumably thinking that once something's dirty you can't dirty it any more. Good worker, mind. Brilliant worker. No complaints there. Always a cobble on. And always black. Few and far you saw Fred dolled up.

For a boaster, for the bastard liar that many of the men at the wagon works thought he was, he could sometimes seem oddly shy. He struck some of them as a very quiet chap. He wouldn't mix with anybody. He wouldn't go to a pub at all. He always said he was too busy if you asked him out for a drink. Said he had too much to do. Colin Price had helped Fred guillotine and bend metal for his house sign and for other bits and pieces for around the house. They traded ornamental fish. Fish, some tools, a few plants. Occasionally Fred would drive over to Colin's at Longlevens but he was itchy and would never want to stay. It was out to the greenhouse, sort a few plants out, and gone. Away.

When the men in his shop stood in a group together for a picture to mark the retirement of one of them, a man called Reg Williams, who the joke was had been born in the shop, Fred didn't want to join in. His workmates all grouped together in their boilersuits and grimy faces and steel-toe-capped boots to provide a memento for Reg Williams who had worked the press on the other side of Fred's drill for many years, but he didn't want to know. Ronnie Cooper and Fred would sit and have their morning break on two wooden stools on the other side from Reg. 'C'mon now, Fred. We're going to have a picture took.' 'Ah, I won't bother, Ron.' He was eventually persuaded to come in on the edge, peeping bashfully over the shoulder of a taller man, his face sooty, a smudge of dirt over his mouth, standing shoulder to shoulder with a smiling West Indian man, a piece of work slung up behind them.

The evening shift at the wagon works was two till ten. And on one occasion that would remain in Ron Cooper's memory Fred knocked off at ten and was back at seven the next morning looking black and dirty and seeming tired. His explanation was that he'd had a rush job on and that he had been up all night concreting and plastering up. Fred was very proud of his house and on Ronnie's lunchtime visits he was always keen to show Ronnie what he'd done. At the beginning the cellar used to be more than seven feet deep. But he kept putting down layer on layer of concrete to beat the damp, and by the end Ronnie, who is not a big man, had to stoop to get in. He used to call it the kids' playroom and he told Ronnie to come and see how he'd decorated it out. The house was like a building site. It was never not like that. Decorating, building, DIY. 'Come and see what I've done, Ron.'

Juanita Mott disappeared and was buried under the cellar at Cromwell Street in April 1975. She was aged eighteen and unlike the others buried alongside her in the cellar – Carol Cooper, Lucy Partington, Thérèse Siegenthaler and Shirley Hubbard – she had a known connection with the people who lived at Cromwell Street and with the house.

Juanita's mother was from the Coney Hill area of Gloucester. Her father was a US serviceman from Texas who probably gave her her Mexican name and dark-hued skin and then returned to live in America without Juanita or her mother when she was still young. She was dark and attractive with a fiery, wilful side and, like dozens of the other girls who washed in and out of Cromwell Street, was trying out what even in those days, just a year away from the anti-hippy rantings and posturings of punk, was still seen as an 'alternative' way of life. Juanita was difficult. Her family found her difficult and on a number of occasions she had been taken into care. She left home when she was fifteen and moved into a flatlet in Stroud Road in Gloucester on the other side of the park (the side of the park where Lynda Gough had also lived and where Anna-Marie was going to school). She was testing herself and feeling her way and she had become pregnant when she was sixteen. But it was an ectopic pregnancy and so she had lost the baby and had gone on having her wayward but in its own way by then conventional young life. Drugs probably came into it as they had come into Caroline Raine's life two or three years before. Another new experience. She was looking for experience and up for it and obviously running a bit wild and always on the go. Nita, as her new friends called her, went around with a girl called Mary, also from the flatlets, and before that a lodger at 25 Cromwell Street. Mary worked at a café and gaming room in the town called the Golden Goose, and Mary and Nita regularly used to go to Tracy's on the bus station and then on to Snobs and the Top Hat club, which used to stay open late. Snobs or the Top Hat. The Top Hat or Cinderella's. Sometimes Maxi's. Their social circle at that time involved a large group of friends, several of whom used to leave the area for several months before returning to stay in the bedsits. And quite often they used to see friends in the night-clubs who they hadn't seen for a few months.

From the bedsit in Stroud Road, Nita moved to 4 Cromwell Street and while she was there she was charged with stealing a pension book and sent to Pucklechurch Remand Centre in Gloucester. She was given two years' probation. She became a regular at the Pop-Inn café in Southgate

Street which the Scorpions used as their headquarters and where Mary Bastholm had worked. She got a job in a bottling factory, and it was there she met 'Jasper' Davis who lodged with the Wests along Cromwell Street at number 25. She visited him there and it's possible she might have lived there for a period. But by 1975 Nita was living with a friend of her mother's called Jennifer Frazer-Holland in Newent and helping to look after her children. Jennifer Frazer-Holland was getting married on 12 April. And on the night before, a Friday, Juanita Mott left Jenny's house, Horsefair Bungalow, to hitch-hike into Gloucester.

Her remains were found at Cromwell Street at midday on Sunday, 6 May 1994, pushed into a narrow shaft in the cellar. He had taken out the bricks and made a hole and buried her head and her legs and the trunk of her body in the floor of the cupboard used by Frank Stephens and his other burglar friends to store their stolen property. Juanita Mott had been bound and gagged with her own clothes. Ligatures made from two pairs of tights, her bra and two white nylon socks were found wrapped around her skull, under the chin and over the top of the head. She had been trussed up with two lengths of plastic-covered rope, one ten feet long, one seven feet long. Loops had been knotted around her wrists and her ankles. Her skull had been massively fractured, probably by a blow from a hammer. Both kneecaps and many other bones had been taken away.

Four years later Juanita Mott's sister Belinda would become a regular visitor at Cromwell Street. Belinda had a friend called Gill Britt. Gill was going out with a boy named Graham George, and Belinda was going out with Graham's brother, Phillip. Gill Britt was living on the top floor at 25 Cromwell Street in the summer of 1979, and Belinda and Gill and Phillip and Graham would sit up there listening to music and larking about and laughing and having a good time. On some of her visits Fred West or Rose West would open the door. But from the limited contact she had with them there was no way Belinda could imagine they would know that her sister was Juanita Mott who they had tied up and murdered and buried under the cellar floor.

When the floor of the cellar was filled up with bodies he concreted it over. In a few years he would concrete it properly using ready-mix which he would pump in through the narrow vent on the church side of the house from a tanker. But just then in 1975 he couldn't afford ready-mix. He couldn't buy it and he couldn't steal it. And so had to do what he always did: he did it by hand. Bodged it using sand and gravel mixed by hand and carried down in buckets. The same process as the cattle ramp in Fingerpost Field that he had poured and made with his father. The ramp under which Ann McFall and her baby's body lay. The field where he had started driving a tractor when he was nine. A temporary solution involving mixing and carrying and covering up. Then it was concreted, but by hand. Sand and gravel mixed. Just brought in the van and bucketed and dumped down there. Making and constructing. Working and making. Buckets of lime. Sacks of cement. Sewer pipes. Shovels. Back axles. Ice-knives. Rakes. The sheath knife that he always carried on his belt. An actual dagger, used for laying felt. They stood at the spot where they had poured concrete on a farm field many years earlier and he told his father what he had done. 'Come and see what I've done, Ron.' He loved the house. He was so proud of the house. Every penny they had for many years went into the house. The house that they built with their bare hands together.

In these first years in the house he was prone to black moods and fits of depression. He was prey at any given moment to puncture or depression. Depression would come in a flood and he would be gripped by a foul mood and grow progressively more violent. Rose wouldn't know what to do to please him. She had to pretend to the man who was with her that she was having a good time. But if Fred thought she was really enjoying it then he'd go straight in and punch her. He was often unable to sleep and would sit up all night in his working clothes or stay up all night working. Not only could he not sleep, he became fretful and depressed to the point of desperation. It was a black mood and condition that would make him physically sick. He wouldn't join the family for meals. It was a problem for her to get him to bed. He would vomit. He was physically sick. On such occasions he was inconsolable.

Chapter Eleven

It is said that no other English city stands more precisely on its Roman plan. Its traffic lights work in the four main streets laid out by the Romans. Northgate, Southgate, Westgate and Eastgate Streets meet at the Cross and all Gloucester life goes on up and down and through and along and across and around them. For his fifteenth birthday, Fred's mother and father had brought him to Gloucester and bought him a suit from Burton's up on the Cross. That was when the old tram-lines used to be up there. It was sort of a family thing, a tra-dition among the Wests. When you were fourteen you got a gun. When you were fifteen you got a suit. And he had always loved Gloucester from that day, the day of the suit.

The cathedral is built like a cross and there are 'period' tea rooms and craft shops and trinket shops in the alleys close to the cathedral precincts. But the only time Rose went anywhere near the cathedral was to spend the night with one of Fred's Jamaican men on a council estate known as 'Colditz' at the bottom of Westgate Street, and to a pub called The Lampreys close to the cathedral cloisters on country-and-western nights. She would sometimes meet men in The Lampreys and have sex with them up against the wall in the deeper darkness close to the cathedral.

All but the extremities of Westgate and Eastgate Streets have been pedestrianized since the late seventies. Cromwell Street lies east and south, just off the part of Eastgate Street that is full of take-aways and still permits traffic, and close to the part of Southgate Street that leads to the docks and the Victorian factories and the new retail parks sprawled out along the Bristol Road. The city-centre branches of W. H. Smith, C & A, Boots and Marks & Spencer were always only a four- or five-minute walk from Cromwell Street and became less than that when the shortcut was opened up across the car park that was once the schoolyard at Tommy Rich's.

The area around the Cross with all the big shops in it and the cathedral and Shire Hall and the museum and art gallery and the lawyers' and insurance offices is the official, public city. Rose and Fred tended to stick to the ancient, unofficial routes. The centre where they lived is riddled with rat-runs and mossy alleys and long narrow walks, like the dark passageways running behind the walls of grand houses in such a way that the servants, ceaselessly running to and fro laden with coal scuttles, baskets of firewood, bed linen and tea trays, never had to cross the paths of their betters. It was possible to run all over the town without going into the streets. And Rose could frequently be seen dragging Heather, who was five in the autumn of 1975, May who was three and Stephen who was two, plus Anna-Marie who was an obstinate, lumpen eleven-year-old, down cobbled shortcuts and narrow passageways, shouting at one or other of them, clipping another, shouting and bawling and disappearing with them down cuts or dragging them in the side or the back entrances to Eastgate market.

Caroline Raine would occasionally see Rose, and each time she saw her she seemed to have become heavier bodied. She was still quite pretty but she wore her hair in a short, plain, single-parted cut, about down to her collar. A middle-aged style, in other words, for what was still really a pretty young girl. Rose turned twenty-two in November 1975. But she didn't seem to put a great deal of effort into her appearance. She didn't seem to care very much what she looked like and she didn't care what people thought. She just didn't care.

Sometimes in the winter months the children would plead with her not to wear her bobble hat and mittens when she took them shopping. But always the answer was the same. 'If you don't fucking like it, you shouldn't be fucking looking.' An eccentric figure pushing a supermarket trolley down the back alleys of Gloucester in schoolgirl knee-socks and a matching set of bobble hat and knitted scarf and mittens.

Rose and Fred were completely unaware of how other people behaved. She answered the phone by saying 'What' and nothing else. Then somebody would say something and she would say 'OK' and slam the phone down. She never said goodbye or anything like that. She was so rude it was funny. In a shop when an assistant would approach her with a smile and 'Can I help you?' she'd snap back, 'Is there a law against looking?' Shopping for a fridge she walked around the shop opening the doors of all the fridges and kicking them shut again with her foot. She bought the one that closed best with a kick. Heather and May and Stephen hated going shopping with her because you always knew something was going to happen. She'd think nothing of going into a clothes shop and trying to tear the sleeves off sweaters. If she could do it she'd shout, 'Rubbish.' The same happened with shoes, but this time she'd rip off the soles. These were her tests of quality. She'd pull the children's pants down in front of customers and give them a slapping when they started crying. You'd be standing there and suddenly your pants would be off. She never used changing rooms.

They wore really old-fashioned clothes. Jeans from Oxfam, big flared things. They were called the Waltons because they wore dungarees. They were cut off in the summer. Heather and May had to wear boys' shoes because they were harder wearing. They'd have short-back-and-sides haircuts because they were told their mum couldn't handle combing long hair. They had one set of school clothes and one set of play clothes and that was their wardrobe. They were allowed one Christmas present. She'd get out the Argos catalogue and they were allowed to choose one present, anything as long as it was under £10. What made them feel bad was that their mum couldn't even be happy at Christmas. She'd still be shouting and bawling. Yelling and laying in to them and going ballistic.

In the summer Rose would take them paddling in the public fountains in the King's Walk shopping centre instead of swimming at the leisure centre where all their schoolfriends went but where it cost money to get in. They would fish about in the water for two-pence pieces that people had thrown in for good luck. The shoppers stopped and looked but she never cared what anybody thought. Children in their bathing trunks playing in the civic fountains and scooping out the good-luck coins. She washed her hair in vinegar and the children used washing-up liquid. It was always Co-op starched shirts and every item of clothing was three sizes too big, like a clown's suit. She told them, 'You'll grow into them.' They wore really old-fashioned clothes.

Anna-Marie started smoking in the summer between St Paul's Juniors and Linden Secondary when she was eleven in 1975. She had been making roll-ups for her father when he wanted them for years. And she always had a packet of ten No. 6 in the big brown briefcase she had been given for starting at the senior school. She was the only one in the school who had a briefcase. Everyone else had a proper satchel. And she had her hair cut so short that she looked like a boy and she was quite big and so she got the nickname 'Tank'. This big heavy-set girl dragging this big brown attaché case like a doctor's.

Going to school got Anna out of the house so she rarely played truant. She liked school but she often wasn't there. Her attendance record wasn't good because Rose would often invent an excuse to keep her at home. All the children as they were growing up would be rewarded for staying away from school rather than for attending. They used to encourage them not to go to school. 'If you don't want to go – don't go.' There were always the younger children to look after and the housework to be done, or perhaps Rose had miscalculated and some of Anna's bruises showed. In her whole school career only once did anybody become suspicious about her family circumstances and that was when she was in junior school. The PE teacher had become anxious when she brought in a note yet again saying she couldn't take part in games. There were bruises on her legs. The teacher made her roll down her socks and hitch up her skirt to expose the big black bruises on her legs. She was allowed to sit out the lesson and for the rest of the day no more was said. But no sooner had she got back to Cromwell Street that afternoon than the doorbell rang. It was one of the people her father was always warning her against. There were people out there who could only do you harm. Buzzing at the door. Standing at the door. She got the hiding of her life when the lady had gone. One of the worst beatings. The smartly dressed woman introduced herself as being from the Welfare Department and Rose was 'Oh, come in' and all this. Hospitality itself. Oh, come in. She went out of the front door quite reassured and never came back again. 'Oh well, that's fine, Mrs West.' One of the worst beatings. It taught Anna-Marie a lesson about the Welfare – they couldn't help and any attempts they made to do so could only rebound on her. So there she was. Really a prisoner. Rose wore the master key on a string around her neck. They knew what time school finished and exactly how long it took to walk home across the park. If she wasn't in that door bang on quarter past four they wanted to know why. They never had people round. You were locked in. If you went to the shop you were followed.

It was rare for Anna to get new clothes. Mostly she wore

Rose's cast-offs. She hated the huge flower-print dresses she gave her but she had no choice but to wear them. It was only when Rose had dished out a real beating or Anna had pleased her in some way with her 'friends' that Rose might buy her something, a lipstick or a packet of cigarettes or some clothes.

One day in the first half of 1975 when Anna was in what was going to be her last term at junior school and so hadn't quite turned eleven, she had been introduced to some of Rose's coloured gentlemen with the funny names. They had nicknames instead of names. 'Bonnie', 'Sonny', 'Sheepy', 'Suncoo', 'Duke Roy', 'Bigger'. She had seen these men in the house waiting for their time with Rose. Passing the time until it was time to do whatever it was they did with Rose. She had a good idea. It was what she had been having to do with her father for three years. She had been submitted to his devices. But it was just an idea. She had heard things. Funny sounds and noises coming out of Rose's special room. But she hadn't seen anything until the day her father took her and made her look. Took the plate with 'Rose's Room' written on it off the door and unscrewed the wood screw and had a look first with his eye pressed up to it and then made her look. Cackled without making any noise, only jiggling his shoulders, and made her put her eye to the hole and watch what was going on. Rose was naked on the bed with a black man who was quite old. He was about thirty years old. And he was doing things with Rose that she knew she was soon going to have to do with the man. With this man and with other men. Her dad didn't say anything to her straightaway. Not then. But she knew. In addition to having sex with her father at houses where he was working and on building sites and in his van, and having sex where and when Rose wanted it with her, she was going to have to start doing things with Rose's black men. With Rose's coloured gentlemen friends. She had been made to perform oral sex with Rose on more than one occasion and all the time it was happening Rose was squeezing and scratching her breasts. She had long fingers and quite long nails and she scratched her until she bled. She grabbed the skin at the base of her throat and twisted it until she could hardly breathe. It was sex on demand with her father and sex on demand with Rose and now she knew it was going to be sex whenever they wanted her to have it with 'Bonnie' and 'Sonny' and 'Suncoo' and 'Bigger' and these black men with the funny names.

She had to have sex with Rose's black men once a week. There were about five regulars and occasionally somebody new. Sometimes Anna went first and then her stepmother. And sometimes her stepmother went first and Anna waited outside. Rose was always in the room when Anna went with them and she would touch Anna and her father was always peeping through the door. Shuffling about outside the door and peeping. He would want to talk to her about them afterwards. Ask her about them. About their size. About their bigness and how it felt.

At least two or three times a week during this period Rose would go out to the local pubs and clubs in and around Gloucester. Rose and Fred never ever went out much together because they would always end up arguing. So she would go and if she met somebody she would either bring them back to the house or more likely go to where they lived. She'd always have to let Fred know once the pubs had closed what she was going to do. That was a steadfast rule. If she was coming home or staying out until the morning. She wasn't always willing to go. She was often reluctant. She was tired. It was tiring looking after a house and four children. By the time she had washed, fed, changed them, got out and shopped, she was drained. As soon as she sat down to have a cup of tea or something she found herself falling asleep. Fred would cuss her if he caught her. Kick her; drown her in hot water or tea. Either it was the children if she was in, or she was out with these other men. It was tiring. He used to send her out night after night. He used to grind her down, telling her she was a bad wife if she didn't do things for her husband. In those days, whenever Rose went out she always looked presentable. She would dress nicely, put on a little make-up and some of the junk jewellery that Fred was always picking up and that he liked to see her wear. She usually went out without any underwear and would quite brazenly sit with her legs open. She hated Anna-Marie wearing trousers and would tell her that she should be letting the air get to her.

Starting in about 1976 when Anna-Marie was twelve, Rose would sometimes dress her up and put make-up on her and take her out with her for the evening. She would apply some blusher and a slash of lipstick and put her in a dress that made her look older than her years. Not tarty, Anna thought at the time, just older. Grown up and quite pretty. This happened one summer night when she was twelve or thirteen and she would remember they were laughing and joking. Anna laughing and Rose laughing and Fred chuckling watching them. She didn't feel apprehensive. The three of them got in the green Bedford van that Fred was driving at the time and he drove them to a pub in the country outside Gloucester and left them.

Anna drank Gold Label barley wine which was very potent. Rose was buying. She was laughing and joking and talking to a few people. She bought some crisps. It was very relaxed. Anna remembers drinking Gold Label. Rose would say it was Malibu and Coke. But the same result. Anna got drunk. She got steamed. Even at twelve she was a good drinker. She was going to pubs with squaddies. She was running around the streets acting like a tramp with army blokes and Rose found it so disheartening to see a young girl wasting her time. She could hold her drink. But she was very drunk and unsteady walking when they set off in the direction of Gloucester on foot. This was strange. But Anna was drunk from drinking Gold Label barley wine which was very potent and so didn't ask why they were walking home. They had walked a short distance from the pub down a country lane into the dark when Anna saw her father's Bedford van cruise to a stop in front of them and noticed Rose's mood change in a very drastic manner. The back doors of the van opened and she was pushed in the back. Rose punched her in the back. 'If you think you're going to be fucking friends with me, you've got another think coming. You're fucking joking.' Anna had a light blue skirt on and a blouse. Clothes that Rose had chosen for her just a couple of hours earlier and made her feel like she was being taken out on the town by an older sister. They had been kidding and joking. She was bundled into the back of the van and her father came into the back and he was hitting her. Rose was scratching at her breasts causing them to bleed and her father was hitting her. It was the van where she would often have sex with her father and that was the secret between them. There was a mattress in the van and the tools were all tidy in the van and never seemed to get in the way. A purple light would go on on the dashboard and it would start. Tongue in the mouth kisses. She hated it. Rose was hitting her and twisting her nipples and her father was hitting her. She couldn't believe what was happening. The viciousness and the names. She had done nothing to hurt either of them. She was only a child. Rose was being sarcastic and calling her names and taunting and laughing and fondling her breasts and squeezing and pinching. She was held down by Rose while her father raped her.

When it was over they just drove home to Cromwell Street where the other children had been left without anybody looking after them. Anna made her way to the bathroom, washed her injuries and crawled into bed.

Her feelings were very deep within herself, she would say. She couldn't relay her true feelings to paper. Her report would show that she had been absent from school on fifty-two occasions that year.

The summer of 1976 was a summer when a few drops of rain made headlines. The crowd applauded when rain stopped play during the cricket at the Oval. It was a scorchingly hot summer and once again Bill Letts took Rose and the children on holiday to the holiday camp in Westward Ho! in Devon. But the holiday was cut short when Rose scandalized her father by working her way through the resident band. It was the joke of the camp and Bill Letts refused to stay and be laughed at, or let her be laughed at, any more. She didn't care, but they packed their bags and drove home.

From somebody who wouldn't have the dirty gypsy Fred West in his house, Bill Letts had been converted into somebody who was to be found at Fred West's house more and more. He took voluntary redundancy from Smith's Industries in 1976. He was fifty-five. And when they got back from Devon, Fred and Rose's father applied to join the National Federation of Master Window Cleaners together.

At the end of 1975 Fred had got rid of the lodgers. One of them had complained to the council about overcrowding. The house was not registered as what was called a house in multiple occupation and he had been given thirteen weeks to install a fire escape and an alarm system. But rather than do that Fred decided to get rid of the lodgers until the heat had gone off, when he would have the lodgers back in again.

There had been some talk at the beginning of 1976 about turning the cellar into a granny flat for Grampy Letts. A place for Grampy Letts and his new lump-sum redundancy payment to live in. You can believe that the whiff of money would have played some large part in the thinking of the compulsive pilferer and handler of stolen goods who was offering. The man Stephen called the incredible thieving machine. Daisy Letts warned her husband of this before he too left her to go with Fred West. 'I warned him that there was always going to be somebody waiting to pick him up with his money.' But who was going to be doing what to who? That's what it came down to in the end. Bill Letts was no helpless bystander in these matters. It had been a trait of his that he would always use whatever means possible to get what he wanted. Whatever he had, he had to have the best. And if he had to con his children out of their savings to have it, that's what he would do. He was ruthless. 'You pay your way first, and what's left you live on.' That had always been Mrs Letts's motto. But not her husband's. She always felt she upheld Dad in a lot of ways. He would always put the money on her, for her to sort out. Bills. He was a spendthrift. He borrowed two hundred pounds off Andrew once when Andrew had just started working and was still living at home, he said to buy a fireplace. Andrew never saw it again. You knew you were never going to see it again. His own father was a regular target. He was always tapping his father for money. Old Bill Letts senior never had any peace with their dad trying to wangle his money out of him.

Andrew, who was trusting and naïve, had grown up thinking of his grandfather just as somebody who used to work for the gentry, the well-to-do kind of people. He'd sort of run the house for these kind of people. A bit of a ladies' man. Used to like the ladies. Always used to put on an impression for the ladies by all accounts when he was younger. After the death of their Grandma Letts, who everybody had known in the Bideford area of north Devon because she had been the midwife in Northam, their grandfather started coming to stay with them for extended periods, and Rose and the younger Letts children came to know him well. He would be given the smallest of the three bedrooms at Tobyfield Road; Graham and Gordon would go in with Glenys and Rose in the back room, and Andrew would sleep on the sofa downstairs. A funny old stick, Andrew always thought, when he thought anything about his grandfather, which wasn't often.

But Graham, whose life was in the street, thought he could see deeper into the picture than Andrew as usual. Graham had heard his grandfather had a reputation for being studley. It wasn't just the car and the boiler he looked after. His father and his mother had told him that separately. That his grandfather got by servicing rich women in Devon. So Graham saw him in that light rather than being the butler and the chauffeur and doffing the cap. As a randy old sod. A dirty old devil. He had seen him in action on the estate. His grandfather had lived with a woman in a 'van on the Lakehouse site when Fred West was living there. Graham used to go down and lay carpets and underfelt and he would see old Bill with this woman 'van dweller. 'Whoa, you should be slowing down at your age!' But he didn't. Randy old bugger. He kept on going. It occurred to Graham and Glenys to wonder whether there might not even be something between old Grandfather Letts and their mother, shut off in the house up in Cleeve on their own there after their father had gone. They also wouldn't have been surprised if he had made off with their grandfather's money as well as whatever he'd pulled down as his redundancy cheque.

It wasn't a lot. Two-to-three thousand pounds in 1976. It wasn't a lot of money. Daisy Letts had been happy to say goodbye to the money if it also meant seeing the back of her husband. They were continuing to go through a bad time. Things still weren't well between them. Her nerves were shredded. She had been living on tenterhooks for thirty years because of his violence. And so this money was really like a key to her. Something to unlock this grinding-down, hopeless situation. It was mental and physical cruelty. He was a cruel man, there were no two ways about it. He was probably a schizophrenic. They were a perfectly happy-go-lucky family when he wasn't there. When he was there, everything changed. And so this money was like a prayer answered and she made it clear to him that he was free to go with it. He could take it and go and she would only hope the best for him. It was the first time he had a bit of money in his pocket and she said to him, 'You've got your chance now. Why don't you go and see if you can't take your chance?' Before the trip to Westward Ho! in the hot summer with Rose and the children, Rose's father had gone with Fred and found a property in Southgate Street in Gloucester. 214 Southgate Street had formerly been a butcher's called Finch's. Mr Finch, the butcher, who had a second shop near the Cross. And they acquired the property and immediately set about turning it into a café, which they would own together. Fred set about it, which was his part of the arrangement. Bill Letts provided the money to pay for the lease and acquire the necessary equipment. And Fred did all the conversion and building work that was needed as his share. He made a start while the others were on holiday in Devon, working nightshifts at the wagon works and doing the rough work for preparing the café for opening during the day. They were close to each other. They were almost neighbours. So he would finish his shift at the wagon works and make an early start, chucking the white tiles and blue tiles off the walls, hardboarding the floor and putting down floor coverings and counters and kitchens and all that. They had all that printed ply panelling all round the walls and they had all the furniture made at a top place at Charlton Kings. It was made out of elm. The backs of the chairs had stars cut out of them and there was a big table along in the window which sooner rather than later would find itself in Cromwell Street as its permanent home. Andrew Letts would have the star-backed chairs when Fred's and Bill's café eventually folded, as everybody connected with it except those two could see it was going to, after about fifteen months.

It was looking well and, although the plan for a granny flat in the cellar came to nothing, Fred offered Bill Letts one of the lodgers' rooms at Cromwell Street in the autumn of 1976 in the run-up to opening day. Rose was continuing to have a sexual relationship with her father, which Fred encouraged and was very happy about. What he claimed at the end of his life to be less happy about was the sexual relationship between Rose's father and Anna-Marie. Bill Letts denied that this was something that had ever taken place. More than that: Andrew was there and heard his father tell his mother that he had been kicked out of 25 Cromwell Street by Fred when he objected to Anna-Marie, who was then still only twelve, sleeping with a much older man. He had gone upstairs after hearing a lot of noise, so the story went, and there was a man up there with Anna. He had told him to get out of there. He had told him to get himself out of it, but on his way back down to his room he had met Fred who grabbed him and told him, 'What goes on in my house is my business, Bill.' End of story. This was Bill Letts's story.

Fred West's story, found among his prison jottings after he had hanged himself in 1995, was the following. 'I stopped home [from work] to see Rose. It was about 11 p.m. Rose was in bed, so I went into the bedroom . . . I didn't put the light on in the room. I sat at the bottom of the bed. I was telling Rose what had happened to my hand at work [he had injured his thumb while using the drill]. Then Anna came running downstairs and said to Rose, "Grampy's going to sleep with me" . . . I went upstairs to him and said, "What's going on?" Anna was with me. Bill said, "Rose said Anna could sleep with me but Anna's playing up" . . . When I got home in the morning Rose and her dad was in the kitchen having breakfast . . . He said to me, "Do I have to go?" I said, "Yes." "Where can I go?" I said, "To the café." There was a flat at the top of the café. "You can go there."'

Rose's attitude to the café was couldn't-care-less indifference. She knew them too well. She knew her father and she knew Fred and all the money they hadn't made. And she could tell that the café, which was officially called the Green Lantern although it was the Cumngetit to Fred, was another money-losing scheme. All that would happen was they would end up in debt up to their necks. She didn't think it was worth wasting her time on. Besides, by the early part of 1977 she would be pregnant again, with the baby due in December. So Rose kept herself separate from this enterprise involving members of her family. It was mostly Fred, who had given up a good job at the wagon works to do it. Rose seems to have decided to hold herself aloof as a vindication of her position: they had ended up camping on her doorstep. In the end they had come to her. She was making a home. She was building a family with a new addition on the way. Rose stayed where she was at home while Fred and her first family played at too many cooks.

It had taken no time for them all to come round. Glenys with Jim Tyler. Graham and Barbara White, his girlfriend from Stoke Orchard, who had got themselves moved into the flat. Andrew and Jacquie who had got married that summer and hadn't invited Fred and Rose to the wedding. Gordon was there somewhere as well. This one and that one. Who was ripping off who? Who could rip off who the fastest? Too many chiefs and not enough Indians. Shake hands with Graham. Now count your fingers.

Ronnie Cooper went in a few times for chips and eggs and

to remind Fred that there was still a job there for him any time he wanted. Ronnie had his chips and eggs cooked for him on one occasion by Fred, which was an experience. Fred standing at the range putting his dirty hands on everything and his white eyes and his red mouth in his dirty face. He was as black as the ace of spades. And of course he had a cobble, working for Jim Tyler. Graham Letts was also working for G & D Services, the haulage company run by Jim Tyler. Fred drove a blue diesel minibus van that had been rigged up for him by the dog man in St Michael's Square who sold them iffy Alsatians. He had built on a roof-rack of scaffolding poles designed to carry eight-feet-by-four-feet sheets of ply that fitted on the top. This van had scaffold poles that they drilled straight through the van and welded on the chassis. It had one massive roof-rack on it. And Fred drove it for Jim, delivering stuff all over the place for him to make money to get the café going. Tyler used to do a lot of ply for this bloody DIY stuff. Working a cobble doing hauling for Jim Tyler. Or perhaps the café was the cobble and this was Fred's proper job. It was hard to tell which was which. And all those Letts together was a shambles. They were shambolic. Rose's family. You could take them but you couldn't leave them. Rose's lot. They were soap-operatic. Every day was like a soap opera.

Just Graham. Even leaving the drink out of it. Leaving the drugs and the drink out of it. Forget the rest and just look at Graham. He had been knocking around with a thirteen-year-old who had one brother who was a bouncer and another brother who was a DJ at Tracy's nightclub on the bus station. Graham lived with Sandra Johnson* for a while at the end of 1976 above the Crown pub in Cheltenham. She was thirteen, he was eighteen and she was very domesticated and wanted

*Not her real name. She was called 'Miss A' when she was a witness at Rose West's trial.

babies. In early 1977 Graham took Sandra down to Bognor Regis in a stolen car for, in his words, a bit of a jaunt. But they ended up being apprehended and Sandra was taken into care as a result of the stolen-car incident. She was placed at Jordan's Brook House, a former approved school, in Gloucester in May 1977. A month earlier Graham had been sent to borstal for four months' recall. While he was there, Sandra wrote to him enclosing the picture of a year-old baby saying he was the father. He knew he couldn't be because the baby was too old and Barbara White had seen Sandra while Graham was in borstal and she wasn't pregnant. Glenys and Jim Tyler were living next door to Barbara White's family in Stoke Orchard and Barbara had first met Graham when he had been living with them. She remembered Charmaine and Anna-Marie when they were little and Fred used to leave them with Mrs Nock, a near neighbour. Barbara had always liked Graham but he was with Sandra Johnson. But then just before he was sent back to borstal and Sandra was taken into Jordan's Brook, Graham ditched Sandra. He came out of borstal in August 1977 and moved into the flat above the café in Southgate Street with Barbara White, who had been working there for just meals and free lodging for Graham's father. Her job was to serve; Graham's mother by this point was doing the cooking. Graham ditched Sandra but she wouldn't stay ditched by him. She wouldn't accept it. She was a hanger-on and kept appearing to see him. Sandra would pop in to the Green Lantern to see if Barbara was still on the scene. Graham and Barbara were woken up one night by Graham's mum because Sandra was there with her friend Yvonne, who used to babysit for Glenys and Jim. Yvonne was another Jordan's Brook girl. Another girl from the home that had been set up to provide care for some of the most difficult and disturbed young people in the country, many with personal histories of degradation and exploitation. By 1977 many girls from Jordan's Brook had started to find their way to 25 Cromwell Street, which had got itself a reputation for being a place where you could expect a sympathetic reception. Rosemary, the woman in charge there, was nice and pleasant and in no way heavy. She seemed to be very understanding and caring, like a young mum or a big sister. The house was always open and you could always cry on Rosemary's shoulder.

Sandra Johnson was still only fifteen in 1977 although she looked – could look – a lot older. When he was younger Graham Letts had this charming talk and people would fall for it at the time. And Sandra had become infatuated with Graham. She needed somebody to take her away from her life and Graham was the person she picked to do it. She needed rescuing from a life that up to that point and continuing had been blasted and often unbearable. But Graham had dropped her. She was very domesticated and wanted babies. But she was living in a home with twenty-three of the most difficult and disturbed girls in the country and Graham had ditched her.

When Sandra found her way to Cromwell Street and Rosemary with the pillowy bosoms and comforting shoulder, it seems to have been a coincidence that Rosemary was also Graham's sister. It is a strange coincidence, but that does seem to have been the case, certainly as far as Sandra was concerned. You had the runaways coming round. The misfits who were of two different sorts: ones who caused trouble and ones who had trouble. Sandra was both. She was very troubled. She was severely disturbed. When her parents separated she had stayed first with her mother, and then with her father. Her father had raped her when she was young and she had suffered further sexual abuse from her brother. She had had many imagined pregnancies and as she grew older she would have repeated hallucinations of seeing people with other people's heads on their shoulders, perhaps suggesting a schizophrenic condition. She was so alone. She had been abused out of innocence. And Rose was so caring and pleasant Sandra let her heart out to her.

Every third weekend the girls in Jordan's Brook were allowed a paid trip home. Sandra usually visited Cromwell Street on a Friday when she was catching the bus home to Tewkesbury to see her mother. Jordan's Brook operated a graded system of supervision in which their status – junior, intermediate or senior – determined how much free time the girls enjoyed. During the period of her most frequent visits to Cromwell Street in the early part of 1977, Sandra was a senior. Her visits were legitimate and nobody could stop her. She would arrive at about ten in the morning and leave about one and Rose would come and sit beside her on the sofa and they would talk about periods and sex and things, which seemed pretty normal for that age. Girls' things. Sandra would particularly remember a dark small notebook Rose used to keep on an occasional table in the living room as if keeping notes or she had another appointment. 'Do you comb your pubic hair? Do you play with yourself?' It just seemed as if everything was supposed to be normal. Girls' things.

But then Sandra started absconding. Running away from the home and going to Cromwell Street. In the summer of 1977, Sandra and her friend Yvonne ran away and slept rough on the streets of Gloucester for a night. The next night they went to Cromwell Street together and were let into the house by Rose who was dressed in just a bra and pants. Yvonne and Sandra stayed that night on the sofa and Sandra kept up her Friday visits to Cromwell Street throughout the summer, still apparently unaware of the link between her new friends and her old boyfriend Graham Letts. On one of these Fridays she would remember many years later Rose answered the door wearing a see-through blouse and instead of going through into the back living room, which is what normally happened, took Sandra upstairs to the first-floor front bedroom which would one day become the Black Magic bar and was the room where the attack on Caroline Raine had taken place.

It was the morning. Sandra's usual time around ten. And the room was filled with people either getting up or getting ready to go to bed, it was difficult to tell. There was considerable nakedness and semi-nakedness. Of course she noticed that. Fred and two young girls. They were both naked. He had some shorts on. One girl was thirteen or fourteen and blonde with bright nail polish on her toenails; the other was a little older with a tattoo on her forearm and dark spiky hair. A whip on the wall. Some strange pictures on the wall depicting animals and people. Saying nothing, Rose West started to remove Sandra's clothes. She started. Saying it was OK, things like that. We are all girls. It felt like a fairground ride where you're stuck against the wall. She started. Relax, it's fun. Enjoy, relax. Sandra was wearing just a sun-dress and a bra. She ended up finishing and she was naked and they were three naked girls. It just seemed as if everything was supposed to be normal. It's all right to touch. Rose got out of her own clothes and started to caress the young blonde girl, whispering it was OK and things like that. It's all right to touch, she said, and led her towards the bed. We are all girls. The blonde girl lay face downwards on the bed and Fred West wrapped brown parcel tape around her wrists and thumbs leaving her fingers free as well as across her chest so that it seemed like bandages. The parcel tape was then wound around her ankles and she was rolled over on to her back on the bed so that her feet could be tied far apart. Sandra wasn't looking but she heard the sound of buzzing. When she looked again she saw that Rose West had a vibrator and a candle and a tube of ointment she presumed was lubricant. Saying relax, enjoy. The girl was crying. There were tears on her face. Fred West removed his shorts and raped her. It was over very quickly. He left the room and soon could be heard downstairs in the kitchen. Rose started aggressively ripping the tape off the girl's body, soothing her when she started crying. All aggressive one minute, then all motherly again. Then she turned her attention to Sandra. She led her to the bed and taped her wrists when she was on the bed. She used words like, relax, it's fun. Sandra sat on the side of the bed, her arms crossed at the wrists, level with her breasts. Fred West came back in the room and Sandra was coaxed on to her front and her legs spreadeagled. She felt things going inside her. She felt fingers probing inside her. She was terrified they were going to put something in her or operate or something. A sexual kiss on the neck. 'Fred, you're enjoying this.' This was Rose. 'Is it turning you on?' She could see Fred West masturbating beside her. Brushed bright bri-nylon sheets. The next thing she was aware of was Rose crouched between her legs. It seemed like for ever. Rose then Fred. Fred had moved and was having sex with her from behind. It was like being on the Cyclone or the Wonderwall. An island of light and noise surrounded on all sides by intense blackness. A fairground ride where you're stuck against the wall. This ride is very frightening and fast-moving. People paying to be frightened out of their lives. Volunteering for that. A gravity ride. She used words like relax, it's fun. Relax. We're all girls, it's OK. It seemed like for ever. It's OK. All aggressive one minute, then all motherly again. It's OK.

Blood had gone down her leg. From her anus, she believed. She grabbed her dress and washed her leg and then she just ran down the stairs and went. She fled in her bare feet down Cromwell Street and across the park and started hitch-hiking home via the Hauliers Arms and the Bristol Road and that way. To her mother's home. She couldn't go to her mum. She couldn't go to her dad. Graham was in the flat over the Green Lantern café with Barbara White. There was nobody now. Because you were in care you were bad. There was nobody.

On another Friday a few weeks later Sandra walked along Cromwell Street carrying matches and a can. There was petrol in the can which she intended to pour through the letterbox of 25 Cromwell Street and set it on fire. Torch the place and burn it to the ground in an act of revenge. But she had forgotten the gates. The high silver painted gates with two opening parts to them and two bells which he would tell them repeatedly it was for their own good they were kept shut up behind and that it was safer and which she found padlocked and closed. She had formed the intention of doing something damaging to the West house and she had gone equipped. She had brought a Castrol GTX can. She had matches with her. She was full of intention. And then these gates. She froze and couldn't go near the house. It was quiet. And the presence of the gates. She kept the matches but threw the can which she had taken from the shed at Jordan's Brook in the back of a food store. She wanted to do it so much. But she threw the can away.

It took them weeks to get the house back to any sort of state where it could be lived in once they got the lodgers out. And Rose thought she had got her house back once they got rid of the dirty hippy lodgers from upstairs. And she had for a while. For most of 1976 while the snoopers from the Council were still snooping about. But in 1977 Fred had decided it was safe to go to bedsits again and had put his two line ad in the *Citizen* offering rooms at £7 a week. He said they would try having girls this time and they were a great deal better. At least they nearly always paid their rent and the money from the rents was useful with another baby on the way.

The Cumngetit as Fred insisted on calling it had opened in the autumn of 1976. But all those Letts together was a shambles and he was back at the wagon works working on his old drill within two or three months. He would remain there without interruption for another seven years. But the café was near enough for him to keep a check on what was happening. And in particular on what Rose's father was up to with the steady stream of young girls from the Jordan's Brook home and elsewhere who had started passing through. The café was open from early morning until midnight most nights. And, following his instinct for spotting any directionless or rudderless person, Fred would usually look in at some point during the day.

The café quickly became absorbed into his fantasy life, as the following paragraph that he wrote in prison shows: 'I was going home from work one morning. I stopped to see Bill. I went to the back door. I looked up to the roof at the back of the café. There was Bill by the bathroom window. He had sacking over him. I said, "What you doing up there?" He said, "Shhhh." He came down to me. He said, "I picked up two young girls in Bristol. They were coming to Gloucester. And they stayed the night. And they're having a bath together. If you get up on the roof you can see them." I said, "No way. I am not into that."'

He met Shirley Robinson, who was to become the seventh person to be buried at Cromwell Street, when he looked into the café one day. She was seventeen and undernourished and spoke with a broad Black Country accent. She came from a broken home. Her father was in the Air Force and she had spent her life being shunted between both parents until in 1974, at the age of fourteen, she had been taken into care in Wolverhampton. Fred West would claim that one of the first things Shirley Robinson told him when he met her was that she was a lesbian and only went with girls, which would have relieved him of some of the anxiety he seemed to feel in the company of all women. At the same time it would have piqued what he liked to regard as his instinct of research into sexual matters. Here was somebody to take home to Rose. A friendless and homeless lemon to take home and put with Rose. He said they would try having girls this time. Shirley Robinson would be eighteen in October and would cease being supervised by Gloucester Social Services, who had taken over on behalf of the Wolverhampton authority, on that date. At Fred's invitation in April 1977 she moved into the small bedroom at Cromwell Street next to the bathroom on the first floor.

Around the same time that Shirley Robinson moved into Cromwell Street, and Sandra Johnson was becoming a regular visitor, John West, Fred's brother who was younger than him by just a year, started stopping by the house most days. John and Fred had stayed out of touch with each other following a row over money for four or five years. But in May 1977 John West started driving what was known as a gulley-sucker for Gloucester Council, and he got into the habit of bringing his sandwiches into Cromwell Street most mornings so Rose could make him a cup of tea to have with his morning lunch. He would start driving a dust cart after a couple of years and would remain a bin man for the centre of Gloucester throughout the eighties and beyond.

The children got used to their Uncle John bringing them presents – stuffed animals and plastic dolls and floppy Raggedy Ann ragdolls that he had rescued from the rubbish. A glass eye would be missing or a seam would have opened showing the nylon filling; the fur of the rabbits and puppies would already be stained from other people's hands and spilled food. They were other children's cast-offs. Dirty toys. But these were their only toys and so they were grateful. Heather and May and Stephen looked forward to these visits from their Uncle John.

Her Uncle John started having sex with Anna-Marie on his visits almost straightaway. She was twelve and a half and he would make her have sex with him in the bathroom off the living room on the ground floor. Her father had made a board for changing nappies on which half covered the bath, and her Uncle John would make her get up on that. He was the only member of her dad's side who would visit them and she had to have sex with him several times a week. He'd come into the house, put the kettle on, and take her into the bathroom. It was a baby-changing rack her dad had made. A foam mattress piece with towel. Always a towel on top of it. She went to Rose about it and she said there was nothing to worry about, it was perfectly all right and was a natural function. He was her uncle. She basically laughed it off. Three times a week for three years, from twelve and a half to fifteen and a half when Anna finally packed her things and ran away from home.

It was her nature at that time to be a violent bully. Anna was a bully at school and had a gang and had started to carry a knife. A gang of them wielding blades. She had come to the attention of the police and was starting to appear to be uncontrollable. She was going out drinking with army blokes and getting absolutely steamed. But then that summer in 1977 when she turned thirteen and the fair came to the park she met Rikki Barnes who was travelling with the Jimmy Rogers Fair and Rikki became her boyfriend. The fair was on the park in Gloucester for three weeks and when it moved on Anna-Marie and Rikki stayed in touch by post. At the end of the season in October Anna invited Rikki to live at 25 Cromwell Street. He was given the room on the first floor at the front, which shared a landing with the small room occupied by Shirley Robinson who was so thin and undernourished Fred used to call her 'Bones'. Soon after Rikki moved in he agreed to help Fred build an extension on the rear of the house. They needed extra room, and in the winter of 1977, with Rose eight months pregnant, Fred, assisted by Shirley Robinson and Anna-Marie and Anna-Marie's boyfriend, started the work of pushing the downstairs walls of the house out at the side and the back, out over the garden. It was as if Fred was always building. The children would come home from school and all join in.

Chapter Twelve

The roof of the new extension was held up by a tree. For an RSJ he substituted stolen railway sleepers. They were supported by the trunk of a tree that he had helped himself to from somewhere – a living, growing thing that he had chopped down and stripped of its branches and planted in concrete at about that part of the garden where Mrs Green's fruit trees used to grow. The evidence of its recent life remained intact: he left the black bark on and the clean white scars of where the limbs used to be were left showing. A tree regarded not in any country way, but as a piece of citified building stuff – dismembered, domesticated, remade. As well as having a useful load-bearing purpose, it formed the centre-piece of the room; a gnarled tree trunk apparently growing up out of the floor of what was the new living room.

Possibly only to Fred did it have associations with the oak tree that sprayed out like an umbrella in the home field where he used to make love to Rena and under which Rena was buried. There was a hunting stile by the side of it and they used to sit up on this stile and just look out over the valley, the woods, Much Marcle. Or perhaps it connected in his mind with another tree that at the end of his life he chose to remember. 'We used to have a fir tree by our back door,' he said, 'and we had the top cut out where the electric came through and we made a house up in there. When my mother used to get at us we'd shoot straight up this tree. My mother was a big woman, and she used to say, "You'll come down when you're hungry." She wouldn't bother with you, but when you came down, she'd have you.'

So anyway he footed it in concrete and it stood there holding up the new part of the house that was on the ground rather than in the ground and set over a damp cellar. He said it gave a bit of character to the place. He knocked all the notches out of it. It was shaped but it was smart, like. He made a good job out of that. It looked like a tree. It was still recognizably a tree. 'Oh, yeah,' he'd say when anybody commented on it. 'Yeah, it's a real old-fashioned.'

When the Sabbath Church was turned from a ramshackle shed into a building made of brick, the new, tall perimeter wall edging his property seemed to offer an opportunity, and opportunities were there to be taken. Without anybody's permission being asked for, the living-room extension would appropriate the wall of the church on one side and would be fixed to the existing kitchen and bathroom on the other. He didn't seem to worry. He plastered all the church wall up and faced it with tongue-and-groove teak-look panelling. He added a porch over the part of the path leading to the front door so that none of what he was doing was visible from the street, in the process adding another locking door and yet another security seal. There were a couple of steps up to the original house, and so there were a couple of steps down into the living-room extension. It extended out from the old back wall over the wooden trapdoor access to the cellar. This access was brought into the house; the sash window that had once looked out on to the garden was blocked in, and now the old kitchen door opened into the new room. The back wall was pushed out until it was brought square with the bathroom extension, so that from the outside the added-to parts of the house looked like a single-storey box rather than an 'L'. The partition wall, which was formed by the extension meeting the existing kitchen, had to be demolished and the hot-water boiler moved from the old scullery kitchen to the new one, which was sited at the garden end of what was going to be an open-plan-style living area emanating from the trunk of a tree.

It was a big job and an ambitious undertaking, especially in the winter, and especially with Rose only a few weeks away from having the new baby. Fred had just got the water boiler off the wall one night – it was three in the morning – when Rose went into labour. It had to be done at night because the tenants would want it back on in the morning. Just as he had got it all apart Rose woke up and realized after having a cup of tea that she was in labour. He took her to the hospital and was with her when Tara was born on 6 December. Tara, who would always be called 'Moses', or 'Mo' – '*De Da!' 'De Mo!'* – in a parody of minstrel speak. Fred's darky routine.

Tara was black. Her father was black. Tara was a half-caste baby and Fred was delighted. They were both delighted, Rose *and* Fred. She was their first baby in four years and she was what they had wanted and even planned for. He called them their 'love children', the children fathered by Rose's black men. And they'd have two more: Rosemary junior (known as 'Roe-Roe') born in 1982, and Lucyanna (known as 'Babs') born in 1983.

Fred West wasn't close to any of his children. He rarely showed them affection and could never remember their names. He couldn't give the police the dates of any of his children's birthdays except May's, which was easy to remember (May June, born June-the-first), when he was questioned in 1994. But he never discriminated between his five natural children and the children Rose had with other men. 'I have never said to anybody that Tara, Rosemary and Lucyanna wasn't my children,' he said. 'I know they're looking at 'em because they're dark and thinking, hey-up, what's this. But it didn't bother me. I couldn't care less. They're my children and that's all there is to it.'

Black children, in fact, were something he wanted and, again casting himself in the role of investigator and sexual experimenter, set out to get. He set up 'experiments' involving the sperm of the black men who slept with Rose. He ordered her to save their semen in condoms and then he mixed the semen of different men together and, using a home-made device consisting of a syringe and a length of copper pipe, injected it into Rose. To keep the semen in what he considered optimum condition, Anna-Marie was made to carry it in knotted condoms inside herself. 'We go up in the hills . . . and use it the same night . . . within an hour and a half,' he said.

In addition to the rituals that involved bottling, and eventually cremating, Rose West's semen-stained knickers, they evolved a ritual between them during which he would video her preparing to go out on the several nights a week he sent her to sleep with Jamaican men. Before putting them on she would hold up her invariably black knickers for inspection by his camera. He would be waiting when she came home early next morning – in time to get the younger children to school – and he would want to film the semen stains before he left for work. She would also hold up a number written on a card, giving the man she had been with the night before marks out of ten. It was a real ritual in that it happened not just once or a handful of times but dozens of times, the same things happening in the same place and time and in the same sequence (the top-floor back bedroom at around nine o'clock at night and seven in the morning), framed and shot in the same way. Filmed evidence not only of her compliance and obedience – her willingness to put herself in bondage to him; but evidence also of the loss of self-control and abandonment that accompanies an orgasm – the kind of little death that Fred West was so compulsively interested in witnessing in other people and so afraid of experiencing himself. Do as you like, Fred said, and she did and liked it and liked telling him about how much she had liked it no less than he liked hearing about it.

Fred's chargehand Ronnie Cooper got into the habit of parking in Cromwell Street when he went shopping with his wife and family in Gloucester on Saturday afternoons. They would leave their children to play with the West children at Fred's and Rose's and come back and collect them an hour or two later. Through the winter months of 1977 and 1978 Ronnie was interested to watch how the work on the jerry-built extension was progressing. He admired Fred's nerve. It wasn't something Ronnie himself would ever risk doing. It was clear that by doing this Fred felt he was going up in the world. 'Where's the cellar gone, then?' Ronnie asked Fred one day, and with one of his sly grins on him Fred showed him. The coal-hole opening to the cellar had been made into a trapdoor with two opening parts to it instead of the single timber lid. Carpet that matched the carpet that had been laid in the new family area had been glued on top of the cellar hatch in a way that made it invisible to anybody who didn't know it was there. Anna-Marie's boyfriend, Rikki, had made a bench table and chairs which were hinged and fitted with the trapdoor and moved with it whenever it was opened from underneath. Heather and May and Stephen slept in the cellar and would need to come up to use the toilet sometimes through the night. The hatch door in the living room was the only way in or out. The door from the hall into the cellar from then on was kept bolted shut.

But the thing that would most stick in Ronnie Cooper's mind about his visits to 25 Cromwell Street around that time had nothing to do with home improvements. Some time around the time that Rose came home from hospital with the new baby at the beginning of 1978, Ronnie and his family stopped by as usual one Saturday and Pam, Ronnie's wife, went straight over to the Moses basket on the sofa where the baby was sleeping. The 'babby' as Ronnie called it, who was asleep in a wicker basket on the settee. 'My missus went all the colours of the rainbow. She went pink and it was jet black. There was a babby on the settee as black as the ace of spades. "Where's the new babby, Fred?"' And Fred thought it was hilarious, of course. The colour Ron's missus went. The look on Ron Cooper's face. Fred knew who the fathers were. Tara's father was one of Rose's regulars called 'Sheepy'. Rose didn't want the fathers to know. That was supposed to have been the point of his 'experiments' when he started doing them. Rose wanted those children to be part of *her* family. But Fred told them anyway. Mouth almighty. Fred couldn't resist letting them know.

It soon got around the factory about Fred West having a black baby. Then two months after giving birth to Tara, Rose was pregnant again, this time by Fred. And this was another big joke in the factory, Fred having a wife and a girlfriend pregnant at the same time.

One of Fred's labourers on the house extension was Shirley Robinson. Frank Zygmunt had died a year or two after they moved into Cromwell Street. But his widow and his son Roger had kept on the properties and it was Fred West they still turned to for odd jobs and maintenance work and emergency repairs. And Shirley Robinson, frail as she was, had become his willing helper at these jobs. Shirley had told Fred that she was a lesbian when he first met her, and this wasn't a lie. Her first sexual encounters after moving into Cromwell Street had almost certainly been with Rose. Rose West denies it. But Anna-Marie and others say it happened and it seems likely to be true. A few lodgers became a part of the family and Shirley Robinson was one of these. She had no family of her own, and she marked her freedom from local-authority supervision in October 1977 by electing herself a member of

353

the West family. 'These are my children, this is my wife and this is my lover,' Fred told the sister of one of the other lodgers in front of Rose around that time. Shirley had been living in the house for six months by October, and things had apparently been going well. But that was also the month she got herself pregnant by Fred West.

His account of how it happened contains characteristic elements of fantasy in it. More convincing is the (apparently inevitable) environment of building dust and building materials and ladders and tools. 'Shirley worked like a man . . . I worked on my job by day [and then] went to work with Shirley till we went home at eleven or twelve at night . . . [One night] Shirley was undressing to change out of her working clothes. She said, "You want to have sex with me?" I said, "You're a lesbian." She said, "Lesbians have sex with men." I had never made love to a lesbian. I wondered what it would be like. So I said, "Yes" . . . We started [on another occasion] to strip the walls. Shirley said, "I will take my overalls off . . . catch them." So I look up. She kicked them off at me to catch them, so I did. I looked up and said, "You got no pants on." She said, "No, it's too hot to wear them." So Shirley said, "Catch me." So she jumped down to me to catch her. I did. We fell on the floor. Shirley held me tight and said, "Please make love to me. I am in love with you." . . . So I made love to Shirley. Then we got on with the work.'

As in the separate but parallel accounts they gave of the happenings at and around the bus stop opposite the Pump Room at Pittville Park, it is probably significant that Fred West's version of how Shirley Robinson came to be pregnant with his baby – the event that would lead to her being murdered – corresponds closely with the story Rose West told people about how she became pregnant with Louise, who was also Fred's. They had been working on the extension when it happened. Fred lifted her down from the ladder she

354

was standing on, made love to her among the rubble, and set her back to work. What a surprise when she found out.

Tara had been born in December 1977. Shirley's baby was due in June 1978. Louise, Rose's fifth, was due in November, five months later. Two pregnant women and four demanding children and a few-weeks-old baby and a house that was still a building site. And Fred as usual was nowhere to be seen. Mr West was the breadwinner and Mrs West was in charge of the domestic scene and childcare. He had taken an allotment in Saintsbridge a couple of miles away and constructed a small shed there at the beginning of 1975. Which gave him somewhere else to go when he didn't want to be around the house, which seemed to be all the time. He could work on the extension at night. He seemed to prefer it that way. Late at night. Through the night. Going back to the wagon works filthy in the morning. There was an atmosphere of tension building and he wasn't able to handle tension very well. His way of breaking the tension was to tell people that Shirley, who was carrying his baby, was going to be his next wife. He'd put his arm around Shirley and tap her stomach and say she was going to be the next Mrs West. That was Fred's idea of a way to lighten the tension. His idea of a joke. As Shirley's pregnancy had started to show more she had started going around the house in only a bra and pants. He'd tap Shirley's bare stomach, cup her stomach and in front of Rose say she was going to be the one to succeed Rose. Shirley who to Rose was silly, carefree and irresponsible. Rose's successor. She was just like having another child around the house. Mr and Mrs West for Ever. The next Mrs West.

It was very tense. Shirley didn't come down so often. There was a jealous atmosphere in the house. Anna-Marie was very much Daddy's girl. Anna would go down to the unemployment office on a Thursday with Shirley. She liked Shirley. Rose wasn't her real mother. She hated Rose. There was a competitive element. Rikki Barnes left the house at the end of February. Anna told him that Fred thought he was being too friendly towards Shirley and this was the reason he would have to leave. Fred was taunting Rose. Shirley was flaunting her relationship with Fred. The children were demanding. The house was a building site. Within a week of leaving Rikki came back to Cromwell Street to live. In April 1978 Shirley had been with them for a year. Her baby was due in two months. She had to come downstairs to use the washing-machine and the telephone. Shirley was becoming emotional, saying she loved Fred. In just briefs and a bra walking around the house. Then one day she was gone. One day Shirley just moved out. She had a girlfriend who lived near by in Gloucester and she went to stay with her. But this was a short-lived arrangement. Suddenly Shirley was back. Her room was small. It was the smallest room next to the bathroom and toilet on the first floor. Liz Parry, top-floor front, had a bigger room and Shirley started spending a lot of time with her. Liz Parry let Shirley stay in her room during the day and sleep on a couch in her room at night when she came back from Tracy's where she had a bar job. Shirley was seeking sanctuary from the rows and the friction and she did that by going to her friend's room. Fred made a special trip to Liz's room and told Liz that Shirley had a fantasy about ripping her knickers off and this was what she was going to do. Shirley told Liz she was frightened of Fred and Rose and she wanted to stay in Liz's room to keep away from them. She was last seen at the health centre in the park for an ante-natal check-up on 2 May 1978 at the beginning of the eighth month of her pregnancy. And she was certainly alive on 9 May because that day Shirley and Liz Parry were in Woolworths in Gloucester and a photograph was taken in a photo booth. Shirley wrote the date, 9 May 1978, on the back of one of the photographs and gave it as a keepsake to Liz. The rest of the strip she kept herself. Woolworths was where they socialized at that time. And the last time Liz saw Shirley was one morning when she went off to meet some friends in the Woolworths café. Shirley seemed fatigued and depressed about everything and she left her drinking a cup of tea, saying she'd see her later.

When she came back later to find Shirley not in her room she thought she must have made it up with Fred and Rose and gone back to them. But Fred told her no. She had gone to visit relatives in Germany. In which case Liz expected her to come bouncing back full of how they were all getting on again. But Shirley never came back. And quite soon afterwards another lodger, Claire Rigby, who was a friend of Juanita Mott's sister Belinda Moore, saw Rose in Shirley's room and a bundle of Shirley's clothes on the chair and other items strewn around the room. The door was open slightly until Rose pushed it closed and she saw Rose on her knees bailing Shirley's belongings into plastic bags.

It was an image of Rose that would stay with Fred. The schoolgirl Rose on her knees in the trailer at the Lakehouse site bundling together the girls' underwear and clothes that were Fred's trophies. She took them and the other women's clothes that were strewn around and put them all in a tea-chest and said to him, 'Dump that.'

Over the years that she knew her, Rose gave her sister-in-law Barbara Letts, Graham's wife, lots of clothes, including skirt and jacket suits and a brown fur coat. She gave her underwear which looked new, bras and knickers, which fitted Barbara – she was size ten – but were too small for Rose, which had to make Barbara wonder what Rose was doing with them in the first place. Graham introduced Barbara to his sister for the first time only in 1978. And on that and future visits to Cromwell Street Rose would go off with Barbara in one room while Graham and Fred stayed together in another. It was something Graham always noticed: the way they would separate them up. Rose would often take her clothes off in front of Barbara, giving reasons such as getting changed or having a bath. She would talk to Barbara while she was doing it and Barbara would answer back but not look. Graham would go with Barbara and Rose would take Barbara to one room and leave him with Fred. You were never allowed to wander about on your own. They'd even go with you into the garden. You hardly ever saw Fred and Rose together in the house. Somehow Graham always had the feeling he was being watched in that house.

After Shirley Robinson's belongings had been sorted and bagged by Rose, Fred took them to the bottom of the garden and left them there for the bin men.

The extension to the house was still being completed in June 1978 when Shirley Robinson disappeared. The last part to be finished was a utility room with a washing-machine in it which opened straight off the garden and led through into the kitchen. Shirley Robinson's body was disposed of in the garden immediately outside the door of the washroom, as it was called. Her dismembered remains were shoved down in the corner made by the back door of the house and the wall of the church so that everybody walked on them every time they went either in or out. She was the only victim at Cromwell Street whose remains were found without any sort of tape or rope, although several fingers and toes had been taken away and her kneecaps were missing. The skeleton of her eight-and-a-half-month-old unborn baby was found down in the hole with her. 'I packed her up,' Fred West said. 'I didn't have much room to put it in, so it had to be packed . . . just pushed her in with a spade.'

The next day Liz Parry was leaving the house with her boyfriend Peter when they bumped into Mr and Mrs West on the stairs. He repeated word for word what he had said about Shirley leaving to visit relatives in Germany and he struck Liz Parry as being very happy. They both appeared to her to be very happy on this morning. That's all she could say, really. Just happy.

The living-room extension started where the old house came to an end. This left him with the part of the alleyway between the right side of the house and the church to fill in. It was a small caravan- or shed-sized space and this became his tool room. It was a good arrangement as far as he was concerned because it meant his materials and equipment were kept close to the front door for easy dumping and loading off and on the van. And there was the added advantage that every time he arrived home or was leaving the house he was brought into unavoidable intimate contact with racked-up hammers and grease guns and hacksaws and car jacks and concrete tampers and cold chisels and planes, and shelves full of sealer and adhesive and polymer varnish and electric cable and plastic-covered washing-line and paints, and lead sheet and pickaxes and mallets and sacks of sand and artex and gripfill and sol-vent cement. Brushing past all this and staying coated in lay-ers of grease and oil and fine debris and dust and hardly or never washing. Forget a bath. The city version of the spores and burrs and pollen and light country rubble that his hair and clothes would collect from the lanes and fields around Much Marcle when he was growing up. As an adult he wouldn't wear new clothes. He refused to wear them. He used a pair of new jeans as a draught-excluder for seven years once before putting them on. That's how much he took care of his clothes and appearance. He preferred things retrieved from skips and dumps. He liked to wear clothes he found while he was out working. He hated spending. He loved hoarding.

His tendency was always to domesticate his working vans, cutting in windows and putting up curtains and adding mattresses and tables. And he had an equal tendency to turn the places where he lived into work spaces, tool rooms, building sites. Building his tool room just off the living room meant that he could keep his tools and materials always close to him. Fred's special room. Rose had her special room. And this was his. The place where Fred felt most completely at home in his home. Locked together with his room like the parts of a gun or a camera in the most easeful way. It acted like a decompression chamber between the public and private worlds; between outside and in. Open the new front door and you turned left and took two steps up into the old front entrance to the house. Into the hall with the now permanently locked entrance to the cellar straight in front. Rose's special room still on the left. Fred's and Rose's mutual bedroom, which used to be the back living room, on the right. Into the bedroom and through a door in the left corner took you down into what was once the kitchen but had now become part of the expanded family area. That was one way into the new added-on part of the house, and the lodgers from upstairs like Liz Parry used it when they wanted to use the washroom at the back, always knocking at the door of the bedroom first before they went in. But the most direct route to what had become the heart of the house was straight in through the tool room, and this was the route Fred always used. Through his special room. His place of maximum refuge. There were two routes into the extension living room at Cromwell Street. One was through the bedroom he shared with Rose. The other was through Fred's special room with its own array of lubricants, fetishes, aids, prostheses and tools he was confident he did know how to use. One of the most disturbing sequences of the many pornographic videotapes he made at Cromwell Street shows Rose lying bound on the floor of the tool room. At first it looks like the back of his van but it's the tool room. She is immobile, lying on her side wearing tights and knickers and surrounded by equipment and materials and pots of paint. She is on a thin mattress lying in the foetal position and Fred steps briefly forward and with one hand rips off her knickers which he turns inside out and brings to the camera. He was not a big man, but he was brawny in the arms and shoulders. He keeps his face out of shot but his prison build is noticeable. Under the knickers Rose is wearing a sanitary towel which has become dark red and bloody. The black knickers that gradually fill the frame are seen to be patchily white with semen. Building his tool room just off the living room meant that he could keep his tools and materials always close to him. This was important. He was always going out to the van during the night to clean it and top up the oil and water. He was always getting up in the middle of the night and going out to the van and putting his tools in order, oiling and greasing his tools and ordering and arranging them. Keeping sand separate from cement. 'Just going out to the van.'

His last act on what can be considered the last day of his life – the day he gave himself up to the police who were about to begin digging in the garden, searching for the remains of his daughter Heather – was to ask Stephen to go outside and bring his tools from his van. To bring his tools and put them in the tool room. To clear all the tools out of his van which was parked outside. To collect them and bring them in the house where they would be safe.

His house was his life. He just worshipped the place. He wanted his tools in the house where they belonged and where he was going he could picture them. He told May once, 'My life begins when you are in bed.'

Chapter Thirteen

Rose made a lot of noise and Fred liked to hear it. Wails. Noises. Shrieks. If Rose was with a man and she wasn't making enough noise – if she wasn't being loud enough – Fred would go in and tell her and she would turn it on. Like touching a button. Just like that the volume would increase. Wailing, thumping, thrashing about. 'I'm going to come . . . *I'm coming!*' You could sometimes hear it in the street. She used to have all the windows open so everybody could hear it all down the road. Noises. Shrieks. These were the night-time sounds of the house once the pandemonium of the male lodgers had been got rid of. Once they went back to bedsits they only had girls and the girls were quiet. But Rose was noisy. The house was her house and she filled it with the sound of her voice. She had a mouth on her. Mrs West was the dominant character of the family. She always seemed to be telling everybody in the house what to do and when to do it. It seemed to be uninterrupted. She never seemed to leave the house.

She rode the children. She was always yelling and screaming at the children. Forever bawling and screaming at them and calling them fuckers. You fucking little this and you fucking little that. I'll fucking have you. Fucking watch it, boy. Watch it, feller. Screaming and carrying on. Sometimes she could be pantomime-like in her red-faced fury, and almost funny. Screaming for them to find the tea towel, and the children all scurrying and looking, scuttling about and searching and expecting to feel the weight of her hand across their face any minute, and the tea towel is over her shoulder. But she would also use knives and rolling-pins and other everyday objects which in her hands would become weapons. She put a knife inside Anna-Marie's mouth. She nicked May with a knife all up under her vest when she was little. She was a taskmaster. Of course it was still the case that in her father she had had the right man to train her. And every task had to be carried out to the letter according to her instructions. 'If you're going to live here . . .' and then she'd give them a job to do. And if it wasn't done properly – if it wasn't done how she would do it – she would blow up. She would go ballistic. She'd hit one of them and then she'd want to hit them all because she was in the mood. She would just lose it.

From the age of seven, just like Charmaine and Anna-Marie before them, Heather and May and Stephen were expected to do the washing, do the ironing, scrub the kitchen, scour the toilet, change the babies' nappies and feed them. There was always something to do around the house – a lamp to rewire, the bins to put out, a floor to wash, cement to shift. She would send them shopping around the corner in Limbars which was the cheapest most horrendous shop ever in the whole world, Stephen thought. Horrible cheap discount food from Limbars. They weren't allowed to have friends around and they weren't allowed to play outside the house. They didn't have many friends for the simple reason Rose told them to fuck off when they came to the door. My children have got more to do than hang around the streets. None of my kids spend their life on the street. They never came again. She exploded on a daily basis. You could hear her from up the street, she was so loud.

Heather and May and Stephen had been sleeping in the cellar since the last body – Juanita Mott's body – had been roughly concreted over in 1975. Stephen slept in the back room almost exactly at the spot where Carol Cooper was buried. The view from his bed wasn't of the familiar and friendly things that are put in children's rooms to make an atmosphere of security and well-being, but of tools. From his bed he looked at a stack of conventional tools spilling out from the cupboard under the cellar stairs, plus a lot of rusty agricultural implements whose claws and spikes and teeth as a child he found frightening. His first spell in the cellar was between the ages of two and six. And Stephen would be quite a bit older before he recognized some of the rusty things he had shared his room with as bolt-croppers for extracting cow and bull horns and other things from his uncle Doug's farm which cast shadows that could be terrifying. At the end was just like a big jaw. These great steel jaws at the end. The handles were so long you could get some weight behind it and in the lamplight spiky frightening shadows.

Heather and May slept in the front part of the cellar closest to the street and directly under their mother's special room with the noises coming from it that didn't sound like anybody was having any pleasure. The most horrendous screaming noises you have ever heard. Before the building of the new extension there were two entrances to the cellar, one inside and one outside the house. And even in the coldest weather and when it was raining, the children would be made to go outside and make their way to bed by way of the concrete steps going down into the old coal hole around the back. Dressed in their pyjamas they would feel their way down the side of the house and around to the trapdoor lit up by the light from the living-room window that was their way to bed. In the mornings they would queue up and wait to be let in at the front door, rain, hail, sleet or snow. This had gone on for nearly three years when, three months after his fifth birthday, in November 1978, Stephen says he led a rebellion. He led a break-out which resulted in him and May and Heather nearly getting away from Cromwell Street one night. They would lie in bed and endlessly talk about the house in the country that they were going to run away to and live in for ever together. And they were halfway over the fence at the bottom of the garden when they were spotted and dragged back inside and beaten and put down in the cellar again. It may or may not have happened exactly like this: like his sisters and brothers Stephen has been damaged by his childhood experiences; like his father he has been known to tell what those close to him call 'porkies', and so some of what he says has to be treated with a degree of scepticism. But the consequences are not in dispute. For a period from the end of 1978 or the beginning of 1979, the children's beds were moved upstairs into the part of the new living area formerly occupied by the scullery kitchen. Their beds were put behind a curtain and the door to their parents' bedroom was left open at nights so they could hear what was going on. Right into Fred's and Rose's mutual bedroom off the hall and through a door in the left corner took you down into what was once the kitchen but had now become part of the expanded family area. That was one way into the new added-on part of the house. It was an arrangement that made the children available to be casually molested and groped by their uncle John and Rose's visitors and other men calling at the house. Men on their way to work in the morning would come in and, while Rose was boiling a kettle, reach behind the curtain and grab and sexually abuse Heather and May. While they were having their tea they would sit them on their knee and touch them indecently.

After Rose had had Tara, her first mixed-race baby, her mother had made it clear she didn't want Rose coming around to her house again. She had taken about as much from Rose. A lot. And it was all she was prepared to take from her. Mrs Letts came from a time when you wouldn't talk about sexual things when you were growing up. It was just something you never spoke about. Her father was a Cambridgeshire man. And once Rose started having half-caste children her mother asked Rose not to come around any more. Which Rose had taken as a rejection by her mother. The second time she had been rejected by her. She had never allowed Rose to love her. When she got too close she pushed her away. She didn't need Rose, like Rose needed her. She didn't think her mother really wanted her any more.

When the Green Lantern café had folded, in spite of Daisy Letts taking over in the kitchen in the last months, Rose's mother and father had gone back to living together, this time in a council block in Lydney in the Forest of Dean: after his early retirement they had had to give up the house that had been their home for fourteen years on the Smith's estate. But they had been living in Lydney for less than a year in May 1979 when Bill Letts died. He was fifty-eight. Rose didn't even know her father was ill. He was rushed to hospital in Bristol and given an emergency operation for what was thought at first to be a chest complaint but turned out to be cancer of the lung. He died after three days.

The funeral was held at the council cemetery in Cheltenham and the family were all together for the first time for a long time. Fred didn't go with Rose and she couldn't understand why he didn't want to pay his last respects to her father, after all they had become close. She was angry with him for not going to the funeral and supporting her. She attended on tottering heels and in clothes that the staider members of the family regarded as the uniform of her profession. It was a right show-up. She was still only twenty-five, but she had had five children, two of them in the past two years, and her body was assuming a slack look as a result of one pregnancy following another. In May 1979 Louise was only four months old but Rose was just weeks away from falling pregnant with her and Fred's second son, Barry.

When Rose went to comfort her eldest sister who she hardly knew, Pat threw her over on to the gravel in the churchyard. Across the gravel and into the dirt as if this was the right place for her. And Gordon was handcuffed between two prison officers or CID looking tranquillized and zombie-like with 'K-a-r-e-n' tattooed across the fingers of his left hand. He would disappear from their lives for many years after this, virtually for the whole of the eighties. Her baby brother Gordon was there, dead-eyed between two policemen. And Andrew and Jacquie and Joyce, who had found religion and was overbearing, and Graham and Barbara White, who were recently married. 'The only reason any of us went was to make sure he was going down in that hole in the ground,' Andrew says. 'Everybody seemed so glad when he died. Gone and out of the way. My mother hated my father intensely,' Gordon would say many years later. Graham and Barbara had moved into the same council block in Lydney as Rose's parents. The week after his father died, Graham would break into his mother's flat, strip it, sell the furniture, rifle the gas meter, etcetera. This was Rose's father's funeral.

Fred had patience. He liked a set routine – he was rigid in his routines – and he knew how to be patient. In 1979 he was working on a house near Jordan's Brook, the home for abused and off-the-rails adolescent girls in Hucclecote in Gloucester. And one of the live-in care assistants at the home started to notice his transit van parked by the gates in the late afternoons and evenings and some of the girls hanging around it until they were called back into the home around bedtime. Alison Chambers, known as 'Al' or 'Ali', was one of the girls and she was thought of as a girl who was particularly inse-cure. The staff at the home thought of her as very clinging. She came from a broken home and she had come to Jordan's Brook from a children's home in Pontypridd in South Wales after running away and threatening to 'go on the game' in London. She wasn't popular with the other girls at Jordan's Brook and had become a target for bullying. They were aggressive and punky – one of them was nicknamed 'Punky', others were Uta and Lil – and Alison wasn't that way at all. One of the tenants who saw her at Cromwell Street would describe her as wearing a suit and carrying a handbag and being almost a professional-looking person. Very slim, dressed smartly. She looked almost official the way she was dressed, with a handbag. Compared to Rose who stared a lot and dressed like a child. The same tenant, Gill Britt, would remember that Alison Chambers 'had lesbian tendencies'. Alison absconded from Jordan's Brook on a number of occasions because of the bullying and inevitably found her way to the house of the man in the transit van who, in the months she had been at the home, had become more or less a permanent presence just along from the gates in the evenings. Jokes and banter. Roll-ups and offers of rides. Lightly, lightly. If it takes a year, it takes a year. He could be tirelessly patient.

He was always scouting. Waiting and recruiting. Watching; scouting. It was like an ever-increasing hunger that supplemented itself, fed itself, on hunger, and could never be content. The *Lustmord*. They were lust murderers. Lustful pleasures are fleeting; they are forgotten almost as they happen. The memory of what happened – the intensity of pleasure, the ache of desire – can't be recorded or stored. It has to be re-lived in order to be remembered. There is a craving for repetition because the intensity is evanescent, it has no life span; it exists only in the moments that it is happening, in the present. You're in this aura of sexual feeling together and everybody else is excluded. The nagging insupportable erotic excitement that would be the hallmark of their years together. Exciting to them both. The secret realm of thrills and concealment. The force that wants more and more. Lust can't know itself; it doesn't know what it is or what it is looking for. It does not discover, but immerses itself. The *Lustmord*. The scandalous perversion of erotic urges in which sexual satisfaction is achieved through the violence of murder. The erotic drunkenness that can't be remembered or stored but only re-lived and re-enacted. The yearning for intensity. The final investment of everything in sex.

Their own daughter Heather would grow up with a longing to live in the country. It was fierce in her. She liked the outdoors and the feeling of freedom. She wanted to be on her own and do things on her own. She wanted to live like a hermit. She never wore shoes; she used to go everywhere in her bare feet. Forest of Dean I Will Live. FODIWL. They told Alison Chambers they had a farm in the country. It was their farm. They owned it and one day – it wouldn't be long – she could leave the children's home and ride horses there and walk in the fields. She could live on their farm when she turned seventeen, which was quite soon. And like Ann McFall who sent pictures back to her mother in Glasgow of the beautiful big house she was living in – the lovely children and the beautiful big house and the successful man; the tremendous man – Alison made a photocopy of the picture of the beautiful big house they showed her and took it back to Jordan's Brook House and drew ivy all up the walls. When she was seventeen. September 1979. So three months.

Dear Judy,
Please, please help me, I am at my wits end, and I'm thinking of putting an end to my rotten worthless life.
My problem is one that I've had for almost 2 years now. Since I came into care, (I was 14 almost 15) I have developed bouts of depression. The least little thing makes me cry.

I am also very self-concience about myself too, this is mainly because the girls in the 'home' I'm in at present, have all got boyfriends, except one who's just not interested and me.

I am not ugly, but I'm not brilliantly pretty either, I am big-boned and I'm always complaining that I'm fat, although I exercise each night, I wear fairly fashionable clothes, although I really can't afford up-to-date clothes, because I am badly paid at work. I am a receptionist-telephonist.

Every time I meet a boy (I am quite shy), and they ask where I live, I am quite honest with them, and say I'm in care, they just clam up, and after one night they don't want to see me again.

Please help! I am getting desperate, not for boys, but through worry of thinking I'm abnormal.

I've known about this problem for ages, but I've no-one really close to talk to.

Thank you, Judy
Yours faithfully
Alison Chambers

When Alison Chambers's remains were recovered from the back garden at 25 Cromwell Street at twenty past five on Monday, 28 February 1994, a wide plastic-leather belt with a square plastic-covered buckle was found strapped under her chin and over the top of her skull. A purple coat belt around her head clamping closed her jaw to stop her screaming, to keep her silent. She had been decapitated and dismembered and many of her toes and fingers had been taken away. The jumbled parts of her body were found buried underneath what had been a paddling pool made of blue engineering bricks immediately under the bathroom window in the garden. 'All I done was lifted him up and packed her underneath him, and dropped him back on top of her,' Fred West said. 'All I done was lifted 'im up and and banged 'er underneath . . . push parts of her body underneath.' Out of 'sheer force of habit' he had used the sheath knife he carried on his belt. 'I mean, it's handy to have a knife with you anyway, for numerous reasons . . . It wasn't carried as a weapon. It was carried as a tool.'

At the beginning of the summer during which Alison Chambers would be taken to Cromwell Street and bound and gagged and sexually brutalized and finally murdered, Fred West had got Anna-Marie, who was just about to turn fifteen, pregnant. It was an ectopic pregnancy, meaning the baby was developing in her fallopian tubes and, without ever being told what was happening to her, she had been taken into hospital to have the baby aborted. Apart from a brief visit from her father who was always telling her, 'You don't want no fucking schoolboy. He won't know what to do with it', but who tried to blame her pregnancy on a boy she knew from school, nobody from the family visited during the week she was in Gloucester Hospital. When she came out, her stepmother, as she wasn't allowed to call her, put her to it doing housework and then set about her using her fists and her feet when she decided she wasn't doing it the way she had shown her. 'You're not doing that right.' 'Sorry.' 'Don't be fucking sorry. Just do it fucking right.' She had been out of hospital only a few days. She still had clips and stitches holding the wound together. But Rose was glaring. It had been ten years now, from the ages of five to fifteen. She knew that glare. And she laid straight into her. She got Anna-Marie on the floor and started kicking her. 'You wait till your fucking father gets home.'

Quite soon after this Anna-Marie was put in the cells at Gloucester police station for knifing a girl. She had been picked up with a nightdress on, heading out on the A40 in the direction of the Forest of Dean. She had a stand-up fight with her father outside in the street when he got her home, and then Anna disappeared two or three mornings after that. When she wasn't there to prepare the breakfasts as usual, they sent one of the younger children to get her up and she was gone. Her bed was made but she wasn't there. She wasn't anywhere in the house. Rose said, 'Cow.' 'I don't think she'll be a problem, do you?' Fred asked Rose.

Heather told Anna-Marie this is what had happened the next time they met. She also told her that Fred and Rose had gone into her bedroom later that day and stripped it bare. They tore her Elvis Presley posters off the wall, bundled up her magazines and books of pop lyrics and burned the lot. The rest of her clothes went too, even the ornaments on her shelves were thrown out. It was as if she had never existed.

She had crept out in the middle of the night and slept on a bench in the park until it got light. She would sleep in the park for several nights, washing in the mornings in the toilets where Caroline Raine had been attacked eight years earlier, until she found a friend to take her in. Like the son of the Victorian anti-masturbation zealot Daniel Schreber, who in adult life wrote a book about 'the tormenting and humiliating bodily sufferings' performed on him by his father, with 'the utmost cruelty and disregard as only a beast deals with its prey', Anna-Marie would one day also put down on paper her account of what it had been like to grow up being constantly preyed upon and sexually humiliated by the people she should have been able to rely on to care for and protect her.

It was only after she ran away that she realized for the first time that 'other people didn't live in the way we did at Cromwell Street'. 'I associated everything with sex . . . To get love you had to provide sex; if someone gave you something or offered to help you in any way, you repaid them with sex.

If you wanted something from someone, you offered them sex. To avoid beatings and provoking Rose, and to please her, you had sex with her or with the men she had chosen . . . The only kind of love and affection I ever knew came from my father after he had had sex with me.' Now, in order to survive, to eat, to find a place to sleep, she was going to have to resort to sex. She was going to go looking for love in some wrong places, and sometimes she was going to have to pay for that.

Rose knew she was made to have children. This was something she had always known and they always said they would have eight. Barry was born in June 1980. Fred used to take them to Barry Island near Cardiff now and again. They all loved it and that's where they got Barry's name from. Heather turned ten that year; May was eight, Stephen seven, Tara two and a half, Louise a year and a half, and then Barry, number-two son. Barry was born at the beginning of the summer. But then, when Rose found herself pregnant again before the summer was over, she did what she had never done before: she had a baby aborted. If that baby was Fred's, it would have been the last baby she would have had with him. Her next two children – Rosemary junior, born in 1982, and Lucyanna, born in 1983 – shared the same Jamaican father. But Fred considered they were his anyway. They were all his. Lucyanna was baby number eight. They had got their eight and they decided to stop there. Eight children in the house. Eight bodies buried in the garden and the house. Rose decided to be sterilized. She had her tubes clipped after Lucyanna was born and said that was it. No more.

For a house with so many children it stayed very quiet. Any visitor to the house had to be pre-announced and the children were warned in advance not to talk to any of the visitors. Visitors were warned never to answer the door unless Fred or

Rose asked, and Fred had wired the phones so that if any extension in the house was picked up it would ring loudly once. They were quiet children and didn't discuss anything. Anybody who was allowed in the house noticed the silence and extreme docility of the children. Their politeness and quietness were often remarked. They came instantly when they were called. They responded. When this failed to happen they'd yell blue bloody murder at them.

As Stephen grew older, Rose's attacks on him became more aggressively physical. There was a more openly sadistic aspect to them. On one occasion she lifted him by grabbing him by both hands around his neck and holding him until the blood vessels burst in his eyes. Her fingerprints stayed around his neck for a fortnight and she had to give him a note to take to school saying he had been fooling around with a rope in a tree and had fallen out. When he was put in the head cage that his father had made at the wagon works and which hooked over the back of the settee so that he couldn't move, it was his mother who hit him in the face with an ashtray or whatever was handy every time he tried to look away from the pornography that was being shown on the television or even blinked. Sometimes it was a video of people having sex with animals and sometimes it was people having sex with children – adults abusing children the way his mother had been abusing Stephen since he was six years old. She had a habit of walking into the living room out of the shower naked. And on one occasion when Stephen dared to say something cheeky like 'Oh for Chrissakes cover it up', she lost her temper, grabbed a wooden spoon and chased him down the road without a stitch on. 'So I let her catch me and beat me so she would just *go in*.'

One day in 1983, when Stephen was ten, his mother phoned his school to say that she wanted him home straight away. He rushed home, but when he got there there was no sense of emergency. His mother seemed very calm. She told him to go into the bathroom and take all his clothes off and shut the door. In the bathroom he saw that his father's wide buckled belt was hanging up and he also noticed electrical wire waiting ready over the bath. Electric flex was something Fred West claimed to have used to strangle several of their victims. 'I turned round and smacked her straight in the jaw and she went straight on the floor. And then I went and got that piece of flex and tied it round her neck,' he told the police about Shirley Robinson. 'There was a piece of electric flex. I believe it was 13 amp. That's two-point-five wiring,' he said, describing how he claimed to have murdered Heather and cut her body into pieces in the bathroom. 'It was a bit I'd cut off when I was rewiring a house. Probably two feet to a metre long. I picked it up and I thought I better make sure she is dead, because I dare not touch her if she's alive. You know, if there's any life still left.'

His mother had planned it. It was obvious from the belt and the three-core wire that this was something his mother had spent some time planning. That the anticipation contributed to the pleasure and was part of it. She wasn't frenzied though, as Stephen had often seen her. Rose in an ecstasy of anger like a performance. Not that. She was calm. She made him hold his hands out in front of him and using the wire she bound them. He was naked. Then she ordered him to lie down face forward on the bathroom floor. Got him to lie on his stomach at almost exactly the spot where Lynda Gough's remains were buried. He kept asking what he'd done; he didn't know. What had he done? What was this for? She had had the electric flex there waiting and now she used a second length to secure his wrists and hands to the pedestal of the toilet. When she had him immobilized at full stretch on the floor in this way she started to flay him. She used the buckle part of the belt and brought it down repeatedly at a point near the base of his spine. Saying, what have you done wrong? Tell me. What have you done wrong? Tell me, boy. They always called him that. They both called him that. Heather got 'big girl'. They called him 'boy'. What have you done wrong? He kept asking what he'd done; he didn't know. The buckle striking his spine. Trial, sentence and punishment all in one. The buckle striking his spine. What have you done wrong? He didn't know so she told him. The answer was blue magazines. She blamed him for stealing blue magazines from one of their private rooms and taking them to school. Beat him until the very painful area at the base of his spine was red and raw. Tried and found wanting. The buckle striking his spine. And when Heather came in with a letter from her teacher saying she had had pornographic magazines confiscated from her at school that day, his mother only laughed and said, well, Stephen's had your beating. He's had yours. Put the belt around her waist and did it up.

Rose would just suddenly go bang and you'd dive for cover. Whereas with Fred you could see it slowly build up. The look in his eyes. It would be a general build-up of several things, or his inner moody. He didn't go very often. But when he did go he definitely had a look about him when you're thinking – his son-in-law Chris Davis thought this, and he never backed off from a fight – 'I really shouldn't be here.' The perfect way to intimidate him was to do something he couldn't do. Stephen was fixing his sister's bike one day and his father told him to leave it until he came home and then he'd sort it out. But Stephen was bored that day and so he thought he'd do him a favour and fix it before he got home. Big mistake, as it turned out. When he saw the bike was fixed his father punched Stephen in the side of the head, knocked one of his back teeth out and walked away. Stephen made a bolt for the back door but his mother locked it before he could get there and his father started punching and kicking him when he was on the ground. Putting the boot in until it was obvious Stephen was hurt. Almost immediately then Fred started almost crying and begging Stephen to forgive him. To make it up he said they would go out tomorrow and get Stephen himself a new bike. 'Silly me, I thought it meant off to Halfords in Cheltenham.' But it was into the van with the cutters the next night, cruising round for a bike to steal. The only reason he ever took Stephen to the park was to steal other children's bikes. His father would walk a hundred yards in front and break the bike lock very quickly without anybody seeing. Then Stephen would ride the bike to the van where they would meet up. They'd get them for the whole family. Like their mother walking into the room naked and their father watching the television wearing only his underpants, it was considered normal. Family life. It was what families did. It was part of family life.

Heather was withdrawn and quiet. She used to rock like her mother used to rock herself in a chair or in bed, backwards and forwards for hours wiggling – rocking. She was growing up sullen – surly even. Heather was difficult. She was known as quite a hard girl at school. She was made to wear her hair in a short back and sides and boys' shoes because they were harder wearing and she wasn't popular. Nobody would mess with Heather at school. People just stayed away. At home she was becoming withdrawn and surly. Just being really quiet and awkward, always wanting to do the opposite to what everybody else was wanting to do. Sitting silently staring into space for hours, chewing her nails. Gnawing her nails until they started bleeding. She was always different and Rose's brothers weren't the only ones who occasionally wondered if Fred West was really Heather's father. Andrew Letts always had a suspicion that Heather's father could have been Graham, who was fourteen when Rose left home. Graham always suspected it might have been their own father. 'She wasn't a West,' Fred's chargehand, Ronnie Cooper, believes. 'She was too select for them. I think she was a pain in the neck to them, I think Heather was.'

Her father was raping Heather all her life. And it showed in the way she acted. She was being casually abused by her father's brother, her uncle John, and others, and raped by her father from an early age. When they were small children their father would put his hands inside Heather's and May's clothes and touch them. It would happen frequently, at any time of the day. These were part of their dad's 'antics'; his way of playing and being affectionate towards them. He told them that he had created their bodies and that this gave him the right to look at them any time he chose to look at them. He talked about the right of a father to take his daughter's virginity. He said that his father had done it to his sisters and he made it clear that he intended doing the same to May and Heather. He told them that because they struggled to push his advances away they would become lesbians. 'I had a good ride last night off your mother,' he'd tell them. 'I screwed the arse off her.' 'There's my daughter,' he'd say to some visitor to the house about Heather. 'I think she's a lesbian.'

After their attempt to run away Heather and May and Stephen had been brought upstairs out of the cellar and put to bed at nights behind a curtain in the part of the new living area previously occupied by the kitchen. Their beds were put behind a curtain and the door to their parents' bedroom was left open at nights so they could hear what was going on. But this could only be a stopgap arrangement and their father had eventually come up with a longer-lasting solution. He used a machine at the wagon works to stamp out six pairs of metal brackets and he brought them home and attached four of the brackets to each of the older children's beds. The beds were returned to the cellar and the brackets fitted and every night from then on Heather and May and Stephen were strapped to their beds. Each bracket had a hole in it and rope was pushed in through the holes and Heather and May and Stephen were tied face downwards on the bed. 'The same way that other kids would go to their mum in their pyjamas and say will you come and tuck us in,' Stephen says, 'we used to go and say will you come and fuckin' tie us in. I still can only sleep on my front.'

May West, who now has changed her name and started a new life, denies that either she or Heather was ever raped by their father. The life-long sexual abuse and pestering she admits. And she also acknowledges that she was raped at the age of seven or eight by one of the men who used to come to the house. But she says that neither she nor Heather was ever raped by their father. 'Heather and I had decided when Dad had first started touching us that we would never give in and allow him to have intercourse with us. We were both determined about it, and I know that Heather would have never given in to him.' But Stephen believes that May, who he still sees, is 'in heavy denial'. That she has been 'brainwashed' by her mother, to whom she remains close, to think that many things that did happen to her never happened. May still believes her mother is innocent of the murders of Charmaine and Heather and Shirley Robinson and of the seven other murders of which she was convicted. 'I block out a lot of things,' May has admitted. 'Sometimes it seems as if I never lived at Cromwell Street . . . I feel I've lived a lifetime since [the arrests] and I've started a new life, so it feels like it didn't happen.' But Stephen was there and he insists it did. 'He was raping Heather all her life. And May. I was in the same room. So I think I would remember that, yes.'

In 1976 when Heather was six or seven and May was five, a lodger at Cromwell Street, Jane Hamer, remembered hearing children's voices in the cellar screaming and shouting, 'Stop it, Daddy!' It was either Heather or May and there were several screams and then just, 'Stop it, Daddy!' Three years later a boyfriend of Anna-Marie's who stayed the night heard 'some rustling around' and then screams of some sort. The screaming went on for ten to twenty minutes, stopping for a while and then starting up again. Screams and then, 'No, no, please . . .' and he found he couldn't sleep. The next morning Rose had told him Heather was having nightmares. Heather had regular nightmares and that's what it was. He had noticed before Heather went to bed that she seemed a bit down; a bit shy. Her mother said she was backward and didn't talk very much.

The three of them slept in the cellar from 1975 to 1982, when Heather was twelve, May was ten and Stephen was nine. And after 1978 when the living-room extension was completed they would lie in bed some nights and hear noisy parties and what they speculated could be orgies going on up there. Whoops and screams. Most nights though they would lie awake waiting to hear the creak of the stairs that meant that their father was sneaking down to force himself on either Heather or May who were lying helpless on their fronts, bound to the bed with rope. The key turning in the door; the creak of the stairs. Their subterranean bunker. A universe of total uncertainty; one in which submissiveness was no shield against even worse outcomes.

The worst night happened when Stephen was six or seven. The lodgers all left finally in 1981 and it was before then. It was a party night. There were people in doing what would come to be known as 'partying'. Noises. Shrieks. Shouts and screams. And they were downstairs trying to keep their heads down. Hoping to remain ignored. Trying not to attract attention. It was when they heard the trapdoor opening in Stephen's part of the cellar and the noise from upstairs grow abruptly louder that they knew they were in trouble. He usually came in through the door from the hall. The noise grew louder and a slice of light lifted the gloom of their bunker and they knew that they were in for it now.

People were wrecked. Their mother used to smoke dope sometimes when she was younger. She liked a hit of a joint and she drank vodka at these parties. And the children were untied from their beds and led up the stairs looking up to what would have recently been the sky but was now a ceiling of artex and railway-sleeper beams. All this noise and bright lights and swirling smoke and the smell of drugs and what Stephen regarded as all these wrecked and druggy bloody useless people. Some of them lodgers. Many of them black. In the noise and the smoke and some of them naked and having sex with each other in corners and under tables. They were untied and led up the stairs into this and then tied again around the base of the tree that stood in the middle of the room holding the extension roof up. Heather and May and Stephen held their hands out as they had been ordered and had rope looped around them and then sat at the base of the tree as they had been told to do. Sitting under the canopy of smoke, tied up together and tied to the tree and confused and frightened. People having sex together on the floor; under tables. They were staring at the floor. It went on for a long time. Heather nodded off until she was woken up by her mother. 'Wake up, you stupid bitch.' It seemed like days and days. 'You're a pretty little girl.' Druggy bloody useless people. Heather was crying. Heather was being raped by a black friend of her mother's. His mother was touching Stephen. The room seemed to get busier. Other women were touching him. The room was packed. Everybody laughing. There was another man. Stephen's dad called him 'Snooty'. He started urinating on Heather. 'He started weeing all over Heather. Then he turned around and weed all over me . . . It never happened again and it never happened before. It seemed to be a one-off idea. The most degrading night.'

Afterwards they made a pact to leave home, live in a big house and not ever tell anybody what happened with their mum and dad.

After being out of their lives for two years, Anna-Marie returned in 1982 with a new name – Anne Marie, to some people just 'Anne' – and a live-in boyfriend who was going to become her husband. They had met through Citizen's Band radio – CB – which was going through a phase of popularity in the early eighties. It had come over from the United States where it was popular with truckers and there was a CB craze. Karen, Anne Marie's friend in Gloucester who had taken her in when she first ran away from home, had got hold of a set. And Anne Marie got on the CB at nights to put it over that she was a girl on her own, sixteen in 1980 when she first left home, looking for a place to stay. Naturally she never went short of offers. And equally inevitably it brought her in touch with many people she decided she didn't want to know and took her to many places she didn't want to be. They would say something like, 'Breaker, come on', then you would identify yourself. Not by your real name but with a made-up CB name called a 'handle'. Anne Marie's handle was 'Cover Girl'. Although her 'wind-up handle' was 'Cream Cake, naughty but nice' when she picked up somebody looking for a gas. She had been through some terrible times via this route and landed herself in some terrible messes, and her latest boyfriend had just turned violent on her when she picked Chris Davis up on the CB. Chris's handle was 'Contractor', which sounded interesting. And he confirmed that, yes, the other side would come into it as well, 'but not as far as snuffing somebody'. He was 'loosely police connected'. They did an eyeball. Anne Marie came over for an eyeball. She wore a light-blue body-warmer covered in badges. One of herself naked made from a badge set, and one of a Page Three girl called Mitzi who Chris was able to tell Anne Marie he knew. He also knew Sam Fox and Linda Lusardi, then the stars of Page Three. He had met them when he was up in London doing business: 'Not drugs – other business. It was within the boundaries of the law. I have a very clouded past, but always on the side of the law,' Chris said.

Just one snag. 'Contractor' wasn't unattached. He was living with a woman who was nearly twice his age and several of her children. But then, as it happened, not such a snag. Chris's girlfriend invited Anne Marie to join them and move in. Anne Marie was at a low ebb in those days. She was on 25 mg. of Valium every four hours. Had been on it for two years. Chris became her counsellor, and very quickly then her lover. The more people who wanted to have sex with her, the more Anne felt wanted. Chris realized this about her straight away. She had sex with people the way she would have a drink with them. He put it down to her needing a bit of extra loving. Obviously his girlfriend whose house they were in didn't see it that way and asked Anne Marie to leave. Told her to get out like many other women in the previous eighteen months. Fred had gone in to the wagon works one day to be told by one of the men who worked there that his runaway daughter had caused a bit of trouble in New Street which wasn't very far away the previous night. She had walked into a house with a man she had just met in a pub and chucked his wife and her small baby out. Physically thrown them on to the street. But when Anne Marie packed a carrier bag and walked out of the house where she had been living with Chris Davis and his girlfriend, Chris walked with her. He wanted to teach her there was a different side to life; help her revert back to the normal way of life and the proper way of things. He tried to show her this. He had a sense of mission. But friendship is like a lame dog you take in and bring back to health, only to have it turn around and bite your hand. He had Oriental interests in his life. He had Japanese and many other knives in his house. He has studied martial arts. There's a bowie in the bedroom. He believes that in a previous existence he may have been Vietnamese. Show him any picture and he can tell you where in 'Nam it is. Maybe he was shot dead in 1959 and born at the same time. He is acquainted with Confucius. And the lame dog having the potential to turn into a biting dog would be one of the lessons Chris Davis would take away from his years with Anne Marie.

They had been living in Stroud but they found accommodation above the Prince of Wales pub in Station Road in Gloucester. The rent was paid by Social Security and they earned extra money working behind the bar and dogsbodying crates up from the cellar. Anne Marie was back living in the centre of Gloucester; an alley connected the Prince of Wales with Cromwell Street only half a mile away. But Chris knew nothing about her previous life and only gradually learned about some of the things that had gone on in it and which had driven her away. But only the physical abuse. He knew she had been beaten stupid. Snippets. But she didn't go near the sexual humiliation and the brutality and the years of persistent rape by her father.

They had been living at the Prince of Wales for nearly six months before Anne Marie lifted a phone to call her father. There was no way she would have turned up at Cromwell Street unannounced. The reception was friendly and she said she was living near by and with a man and the man she was with was keen to meet him. Meet them. Her dad and the children. Chris was keen to meet her family and felt she should make it up with them. He was pretty persistent. And so it was arranged.

It was 1982. The last of the lodgers had been got rid of the previous year and the house which was in a constant state of becoming had undergone one of its regular remouldings in

Anne Marie's absence. It hadn't been a voluntary decision: the council had come around sniffing and applying their rules and the lodgers had had to be got out. From now on they would take in lodgers only occasionally, and these for a time would include Chris Davis and Anne Marie.

The older three had come out of the cellar and taken over the upstairs rooms. Stephen shared the top-floor front with his baby brother Barry, and Heather and May were underneath. Rosemary and Lucyanna were put in Shirley Robinson's old room, the small room next to the bathroom on the first floor, with Tara and Louise sharing the back room directly overhead. The door to the right off the hall was Fred's and Rose's mutual bedroom (although Fred tended to doss on a sofa in the extension living room most nights). The back of the cellar was now the children's playroom and Fred stored decorating stuff and junk in the overspill at the front. The painted plate and the core-screw were still part of the door leading to the front room on the ground floor, but this had undergone a change of use from Rose's special room to a private bar/living room for Rose and Fred. He had put up a wall-sized forest mural of red leaves and the Rockies and installed a curved velour sofa and a curving cocktail bar with a dimpled plastic front. Fred's and Rose's private living room linked up with their mutual bedroom through a cupboard under the stairs. A cupboard full of porn. Packed with porn. It was the promise of the lace dress and the fur coat all those years ago – the promise of racy living and city sophistication the high life – coming good, and it was quite smart.

They took Chris Davis through to the eighteen-foot-by-eighteen-foot family room on his first visit and he was impressed. It was spacious. Fred had put in ranch-house arches either side of the timber support post by then, and this room opened on to a kitchen with a utility room beyond it and pink-and-white, chequerboard-pattern patio paving going out over the narrow garden to about the halfway point. Rose made no impression that first time – she spent all the time Chris and Anne Marie were there pottering in the kitchen, hovering around the sink. But Fred went on the brag straight away, reminiscing about how he had known the singer Lulu when he lived in Scotland – she had been a friend of his first wife, Rena – and how Charmaine's father had been a Mister Big in the Gorbals underworld and so on in that vein. Bullshitter, Chris Davis thought. And not a good bullshitter, either. A bad bullshitter because he didn't have a very good memory. Contradictions all the way through. But he said nothing to Anne Marie because he could tell there was a strong bond there. He could see Anne loved her father.

When he heard that they were living in bed-and-breakfast accommodation which meant that they had to stay out walking the streets all day, Fred invited Anne Marie and her boyfriend to move in with them until they found somewhere more permanent to live. They had her old room on the first floor at the front of the house and Chris Davis moved in with two suitcases full of war books. Hundreds of them. It didn't escape Fred that that's all his luggage was. War books and the conviction that in a previous life he had grown up in the mountains and forests of Vietnam. He spent hours telling Fred the story of being shot dead in 1959 and being born at the same time and there's Fred sitting there saying it must have been frightening for you, and all that. 'The murmuring souls . . . The howls of the unburied . . . The souls condemned to wander unhappily until their mortal remains have been laid to rest.' What a way-out bastard. Takes all sorts.

Although there was a toilet and bathroom on the same landing, Chris and Anne Marie had to use the bathroom downstairs. The one on their floor was now Rose's private bathroom and it was decorated with framed ten-by-eight black-and-white photographs of Rose in explicit poses with black men. There was no lock on the bathroom off the living room on the ground floor. And having a bath with Anne Marie around six o'clock on their first night, Chris Davis was surprised when some of the younger children started wandering in and out using the toilet, cleaning their teeth, not to mention Rose traipsing backwards and forwards while they lay there. 'The next train standing at platform two will be bloody busy!' Chris had grown up in an atmosphere of sex-is-a-word-you-don't-mention. Whereas in the West house it was a go-with-the-flow natural thing. Sometimes the conversations. My God. Unbelievable. You got used to conversations about sex. Chris had also noticed of course that Anne Marie's stepmother liked to sit around with no underwear on. T-shirt, no bra, no knickers. That was Rose. There was only six years between Chris Davis and Rose. She was twenty-nine in 1982; he was twenty-three. And Chris was aware with Rose that it was all set out in front of him but he didn't want to know. But they used to have some fun-time moments as time went on. 'For fucksake, close your legs, Mum, I can see what you had for dinner.' They made it seem normal and natural and quite OK. The two lives Rose was leading, and the carefree attitude to sex that Fred portrayed.

After six weeks Fred got Chris and Anne Marie a bedsit in Cromwell Street. They were on the other side of the church with Mrs Taylor. And on Saturday nights they started to make up a regular threesome with Rose to go around the Crown and Thistle, the New Inn, the Cross Keys in Cross Keys Lane, the Bierkeller in the Fleece Hotel and other Gloucester city-centre pubs, generally ending up at the Wellington where there was a band and dancing to traditional Irish tunes on Saturday nights. Sometimes Rose and Anne went on around the clubs. But Rose would always be up early the next morning whatever happened preparing a big Sunday lunch. Chris and Anne would go next door to number 25 for lunch on Sundays, and that would be the day they would see one of Rose's Jamaican regulars. 'Suncoo' (from 'Sunday cooking') was one of Rose's freebies. He was the father of Rosemary junior who had been born in April 1982 and he was one of the men Anne Marie had been forced to have sex with in the last four or five years she was living at home. Suncoo would go off in her room with Rose for an hour or so and do what Fred had told him to do. It was around this time that Rose had signed the document beginning, 'I, Rosemary West, known as Fred's cow, give my cunt to be fucked by any prick at any time he so desires without ever saying so' and ending 'I must always dress and try to act like a cow for Fred.' And Suncoo was one of her regular partners in the van when they drove out to the disused airport at Stoke Orchard or to Painswick Hill. Sometimes Suncoo would turn up when she was still cooking the Sunday lunch and then the family would have to wait. They knew they didn't dare complain. 'There was a weight on their shoulders inside Cromwell Street,' Chris Davis says. 'Although it was a relaxed regime, there was a weight there. Outside the kids seemed to be lighter, but Fred and Rose seemed to be carrying a lot. Outside they would be quieter, whether the kids were present or not. So it was totally reversed.'

By the time May was twelve and Heather was fourteen their father had bored holes in the door of their room and punched holes in the walls so that he could watch them dress and undress. He would burst in in the morning and pull the bed-clothes off them while they were sleeping and throw himself on top of them. He reached under their skirts and touched their breasts in front of the family and tried to pull their tow-els off them when they came out of the bathroom. When they complained he would tell them they were lesbians. He would keep a record of their periods and when he decided they were being what he called 'hufty' he would tell them they needed a good seeing to. They needed a man like him to sort them out. Heather and May made an arrangement to take it in turns standing guard for each other outside the shower. He used to come in and reach around behind the curtain and they wanted to try and put a stop to that. He used to sit them down and go on for hours about how fathers had to break their daughters in because boys of today didn't do it properly. He used to say he wanted his daughters to have his baby. He'd say, 'Your first baby should be your dad's.' He'd say, 'Dads know how to do it right.'

Anne Marie discovered she was pregnant in October 1983. It was four years since her ectopic pregnancy by her father. The baby was Chris Davis's. And the families – Chris's parents and Anne Marie's parents, her father and stepmother – decided they should get married. The wedding took place at the Register Office over the park in January 1984, almost twelve years to the day since Fred and Rose had got married there, and Fred wore a tie for once in his life. Anne Marie wore a fluffy white jacket and a flower in her hair and carried a bouquet of artificial flowers. Rose didn't attend. Afterwards there was sherry and snacks back at Cromwell Street and a wedding cake it proved difficult to cut. The icing was like rock. It took three knives. Chris joked about getting the chainsaw out. Chris was a big drinker. He would declare himself an alcoholic in 1986. Fred didn't drink. He drank once a year at Christmas. He would have a sherry at Christmas with his dinner and it would last him all day. Then he would fall asleep on the floor.

Michelle, Fred West's first grandchild, was born in June 1984, the summer he was laid off work. The wagon works went bankrupt that year after being in existence for a hundred years and employing Fred for the last ten; the site was slated to become a trading estate. It was a blow to everybody who earned a living at the wagon works but it was a very hard blow for Fred who liked so much to work. He depended on work. When he wasn't at work he was working on the house. And he had his cobble work. His odd jobs and call-outs. He still did jobs for Mr Zygmunt's widow and his son, Roger. But most of his work at that time was for Alex Palmer who had picked up three or four properties in Cromwell Street. Alex Palmer, who was of mixed race, had been a nurse at Coney Hill mental hospital. He had contacts. And he filled his houses with recently discharged Coney Hill patients.

Fred did little fixing jobs for them and got to know some of them. He would see them surrounded by their belongings in their shoebox rooms when he went in to fix a fuse or a leak. A few of them became dependent, which he didn't mind. He had the time. The bell would go at home at odd times of the night and it would be one of the Coney Hill people to borrow for instance a tea bag. A roll-up cigarette, say, or a tea bag. And Fred would be all yeah, come in. Opening the door and offering this sad and usually strange-looking person a drink. That was if Fred went. If Rose went it was a different story. If the bell went at eleven at night and it was one of Alex Palmer's tenants asking to borrow a tea bag, say, Rose would go bananas without even opening the outer gate. 'Fuck off, you nutter! Fuck off out of it.' Scared the life out of them. One of Fred's hard-luck stories. One of Fred's down-and-outs. Who Fred came to resemble, as it happened, the longer he was out of a full-time job. He liked a routine.

When Fred got depressed or had a strop on him he grew his hair. He didn't bother cutting his hair. Chris Davis noticed this about him. Every time he let his hair go into a bush it was a reflection of his inner moody. He would have bushier hair at those times and he also had a bit of a beard with him. A scruffier appearance, anyway. Then he'd have his hair cut and he'd be back to his natural self.

After the wagon works, work was sporadic. He liked a routine and he liked to work. Rose noticed that he got a lot more miserable than in earlier years. Although they didn't physically fight like they used to, it seemed like nothing was good enough for him. He used to sit and watch the television with them but he didn't do that any more. Unless it was the news. He liked a steady job as well as being a Mr Fixit man for Alex Palmer. Driving Alex Palmer around and about and sitting in cafés waiting until Alex had completed whatever business he was doing. This was being a casual. He didn't like being a casual with time on his hands. So he started on the house. Again on the house. Another refit. Another rethink. Three years ago the children had been moved to the top from the bottom. They had been given the upstairs of the house. Which meant children running up and down all night to the kitchen and back. Non-stop traffic of children up and down the stairs and through Fred's and Rose's bedroom and through the tool room going to the kitchen and the bathroom and the toilet. So he decided to reverse it and put the children in the cellar and the downstairs rooms again. Confine them to the ground floor and the cellar and take over the first and second floors for Rose and himself.

He was still pushing Rose out to go with other men at night and she was still having men come to her at the house during the day. But from around 1985 onwards she decided to put the Cromwell Street part of the operation on a more business-like footing. She decided that the men coming to see 'Mandy' from now on would pay. The money would go most of the way to making up the shortfall they had been experiencing since Fred had been forced to become self-employed. And to begin the move towards what was to become the house's final incarnation Fred moved the four-poster bed into the top-floor front bedroom. The four-posted Black Magic bar would eventually be installed in the room underneath it, and Rose's visitors would be taken into there first and offered a dirty video to look at and a drink. Fred had hidden microphones in the headboard of the heavy oak bed. And as soon as a red light went on in the family room to indicate Rose was with a customer, Fred would dive in there to listen in. The monitoring equipment he installed was primitive at first – baby intercoms from Boots. But rapid developments in the technology meant that it became increasingly sophisticated. He would progress to a multi-speaker transmission box concealed in the top of a built-in cupboard: he could turn the dial to choose which room he wanted to listen to. He would tape it all as well. There were two cassette tapes and the intercom coming in and he used to tape it. The older children knew it was all going on because they had to sit and listen to their father listening to their mother going with a man upstairs. He used to have this square intercom thing on a massive piece of cable and he used to make his tea and listen to it. He would sit on the sofa with the speaker next to his ear just listening. There was a squawk box with a cable coming out of it going to the master unit which was in the cupboard. And he would just walk round listening to it, sit down listening to it. And it was really loud. So everybody else could hear it as well. Everybody could hear it. Half the street could hear it. So it was impossible not to know what was going on.

Heather and May and Stephen would have to listen to their mother making the noises she knew their father needed to hear. And if by some miscalculation Heather or May happened to be left in the house with their father on their own, he'd make them sit on the sofa and watch a porno tape with him. He would touch them. When the others were around he would chase Heather and May and touch them; grab their breasts or grab them between the legs. He was short but he was strong and he would get them and pin them to the floor with his body, grabbing at their breasts and grabbing them between the legs. This was often. Sometimes every day. He said he was proud of his daughters' bodies. 'What sort of girl is it that won't let their dad touch them? Every girl should let their dad touch them.' He used to call them bitches and frigid and Rose used to laugh. He used to call Heather a lesbian. 'Did you know your sister was a lesbian? I caught her pissing on the bed.' After she turned thirteen or fourteen he was always on at Heather about being a lesbian. About Heather hating men. About never wanting to be near men and hating them. And not surprisingly she did. Stephen thought so.

After their mother turned what she called 'professional', May and Heather were given the job of answering the phone if 'Mandy' wasn't available. They would have to answer the phone and make appointments and ask the men about the kinds of things they wanted and any special requests or requirements. Rose told them to ask these things and write the answers in the books provided. A black book for the black men; a red book for white people. It had their age, penis size, what position they liked and any special aids or requirements, and May or Heather had to fill that in. These men would tell them over the phone, unless they were regulars, when all that information would already have been recorded. Heather hated men. Just hated them. She couldn't stand to be in a room with men. Couldn't stand them near her. It showed in the way she acted. Stephen could read it in her face.

Being a married couple living in a single room with a baby, Anne Marie and Chris Davis were rehoused by Gloucester Council in 1985 on the White City estate. Although it wasn't far away none of the West children was allowed to visit their half-sister. May had been given a beating for talking to Anne Marie in her bedroom at Cromwell Street after she came back. And they had been warned not to allow Anne Marie in if she called when neither Rose nor Fred was at home. The children would turn her away at the gate as they had been instructed to do by their mother.

After Anne Marie had moved to White City, though, Heather and May and Stephen would sometimes sneak up to visit her. Chris Davis was in on his own doing some work on the house one day just after they had moved in when Heather came around. He was up in the loft laying a floor and Heather climbed up with him and said she'd had enough at home. She was miserable and she wasn't going to take it. She said she was seriously thinking of leaving and going to live in the Forest. She had recently been on a two-week camping trip to Clearwell Caves in the Forest of Dean with her school. Which struck Chris as a turn-up for a start – Rose and Fred letting Heather out. And she had made her mind up that was where she wanted to live. On her own. In the Forest. FODIWL. Be a hermit. See nobody and be a recluse. And she meant it. Her face was clenched. Her nails were bitten to the quick. She wanted to live actually *in* the Forest so she could be totally lost. Away from everybody and all this. She seemed shaky and nervous. So he did the would-you-make-a-good-castaway thing to lighten it up. If she could trap animals, if she could skin them, what berries to eat, how to get fresh water out of a running stream. Told her about warm deer brains just after the kill. The most delicious thing you could ever eat. She got a bit squirmish but that was a relief, knowing what you could sometimes get with Heather. She was a difficult character. She could be cussed. When she was in a good mood, she was fun. But when she got a strop on, by *God* did she get a strop on. You took to the hills. Hell or high water, if she didn't want to see you she would look straight through you. Chris Davis put a clown's outfit on one day – tried it on one day. 'I did everything *but* jump on her head, if you like. Looked straight through me as if I wasn't there. Then again, if you've been

394

molested, you switch off. That ability to distance themselves from reality.'

Before she left, Chris got Heather to promise that if she did run away to live in the Forest, she would contact him so he could reassure Anne Marie she was all right, and she said she would. That was the agreement then.

Fred would never have bothered to take the family away if it was left to him. He liked Gloucester and he liked his house. But Rose nagged and nagged. So he bought a little two-berth caravan that he kept parked behind one of Alex Palmer's properties at number 11, and in 1985 he swapped his old green Bedford for an ex-Group 4 security transit which he converted to a living van. He put in transit seats that clicked in and dark-glass windows and a table that would drop down between two benches to make a bed. He towed the caravan behind the living van and took the family to a holiday camp in Barry Island every so often. Occasionally they went somewhere different like Craven Arms in Dorset. Rose liked Cardiff Airport. She thought it was great parking up there and watching the planes coming and going. But Fred's favourite was Barry outside Cardiff and they went there seven years in a row. One of these years Fred got Anne Marie and Chris and the baby to move in and house-sit Cromwell Street for a week for him while he was away. He had a lot of stuff in at the time, new videos and TVs and suchlike that he was 'looking after' and that were probably hot enough to cook eggs on, as Chris pointed out to Anne. Dodgy gear.

Being back in Cromwell Street after she had got her own household going seemed to have a profound effect on Anne. It seemed to unhinge her, although 'unearth' was the word Chris used. It seemed to unearth her being back living there, even if it was only for a week. A hell of a change came over Anne. On the second or third day Chris had to pin her down on the breakfast counter because she was being so violent and moody. 'It's the place,' she told him. 'It gives me the shits.' They were using the four-poster bed with the 'Cunt' sign on it in the top front room with all the magazines piled up in the corner. 'Fucking weird bastards' did cross your mind. They threw this video in. It turned out to be two females, one wearing a mask – a henchman's mask; a henchman being an executioner. There was shitting involved. One female eating the other female's shit. They switched it off rapidly.

Poking around in the cellar one day, Chris discovered what he took to be a museum-piece chastity belt. The back part of the cellar was for the children; the front was for junk. In among all the tins of paint and wallpapering tables and junk and rubbish was what looked like a metal chastity belt – welded ribs of metal with a fabric tie-around belt. Anne Marie went extremely quiet, red-faced. She told him all about it within a week. Went into one of her talk modes. These periods of letting on or telling. 'For Chrissake don't do anything.' Chris could see she was scared shitless. She was as white as a sheet. Red first then white and shaking. 'He'll come up here and kill me.' That week was a fantastic horror week.

Anne Marie had a second baby at the beginning of 1987. Chris Davis wasn't the father. She had had a holiday every year they had been together and it was always a boyfriend who took her. Chris accepted this and they were still in the house at White City and still together. After Carol was born, Anne had to have a hysterectomy, which meant no more children. And it was while she was lying in bed in her living room recovering because she was unable to climb stairs that she decided to arrange a confrontation with Fred and Rose and ask them to tell her why she had been abused as a child. The result was predictable: violent denials from her father – 'I'm not standing here and listening to this fucking rubbish'; a lot of staring into the carpet and blank silence from Rose. Rose said she never wanted to see her again as they both stormed out.

That happened in March 1987. Michelle had her third birthday in June, three months later. And in an attempt to mend the breach in the family, which she hated, Anne invited Fred to a birthday party for his first granddaughter on 17 June. Fred and Rose of course and all her half-brothers and - sisters. And to her delight they all came. They were all there. The whole clan. For all the time they were there, for all the clan to descend, it had happened only twice. But it was noticeable things weren't well with Heather the minute they arrived. She was in a ratty mood. Hufty. A face like thunder. And she was being bullied by her father. Pushed by him to join in. 'Don't fucking stand there like a lemon.' 'Why don't you just fuck off and leave me a-fucking-lone.' She was never allowed out. None of them was allowed out. They were all basically kept at home.

Heather was four months away from turning seventeen. She had left school a few weeks earlier and she had got good results. She had eight GCSEs and could have got a job if she had been interested but she seemed like she couldn't be bothered to look. She was lethargic. She sat around the house all day staring into space. She had few friends. She had no boyfriends. Her father was still touching her and molesting her. Still raping her in the cellar where she had gone back to sharing part of it with May. Stephen was in the cellar as well. She said if a boy touched her she'd put a brick over his fucking head. If a man came near her.

On the day of Michelle's party, Heather seemed agitated. Also very distant. Heather was a quiet one anyway. But on that day, which was a Wednesday, she seemed particularly shut off and distant. Chris Davis had a friend, Charlie, with a video camera and he was going around filming. He filmed Michelle and her friends having their party in the house and in the garden. But for a lot of the time Heather stood with her back to the house at the bottom of the garden on her own and didn't want to know. When Rose turned up she had been in a bit of a funny mood. She mentioned to Anne they'd had problems with Heather before they left, and Fred seemed to be keeping a close watch on Heather all the time they were there. Part of Heather's agitation came from the fact that she had just found out who the father of two of her half-caste sisters was and realized that she was at school with one of his other daughters. Although she must have known it wasn't true, Fred and Rose had always explained away their mixed-race children by saying they were throwbacks to Fred's gypsy past, and that is what Heather had chosen to believe. When she found out the truth she had had a go at Suncoo's daughter and Suncoo had come around to Fred and Rose and the result of it all was that Heather had taken the beating of her life. They wanted to keep the family tight. They didn't want their affairs out in the street.

At the party Heather stayed off on her own and was sullen and morose. Giving her mother looks like: Just you wait till I'm out of here. A major strop on. 'Why don't you just fuck off and leave me a-fucking-lone.' There were complaints from next door about Heather's language. It was a rough estate. It wasn't Harrods. They were rough. But. They had several complaints from the mothers of the other children about the foul-mouthed swearing. A mule skinner's ears would have been burning. Anne phoned up and said to Fred and them about it later that evening. And it was a day or two later Heather buggered off. 17 June 1987, Michelle's birthday, was a Wednesday. 19 June 1987 was a Friday. And that was the day Heather threw her things together in a bag and got into a red Mini belonging to a lesbian and set off for Wales, if you believed Rose and Fred.

The day after Michelle's birthday party Stephen played a mean trick on Heather. He told her to hang on to the metal grille in front of one of the electric fires in the cellar and stupidly she did and she ended up being hurled across the room. She got an electric shock and shot across the room. So she had already been crying when the phone went shortly after that at about nine o'clock to tell her that the holiday-camp job she had been given had fallen through and Heather really started crying then. She had found a job cleaning chalets at a holiday camp in Devon. It was the first thing she'd taken an interest in since she'd left school. A holiday camp in Torquay. She had found a way of leaving home and getting out of the house and now it had been snatched away from her. She cried. She crumpled up in tears. She sobbed all through the night.

May and Stephen left for school at eight the next morning. They walked the four miles to Hucclecote School and the four miles back every day to save the bus fare which was the only money they had. It was something they had been doing for the past few years with Heather. When they came back from school at around five o'clock on the Friday, Heather had already gone. 'Oh,' their dad said, 'your sister's gone.' They could see that their mum had been crying, which was unusual. And their dad took May and Stephen outside to the converted security van that was his work van and sitting in the back at the bench table told them the holiday-camp job was back on and that Heather had left at lunchtime with a lemon in a Mini. He took them up into the van and said, 'Look, your mum's a bit upset 'cause of Heather's leaving.' He was quite upset as well, shaking a lot and quite tearful. Rolling a roll-up in his chipped working fingers. 'It's just me and you now.'

Fred West in these years had become an addict for the news. The news was all he watched. The one o'clock, the six o'clock, the nine o'clock, the ten o'clock, the graveyard-shift news. Peter Kurten, the German mass murderer, was a similar addict for the news, although it was the radio news in the twenties in Weimar Germany when Kurten was prowling the streets of Düsseldorf abducting and murdering scores of women and children. Kurten claimed to derive as much, if not more, sexual satisfaction from the response to his murders as from the actual killing. He claimed that the excitement and outrage expressed by participants in a spontaneous protest staged after the discovery of another corpse had aroused him sexually and led to ejaculation.

Fred West would come in and switch off whatever anybody else was watching to watch the news. The one o'clock, the six o'clock, the nine o'clock, the ten o'clock, the graveyard-shift news. Watching to see if he was on it yet. Watching to find out if he had been caught. Like a child playing hide-and-seek who doesn't know what he fears or wants more: to stay hidden, or to be found.

Chapter Fourteen

In his first interviews with the police in 1994, seven years after he had murdered Heather, Fred West would tell them how he had strangled her while she was lounging with her hands in her pockets against a washing machine he was working on in his tool room. It was the Friday morning. Friday, 19 June 1987. He had waited until Rose had gone out to do her shopping. Heather was standing with her hands in her pockets cheeking him. Her belongings were packed in a suitcase and carrier bags and waiting by the front door. She was lounging and leaning (he said) and cheeking him. 'And I said to her . . . now what's this about you leaving home? . . . You know you're too young. You're a lesbian and there's AIDS and all that. I mean, you're vulnerable for anything.' But Heather just stood there and looked at him.

He told them that he had said, 'Well, Heather, I'm not going to let you go', and she had said, 'If you don't fucking let me go I'll give all the kids acid and they'll all jump off the church roof and be dead on the floor.' He told them how he had gone to slap her face and had suddenly remembered a previous occasion when he and Rose had had an argument 'and I slapped her across the face and I dislocated her jaw . . . moved 'er jaw over'. So he had grabbed Heather by the neck instead. He had grabbed her by the neck and held her until she turned blue. 'I'm strong in the hands because of the job I do . . . When you're using big spanners an' things like that, you get strong in the arms . . . I spotted she'd gone blue. So I let go of her quick and, of course, she just started to fall backwards on to the washing machine and slide forward.'

He told them how he had dragged her through the tool room and down the few steps into the living room and how he had gone and got wet cloths and flannels and put them on Heather's face. He had taken a brass mirror off the living-room wall and put it over her mouth to see if she was breathing 'and there was nothing on it'. He told them how he had dragged her body into the bathroom then and stripped Heather and put her in the bath and run cold water on her 'and still I couldn't get nothing . . . So I can remember standing there and thinking, how do you know when somebody's dead?'

He told them how he had taken Heather's body out of the bath and dried it and then 'put something round her neck . . . to make sure she was dead . . . I mean . . . if I'd have started cutting her leg or her throat or something and she'd have suddenly come alive . . . That's what I was thinking.' He had taken a pair of tights and tightened them around her neck. And then he had brought a dustbin in from the small con-creted-over space at the front of the house and dismembered Heather and put the parts of her body in it. He told them how he had cut and twisted off his daughter's head ('I remember it made a heck of a noise when it was breaking') and cut and twisted out her legs at the groin. She 'filled the bin shoulder-ways'. He had hidden the bin behind the Wendy house that was actually a bicycle shed at the bottom of the garden and buried the remains by the interwoven panel fence by the Leyland pines under cover of darkness.

He told them all this over many days in a circular, self-contradicting, always revising and backtracking way. People often do this as a way of coming close to a difficult or elusive truth. He did it, he thought, as a way of keeping people away from one. He spoke in a becalmed, dissociated voice and with the degree of extreme detachment that the police and others who come into contact with them have come to expect from psychopathic killers. What was striking about Fred West's account of how he had murdered and mutilated his daughter was the way in which the close details of how exactly he had decapitated and dismembered Heather and disposed of her remains frequently slipped into animated soliloquies on ordinary household things. With a sort of compulsion, a description of cutting or carrying would turn, within one or two sentences, into a hymning or inventorying of the objects he had done the cutting or carrying – or tying or washing or concealing – with.

He said at one point he had left Heather's body in the bath and gone into the tool room to look for something to take her head and her legs off with. 'I looked up an' I seen this knife sticking out an' he was brand new. He came with something from Icelandic – summat we bought from Icelandic an' the knife was free with it. And he was put up there out of the way of the children. Because he was deadly, this thing was. I mean the blade on it was *terrible* . . . So I just shoved him up in there. What I was going to use him for was trimming the trees. That's what I was actually going to use him for . . . I was going to try an' break him up, just bust him through an' chuck him in the bin, because it was such a deadly weapon to have about . . . [But] it just ripped. It didn't actually cut across. It just ripped across the skin, like. Cut bits out. So then I went in the kitchen and got the bread knife . . . I run the knife round the neck through the skin, and then just twisted the head round. And whatever bits was left, just cut that off.'

He said he chose a knife because it minimized the possibility of damaging the bath. 'The body was in an enamel bath. Pressed-steel enamel bath. So if you tried chopping in that, the thing would splinter all over you. The enamel . . .'

In one interview he said he thought he had knotted a pair

of tights around Heather's neck. In another he said it could have been a length of flex. 'It was thirteen-amp, ring-main cable. Grey. Three-core. Plain copper wire . . . We use it for pulling posts out of the ground, things like that. All you do is just pull it round and twist it. You can't tie knots in it . . . I may have chucked it in with her; I don't know what I done with it. Because there would have been blood on it . . . I mean, I knew she was dead before I did it, or as good as . . . It was a bit I'd cut off when I was rewiring a house. Probably two feet to a metre long.'

He had rolled the dustbin containing Heather's remains outside and hidden it behind the Wendy house at the bottom of the garden. 'Stephen made the Wendy house – part on the lawn, part on the patio. Eight-be-four. Made out of eight-be-four sheets. I put her behind the Wendy house and covered it over with that blue polythene again . . . That blue membrane polythene, you know, they use on the floors . . . 'Cause there was loads of that down the bottom. Stephen had it all over the place down there. Pulled across on strings from the front fence to the back fence. Stephen had a load of parts – spare wheels and handlebars an' all that – behind the Wendy house.'

When the time came to dig a hole in which to bury Heather – to make the narrow shaft to force the pieces of her body in – he found his spade kept hitting metal. 'When I dug, these base bars went right across . . . [There used to be] a climbing frame in the garden – tubular steel. There was a scaffold bar attached to it, across to the church wall with an ordinary lorry tyre hanging from it on three chains, an' they used to swing round in it. We found that on the corporation tip or somewhere. The chains were all on it when we found it . . . [Then] the frame finally got disintegrated and busted up . . . What's sticking up there now is one of the angles off the corner.'

After he had buried the remains of Heather's body that night, he had swilled out the inside of the dustbin and washed himself with a hose attached to the side of the house. 'I took the dustbin to the 'ouse and washed him, because we had a tap on the side – I'm not sure if he's still there now – an' put him back out the front. I washed off at the hosepipe outside. Washed wellingtons an' that in the bin full of water and then tipped him over across the yard.'

Not very long afterwards the family had helped him to extend the patio over the rest of the garden, covering the place near the pines on the left-hand perimeter where Heather was buried. 'We patioed it. Innsworth Patio Slabs. They come from out by the airfield there, where all the Air Force is . . . The ground has been levelled down, or hammered down. Refilled. As the end of the slab sunk, you put more soil under, or gravel, to level him. As the body sinks, then the slab was tipping . . . Actually I did it not so very long ago . . . Heather helped me put the original one down – just a toddler, like, but she was there rakin'.'

These displays of intimacy and affection for inanimate objects – spontaneous declarations of the companionship he felt with objects; the easy friendships he made with things – contrast forcibly with the emotional nullness that Fred West's children associated with their father. He never showed them any affection. He couldn't remember how many children he had and he couldn't remember his victims' names. He was emotionally null. Morally delinquent. A moral vacuum. He was a moral blank.

Different people were given different reasons as time went on for why Heather was no longer around. Mrs Knight, a neighbour, was told by Rose a couple of days after Heather's disappearance, 'There was a hell of a barney here a couple of nights ago. We found out that she was going with a lesbian from Wales, and she has gone to Wales with her.' Erwin Marschall, a window-cleaner (and a former boyfriend of Anne Marie's), was told that Heather had gone away from home – she was uncontrollable and had run away and there was nothing much anybody could do about it. Ronald Marshall, a friend of Fred and Rose for twenty-five years and whose daughter Denise was Heather's best friend at school, was told when he asked about Heather that she had run off after being given a good hiding by Rose for knocking the small ones around 'and putting scratches in their face'. (This was the same reason they had given for the disappearance of Lynda Gough fourteen years before.) They said Heather was living in Brockworth in Gloucester. They didn't know where in Brockworth but she was always phoning to say she was all right. The phone would go and Stephen and May and the younger children would often be told that it was Heather on the phone. If they asked to speak to her they would be told that she would speak to them some other time. In the years ahead their father would occasionally come home and report sightings of Heather – chance glimpses of her and a few times meetings with Heather in Birmingham, Devizes, Bristol, Weston-Super-Mare. She had turned into a drug-dealer. She was involved in credit-card fraud. She had gone blonde. He started a new job with a firm called Carsons Contractors in Stroud in 1988 and he would tell his employers, Derek and Wendy Thomson, that he had been to see his daughter Heather in Weston where she had got in with a bad lot of glue-sniffers and drugs users and a what's-her-name drugs-running what's-it. Bloody cartel. But the Thomsons, who had got used to Fred by then, would just go, Oh right. Walter Mitty, Wendy Thomson called him. He was just a character to himself like most people are. He'd screw up the dog-ends and put them in his donkey-jacket pocket. He was just a mucky little man. An excellent electrician. A very good decorator. Always on about his orgies. Orgies he had been to in London with the most unlikely of their customers. They were in the haute Cotswolds. Royalty and writers. People off the television and very well-to-do people. 'They invited me up to London and oh it was a big orgy.' Oh right. Oh yeah.

Not long after Heather disappeared, Graham Letts and his wife Barbara received a visit from Rose and Fred, which was very unusual. They drove out to see them to say that Heather had gone away and that she was a lesbian. Rose did all the talking. 'Heather's left us. She's disappeared. She's a lesbian. And that's it closed. I don't want to hear any more about it. We won't mention it again. I don't want you coming round in future if you do mention Heather.' That's the way Rose was. She hardened up. She got very hard.

When she was little, about six or seven, May saw her father making a cat-o'-nine-tails. Of course she was too little to know what it was. But many years later, after Heather had gone away and the upper floors had been converted for their mother's private use, Stephen and May came across the cat-o'-nine-tails on one of the days that Stephen picked the lock to the upstairs flat. It was a cut-off broom handle, and then just strips of leather nailed to it. Leather and plastic belts that Fred had spotted and collected with his scavenging eye. 'About 13 million strips of leather. I think it's supposed to be nine strips but he got carried away,' Stephen says. A peculiar thing that looked like dreadlocks.

There were now two locked doors facing the old front door in the hall. One was the door going down into the cellar. The other was the door going up into Rose's private part of the house. This part had been made totally self-contained. The small room at the back next to the bathroom had been turned into a kitchen; the room on the first floor at the front had become the Black Magic bar. There was a king-size bed with a white lace canopy over it and a convex mirror in the canopy roof, in the top-floor room overlooking the garden. The four-poster hand-made by Fred out of Dean oak timber had been installed in the top-floor front, which is also where their collection of vibrators and bondage suits and the other things they had amassed for their life together was kept. A built-in cupboard along one wall contained clamps and whips and harnesses and leather and rubber masks and full skintight second-skin latex and leather suits and other S-and-M paraphernalia.

The house was full of blue magazines and blue movies. Dirty books and dirty films. There was hard-core pornography in magazine and video-cassette form all over the house. Fred was always keen for other people to borrow it and watch it. And Rose kept a written record of where each tape went – a title and who had it and when it was due back. Like a library, in fact. Fred liked the little ones to sit down with him and watch pornographic films and Rose had porn on in the kitchen while they were eating their tea. Chris Davis tuned in the video channel on his televisions for him because Fred wasn't able to do that and borrowed a few tapes. Around 1988 a small video shop opened on the corner of Wellington Street and the connecting road into Cromwell Street, and Fred started more or less to live in there, offering pornographic Polaroid photographs and pornographic tapes for sale or hire to the regular customers.

The brothel style of the rooms in Rose's flat at 25 Cromwell Street was based on the tacky glamour of the rooms in the videos that, by the late eighties, Rose and Fred had been watching together for years. The avocado corner sinks, louvred cabinets, velour headboards, lace canopies, marbled vanity units, faceted mirrors and flouncy touches were directly traceable to the room sets in *Disco Audition* and *Big Bill Banana* and *Debbie Does Dallas* and *Bangkok*

Boobs. The bedrooms had fake black beams in the ceilings and arched, ranch-style doors with latch handles and were separated by a heavy curtain from the lower floors. The life-size poster on the back of the door leading to Rose's private part of the house showed a girl in a black négligé posing with blond-wood louvred doors and could have been taken in the room Rose took her clients to on the top floor. A gap eventually became apparent between the smudged bright colours and motel-room finishes and boudoir lighting of the rooms upstairs, and the downstairs rooms where the children were living which were neglected and sticky-carpeted and brown.

At his granddaughter's third birthday, two days before he murdered Heather, Fred West had gone up to the neighbour of Chris Davis's who had volunteered to video Michelle having her party and asked him if he would be interested in coming round and filming sex scenes at his house. He hadn't had a video camera until then, and had possibly never seen one being used. But he soon went out and bought one on hire purchase and used it to start photographing what he had always and only been photographing: human parts. Male and female genitals, only now with sound and in living colour. Rose was always a performer. She had never minded being watched. And she was an enthusiastic performer in this medium, alone and with others. Occasionally Fred would be present in the room with his camcorder, moving around the bed. But mostly he would set up the camera in the top back room and leave her having sex with a man while he listened on the intercom downstairs. The camera was simply there and things took place in front of it. It was a bare style that gave what he was doing the clinical, 'scientific' gloss that he always liked.

There seems to have been no shortage of men who were prepared to be taped having sex with Rose. But there was also a lot of footage of Rose with devices in a room on her own performing solo. Rose bringing bigger and bigger and increasingly outlandish objects inside herself. Rose urinating on towels on the bed, on a sofa in the Black Magic bar and flamboyantly on the kitchen table. They evolved the ritual of him filming her dressing to go out to spend the night with one of the men he had approved for her, and then filming her undressing the next morning on her return. In addition to recording the semen stains on her underwear, he would carry out a gynaecological examination before she set out and again when she came home that involved a video camera in place of a speculum. She would lie with her feet pulled backwards over her head and wide apart and he would tape four- and five-minute close-ups of her nothing-to-be-seen. An obsessive, fixed stare into an absence, a lack, a nothingness – a hole. A torso and a hole which, because of how close he came in, could have been the hole where a head had once been. Blackness filling two-thirds of the frame. This was something even his children knew about him. He had a thing about women's bodies – he was into internal bits. He wanted to go right into the body and look at the internal organs. He really wanted to get inside them. He wanted to come as close as he could.

And Rose seemed happy always to co-operate in his probings and schemes. To give him what she knew he needed to have. To assist and comply. It was a go-with-the-flow natural thing. 'That is why our marriage worked out so well, for the simple reason that Rose had had no wild life, and she just blended in to my way of living,' Fred West said. 'I met Rose at sixteen an' trained Rose to what I wanted. And that's exactly what has happened.' He had trained her, down to letters and commands, and she had complied. She was his slave in a way. But she was his willing slave. This was her life. Striving for abasement and humiliation in all her life with Fred. Striving to submit. Going with his men. Letting the men do to her what he had told them to do. Holding herself open to his gaze. Enabling him to stare right into her. Being interrogated by his camera. Surprising herself as well as him sometimes in how far she was prepared to go. And somewhere understanding that her submissive surrender had more power over him than if she were to refuse or rebel. To kick out. The obedience of the slave kills the commands of her master. Because she didn't resist her enslavement she proved she could endure anything. He treated her coarsely. He made her into something compliant and corrupt. A second document in her handwriting found in the attic at Cromwell Street said, 'I, Rose, will do exactly what I am told, when I am told, without questions, without losing my temper, for a period of three months from the end of my next period, as I think I owe this to Fred.' There can be surprising shifts in roles between dominator and dominated, between 'hammer' and 'anvil'. In a sense the dominated seeks indirectly to dominate as well. Her exhibition of her masochistic submissions became her badges of triumph.

Whenever Fred West was in the room working the camera, he would focus almost exclusively on her vulva. But even in the long shots he tended to depersonalize her by framing her in a way that kept her face and head out of the picture. She was prepared to play dead for him. Become an object to be investigated. Even her self-pleasuring – on those occasions when it was performed in front of a camera – was done first and foremost to please Fred and confirm him in his position of power. At one point during one of the sessions she would grab the ankles of a Jamaican man who was lying naked on his back on her bed and haul his dead weight further into what she knew would be the centre of the picture, repositioning him in front of Fred's camera.

In the same way that Rose seemed capable of continuing her pleasure indefinitely (compared to Fred whose sexual performances rarely lasted more than a minute), he could never get enough of listening to and watching Rose have sex. As soon as he came in from work he would start unwinding the speakers and listening to Rose having sex. He would sit on the sofa with the speaker next to his ear, just listening. Nobody was allowed to speak to him while Rose was with a client. There would be a lot of talking and screaming, and the children used to keep turning up the television to drown out the groaning noises from upstairs. Wails. Noises. Shrieks. Wailing, thumping, thrashing about. If a man stayed overnight Fred would sleep on the settee downstairs listening to the close-up sounds of their pleasure.

He preferred to listen and watch in this technologically distanced, sanitized way than to take part or even be present. It could be switched off and on. Turned up and down. Fast-forwarded or rewound. Saved or wiped. He stayed in control of these aural fetishes originating from inside the body. The sounds of pleasure erupting from the invisible places deep inside the body. The out-of-control confessions of pleasure.

Kathryn Halliday left her husband in October 1988 and moved into Cromwell Street with her lesbian lover, Kimberley Stanton. They rented a bedsit at number 11, which was one of Alex Palmer's houses. And they had been living there only a few days when Fred West was sent round to take a look at a leak in the ceiling. He came one morning when Kim wasn't there. But Kathryn Halliday made no secret about her domestic set-up and the cheery little man said straightaway, 'If you see my missus, she'll sort you out. She likes a bit of both.' He invited Kathryn along to number 25 for a drink that night and she went. Fred came to the door and took her upstairs to the lounge with a bar in it on the first floor and offered her a video to look at and a drink. There was a large mural of a tropical island and the sea, and a well-stocked bar. A tiger-pattern rug under her feet; a plastic pendant chandelier over her head.

There were what she estimated to be a couple of hundred videos in a dark wood unit in the window corner, and he said, anything she wanted, he could put on. What was her taste? She said just straight would be fine – just a straight blue movie, and he threw one in. A few minutes later a woman came in and the woman's manner left no room for doubt that she was the woman of the house. Rose came in and sat down next to Kathryn. It was a small, two-seater sofa and she sat down close to her wearing a very short skirt and a low-cut T-shirt and nothing else. She could see that. She started taking Kathryn's clothes off straightaway. She was very pressing. No niceties, no formalities. Very urgent. Within a matter of minutes Rose had taken off all her clothes and stripped Kathryn and was dragging her – this was the word – to one of the bedrooms upstairs. They all went into the back bedroom and Fred took his clothes off and brought a camcorder camera. There were mirrors on the wardrobes and there was a double bed. She was pushed down on the bed and Rose joined her. She was quite aggressive. Fred joined them on the bed and had sex with her while Rose sat astride her, on top of her. He climaxed very quickly and went downstairs to bring another drink. He was very wham bam. Rose now became the aggressor. She became very aggressive and demanding. She held Kathryn down on the bed very hard and began to taunt her. Was she woman enough to do all the things they wanted her to do with them? There were various vibrators, all sizes and shapes. There were dildos, battery-operated and not battery-operated, and various shapes and sizes. 'She wanted me to use them on her, but also to take them,' Kathryn Halliday said seven years later. 'I couldn't physically take some of them . . . The ones she preferred were exceptionally large.' He came upstairs and in and out but he didn't join in again.

The relationship with Kathryn Halliday lasted for four months, through the New Year and into 1989, until the threatening edge to the violence got too much for her. Rose would knock on the window at number 11 every morning on her way back from taking the children to school, although she told Kathryn not to come around on a Thursday in the morning because that was kept for men visitors who paid. There was a pattern that Kathryn Halliday came to recognize. Their meetings always started very gentle. Rose was very persuasive. But once she got you into the bedroom, she wanted to make you vulnerable. Vibrators were there to be used 'very, very physically'. 'When she got you into a vulnerable position physically and mentally she would use that against your person.'

If she visited in the evening and Fred West was there, a video would always already be playing in the bar room upstairs. There was always a video in the background like background music. These tended to be home-made videos rather than the pre-recorded sort. One showed a woman tied to a bed in a spread-eagle fashion on her back. A very large dildo was being used on her. She seemed distressed and not just acting distressed. They looked like involuntary flinches of pain. Kathryn Halliday recognized the room as the top back room at Cromwell Street because of some of the furniture and by the wallpaper which she had come to know. Other videos showed other girls being subjected to various forms of sexual abuse. There was one of a girl with fair hair being whipped and tied to the bed by a man. There were others of girls being tied to beds with chains and straps. Kathryn was tied to the bed on many occasions herself and was then either blindfolded or stopped from seeing by having Rose lying across her face. Rose straddling her. Rose was quite a big woman by then and very strong. Most times she went in the evening it would end up with Kathryn having her hands and feet tied. It felt like dressing-gown cord. They blindfolded her several times and forced a pillow over her face twice. Fred would watch rather than take part. He took part sometimes, but not very often at all. He would be downstairs with the children. Rose threatened her and taunted her and pressed what felt like cold metal against her skin. On one occasion Fred used a bullwhip so hard it left marks. 'They got more and more violent. They wanted to do more and more all the time. They pushed me beyond my personal limits, and they hurt me . . . Rose West wanted me to do things to her which were very, very aggressive . . . She wanted orgasms all the time, like a machine.'

One night after she had been going to the house for about two months they took Kathryn across the landing into the top room at the front of the house which she had never been in before. It was quite darkly decorated. She saw a four-poster bed with large hooks in the pelmet, and then she was shown the contents of the wardrobe. There was a cat-o'-nine-tails. Whips. Clamps and whips and harnesses and leather and rubber masks and latex and leather suits. There were clothes on hangers. All dark and black and sexy clothes. Little bits of lingerie like slips. Like nylon. Masks and hoods. In a suitcase in the wardrobe were black rubberized masks and suits. These smelled sweaty. Suits all-in-one with two little slits for the nose and some with no nose holes at all. They were giving off that body smell and had obviously been worn. Some zips across the mouth. She was frightened. 'They played with me and the idea that I was frightened. They got their thing from seeing other people frightened.' She never went into that room again and soon stopped going along to number 25 to see Rose and Fred. She ignored the raps on the window. Fred had the keys to her door. In March 1989 she moved out of Cromwell Street altogether.

Stephen West was going to be sixteen in August 1989 and his present from his mother that year was the news that she wanted him out. 'Got a good present for you this year – I want you out.' He was told, 'You're on your own, feller. Sling your hook. You're out.' And one day when he came home his things were packed and waiting by the door and he was told that from now on he was living in Mrs Taylor's house on the other side of the church. He was given Anne Marie's and Chris Davis's old room. He recognized it from the cork tiles around the fire and he was out and living with Enid Taylor.

At the beginning of the year, in March, a teacher at Stephen's school had suspected that he might be being physically abused and had reported his suspicions to the NSPCC. Stephen had a series of meetings with people from the NSPCC between March and May, but they didn't take it any further because Stephen insisted he was fine, he was OK and he asked them not to.

Stephen had learned to cope with the way they were having to live at home by turning off when he was in the house and mentally shutting down. 'I started my mind again', he says, 'when I was fifteen.' It had always been going to happen. It was bound to happen. But when they saw Stephen starting to become alert to what was happening around him, obviously his mother and father took it as a warning. Like Heather, Stephen had never been comfortable with the idea of having three half-caste sisters. When people used to ask him about them he never knew what to say. He knew there was talk. And he started playing up at home, making remarks to Tara and Rosemary and Lucyanna about their colour. Abusive, hurtful remarks that would make them cry. Starting fights and making them cry. And they used that as the reason to get rid of him and make him move out. He had been running away anyway. Disappearing for a week, two weeks. He was told he could come back in if he wanted for one hour every Sunday. That would be his family time. An hour and then fuck off out of it.

May – who had started spelling her name 'Mae' by this time after years of being mocked at school – also moved out of Cromwell Street in 1989. She had a boyfriend, Rob, and they moved two streets over to Belgrave Road. Mae had been sharing the back part of the cellar with Rob. Stephen had been sleeping in the front part with his girlfriend, Nicki, and they had put a curtain up between them. Mae didn't sleep with Rob for the first weeks he was in the house. He was her boyfriend and she liked him. But in many ways she had brought him in for protection. Ever since Heather disappeared, Mae had become the main object of her father's attentions. He was still grabbing and touching her. Pursuing her and using his body to pin her to the floor. Spying on her through holes in the floor. He carried pictures of her wearing only her underwear. He forced her to watch videos of her mother having sex with other men. He would grab her and take her bra off and fondle her. When she found a boyfriend they almost dragged him into the house to live. 'How was she?' her father would ask Rob in the mornings. He insisted on lending them videos. There was no way you could refuse. When Rob and Mae moved out she was told she could come round only on a Sunday and she had to hand over the keys to the house. Once they had left home, if they returned, it was the rule that they were not to talk to any of the other children, who ranged in age from six to eleven in 1989: Lucyanna, the youngest, then Rosemary, Barry, Louise, Tara. Three of them their 'love children'; two of them Fred's own.

There was a phone on a bracket shelf in the living room and when he was waiting for work Fred would spend the whole time pacing backwards and forwards in front of it. He was always waiting for work. He would put his boilersuit on even on a Sunday and if there was no job lined up for him to go to he would start pacing. Drove them all crazy. Backwards and forwards. Up and down. Pulling on a roll-up. Wearing a hole in the carpet. Then the phone would ring and he'd be off. A roofing job in Birmingham, Bournemouth, Nottingham, it didn't matter. The phone would ring and he'd run for it and he'd be out the door. Derek Thomson still says it at least once a week now: 'If only Fred West was here.' An excellent electrician. A very good decorator. Brilliant worker.

Sometimes Stephen would go off on weekend jobs with him. Sometimes Rose. It was the only time she got to see Fred. But Fred's employers at Carsons Contractors, the Thomsons, had to put a stop to that because their customers didn't like it. Their customers were well-to-do people in nice houses in the Cotswolds and they had complaints. When Fred had come for an interview for the job as a general builder he had turned up with his wife and kids. They had sat outside in the security van-turned-minibus while he was being interviewed in the house. They gave every appearance of being a normal working family, and he had got the job. He told them he could do all sorts of things that they didn't necessarily believe, but give him his due he basically could. He could turn his hand to everything, not always to perfection, but he could get around it. He had difficulty reading and writing. But he would make notes and his wife would write them up, with the extras always in red. His wife filled in his time-sheets and his claims for incidental expenses which he'd get reimbursed for and which were always written neatly in red.

The Thomsons had a contract to look after a home for the autistic in Minchinhampton, seven miles from Gloucester. And in the first four years he worked for them, from 1988 to 1992, it was Fred's job to be on twenty-four-hour call to do odd jobs and emergency repairs at Stroud Court, where he had keys to all the buildings. Stroud Court was an old and rambling building with an underground network of passages, corridors and cellars. And Fred would use any excuse to drive there late at night. He would often be discovered wandering the narrow passageways and underworkings at Stroud Court apparently locked in some kind of reverie. He could stay down there for hours just wandering and never offer an explanation or feel the need to offer one. He couldn't sleep. He was always getting up in the middle of the night to sort his tools or see to his van or go round the patio in an apparently zombie-like way, pushing a broom. He was prey at any given moment to puncture or depression and to patterns of compulsive behaviour. It was a problem for her to get him to bed. He was a bad sleeper. He had problems sleeping.

Apart from when she went with him to unblock a drain or fix some guttering, Rose and Fred never saw each other. He was forty-nine in 1990 – coming up to the half-ton; she was thirty-seven. They weren't old. But he wasn't interested in making any kind of social life. All the social life he needed was in the house, watching Rose; filming Rose and watching her and listening to her going with women and other men. He would put her out on at least two nights a week to go with West Indian men. They had their video ritual while she was dressing, then he would drive her to them and expect her to stay away all night. She wasn't to have any life apart from the family and his other men. He always brought the subject up. It was a daily thing he talked about. This very, very strong persuasiveness and reasons why she should. He could be very persuasive. 'I provide you and the children with a good home and all the money I earn goes to you. But you can't do something for your husband.' He could talk the birds out of the trees. And so she would go on doing it for their marriage. For her husband.

He would never take her out. She had black men to take her out. Take her to pubs and buy her drinks and bring her presents of sex toys and clothes. Little bits of lingerie like slips. Like nylon. The black men were well aware that in having sex with Rose they were doing Fred a favour. They never paid. Only the white men paid. She would go through her book and look a black friend up sometimes and invite him around. Which was all right. But they were Fred's. They could be relied on to report back to Fred what had happened. As if he controlled them the way he controlled everything. She did like sex. But she liked other things such as music. She liked country and western. She liked a change of scenery sometimes and a chance to meet some different people who weren't totally answerable to Fred. Controlled by Fred and having their strings jerked by him, telling him where they were going and for how long and when they would be back. Rose had had her sterilization operation reversed at the end of 1989 and very soon afterwards had become ill with a pregnancy in a fallopian tube. It had left her house-bound for a while and depressed. She told Fred that she wanted more than just going out with other men. There had to be more to life. There was no baby on the way. The younger children were growing. She started to think of a life away from the house.

He didn't like it and didn't want to listen. He would hit her every time she tried to bring it up. There were fights. Constant arguments. Fist fights in front of the children and endless bickering. Until she threatened to stop seeing the men he wanted her to see unless he relaxed his grip on the leash just a little; stopped reining her in all the time. She noticed in the paper that they had started having singles nights at the Bristol Hotel on the Bristol Road where Fred used to go to watch the stag films and strippers on Sunday afternoons when he was a teenager. They used to have the blue films on a Sunday and Fred used to ride in on his grey Triumph, his small body at full stretch astride the big frame and the massive tank. The Bristol always had some entertainment going on of one sort and another and she read the ad out to him. It was summer. She could walk there across the park. It was going to be country and western. That was her favourite. It was only the Bristol. So, although it creased him to, he allowed it. He let her. She went on her own and she had a really good time. The barman, Alan, was really nice. And the landlady, Yvonne, was really friendly. She was made to feel really welcome. And after a couple of drinks her new friend Yvonne introduced her to her cellarman Steve who wasn't everybody's cup of tea – he had bright ginger hair and sticking-out ears and was known by the nickname Lurch. But Rose liked him. And he liked Rose. And once Yvonne introduced them it was obvious they seemed to hit it off straightaway. It was a singles night, after all, their second or third of the summer. So: mission accomplished.

Rose became a regular at the Bristol not just on Thursday nights but on other nights of the week and was soon on first-name terms with Yvonne and Alan and a few of the others, and she would often go to Steve's room with him. They would go out for a stroll around the block or she would slip off to Steve's room upstairs with him. Needless to say, Fred wasn't slow to spot the change in her, and he didn't like it. He was jealous. He was boiling. 'Fred's got it on him,' Rose would tell her friends at the Bristol, who knew she lived with Fred, her crabby brother, and Fred's children. With Fred you could see it slowly build up. The look in his eyes. It would be a general build-up and then – watch out. She started going to parties and country-and-western dances. They argued almost every day. She was taking the family money and pissing it away – spending it on her friends. Couldn't she see? They were milking her. Most days he'd kick her or hit her. So to stop it she stopped going to the Bristol and stopped seeing Steve. But she also stopped seeing Fred's men at the house. If he wouldn't agree to her doing anything she wanted, then it would all stop. So it did for a while. But she knew it wouldn't be long until he was back to his other men. Back to his persuading. And of course she was right. To get her revenge she took a flat in Stroud Road without telling him in March 1991. A place of her own. Although it was more a statement of her separateness than somewhere to go. She intended him to find out eventually. She wanted him to know. And he found out what she had been up to when the doorbell went one day and Fred answered it and found himself talking to a man who was looking for a Mandy West of that address. The Mandy who had been renting a flatlet from him in his house in Stroud Road for five months and had disappeared leaving all her belongings behind, including a new hoover in its box. Being the kind of combative character Rose was, she always felt the need to offer something back. Something to indicate that she understood the game they were playing. Something to show that she was not quite the doormat to wipe his feet on that, even after twenty years, he might sometimes suppose she was. He had beaten her up when she came in late from a party at the Bristol on New Year's morning in 1991. Ripped her clothes and laid into her and pummelled her black and blue. And the flat in Stroud Road had been her reply. He went up the wall, and that pleased her. It was a small victory, and he was sore about it for months. He retreated into the world of his blue books and his sound-box and his other compulsive behaviours. Sweeping the patio in a set pattern. Chasing the television news. He got up in the night to wander the cellar corridors at Stroud Court and grease his tools. He started seeing crashes on his way to work at Carsons Contractors every morning – flowing blood, legs and arms floating about: he'd hear the report of an accident on Severn Sound and talk about it as if he'd been there. He let his hair go into a bush.

In March 1992 Fred's father died. He had been living with

his youngest son Doug and his wife at Moorcourt Cottage in Much Marcle where the children had all grown up. Walter West was seventy-eight and Fred hadn't seen him for quite a long time. Fred hadn't spoken to his brother John since the late eighties following a falling out over money. And he went on ignoring John's messages that his father was ill in hospital and kept asking for him: 'Fred hasn't been to see me.' Where was he? John West called Fred on the Wednesday and he said he'd go in on the Friday. When his father died on the Saturday, Fred still hadn't been. There were drinks after the funeral in Marcle village hall. Rose and Anne Marie went with Fred. John told his brother that as far as he was concerned he didn't like the way he treated their family. His mother was dead, his father was dead now and that was it over and he'd never speak to him again.

By the summer of 1992, Heather had been gone for five years. Mae and Stephen were hurt that Heather had never been in touch. They had always been so close. Five years was a long time and they did worry about her. But every time they brought the subject of Heather up at home their mum would tell them that if Heather wanted to contact them she would contact them. She knew where they lived. Mae and Stephen filled in a Salvation Army form for missing people. They wrote to Cilla Black at *Surprise! Surprise!*, the TV show where she brings people together who haven't seen each other for years. And they wrote to another TV show called *Missing*, which tries to find missing people. They never heard anything back. When they told their father that they were going to report Heather as missing to the police, he sat them down and told them that Heather was involved in credit-card fraud and that if they went to the police it would be like grassing her up. They had been brought up to resent and distrust the police.

One day at the beginning of August 1992 Stephen got a visit from some policemen at work who told him that his father had been arrested for raping one of his sisters (who for legal reasons can't be named). His mother had been taken into custody as well for her part in what had happened. The story as Stephen pieced it together was that several weeks earlier his sister had been vaginally and anally raped by their father on three separate occasions. On the first occasion she had been ordered upstairs into the bar room in Cromwell Street. Her father had told her to carry a bag of wine bottles upstairs. He had told her to sit on the small sofa with the hand-crocheted coverlet over it and had then turned on his video camera and raped her and buggered her while she kept her eyes fixed on the television as he had ordered her to do. Two of the other children who were watching television in the family room downstairs had heard screams and shouts and had started banging on the locked door to their mother's private part of the house but their bangings had been ignored. Their father had then been seen having long conversations with Stephen's sister at the bottom of the garden telling her (she told them later) that he had done it wrong and would have to do it again. He hadn't done it properly and it would cause medical problems if he didn't finish the job. He raped her again in the upstairs Black Magic bar and this time her mother was in the house. She had gone to talk to her afterwards in the bathroom and told her what did she expect, she had been asking for it. The next morning, a Saturday, Fred West had taken his daughter with him to a place near Reading to a warehouse he was painting. As soon as they arrived he forced his daughter to have sex with him for a third time in the deserted building. It seems that he frequently wavered in his idea of himself as invulnerable and special and that those of his actions which seem most irrational and ugly had to be attempts to defend his faith in his powers. Depression would come in a flood. Sitting alone in the van at the end of the day he had patted his daughter's thigh and said, 'I'll leave it alone now.'

At the end of the first sexual assault on her, Stephen's sister had been told by their father, 'You mustn't say anything, you know, because I'll go to prison for five years. We'll all be split up, and you need a mum and dad at your stage of life.' But when she had recovered enough to go back to school, the girl piece by piece told another girl, and the other girl eventually, some weeks after the rapes had happened, in a roundabout, would-be casual way told a policeman. He was the Cromwell Street community policeman and around six o'clock one summer Sunday evening in 1992 the twelve-year-old asked him, 'What would you do if a friend was being assaulted?' It was banter. It was an English summer evening. But then the girl told him that actually she had a friend and she was worried that her friend might have been 'mucked about with' by her father, who had made a video of what he was doing. The policeman made some notes in his book.

Four days later, on Thursday, 6 August 1992, Rose West opened the door at Cromwell Street just before nine o'clock in the morning. Fred had already left for work. It was the school holidays and the younger children were in their pyjamas in the living room watching television. There was a team of two detectives and four policewomen and one of them explained that they had a warrant to search the premises for pornographic material following a serious allegation of child abuse. Rose immediately threw a fit. She had physically wrestled women police officers out of her house in the past when they had turned up without a warrant to make inquiries about the activities of Anne Marie. 'And good fuckin' riddance!' Her instinct was to go on the attack. It was a small army. And she started kicking and lashing out and had to be physically restrained by one of the men grabbing her and twisting her arm up her back. She was arrested and taken to Gloucester police station and the children were dressed and taken to a local-authority home near by to be introduced to the team of social workers who would be looking after them. 'Don't you dare say anything' had been their mother's last words to them as she was taken away. The main aim was to find the video cassette that had apparently been made of Fred West raping his daughter, and the search team were very thorough: they looked in vacuum-cleaner bags and in the freezer as well as the more obvious places, and they would search behind the skirting boards and under the floorboards before they were through.

They didn't catch up with Fred West until later in the afternoon. He was arrested in the garden of his employers, Derek and Wendy Thomson, in Water Lane, near Bisley, near Stroud, seven miles south of Gloucester, around half past two and there was no resistance with him. He didn't struggle or try to fight them off. Their elderly customers loved Fred. He was very kind to old people. If they had a problem, Fred would sort it out. They were always asking for Fred. 'Nothing you need worry about,' he said. 'Nothing you should worry about.' It was a lovely day in August. Another lovely day. Slightly humid. The birds that Derek bred were singing in the aviary. A lovely day in high summer in one of the most beautiful places in England. He was almost affable as they took him away. 'Absolute rubbish,' he scoffed when they told him what the charge was once he was in the car. 'Lies, all lies . . . I never touched her.'

Under questioning at Gloucester police station throughout the afternoon and into the evening he remained composed. 'Me and my wife leads an active sex life . . . We make love every night, I mean perhaps twice, it just depends on what happens,' he said. 'I mean, you'll find harnesses, you'll find bloody God knows what in my home that we make up and things we do. You'll find tapes where we've been out in the van, out in the lanes, making love, and we're not frightened to show it. We enjoy our sex life, but not with our children . . . I mean, we got what we want. We don't mess with our kids. We've got everything.' But the officers searching 25 Cromwell Street had found photographs of two of the West children posing naked and home-made videos of Rose West having sex with both women and men. They were part of a haul of ninety-nine amateur and commercial pornographic videos that they had brought away, along with an extensive collection of rubberized suits and masks, a rice flail and a bullwhip, vibrators and dildos. The other visual evidence would also eventually include photographs of the erect penises of a number of naked men and Rose West sitting astride the gearstick of a car. The following day, Friday, 7 August, Lucyanna, Rosemary, Barry, Louise and Tara were made the subject of Emergency Protection Orders and removed to local-authority care. Their parents were forbidden to make contact with them and weren't even told where they were.

Rose West had been held at the police station overnight. The first thing she did when she got back to Cromwell Street on the Friday morning was pick up the phone and warn Anne Marie to keep her mouth shut to the police. 'If you think anything of me or your dad, especially your dad, you'll say nothing and keep your mouth shut.' It was eight o'clock. At the same time as Anne Marie was talking on the phone to Rose, Detective Constable Hazel Savage was ringing the doorbell at her house on the White City estate. Hazel Savage had been in the police force in Gloucester for nearly thirty years. She had had a number of run-ins with Anne Marie in her knife-carrying, tearaway teenage days. In 1966, when she was a WPC, she had brought Rena, Anne's mother, back to Gloucester from Glasgow to stand trial for breaking into caravans on the Watermead site. She knew Fred West well and over twenty years had become familiar with the house in Cromwell Street where he lived. Hazel told Anne Marie about the accusations being made by her half-sister against their father. And for the first time in her life Anne Marie found herself opening up. He had done the same thing to her, she told Hazel Savage, when she was eight, and it had continued until she was fifteen and had run away from home. Her stepmother had also been involved. She accompanied DC Savage and another officer to Tuffley police station and for a large part of the rest of the day found herself telling what seemed, even to her, the person who was telling them, the most barbaric, unbelievable things.

Her father meanwhile, in another interview room in another police station just two or three miles away, was accusing his children of 'ganging up' on him and making it all up. He suggested that his daughter was making the allegations against him because, among other reasons, she was jealous that he was paying more attention to one of her younger sisters than to her. 'It's all made up,' he said. 'She copied it from somewhere . . . There ain't one blade of truth in it as far as I'm concerned.'

When Stephen went to see his father towards the end of the Friday, he found him in a bad way. He was worked up and crying in a way Stephen had never seen him cry before and seemed scared to death. He was crying his heart out and saying that he'd done stupid things at night when they were in bed. At the same time swearing that he hadn't done anything and God-knows-what-else and that the police were trying to set him up. And he almost convinced Stephen that that was the case. But Stephen knew it wasn't. He had had a chance to talk to his sister and she had told him what he believed was the truth. Knowing what he did about his father and wishing he didn't, he knew it had to be true.

His father said, 'They've got medical evidence that I

touched [your sister], but I haven't touched her, it was one of her boyfriends.' And Stephen said, 'Well, I doubt it, she's only [a schoolgirl], Dad.' And his dad said, 'No, c'mon, it is one of them. But they're going to have me for it.' He said, 'You got to say *you* done it when you were a kid.' He said, 'I'm telling you. You've got to say it.' Pleading with him. A pathetic plea. Then he got a bit nasty. 'Look, you either do it, or I'll kill you when I get out of here' is basically what he was saying. His hard face now. Under his tears he put his hard face on. And Stephen said, 'Don't be stupid. I'm not sticking my neck out. I'll get put in prison.' But Fred said, 'No, you won't.' He'd worked it all out. If Stephen said he was, like, twelve years old when it happened, they wouldn't be able to touch him. The case would crumble. He had to do it. Stephen stood to leave and his dad cuddled him goodbye, another first. And as he cuddled him he said, 'I mean it, boy. I *mean* it.' And after two days Stephen went back to the police station and sat down and gave a statement saying it was him who did it and they more or less laughed in his face. When they turned the tape off they told him they knew he was making it up. And two weeks later he thought 'What are you doing?' and went back and told them that, yes, they were right, and the charges against his father stood.

Over that first weekend of 8–9 August, Mae and Stephen moved back into Cromwell Street to be with their mother who was now in the house on her own. On the Tuesday she was formally charged with 'causing or encouraging the commission of unlawful sexual intercourse with a girl under the age of sixteen' and with 'cruelty to a child'. She spent the night in the cells and the next morning appeared at Gloucester Magistrates Court where she was granted bail on condition that she did not communicate with her younger children, her stepdaughter, or her husband. She returned to Cromwell Street early on Wednesday afternoon and on Wednesday night washed down forty-eight Anadin tablets with several drinks and had to be rushed to Gloucester Royal Hospital in the early hours of the morning to have her stomach pumped. Mae and Stephen found her slumped on the sofa in the extension living room, and to Mae she looked old and frail and nothing like Mum. It was as if all the energy had drained from her body.

Fred wasn't told what had happened to Rose until some time later. He didn't find out what Rose had tried to do until he was sent to a bail hostel in Birmingham in October where Rose was finally allowed to visit him. By then Mae, thinking she was doing what all the family wanted, had given a statement to the police saying her father was a brilliant father who would never do any of the things he was being accused of doing. She had had a secret meeting with her sister who had been raped and they had agreed that to keep the family together they would both lie to the police. The evidence removed from Cromwell Street had been enough to ensure that the younger children were never going to be allowed to return to live with their parents again. But Mae thought that if the charges were dropped her brother and all her sisters would be able to come back and pick up their lives where they left off. So she said her dad was a brilliant dad and couldn't be persuaded to say any bad thing against him. And also by then Anne Marie had retracted the statement that she had given over so many hours to Hazel Savage and which had cost her so much pain. She was scared. She had got frightened. She knew that neither her father nor Rose could get at her half-brother and her half-sisters who were in the care of the local authority. But what about her own two children? 'I knew who Fred and Rose could get at,' Anne Marie wrote in her book about her life. 'And I knew they wouldn't hesitate to do it . . . So I retracted my statement, saying it was all a figment of my imagination. I claimed I had lied.'

She'd lied. She had dreamed it. Anne Marie and Chris Davis had separated by then. But when he found out about her withdrawing her statement, knowing what he knew, Chris Davis was angry. 'We had one helluva fight in the street about it. One fuckin' helluva row . . . I wouldn't say that she had been threatened by them. What I would say was that she was scared shitless of Fred and Rose. If they got off, she was dead. That's how she put it . . . DC Savage came to see me at my mother's. I told her if she wanted any information about what went on from 1987 onwards she better find Heather. I said Anne and me had tried to track Heather down without any success. I'd made inquiries up and down the fence. She gave me a very knowing look.'

Rose was allowed to visit Fred at Carpenter House, his bail hostel in Birmingham. And she would take the train up to Birmingham and back two or three times a week. Sometimes Mae or Stephen would go with her. But it could be embarrassing if they did. Once they were away from the hostel and somewhere like Edgbaston reservoir, Fred and Rose would fall on the ground and start having sex with each other more or less in full public view. They would jump in a bush and start having sex and Mae and Stephen would be left standing there and half the road could see them. 'We bought them a little tent in the end,' Stephen says, 'a little igloo tent, and said, "Right, fuckin' go in there and stop embarrassing everybody, for Chrissake."' After one visit Rose wrote to Fred, 'To my darling. Well, you really tired me out on Saturday, but it was a wonderful day . . . Remember I will love you always and everything will be alright. Goodnight sweetheart. Lots of love, Rose.' She had drawn a large heart on the letter with an arrow through it and the words 'Fred and Rose'. On the phone at home she started calling him 'darling' and 'sweetheart', words they had never heard her use before.

They were finally committed for trial on the charges

against them on 19 November 1992. Five days later full Care Orders were made at Bristol Crown Court in respect of the five younger children. Rose and Fred were denied access unless the children themselves officially requested it; neither of them was to be allowed to see their children at any time without a social worker being present during a supervised visit, which they weren't prepared to do. If it meant not seeing their children then they would rather not see their children than comply. They wanted to see their children alone and that was all they wanted. They refused to compromise.

Fred was allowed home for Christmas. And then in recognition of his exemplary behaviour he was transferred to an even more self-regulating hostel in another part of Birmingham in March 1993. Rose still went on making trips to see him. But now under the more relaxed regime he started to sneak down to Gloucester by train every few days. He kept coming back to Cromwell Street from Birmingham and then nipping back to be there for the check they made on him every three days. He started meeting up with the younger children in Gloucester Park. He had brought them up to believe that anybody in authority was evil and wrong and would try and take you away from the family who were there to protect you and look after you. And the children started wandering back to Cromwell Street from the foster families they had been placed with in other parts of the city. They would sneak out of care to come home and he'd warn them to keep their mouths shut. He'd tell them to say nothing to nobody about anything that had gone on. If they cared anything about the family. If they loved their mam and dad and wanted to be all living at home with each other together again. They would sneak out of care to come home and he would say to them then, 'Look, keep your mouths shut. If this goes to court, you keep your mouths shut.' Anne Marie had already been kicked out of the family. They put the phone down on her whenever she rang. Then when it came to court they just said nothing. Said nothing happened and all this. But they still had enough evidence to keep them in care.

Fred West was charged with three offences of rape and one of buggery. Rose West was charged with causing or encouraging the commission of unlawful sexual intercourse and cruelty to a child. When the case was heard in Gloucester on 7 June 1993 the witnesses indicated that they were not prepared to give evidence against their parents. The barrister in the case asked the children directly on the day in court if they were prepared to give evidence. They had been prepared for giving evidence by the staff in the residential children's home where by then they were staying. But on the day they declined to go ahead with it. The decision not to proceed was taken by the judge. Not guilty verdicts were recorded. Fred and Rose hugged each other in the dock and walked out of the court and walked hand in hand with each other the short distance home.

He couldn't believe what they had done to his house. What the bastard police had done when they'd come and ripped it apart. They'd been very thorough in their search for the tape of Fred West raping his daughter, which they had never found. Nine months later when he was being questioned on suspicion of murdering his oldest daughter, he would still be complaining how it had cost him three thousand pounds to put the house right. 'The police have ripped my home apart so much over the last eighteen months . . . The people who went there in the big gangs and *tore* my home apart. *Tore* the floorboards up an' just stuck it back down. *Pushed* the units on top of each other – there's one unit upstairs, it's cost us a fortune. There's a massive unit upstairs, we saved up *years* to buy. Broke the top all off it . . . I've had enough.'

He had to borrow off work. He had been working twenty-four hours a day to pay it back. But he had put it right. Put it compulsively back together again. First the house, then the old life of the house. Rose had signed a release allowing the police to destroy all the pornography and sexual paraphernalia that had been taken from the house, which he couldn't believe. Could not believe. She had taken the video camera back to the Midlands Electricity Board where it had come from, saying it had cost her her children. But he soon started to make noises about wanting to start their collection up again. He started to go on again about Rose going with other men. On and on. Using emotional blackmail. He could be very, very persuasive. Pushy. He couldn't leave it alone.

He had gone back to working for Carsons Contractors. He was an excellent electrician. A very good decorator. The old people loved him. Carsons had taken him back on. He couldn't get enough work.

The extension living room was like a den or a bunker. An overground cellar. Apart from a narrow skylight at the end of the kitchen area there was no access for natural light. A window had been cut into the tongue-and-groove teak-look panelling running down the church side of the room, but it was a false window with a view only six inches away of the bricks of the church wall. The overhead lights were always burning in the family room and he went back to his old habit of pacing backwards and forwards in front of the small shelf with the telephone on it waiting for the phone to ring. By 1993 Carsons was affiliated to UK Maintenance, which meant he could be sent to any part of the country where there was a job to do. The phone would ring and he'd run for it and he'd be out the door. It was work that involved the possibility of call-outs at any time. Ideal work for Fred. Through the tool room into the van and away.

Chapter Fifteen

Hazel Savage had been around long enough to remember Rose when she had been young and thin and not wearing glasses yet and not yet a lump. Not the brass-mouthed mother of eight that she had in the cells at Gloucester police station on a humid warm night in August 1992. DC Savage had been part of the team who had arrested Rose at home that morning, and Rose was wearing what she had been able to grab before she left the house – a baggy T-shirt of grey or white or anyway a seedy, used-up colour, and leggings and sneakers. She also had a tracksuit-type top with her. The leggings had cotton knots clinging in various places as a result of indoor rummaging and domestic chores. These were the observations of Leo Goatley who hadn't known Rose when she was slim and attractive and was meeting her that night – the night of 6 August – for the first time. Leo Goatley himself would usually have been wearing shorts and painter's sandals on a night like that at that time of year. He did paint, and was tall and burly, occasionally bearded, rumpled and vaguely bohemian in appearance; he was an accomplished painter. But his full-time job was being a local solicitor. He was part of the duty-solicitor scheme that operated in Cheltenham and Gloucester and when he had received the call at home at half past seven he had changed into something more appropriate for a visit to the police station. The woman who was going to turn out to be more infamous than any client he could ever have expected to represent struck him on their first encounter as pleasant and housewifely if a bit sad-eyed and sallow. He would find out as time went on that

435

she had a comical and engaging laugh and reminded him at those moments in her big glasses of the comedian Roy Hudd. Rose had eight children; Leo had nine young children and one or two of their children even had names in common. She made it absolutely clear to him that at no time had she ever sexually abused any of her children, and he wrote this down.

DC Savage had taken an interest in the Wests at the time of the Caroline Raine case in 1972 and she had been in and out of the house over the years investigating drugs-related offences and offences involving the lodgers such as Frankie Stephens who used the cellar as a place for storing stolen goods. In Rose's opinion, DC Savage was a vindictive, interfering cow. On one occasion in 1977 she had physically wrestled her out of the house. Whatever opinion Hazel Savage held of Rose would undoubtedly have been coloured by the materials that had been removed from Cromwell Street in the course of the day. In addition to the obscene video-tapes of Rose, which she wouldn't have had a chance to see, they included the photographs of erect penises and an album containing Polaroid pictures of anonymous vaginas.

One of the main lines of questioning that Hazel Savage pursued in August 1992 was the whereabouts of Rose West's oldest daughter – the oldest of all her children – Heather. There was no suspicion at this stage that Heather had been murdered. Heather's whereabouts were of interest only because she might be able to provide additional information regarding the child-abuse investigation. It was important to know, for example, whether Heather had been sexually abused by her parents in the same way that her sister was alleging they had abused her. There was no concern as to her current safety. But from the outset DC Savage found it difficult to get any satisfactory answers from Rose. Even on basic questions such as Heather's age and whether she had ever been reported missing, Rose seemed evasive. She had come home from doing her shopping one Friday about five years earlier 'as per usual' and Heather had simply gone. 'She took whatever she had in her room,' she said. 'Her personal things. Clothing . . . She refused to know about all the normal things of living . . . She went off to Devon with a lady . . . I didn't want her to stay here, not in those circumstances, not if she was going to practise what she was doing. She was a lesbian . . . And that was why she wanted to leave. She said it wasn't good for the rest of the children.'

DC SAVAGE   'Are you a lesbian?'

ROSE WEST   No.

DC SAVAGE   Have you ever been a lesbian?

ROSE WEST   No.

In another interview a few days later, Rose West told Hazel Savage that one of Heather's friends had told her that Heather was 'getting on with her life'. Rose went on to explain how she had spoken to Heather on the telephone and she had said she was all right. Sometimes, she said, Heather would be drunk or something. She was the only one who spoke to Heather. She refused to talk to her father.

On the day that Anne Marie had given her statement to DC Savage at Tuffley police station, she had told her about her missing sister Heather and how some time after she disappeared she had taken the train down to Torquay to the holiday camp where she was supposed to have gone to work, looking for Heather. She had travelled the West Country looking for her, and she had even contacted the Salvation Army. When she interviewed Mae and Stephen about their father's alleged rape of their younger sister, DC Savage told them that the one good thing that was going to come out of the investigation was that she was going to find Heather.

But she hadn't found Heather by the time the rape case came to trial in June 1993. She hadn't found even a trace of Heather. No use of her National Insurance number to claim benefits in the past five years, no reported contacts with the DSS or the Inland Revenue, no visits to a hospital or a doctor or a dentist, no sightings, nothing. The only logical explanation was that Heather had changed her identity, left the country, or was dead.

From about March 1993, when Fred West started slipping away from the bail hostel in Birmingham to spend days at home, the residential social workers looking after the West children started to pick up brief comments from them about the patio being laid at the same time Heather left home. Also about the family 'joke' of Heather being under the patio. If they were open with their mouths about what went on in the house, their father told them they would end up being buried under the patio like Heather. Or when the kids were going on about Heather he'd say, 'Anybody would think I'd buried her under the patio', and laugh. It was like a family saying. Anne Marie had mentioned this to Hazel Savage in the statement that she had subsequently withdrawn. Mae's boyfriend, Rob Williams, taking his cue from Fred, used to say he knew which slab Heather was buried under. 'It's three up and nine across.'

After the rape charges against him were dropped and he came back to Cromwell Street to live, Fred West would sometimes tell Mae and Stephen that he had had visits from Heather while he was in Birmingham or that he had seen her at a community centre in Gloucester. But Rose would just tell him to shut up. Mae and Stephen were continuing to have unofficial contact with their younger brothers and sisters without Fred and Rose knowing. And on a night when *Prime Suspect* 2 was being repeated on television, which Mae and Stephen knew was all about a girl that's found under a patio and the trade in pornography, because they had seen it, they decided to test Fred and Rose by getting them to sit down and watch it with them. It was in two parts, with the news in between, and they knew he would be waiting for the news. And they sat in armchairs on either side of the sofa with Fred and Rose in the middle, but neither of them could detect any obvious reaction. The same happened when they got them to watch an episode of *Brookside* which was about a family murdering an abusive father and burying him under the patioed back garden. Not a flicker. Nothing. That seemed to prove to them that that's all the rumours were: just rumours. The younger lot letting their imaginations run away with them.

In those months Mae and Stephen did notice an uncharacteristic side to their mother. They had never known her be shy or bashful before. But one day they were up in the bar room on the first floor messing about with the pots with their lids super-glued shut which stood on the mantelpiece, when she came in and caught them. Normally this would have triggered one of her eruptions. Instead she seemed embarrassed. 'What is it?' 'Put it back.' 'Go on, tell us.' 'Just put it back.' 'Oh, come on.' 'No, I can't tell you.' 'Oh, go on.' Finally she says, 'All right, I'll tell you. I burn my knickers, right?' 'Oh, right. Is there any reason you do this?' She almost blushed. 'Shut up. I can't tell you why.' It had been on the fireplace like an ornament for ages.

It was a side of Rose that her solicitor Leo Goatley would see on a number of occasions. The first time had been during one of the interviews between Rose and Hazel Savage in August 1992. The album containing small Polaroid close-up shots of female genitals had been produced and Rose's reaction had been what it always was when she was invited to respond to any of the pornographic material: 'What's all this then – these are flippin' private pictures. All of these items were kept in our private accommodation upstairs and away from the children.' But Leo Goatley noticed that Rose gave him a curious look and was reluctant to look at the photographs. (Unlike the pornographic videos removed from Cromwell Street which were preserved, the obscene photographs in the possession of the police were destroyed between 1992 and the Wests being arrested for murder in 1994.)

The care workers kept overhearing the same stories about Heather and the patio from the younger West children through all the summer and autumn of 1993 after the rape and cruelty charges against their father and mother had been dropped. Eventually they became sufficiently concerned to feel they should inform the police. As a result, Detective Constable Savage was appointed to investigate Heather's disappearance in a more systematic way. She revisited all the sources she had originally visited the previous year, and with the same result. Heather West didn't exist in any official record. She seemed to have ceased existing.

Before the end of 1993 DCI Terry Moore, the head of CID in Gloucester, was appointed to co-ordinate the inquiry into Heather West's disappearance. Early in 1994, formal witness statements were taken from social workers closely connected with the West children relating to the 'family joke'. On 23 February 1994 successful application was made to Gloucester Magistrates for a warrant giving the police permission to search 25 Cromwell Street. And at lunchtime on Thursday, 24 February, the doorbell went while Rose and Mae were in the living room watching *Neighbours* on television. It was what the police would log as Day 1 of the Cromwell Street inquiry. They went in expecting to find one body. Privately, some of those involved expected to find no body. The search for bodies would continue until Day 104, three and a half months later, when Ann McFall's remains and the remains of an eight-month-old foetus were recovered from a valleyed field, Fingerpost Field, in Much Marcle. On Day 155, a Thursday at the end of July when Rose and Fred West made one of their by then routine appearances in court together to be remanded in custody, they would stop counting.

Mae had come home to Cromwell Street for lunch, which she had started to do since the removal of the children. She was watching *Neighbours* with her mother when the doorbell went and the dogs started barking. Rose had got two mongrels, Oscar and Benji, from an animal-rescue place while Fred was being kept away from the family in Birmingham, and they were yappers. Oscar was wiry and white; Benji was a small wire-haired terrier type and they were yappy bastards. Mae answered the door with the dogs still barking and found DCI Moore, DC Savage and three male police officers who said they had a warrant to search the premises for the body of Heather West. They passed through to the living room and served the warrant on Rose who read it and instantly went berserk. Screaming and shouting. Calling them bastards. Cunts. The dogs were barking. The television was on. It was quarter to two, five minutes into *Neighbours*. And then Stephen walked in. He had a day off work and had just been taking it easy, wandering around town, looking in the shops. He asked one of the officers what was going on and he told him they were looking for Heather and thrust the search warrant into his hand. Stephen read it and told them to wait until his dad came home. They were to do nothing until his dad got back. The writing on the blue form was a blur to Stephen apart from the words 'search for the body of Heather West'. But the officer told him they didn't have time for that. They were digging up the garden whether his dad was there or not. Stephen tried to get his father on his mobile phone. It was ringing but there was no reply. He tried again and it just rang and rang.

They were all coming in with their tools and spades.

The job Fred was working on was out of range. He was working at an address called Hatton House, in Frampton Mansell, which was in a 'black spot' for cellular phones. He had arrived in the morning in the long-wheel-base white Midi with 'Carsons Contractors' and the telephone number along the side and gone straight upstairs to start work. The roof cavities needed spraying against woodworm. And that is what he was up in the loft wearing a facemask doing when Mr Gerrard whose house it was called up to him shortly before two that he was wanted on the phone.

When he couldn't get his father to answer, Stephen had called Derek Thomson in his office at home. As soon as he got through Rose had come on in an excitable state saying that the police were at her house and she wanted Fred home now. She was quite excitable and was shouting and she told Derek to contact Fred and get him home straightaway. She wanted him *now*. Derek Thomson rang the customer and asked for Mr West who was doing work on his house. After a few minutes Fred came to the phone and Derek told him that he had better ring home because his wife was after him. He couldn't call out direct. Apart from being in a black spot for the signal, the phone was on lock-out as far as outgoing calls were concerned. Derek Thomson's home number, mobile number, and a couple of others were programmed in; the rest of it was locked out. Only two or three numbers were programmed into the memory, and his home number wasn't one of them. Mr Gerrard allowed him to use the house telephone. He rang and spoke briefly to somebody at the other end. But he managed to cut himself off and couldn't work the redial. So Mr Gerrard told him to ring again. But for a moment he couldn't seem to remember what his home number was. It was obvious that there was a big problem at home because he appeared quite shocked. Mr Gerrard told him to sit down for a moment, then try again. He rang again. 525995. Again spoke to somebody briefly, then went to gather his things. Within quarter of an hour he was gone. It was wet. It had been raining all day. And he drove off into the rain.

As soon as he was within range Stephen got through to him in the van. Said the police were there and they were going to start digging the garden up looking for Heather. That was just after two. He was about twelve miles from Gloucester. He should have been home by half past two but he didn't get there until more than three hours later. Nobody has been able to discover what he did in those missing three and a half hours. Nobody was able to contact him. Nobody knows where he went. He had been in a black spot. It was as if he temporarily disappeared off the face of the earth.

The police left Cromwell Street at five thirty. They had lifted many of the slabs off the garden in preparation for the digging to start the following day. A mini-digger had been brought in to plough up the garden. It was raining heavily and the exposed surface soil was quickly turning to mud. When Fred walked in there was only Rose and Mae and Stephen, and the yapping mongrels, Oscar and Benji. The dogs were barking and frantic. There had been constant comings and goings through the house. A lot of strange people. They weren't used to people. Rose had been crying. Fred seemed very calm. Transcendentally calm. Rose and Fred talked quietly to each other over by the sink in the kitchen and after a while went upstairs for a bit so that they could talk on their own. Then, at about quarter to eight, Fred left the house to go to Gloucester Central police station not very far away in Longsmith Street. A few minutes later DS Terry Onions and WPC Debbie Willats arrived at Cromwell Street and tape-recorded an interview with Rose in the first-floor Black Magic bar. She was belligerent and aggressive and made out she couldn't remember much about the circumstances surrounding Heather's disappearance: 'What do you think I am, a bloody computer . . . I was upset at the time. I cannot fucking remember . . . If you had any brains at all you could find her. It can't be that bloody difficult.' She repeated almost all the things she had said in 1992. Except that, whereas then she had said that Heather refused to speak to Fred, now she was saying the opposite: 'I know he had several phone calls off her but she didn't want to speak to me . . . She was all her father, not me.' Now she said that she had neither seen Heather, nor heard from her, nor made any efforts to find her. Reporting Heather as missing to the police would have been 'snitching' on her daughter, she said.

At Gloucester police station Fred announced himself at the counter and was taken for interview by DC Hazel Savage and DC Robert Vestey. He seemed very calm. Almost affable for somebody at the centre of a murder investigation. Almost breezy. He knew Hazel. It wasn't as if Gloucester police station was new to him. He'd been there before. So why all the fuss? Heather was alive as far as he was concerned, he said almost as soon as he'd sat down. He'd seen her recently in Birmingham. 'She was more of a lady . . . Her hair was expensively done.' Like Rose, who was busy telling the interviewing officers that Heather had always been all her father, he confirmed that Heather was all him. 'Heather had summat against Rose, for some unknown reason . . . Every time Rose spoke to 'er, she bloody insulted her, and walked away. But me and Heather was *very* close, which all of them will tell you. I mean, me an' Heather built half our home together.' Also like Rose, he said they had never reported Heather missing because they didn't want to snitch on her to the police. 'You don't go inside just because you're a missing person,' Hazel Savage told him. 'Ah!' he said with a throaty chuckle. 'What Heather's up to is a different story . . . You name it,

444

Heather's up to it . . . *I* think Heather was supplying Cromwell Street, somehow . . . Lots of girls who disappear', he added, 'take different names and go into prostitution.' From speaking to her on the phone he knew that Heather had 'umpteen names'.

He was quite happy to reminisce with Hazel about Frankie Stephens and the druggy lodgers and the life at Cromwell Street that Hazel had known. She wanted to know about Heather. 'Where is Heather, Fred?' 'You find her,' he said. 'An' I'll be happy. That's all I can say.' And then he was off on another anecdotal ramble. 'What can we do to find Heather and find Heather quickly?' Hazel Savage asked him some time after nine o'clock. 'I'm going out from here in a few minutes,' he told her, 'an' see what I can do.'

'If you want me I'll be at home all day tomorrow. I ain't goin' to work tomorrow,' he said before walking out of the police station at nine thirty to begin what he must have known was going to be his last night in the house with Rose. Back at the house he asked Mae to make him a cup of tea and then set about undoing the fiddle with the electric meter that he had been running for years. One policeman had been left behind reading a book under a plastic shelter at the bottom of the garden. And he wanted to change the cable over on the meter without the policeman noticing that the house had suddenly gone dark. A team of fifteen men was due to start digging in his garden in the morning, searching for the body of his daughter. But rerouteing the electricity supply back to the legitimate meter was the thing that seemed to possess him. He became calm again once he had done it and took the dogs for a walk in the park with Rose, something neither Stephen nor Mae had ever known him do before. When he came in he had a shower and sat on the sofa in his underpants watching the news. They were already getting some idea that there was going to be some publicity of what was happening in their back garden and that it was going to come out on the news. When it was over he went upstairs to sleep with Rose in the bed made out of dark Dean oak timber that he had cut and put together with his own hands.

The next morning he asked Stephen to clear all the tools out of his van which was parked outside. As the day progressed Derek Thomson would ring and ask Stephen to move the van because the press who were starting to gather in Cromwell Street had seen the number on the side and had started calling him at home.

There was no press when Hazel Savage accompanied by a young detective constable, Darren Law, returned to the house at eleven fifteen. Rose was watching the television in the living room when they went to her and asked her to tell them where her mother lived. They wanted an address for her mother. Which really upset her. She didn't want them to speak to her mother. Her mother was ill and she didn't want her involved. To quiet her, Fred took Rose into the tool-room passage off the living room and closed the door. Hustled her in there and told her he'd go and persuade Hazel not to go up and see her mam. 'I'll kill that bitch if she ever speaks to my mum!' He was well worried what was going on. But once he'd got Rose settled and upstairs out of the way, he said to Hazel Savage, 'Can we go to the police station?' He collected what he always referred to as his 'prison lighter' and his cigarette papers and tobacco. And as soon as he was in the car with Hazel he said to her, 'I killed her.' The ignition hadn't been turned on. They were sitting in the car in front of the Sabbath Church in Cromwell Street. He admitted that Heather was in the garden but said they were looking in the wrong place. It was twenty past eleven. Detective Constable Savage arrested Fred West for the murder of his daughter. He was then taken to Gloucester police station and detained. An hour later Rose West was arrested on suspicion of the murder of Heather West by Detective Sergeant Onions and taken to Cheltenham police station. She arrived at quarter to one.

Mae and Stephen couldn't take seriously what was going on. They weren't allowed in the garden but they watched from the windows, sitting on stools eating crisps and drinking cups of tea and taking the rip out of the police. They found a chicken bone that Stephen could see was obviously a chicken bone and he started making loud chicken noises and jumping about and fooling around, taking care that he was seen by the searchers in the rain and the mud. It was only around tea-time that they got a call asking them to come to Gloucester police station. And when they arrived their father's solicitor, Howard Ogden, told them that Fred had confessed to killing Heather. In fact he was back at Cromwell Street as they spoke, pointing out where Heather was buried in the ground. He was handcuffed to DC Law and sliding around under the tarpaulin roof that had been erected. He seemed dazed and unsteady and kept falling off the duckboards that had been laid across the garden like somebody disoriented by drugs or drink or by the familiar suddenly turned strange. His legs had already given way under him at the police station earlier in the day. He had had to be helped on to a seat soon after he arrived and brought a glass of water. He had walked around the station's exercise yard for more than an hour holding his head and looking blank. 'My head hurts,' he had said when he was asked if he was all right, 'and I keep seeing stars.' He kept falling off the duckboards that had been laid across the garden. Sliding in the mud. It didn't look like his house.

Mae and Stephen had reacted to the news that Heather had been murdered by their father in different ways. Stephen had slipped down the wall in the police station on to the floor and started crying. Mae didn't cry. She didn't believe it. She was sure her father had cracked under the pressure and was making it up. Although they didn't know it, their mother as well as their father was present in Gloucester police station at that point. It was around six. She had also had the news broken to her that Fred had confessed to killing Heather. She had been told by DC Onions in an interview room in Cheltenham just before five o'clock. 'So she's dead? Is that right?' 'I'm telling you,' DC Onions repeated. 'Fred has confessed to murdering Heather.' '*What!*' 'He's told us where she is. Where do you think she is?' 'She's *dead?*' She was crying. 'That automatically implicates you.' She stopped crying. 'Why does it implicate me? . . . It's a lie.'

If Rose had been genuinely upset by the news that her daughter, who had been missing for seven years, had been murdered by her husband and had been lying buried in their garden all that time – 'You are the wife of the person who's confessed to killing her. You live in the house on whose land the body is allegedly lying at this very moment,' as DC Onions reminded her – she had rallied by the time she was interviewed for a second time at Gloucester police station a couple of hours later. 'Do you feel that perhaps you've been a bit naïve over this [seven-year] period?' she was asked. 'Looks like it,' she said, 'don't it?' Adding a few minutes later, 'I feel a bit of a cunt, to be blunt with it.' 'What's your feelings towards Fred now,' Onions asked, 'now that you know he's slain your eldest daughter?' 'Put it this way,' she said. 'He's a dead man if I ever get my hands on him.'

The next day, Saturday, 26 February, he took it all back. In an interview that started just after two in the afternoon he said that everything he had told them the day before about how he had killed Heather – strangled her while she was lounging against the washing machine 'coming the big lady', and dismembered her and hid her remains pushed into a dustbin behind the Wendy house; his soliloquy on the ice knife – that had all been a lie. 'Heather is not in the garden.

Heather's alive and well. She's possibly at this moment in Bahrain. She works for a drugs cartel. She's got no identification – that's why you can't find 'er . . . They're looked after like queens. I have *no* idea what her name is, because I will not let her tell me. She contacts me whenever she's in this country. Now whether you believe it or not is entirely up to you. As far as I'm concerned I'd like to see them all still over there digging in my garden . . . They can dig there for evermore. Nobody or nothing's under my patio.'

Asked why he had confessed the day before, he said he was getting back at the police for what they had done to his house between 1992 and then. He also said he was taking his revenge for the way they had upset Rose by saying they were going to see her mother. 'When you come in yesterday and upset Rosie, when she *begged* you not to have nothin' to do with her mother 'cause her mother was an old lady . . . Rose was so upset over her mother, an' mind I love Rose, an' no messin'. We're devoted. An' when I see anybody hurt that woman then I want to get them back an' make sure they pay 'ard for touching her. She's an angel . . . If Rose was all right, then I was quite prepared to go on with it. Let 'em go on digging out there . . . I feel a lot better for it.'

A few minutes after four o'clock one of the search team digging in the garden at Cromwell Street found a human bone. He had been digging in a different part of the garden from where Fred West had indicated they would find Heather. The bone was taken to Gloucester police station where it was examined by the Home Office pathologist, Professor Bernard Knight. Professor Knight confirmed that the bone was a human thigh bone. He then went to Cromwell Street and excavated the remains which would eventually be shown to be those of Heather West, which had been discovered simultaneously in roughly the place where Fred West had told them they should be digging. When the remains were excavated both thigh bones were found to be present. They had three thigh bones. It became obvious that there might be a second set of remains buried in the garden. It was a possibility that nobody had considered until that moment.

Fred West was brought back into the first-floor interview room at Gloucester police station just after half past four. Hazel Savage told him the police were experiencing difficulties digging. The hole kept filling up with water. And he told her about the water table and the moat around Gloucester. About the moat being filled in and the very high water table. 'I understand that you have been told by your solicitor that we have found something,' DC Savage said to him when he was finished.

FRED WEST   Yeah. Bones.

DC SAVAGE   Would there be anybody else's bones there? Would there be anybody else's bones in any other part of the garden?

FRED WEST   [after a long silence] That's a peculiar question to ask, isn't it? . . . Heather is in there. An' there ain't no more . . . There's *nothing* else.

In another interview at quarter past seven, two hours later, he was told about the third human thigh bone found in his garden. It would eventually be matched with the skeletal remains of Alison Chambers. It had been found buried under the filled-in paddling pool, immediately under the extension bathroom window.

DC SAVAGE   Fred, the question is, is there anybody else buried in your garden?

FRED WEST   Only Heather.

DC SAVAGE   You've never said to us that you scattered

Heather all over the garden. And Heather didn't have three legs.

SOLICITOR'S CLERK   [breaking a long silence] Have you any knowledge of where this other bone might have come from at all?

FRED WEST   [almost inaudibly] Yes. Shirley.

DC SAVAGE   Shirley who?

FRED WEST   Robinson. The girl who caused the problem.

That Saturday Anne Marie was having a birthday party for her younger daughter Carol, who was seven. She had fifteen children in the house plus Carol's teacher when she took a call from a policewoman at Gloucester police station who told her that Heather's body had been dug up in the garden at Cromwell Street that afternoon; her father had been arrested for Heather's murder. 'I was shaking. I wanted to cry,' Anne Marie wrote later. 'Instead I . . . found a bottle of sherry . . . and poured some into a tumbler . . . I made one phone call to my boyfriend, the father of my youngest child, and asked him to leave work as soon as possible and come to my house. Then I pinned a smile on my face, took a gulp of sherry and organized another party game.'

In 1994 Andrew Letts and his wife Jacquie were living in a tiny flat on a council estate outside Cheltenham. It had been built as accommodation for the carers at the home for the physically handicapped opposite. They had known better times. Andrew was always on a catch-up, as he put it. Always broke. He liked the horses. He liked gambling. He was always trying to get on his feet. 'I thought we'd come as low as we could get,' he said when he heard about Rose, 'then this happens.' That weekend they drove over to see Graham and Barbara at their house in Nelson Street in Gloucester. Graham had come out of prison on Christmas Eve. Seven weeks. He looked very pale. That prison pallor. He was smoking heavily and drinking. To Andrew and Jacquie that day Graham looked terrified. He was physically shaking. Rose's mother was living in Reading. After Rose's father died she had moved in as a companion/housekeeper to a widower in his house near Henley. He suffered from Alzheimer's in his final years and she had looked after him until he died. 'Glenys had bought a paper,' Mrs Letts says. 'I see "digging up the garden". And then I see "25 Cromwell Street". Glen looked across at me and said, "Mum, what's wrong? Mum, *what's wrong?*" I run down the telephone to phone Andrew. Andrew came over. I'd worked for all nice people and I couldn't face anyone. I did work for some really nice families. I had really nice people around me. Don't put where it was. The name of the village. I wouldn't like them to know.'

Rose was released on bail on the Sunday night. At twenty past nine on Sunday, 27 February, she was let go from the police station and taken to Cromwell Street and Stephen and Mae. They had been living with the curtains drawn since late on Friday. There were cameramen and reporters camped in the street. TV crews. Transporter vans with cranes and satellite dishes parked around the corner. The police had taped black bags over the windows at the back of the house. It was blacked out. Mae and Stephen were under siege. When their mum came in she was very quiet and she just sat down. Superintendent Bennett had already told them that they were going to have to take over the whole of the house. They were going to have to be moved out of the house. The police needed to search all of it. A safe house was being set up. 'I'm spending one night here and then we're off,' Rose told them, 'and we're never coming back to Cromwell Street again.' That night all of them – Mae and her mum and Stephen and his girlfriend

Andrea and the cat and the two dogs, Oscar and Benji – all slept in the same room together. It was still wet outside. It had never stopped raining. Water was being pumped out of the pits and trenches where in the morning they would resume looking. Oscar and Benji would have to be taken to the RSPCA.

'The thing I'd like to stress, I mean, Rose knew nothing at all . . . She hasn't done anything,' Fred West had said in one of his first interviews with the police, and it was a position from which he would never waver. At one point Hazel Savage asked him, 'Who else is aware of Heather being under the patio, Fred?' His answer was instant: 'Nobody. That's a secret I've kept myself for eight years. And never told *anybody* . . . Anybody can say what they like about Rose, but she is a perfect mother . . . I mean, we both loved Heather. I love my wife as well. I don't want to destroy the love that I had there, when I've destroyed one love already . . . I mean, Rose is not going to let me say to her, "I've strangled Heather", without coming straight to the police. Don't get Rose wrong. Rose lived by the law. Properly. I mean, I know she doesn't like the law, but she will not have it broken.' All the time he was disposing of Heather, he said, 'All the time I'm thinking, "If Rose walks in, that's it. I'm 'ad . . ."'

In an effort to find out how much Rose did know about what had been going on and to establish the depth of her involvement, she was installed with Mae and Stephen in a series of police safe houses that had been fitted with surveillance equipment in and around Gloucester. Microphones had been hidden in the sofas and the ceilings. And although most of what was said was drowned out by music from the radio and soaps on the television, in two months she said nothing that was self-incriminating.

The police continued digging. And over the days that followed, the skeletal remains of eight other young women were found under the ground at 25 Cromwell Street. Each one had been dismembered, decapitated, and in every set of remains bones were missing. The bones were embedded in black glutinous material quite different from the redder, undisturbed soil outside the obvious shaft which had been prepared.

At twenty past five on the evening of Monday, 28 February, Day 5 of the inquiry, the remains of a person who was subsequently identified as Alison Chambers were found in the back garden at 25 Cromwell Street.

At 9.00 p.m., also on Day 5 of the inquiry, the remains of a person who was subsequently identified as Shirley Robinson were found in the back garden at 25 Cromwell Street.

At 11.47 a.m. on Day 10, Thérèse Siegenthaler's remains were found in the cellar. It was a Saturday. The second Saturday of the inquiry. A service was in progress at the church next door.

Three hours later Shirley Hubbard's remains were unearthed close to what would come to be known as the Marilyn Monroe wall.

The following day, Sunday, Day 11, Lucy Partington's remains were found in the cellar in the morning at nine o'clock. Just under two hours later Juanita Mott's remains were found under the stairs going into the cellar.

The remains subsequently identified as Lynda Gough's were found under the ground-floor bathroom area at Cromwell Street at 2.25 p.m. on Day 12.

Carol Cooper's remains were found in the back part of the cellar at ten past seven in the evening on Tuesday, 8 March, Day 13.

On Friday, 18 March, Rose West was moved to new accommodation behind the country court room and police station at Dursley. She had to be moved at short notice to other police accommodation in Cheltenham when she was photographed coming out of the KwikSave supermarket in Dursley a week later. She used to read nearly every newspaper every day and point out to Mae the bits that were wrong in the stories.

At twenty to four on the afternoon of Saturday, 23 April, she was arrested at the safe house in Hales Close in Cheltenham for the murder of Lynda Gough. She was interviewed by Detective Constable Stephen Harris and Detective Constable Barbara Harrison in the cells complex at Cheltenham police station the following evening. 'Would you accept that the remains of Lynda Gough were found in your former home at 25 Cromwell Street, Gloucester, Mrs West?' DC Harris asked her. 'Would you accept that Lynda Gough lived in your house at 25 Cromwell Street, Gloucester, Mrs West? . . . Would you accept that, following the disappearance of Lynda Gough, you were seen wearing her slippers? . . . Would you accept that you seemingly told lies to Lynda Gough's mother when she called to speak to you at 25 Cromwell Street, Gloucester, following the disappearance of her daughter? . . . Do you accept that you told Mrs Gough that her daughter had gone to Weston? . . . Were you told by your husband, Frederick West, to tell Mrs Gough that Lynda Gough had gone to Weston? . . . Were you threatened or pressurized in any way by your husband, Frederick West, to tell Mrs Gough that her daughter, Lynda Gough, had gone to Weston? . . . Was it your idea to tell Mrs Gough that her daughter, Lynda, had gone to Weston? . . . Would you accept that Mrs Gough pointed out to you that her daughter's clothing was on your washing-line?'

To all these questions her answer was the same: 'No comment.' She was charged with the murder of Lynda Gough and replied, 'I'm innocent.'

The next day, Monday, 25 April, Day 61, she was interviewed about a second murder. 'Mrs West, would you accept that you have an unnatural interest in sex?' DC Barbara Harrison asked her. 'Do you accept that you have featured in sex sessions recorded on video tape? . . . Were you forced into making these sex videos, Mrs West? . . . Did your husband force you to make these sex videos, Mrs West? . . . The police are in possession of a copy of a videotape seized from your home at 25 Cromwell Street in 1992. This videotape depicts a female being tied to the ceiling area of a room and then abused by two men. Do you know the film I am talking about? . . . In the cellar area of your home at 25 Cromwell Street, Gloucester, there are two holes in the rafters. These seemingly are similar to the scene depicted in the film. Is that what those holes were used for, Mrs West? . . . Were any of the holes used to facilitate the torture of [victim's name]? . . . Were any of those holes used to facilitate sex with [victim's name]? . . . When you picked up Caroline Raine in the car with Fred, was that a practice session? Was that a practice session with her before you started killing people? . . . Had you done acts of lesbianism before Carol Raine? . . . Fred has told me that the incident with Caroline was a practice session. Is that right?'

To all these questions she replied, 'No comment.' DC Harrison continued. 'We also have some other videos seized from your house in 1992 and they could be described as porn videos. Did you get your ideas for sex from these porn videos? . . . Did you practise anything that you saw in the porn videos? . . . There are some unusual acts shown on the films, such as someone being tied up. Is that an idea that you got from a video? . . . One of the videos shows a woman seemingly in a cellar and she's having sex with a black man and a white man and she doesn't appear to be enjoying the experience at all times. Do you remember that video? . . . She is then whipped with I think you'd describe it as a cat-o'-nine-tails whip and whipped with a cloth. Do you remember that on the video? . . . Did you take ideas from that video and put them into practice in your own basement at 25 Cromwell Street? . . . Did you kill [victim's name]? . . . Were you present when [victim's name] was killed? . . . Was [victim's name] tied up in your house in Cromwell Street? . . . Was she taken down to the basement and held there as a prisoner? . . . Did you tie her up? . . . Did you tie her hands with rope? . . . Did you tie her feet with rope? . . . Did Fred tie her up with rope? . . . Were you present when she was being tied up? . . . Did you gag her? . . . Did you put cloth round her face or over her eyes? . . . Did Fred put any cloth round her face or eyes? . . . Was she tortured while she was still alive? . . . Was she cut at all while she was still alive? . . . Did you take part in cutting her head off? . . . Did you take part in cutting her head off after she was dead? . . . Did you cut her legs? . . . Did you cut off her legs? . . . Did you cut off her arms? . . . Did Fred cut off her legs? . . . Were you forced to do any of these things to [victim's name]? . . . Did you bury [victim's name]? . . . Did you assist at the burial of [victim's name]? . . . Did you dig the hole in your basement where [victim's name] was buried? . . . Were you present when that hole was being dug? . . . Did Fred dig the hole? . . . Was the hole prepared already? . . . While [victim's name] was still alive, did you cut her hands? . . . Did you cut her fingers? . . . Did you cut any part of her hand off? . . . Did you cut off her feet? . . . Did you cut off any part of her feet? . . . Did you cut off her toes? . . . Were you present while any of [victim's name]'s fingers or toes were cut off by another person? . . . Were you forced to cut off [victim's name]'s fingers or toes? . . . Some of [victim's name]'s bones are missing. Can you explain what happened to them? . . . Did you assist in the disposal of any parts of her body? . . . Did you assist in the disposal of them in a place other than in your basement? . . . Fred has told us that he had control over you. I think the time is now if you could perhaps confirm that to us, if that is the case . . . We've spoken about some horrific things and we've heard some horrific things in these interviews and if there's anything you can tell us which might help us understand what happened there, then we'd be grateful to you for an explanation. Is there anything you would like to tell us about your relationship with Fred and any force that may or may not have been used on you to perform any of these awful things?'

She said nothing. She never said anything. If anybody grumbled at her, she'd hold herself tight. She wouldn't make a conversation. She never had a lot to say, actually. She'd always hold herself. And to all these questions she replied, 'No comment.' A second charge of murder was added to the first charge of murdering Lynda Gough and she replied, 'I'm innocent.'

Apart from with her solicitor Leo Goatley and counsel preparing her defence, she refused to discuss any aspect of her past or her children or her relationship with her husband or their life together in the house or the women they were jointly accused of killing. Between 20 April 1994 and her trial in October 1995 she refused to say anything to anybody about anything. In fifty-nine interviews totalling almost fifty hours up to 2 June 1994, she said nothing but 'No comment'. 'I'm innocent' when the charges were put to her – a total of ten charges of murder. Otherwise: 'No comment.'

She said nothing to anybody until the day came for her to give evidence in her own defence in number 3 court at the Crown Court in Winchester. She wore the black jacket and white shirt and long dark skirt that Mae had picked out for her and that she had worn every day of the trial. Clothes that made her indistinguishable from the female prison officers who sat either side of her in the dock. Women of a similar age and background who probably also brought knitting patterns and pictures of their grandchildren to court in their bags with them. She outdid them in the deference of her bows to the judge at the beginning and end of every session and by wearing a poppy in the week before Armistice Day. When the day came for her to cross the well of the court to the witness box she could be seen to be wearing tiny black-leather pixie boots with gold zips up the side and gold metal fasteners that moved with her body and clicked in the silence. She wept when she talked about being abandoned by her mother when she was fifteen and a half and she cried reflexively whenever Heather's name was mentioned, poking a finger up behind her enormous glasses. Asked for her reaction to various atrocities, her answer more than once was: 'Shock-horror.' She had put on a considerable amount of weight in twenty months.

Fred was dead by then. Fred had hanged himself. She had had no contact with Fred since the morning when he had told her that he would persuade Hazel Savage not to contact her mother and had picked up his prison lighter and gone out and sat in the car and turned to Hazel Savage and said, 'I killed her.' She had made no attempt to get in touch with him. He had written to her but she hadn't acknowledged his letters. He had sent her messages through Stephen but she hadn't responded to them.

After his first admission that he had murdered Heather they didn't see each other for four months. Then on 30 June 1994 they appeared together at Gloucester Magistrates Court. It was a small dock. He was brought from the cells first. When she was brought up she had to squeeze past him. He went to touch her but she recoiled. He reached out to touch her on the neck but she made it clear with her body that she didn't want to know. It was a short hearing. Only a few minutes. He stood, slightly swaying. She sat and stared at the floor. When it was over he again made a move to touch her but the policewoman who had been put between them knocked his hand away.

'Rose Luckd Well,' he wrote to Stephen afterwards. 'I have not herd Watt Rose Wanted to do With the House,' he wrote in another letter. And in another: 'That all you got of your pased . . . We had go time . . . all I Love and x.' There was a PS. 'I have got tobacco I need R6 battery get Rayovac VIDOR Longer Life alkaline.'

Chapter Sixteen

The extensions had been collapsed like boxes, which is what they were. They had been very easily demolished. The windows had been filled in with breezeblocks and the doors walled up. All the openings had been blocked and with number 23 adjoining also a void property the house looked like a box from all sides. Impenetrable then. Blank. As each site in the house had been excavated and the human remains removed, the cavity that was left had been filled with quick-drying concrete before another area was dug. Ready Mix road fill had been chosen because it was a highly fluid material which combined the benefits of high flowability with a controlled low strength. It was important to keep the house standing until it was time to pull it down.

It was important to keep Fred West alive until he could be brought to trial. But he had always been devious and thorough and very patient and from nothing he managed to get enough scraps together to make the device that he would use to hang himself. On the one hand he was unravelling. One of his few visitors, Stephen, could see that. His personality was coming apart. He was often incoherent. Tearful and rambling on these visits. On the other hand he was focused enough to write letters that when he saw them Stephen couldn't believe the writing. He found it hard to believe that these had been written by his father who couldn't write. Who just a few months earlier had been writing 'Rose Luckd Well' and 'had Watt she wonted'. 'Will Boy Been a father is no so easy.'

'We will always be in love,' Fred wrote to Rose on her

forty-first birthday in November 1994, a month before he killed himself. 'The most wonderful thing in my life is that I met you. How our love was special to us. So love, keep your promises to me. You know what they are.' This letter ended, 'Well Rose, you will be Mrs West all over the world. That's wonderful for me and you. I have not got you a present, but all I have is my life. I will give it to you my darling. When you are ready, come to me. I will be waiting for you.'

A few weeks later and only days before he died, he wrote: 'To Rose. I loved you forever. I made mistakes. I am so upset about you being in prison. Please keep your promise to me. I have kept mine.' The letter ended: 'I can't tell what I know. You are all free to go on with whatever you want to, but think of what I did for you all, and never complain. I love all of my children. They were all mine.' He signed it: 'All my love and kisses to you darling, Fred.'

It seemed just perfect to Stephen. 'It was spelled correctly, it was just . . . It was like he was *so* relaxed and he just wanted to go so much that he was just like . . . It was all off his shoulders then. Because there was no doubt that he couldn't wait to tell people . . . He drew his gravestone and he wrote what he wanted on there and everything.' He drew a gravestone at the bottom of his birthday letter to Rose with the inscription: 'Fred West and Rose West. Rest in peace where no shadow falls. In perfect peace, he waits for Rose, his wife.'

He wrote these letters but he never sent them. They were found in his cell after his death along with a razor blade that had been concealed in the leg joint of a table. He could have used the razor blade to kill himself but he didn't. He saw another opportunity. A more protracted opportunity that involved pulling the wool over, making a monkey of and raising himself to a position of power over the people who felt they had power over him. He made an opportunity by volunteering to mend the shirts of the other prisoners at Winson Green prison in Birmingham where he was being held on remand. His previous prison experience coming in useful. He was an old con. He knew how to be patient. He could be tirelessly patient. He was rigid in his routines.

He volunteered for shirt-mending duties at Winson Green. And having volunteered he started cutting off and collecting strong cotton tapes from the laundry bags the shirts arrived in. At the same time he was also stealing narrow strips of material from the hems of his prison blankets and twisting and sewing them together to make a noose. A ligature measuring eighty-eight inches by seven-and-a-half inches thick when he finished, put together from slyly snipped off, scavenged, stored and plaited bits. Innocuous pieces and fragments collected and concealed over days and probably weeks and made into the means by which to take his own life.

He chose his moment with care. New Year's Day was a public holiday and many prison officers weren't at work. Lunchtime was the changeover time for shifts and there was a natural lull then. He had had his morning exercise in the yard and when he was back in his cell had written a note to Rose: 'To Rose West. Happy New Year darling. All my love Fred West. All my love for ever and ever.' Shortly after eleven thirty he had collected his 'special' meal of soup and pork chops and gone back to his cell. He knew he would be left alone for at least an hour to eat. Instead he retrieved the rope he had made which, like the blankets it was twisted together from, was bright acid green. The reinforced ties he had stolen from the laundry bags were sewed on to one end. And it was the ties he threaded through the bars in front of the ventilating window directly above the door of his cell. He could have used the chair to stand on. Every cell on D3 landing had a chair. But he used the filled laundry bag to stand on to make the knots. And it was the laundry bag he kicked away from when he secured the ligature around his neck. The chair would have made a noise and brought people running so he didn't use the chair. The laundry bag was soft and silent and would have made only a small disturbance of dust falling over on the floor. The dust lifting and settling again before he had time to be found.

His death was a silent event. The demolition was a full media event; a public spectacle that Gloucester Council who organized it hoped would have a cleansing effect on the city. There was a consensus about demolition. Obliteration. The feeling was that people wanted to see the site made anonymous and ordinary. Demolition started on 7 October 1996 and it was packaged and press-conferenced and shown via live links and cut-aways on breakfast television.

The contents had been removed and taken away for storage at an early stage. The four-poster bed and the bar and the black-and-white-painted wrought-iron signs from these and the '25 Cromwell Street' sign from the front of the house had been put in vans along with 1,300 other inventoried items and transported to RAF Quedgeley where most of them were eventually destroyed in controlled conditions to cheat souvenir hunters.

The job of taking the house down was given to the local family firm of the Bishops whose lorries carry the slogan 'We'll bring it down to earth'. The doors and windows were unbricked and unboarded and as this happened the glass of the windows could be seen to be still intact in the jungle-green frames. The Bishops had been commissioned not only to remove all the materials from the site but to destroy them. There was a crushing machine at the Gloucester tip in Hempstead by the docks. And every brick and piece of rubble was dismantled and driven to Hempstead and crushed to dust. Timber and everything flammable was taken to RAF

Innsworth and put in an incinerator and burned there and the ashes crushed. The cellar was backfilled with the bricks off the walls and sealed with quick-drying concrete.

Anne Marie had been allowed a final visit to the cellar shortly after dawn. And soon after that Mae and Stephen had laid flowers by the front gate on the pavement with a hand-written card attached containing a poem for Heather,

It seems we lived a seven year con
since we came home to find you gone
For all those years we tried in vain
In hope we could ease the pain
But how were we to have ever known
That someone close and in our home
Took you from us that sad day
In such a sad and awful way
No-one could love you the way we do
And know how much we miss you.
I hope one day we meet again
And then at last there would be no pain –

'The sad memories of this house will go with it. But the memories of you will always stay – Love Stephen, Mae and Tara.'

After a long consultation process, the decision was made to turn the site into a walkway or cut-through connecting the street to St Michael's Square and the busy centre of Glouces-ter. Other alternatives were considered and rejected: a com-memorative plaque at the site, a memorial garden. But nobody wanted to keep those memories. A permanent reminder.

When the house had been levelled and the cellar filled in, block paving was brought and laid in a herring-bone pattern, three small trees planted, edging cobbles set in thick-grade concrete: ST4 concrete on 150-mm.-type figure-1 granular material. They installed 'Urbis'-model lamp columns painted gloss black and 'Son-T' lanterns on five-metre steel columns. Four of those. They put in cast-iron bollards across the entrances at both ends to prevent vehicle access – seven at the Cromwell Street end; four at the St Michael's Square end; five down the middle to discourage ball games. They laid a blue-brick on-edge soldier course channel and feature between the block-paved areas and the grass verge. They fixed close-boarded fencing to a height of twelve feet on the exposed flank wall at 21 Cromwell Street and the flank wall of the church where the Wests' tongue-and-groove teak-look pan-elling used to be. Larch close-boarded fencing stained chest-nut brown. Tough spiked pyracantha bushes were planted to run the length of it and discourage graffiti-writers and van-dals. A country lane introduced to the city. The bends and shadows in the narrow road. The country-lane effect familiar from shopping-centre corridors and the rest areas on motor-ways.

The intention is that it will be impossible to distinguish between parts that have been added and those that already exist. Underneath is the cellar void. And under the cellar five cores of concrete buried in Severn clay. The fact of something behind. Something that is inaccessible, unknown. Beyond a doubt there is something behind. It imposes itself and won't go away. You look at the walls. You listen to the space.

Acknowledgements

I couldn't have written the book without the help and in many cases the friendship and encouragement of the following people:

Caroline Raine (now Caroline Roberts), Ian Roberts, Mrs Daisy Letts, Andrew Letts and Jacquie Letts, Graham Letts, Gordon Letts, Stephen West, Leo Goatley, Katherine Goatley, Chris Davis, Brian Fry, Eddie Fry, Derek Thomson, Wendy Thomson, Ron Cooper, Colin Price, Syd Mills, Costadinos ('Nicki') Neocleous, Joyce Dickins and Iris, Tracy Green, Phil Green.

Duncan Campbell, Will Bennett, Brian Masters, Geoffrey Wansell.

Richard Clegg, John Tennant, Marcus Harvey, Paul Green, Allan Jenkins, Alicja Kobiernicka, Sarah Lucas, Angus Fairhurst, Maia Norman.

Damien Hirst and Hugh Allan who did the cover. Fanny Blake who originally commissioned the book. Gillon Aitken, my agent.

At Faber: Jonathan Riley, Joanna Mackle, Chris McLaren, Sarah Hulbert, Rachel Alexander, Jill Burrows.

Carol Gorner.

The title *Happy Like Murderers* comes from a line in David Hare's play *Skylight*.

The second paragraph on p. 280 is a quotation from Elaine Scarry, *The Body in Pain*.

Other books that have been indispensable in various ways, and which I have quoted either directly or indirectly, are:

Anne Marie West, with Virginia Hill, *Out of The Shadows*
Stephen and Mae West, *Inside 25 Cromwell Street*
Geoffrey Wansell, *An Evil Love*
Brian Masters, *She Must Have Known*
Andrew O'Hagan, *The Missing*
Howard Sounes, *Fred and Rose*

Also:

Jonathan Sawday, *The Body Emblazoned*
Louise J. Kaplan, *Female Perversions*
Linda Williams, *Hard Core*
Elizabeth Grosz, *Space, Time and Perversion*
Elaine Showalter, *Sexual Anarchy*
Elizabeth Wilson, *The Sphinx in the City*
Judith R. Walkowitz, *City of Dreadful Delight*
Rachel Whiteread, *House*
Anthony Vidler, *The Architectural Uncanny*
Gaston Bachelard, *The Poetics of Space*
Maria Tatar, *Lustmord*
William Ian Miller, *The Anatomy of Disgust*
Ann Douglas, *Terrible Honesty*
Arthur Mee, *The King's England: Gloucestershire*
Marina Warner, *Richard Wentworth*
Graham Fuller (ed.), *Potter on Potter*
V. S. Naipaul, *The Enigma of Arrival*
Norman Mailer, *Oswald's Tale*
Phillip Roth, *Sabbath's Theatre*